# Web-Based Learning through Educational Informatics:

## Information Science Meets Educational Computing

Nigel Ford
University of Sheffield, UK

**Information Science Publishing**

Hershey • New York

| | |
|---|---|
| Acquisition Editor: | Kristin Klinger |
| Senior Managing Editor: | Jennifer Neidig |
| Managing Editor: | Jamie Snavely |
| Assistant Managing Editor: | Carole Coulson |
| Development Editor: | Kristin Roth |
| Copy Editor: | Holly Powell |
| Typesetter: | Michael Brehm |
| Cover Design: | Lisa Tosheff |
| Printed at: | Yurchak Printing Inc. |

Published in the United States of America by
Information Science Publishing (an imprint of IGI Global)
701 E. Chocolate Avenue
Hershey PA 17033
Tel: 717-533-8845
Fax: 717-533-8661
E-mail: cust@igi-global.com
Web site: http://www.igi-global.com

and in the United Kingdom by
Information Science Publishing (an imprint of IGI Global)
3 Henrietta Street
Covent Garden
London WC2E 8LU
Tel: 44 20 7240 0856
Fax: 44 20 7379 3313
Web site: http://www.eurospanbookstore.com





Library of Congress Cataloging-in-Publication Data

Ford, Nigel.
Web-based learning through educational informatics : information science meets educational computing / Nigel Ford.
p. cm.
Summary: "This book explores the role of information seeking and retrieval in the development of information systems to support personalized and autonomous learning by introducing key concepts from information science"--Provided by publisher.
Includes bibliographical references and index.
ISBN-13: 978-1-59904-741-6 (hardcover)
ISBN-13: 978-1-59904-743-0 (e-book)
1. Computer-assisted instruction. 2. Internet in education. I. Title.
LB1028.5.F623 2008
371.33'44678--dc22

2007039591

British Cataloguing in Publication Data
A Cataloguing in Publication record for this book is available from the British Library.

# Web-Based Learning through Educational Informatics:

## Information Science Meets Educational Computing

# Table of Contents

# Foreword

The digital resource environment arising out of ongoing developments in information and communications technology (ICT) is diverse, complex, and in rapid evolution. Learners and teachers have at their disposal an ever-increasing array of both structured and unstructured digital content in a wide range of multimedia formats. The use of digital resources created by others—whether accessed via institutional repositories, virtual learning environments, library services, or the open Web—has, in recent years, become a fundamental part of educational practice. At the same time, learners and teachers are increasingly empowered to become active producers of digital content that can be widely shared. New systems and standards are being developed to support structured practitioner exchange and reuse of content-focused "learning objects" and process-focused "learning designs." In the open environment of the Web, social networking tools and virtual worlds that connect people in communities of interest and resource exchange have become widely and freely accessible and are creating rich new possibilities for resource access and sharing for both formal and informal learning. However, the need for effective pedagogical mediation of learners' engagement with resources presents a key challenge to designers of digital information and communication systems and tools, as it does to teachers and others—including librarians, learning technologists, and educational developers—who support learning.

As Professor Ford demonstrates in this timely and groundbreaking book, this context gives rise to an important agenda for research and development in a new interdisciplinary field—that of educational informatics. With roots in the research traditions of education, ICT, and information science and situated at the intersection of these three disciplines, this emergent field has, up to now, lacked a coherent and integrated theoretical framework. Professor Ford's considerable scholarly achievement in this book is to comprehensively survey the contours and parameters of the field and to provide such a framework—thereby offering an essential point of stimulus and orientation for new research and development initiatives. Distilling his own, extensive previous research in learning-related information behavior, systems, and retrieval, the book draws on the historical research traditions of each of the three contributing disciplines to provide a systematic exploration of those areas in which education; library and information science; and ICT interconnect. Following a discussion of foundational concepts, concrete examples of existing educational informatics systems are examined and important directions and issues for future research and development are explored, including issues of research methodology. The question of how personalised and autonomous Web-based learning may be facilitated through pedagogical mediation of information seeking and retrieval is at the heart of the book, and of the new research field that it delineates. The distinctive nature of educational informatics as a research field is clarified, and the numerous illustrations of the way in which it integrates the central concerns of librarianship and information science are particularly useful in differentiating it from the adjacent field of educational computing.

With this invaluable book, Professor Ford has made a major contribution to the development of a new interdisciplinary domain and enhanced collaboration among specialists in the three contributing disciplines of education, librarianship/information science, and ICT. In addition to its in-depth, state-of-the-art review, synthesis, and critique of relevant knowledge and development initiatives, the book provides a theoretical framework that will inspire and guide research and development in a domain that is crucial to learning and teaching in the "knowledge society."

*Dr. Philippa Levy*

*Academic Director of the Centre for Inquiry-based Learning in the Arts and Social Sciences (CILASS)*

*University of Sheffield*

***Philippa Levy** is the academic director of the Centre for Inquiry-Based Learning in the Arts and Social Sciences (CILASS), based at the University of Sheffield. CILASS is a national Centre for Excellence in Teaching and Learning funded by the Higher Education Funding Council for England. In her role, Levy leads a programme of development and research for innovative teaching and learning, with particular reference to inquiry-based learning. She has also recently led a "Design for Learning" project funded by the Joint Information Systems Committee, focusing on issues of learning design, sharing, and reuse. She has led other funded research projects and has published extensively in the field of teaching and learning in higher education.*

# Preface

## What is "Educational Informatics"?

A Google search for educational informatics reveals a burgeoning interest in the subject, with an increasing number of higher education courses, research groups, and institutes being established in the area. However, such a Google search will also reveal that there is much imprecision in the term *educational informatics*, which is commonly used simply to signify the application of information and communication technology (ICT) to education.

This book seeks to establish a more rigorous definition of—and an integrated conceptual framework for—educational informatics. It is not simply about the blend of ICT and education, although this is a central pillar. Rather, it represents the integration of three major areas of research and development, namely: ICT, education, and library/information science. While it is a relatively new field of endeavour, at the same time it builds on, integrates, and extends existing areas of work. It is thus relevant to these existing areas as well as representing a new area of research and development in its own right.

Educational informatics is defined here as:

*The development, use, and evaluation of digital systems that use pedagogical knowledge to engage in or facilitate resource discovery in order to support learning.*

This definition indicates that educational informatics is about computer-based systems that support people's learning. This support may be given *directly to learners* themselves—or *to teachers* whose role it is to help people learn. However, educational informatics systems also "engage in or facilitate resource discovery." *Resource discovery* is used here to embrace the seeking or encountering of any informational materials that may be useful to learners. It thus includes both information that has been carefully structured to create formal learning resources, and less structured informal information.

The volume and diversity of such resources available via the World Wide Web (the Web) are growing rapidly. Search engines like Google are increasingly becoming a first port of call for many students faced with an essay or other learning task—as it is for many people who are seeking the answer to some question or problem outside the context of any formal educational course. Much useful information may be located in response to a search. However, carefully constructed learning resources are also becoming increasingly available via the Web. They may be located in specialist repositories available only to particular users, or available freely to all—for example, open educational resources (http://www.oercommons.org/) such as Massachusetts Institute of Technology (MIT)'s *OpenCourseWare* (http://ocw.mit.edu/index.html) and the United Kingdom Open University's *OpenLearn* materials (http://openlearn.open.ac.uk/).

However, a tool that enables people to search for resources does not necessarily fall within the definition of an educational informatics system. To do so requires that it "uses pedagogical knowledge," which is used broadly here to mean "knowledge of teaching and learning." Thus pedagogic knowledge includes not only knowledge of teaching in the traditional sense (i.e., knowledge used by educators in order to help *others* learn), but also the sort of "self-teaching," or "meta-cognitive" knowledge, that people need in order to engage in autonomous and self-regulated learning outside any formal educational institutional context.

As we will see in this book, the types of pedagogic knowledge used by educational informatics systems may be of varying types and levels of complexity—from education-specific metadata, through pedagogic ontologies to academic argumentation structures. The techniques used by educational informatics systems for processing such knowledge also varies, from complex inference mechanisms designed to discover learning resources which match individual learner's needs and characteristics to devices designed to enabled learners to become aware of and use their powers of meta-cognition. In the former case, the system is using pedagogical knowledge to *engage in* resource discovery. In the latter case, it is using pedagogical knowledge to *facilitate* resource discovery, that is, to help learners search more effectively. Thus, educational informatics integrates the notions of learning and resource discovery. It is distinct from educational computing in that it integrates, as essential ingredients, a central concern of library and information science, namely: how to seek and discover information from large, diverse collections of sources such as databases, libraries, and of course, the Internet.

Educational informatics adds a library/information science perspective to the notions of *personalised* and *autonomous* learning. Within education, there is a long history of attempts to devise computer-assisted learning (CAL) systems that provide a level of personalised learning. These range from relatively simple early branching devices to more recent intelligent tutoring systems (ITS) and adaptive hypermedia systems (AHS). Autonomous learning has also been a prominent concern in education over many decades, being manifested in a number of vogues including resource-based, independent, project-based, and inquiry-based learning. Such forms of learning have emphasised the type of relatively autonomous information seeking of more traditional concern to library and information science.

Educational computing systems such as CAL, ITS, and AHS have provided relatively highly "pedagogically mediated" access to information—but until recently, typically to a relatively small set of information sources customised for a particular system, and not readily available for sharing or reuse. Conversely, the information retrieval (IR) systems developed within library and information science to support information seeking and resource discovery have typically provided access to very large diverse, remotely distributed, shared sets of information sources, but have offered no pedagogical mediation.

However, relatively recent developments mean that information systems are decreasingly restricted by the need for such a trade-off between (1) diversity, volume, openness, and shareability of information content, and (2) the level of pedagogical mediation provided by the system. These developments are being enabled in large part by the emergence of: (1) metadata standards relating to how information sources and combinations/aggregations of them should be described, thus enabling the discovery of shareable reusable resources by educators; (2) standards specifying how they should constructed as "learning objects," enabling sharing and reuse via their integration into different learning environments; (3) standards enabling the interoperability of ontologies; and (4) standards specifying how procedures can be shared in the form of Web services.

Although there is a long history of development relating to adaptive and intelligent CAL systems, more recently such systems have incorporated the notion of Web-based resource discovery via standardised metadata (relating to learners as well as information and learning resources) and ontologies. Such systems are capable of providing relatively high levels of pedagogical mediation in relation to information presentation and access to support personalised learning, based on access to a much greater volume and diversity of potential information sources and learning resources.

However, educational informatics is also concerned with the question of how we may facilitate *autonomous* Web-based learning by providing increasing levels of pedagogical mediation to information seeking and retrieval in response to individuals' relatively free exploration of the Web in pursuit of their own "personal learning goals." This represents a convergence of the "learning objectives" often associated with formal educational situations and the more autonomous "information needs" associated with library and information science.

## How This Book is Organised

Chapters I-VI of this book are organised to reflect the main components making up educational informatics. Recall that educational informatics is defined here as:

*The development, use and evaluation of* digital systems *that use* pedagogical knowledge *to engage in or facilitate* resource discovery *in order to support* learning.

Chapters I-VI explore the key concepts included within this definition (and italicised previously). *Learning* is explored in Chapters I and II. Chapter III focuses on educational issues including *pedagogical knowledge*, while Chapter IV introduces *resource discovery*. *Digital systems* are the subject of the next two chapters, which describe ICT-based systems and approaches designed to support education (Chapter V) and resource discovery (Chapter VI).

Chapters I and II explore the basic processes entailed in *learning*—support of which is the goal of educational informatics systems. Chapter I introduces basic processes of learning that we all share. Chapter II focuses on the ways in which different people may use these basic processes in very different ways, often with very differing results in terms of the quality of resultant learning.

Chapter I begins with some basic definitions. Learning is the processing of information in order to generate new knowledge. At a fundamental level, learning begins even before we are born, developing rapidly after birth as we try to make sense of the world around us. As we get older, a significant part of our learning may take place in the classroom, and the information processed may include that supplied by teachers, textbooks, and other learning resources. As we progress, we may experience increasing levels of autonomy in finding the information that fuels our learning both within formal educational environments which emphasise, for example, project-, problem-, and inquiry-based learning.

Learning also takes place, however, outside the context of formal education, and as part of our everyday life we seek information in order to answer questions and to help us solve our problems. The information processes discussed in Chapter I underlie all of these types of learning, and they form the basis for a model, which is developed as the book progresses, and which seeks to provide an integrated conceptual framework for educational informatics. This framework brings together key aspects from the fields of education, ICT, and library/information science, which form the three pillars of educational informatics.

But before going on to explore each of these pillars in detail (in Chapters III, IV, V, and VI), Chapter II focuses on a dimension of learning that is very important in the design of learning experiences and activities, and of systems designed to support learning. This dimension relates to human "individual differences." Although to an extent we all share common physiological and psychological components and processes, these may be developed and deployed very differently by different individuals. Thus we are to a degree all the same, and to a degree all different. Different individuals may bring to the learning process very different kinds and levels of prior knowledge. They may also bring with them very different motivations for, confidence in, and styles of learning. All of these factors may affect how information might best be presented to them by teachers, and how systems might best be designed to support them in their learning. Chapter II explores such differences and extends the framework introduced in Chapter I to take account of them.

While Chapters I and II discuss theories of *how* people learn, Chapter III sets these in the broader context of different views relating to *what* they should learn, and *why*. Educational philosophies are concerned with the purposes of education. Differences in such philosophies map, to an extent, onto differences in learning theories to form broad perspectives on how teaching and learning should be organised—for example, behaviourist, humanist, cognitive, constructivist, and social constructivist. Such perspectives greatly affect views on how learning may best be brought about via appropriate teaching approaches and exposure to appropriate learning experiences and activities. Achieving this is the goal of "learning design," which is also discussed in this chapter. Learning design is sometimes loosely referred to as *instructional design*. The difference between these two terms is explained, as is the choice of the former in this book.

Increasingly, learning designers are able to share, repackage, and reuse learning resources—and learning designs. However, to be effective on a large scale, this process requires agreement on standard ways of describing them. For example, imagine a teacher searching the Web to find learning resources on a particular topic, suitable for a particular age range. If he or she is to find an appropriate resource, then that resource must be described using words which either match—or can be linked to—the words he or she uses when searching.

Chapter III discusses such standard descriptions in the form of educational metadata. However, at a more complex level, if learning designs are similarly to be shared and reused, then agreement is also needed on standard ways of expressing more complex aspects, such as structural features and inter-relationships between elements of design. Such structural specifications are handled by ontologies, and the Educational Modelling Language (EML) enables the creation of such ontologies. The EML is also introduced in this chapter, which goes on further to develop the conceptual framework introduced in Chapters I and II.

Chapter III focuses primarily on formal, mediated learning, that is, learning designed and delivered by teachers. However, as we will see towards the end of that chapter, even within such mediated contexts, learners may be allowed varying types and levels of autonomy, particularly within project-, problem-, and inquiry-based learning designs. A key element of such autonomy entails learners engaging in their own resource discovery—seeking information and resources for themselves, whether from libraries, intranet-based repositories of learning materials, or the open Web. This may be contrasted with situations in which information and resources are largely prescribed or recommended for them by teachers. Resource discovery is also a key component of autonomous, self-regulated learning taking place outside the context of teacher-mediated education

Resource discovery within both contexts—formal education and autonomous self-directed learning—is a central concern of library/information science, and this area of research, practice, and development is the focus of Chapter IV. The chapter begins by introducing key techniques, tools, and standards developed within the library/information science community to enable and facilitate resource discovery, including cataloguing, metadata, classification, thesauri, and ontologies. The chapter goes on to explore the nature of information needs, and models of how we go about trying to satisfy them through information seeking and information encountering.

The relationships between information seeking and learning, and between knowledge behaviour and information behaviour are also discussed. The conceptual framework, which was presented in evolving form in each of the previous chapters, is then further extended in order to integrate the notions autonomous information seeking and encountering with those associated with mediated learning already introduced in the previous chapter.

ICT is the third pillar of educational informatics. Chapter V focuses on ICT-based tools, techniques, and standards developed to support resource discovery—whether by teachers looking for learning materials to support them in their learning design, or learners seeking information and resources in an autonomous self-directed way outside the context of any formal course of study. Chapter VI explores ICT tools, techniques, and standards to support learning. This exploration covers developments in CAL and ITS and goes on to discuss learning management systems and virtual learning environments, the notion of learning objects and the move to an ethos of inter-operability, sharing, and reuse. The ability to share and reuse learning resources created by others on a widespread scale across networks builds on the developments outlined in the previous chapter.

Chapter VI goes on to review more general ICT-based developments including mobile and ubiquitous computing; virtual and augmented realities; and so-called

"Web 2.0" developments. Although more general in the sense of not being specific to education, these developments have a major impact on the way learning can be designed and delivered. The chapter explores the educational affordances they offer and ends with further development of the integrated conceptual framework to take account of ICT-related issues.

Building on these foundations, Chapters VII and VIII introduce a number of examples of educational informatics systems in detail. Chapter VII focuses on educational informatics systems primarily from an individual learner perspective. Examples include adaptive systems designed to search learning object repositories for materials appropriate to individual learners in terms of their personal needs and characteristics, and systems which attempt to discover resources not only from such specially structured repositories, but also the unstructured open corpus Web. These systems engage in resource discovery on behalf of their users. However, research is also described, which seeks to *facilitate* rather than directly engage in resource discovery. The goal is to enhance learners' own powers of resource discovery through the use of "meta-cognitive enabling devices" linked to retrieval systems.

Chapter VIII is concerned with collaborative and community-based learning aspects of educational informatics systems. The limitations of current metadata schemes in accommodating a range of pedagogical approaches—in particular those entailing participation and knowledge creation perspectives on learning—are discussed, along with attempts to devise alternative schemes. A number of educational informatics approaches are introduced, which exploit collaborative aspects of learning. These include systems which derive metadata to describe learning objects from learners' interactions with these objects. User-centric metadata is attached to learning objects as they are used by different learners. The resulting data can then be analysed using data-mining techniques in order to discover patterns, which may be useful in a variety of ways, including helping learners find learning resources suitable for their own particular needs. Systems are also introduced that map argumentation structures inherent in academic argumentation and debate in the form of "knowledge charts." These are supported by ontologies relating to different forms of argumentation.

Chapters IX and X explore a number of key themes to emerge from this review of research and development within educational informatics and discuss what may lie ahead as the field of educational informatics develops. Chapter IX focuses on the limitations of much educational informatics research in terms of "real-world" needs. It discusses the need to overcome the limitations in our knowledge of learning, learning design, and the design of ICT-based learning support systems so that we can improve our own learning, the design of other people's learning, and the design of learning support systems that will work effectively in the real world. The chapter goes on to explore limitations in the extent to which digital systems can support higher order creative thinking processes and discusses the importance of helping learners to develop their own meta-cognitive and "learning to learn" skills.

Chapter X focuses on a number of themes that emerge from an analysis of the research and development presented earlier in the book and discusses how research and development in educational informatics might effectively be progressed. Issues are explored that relate to the generation of different types of "evidence" on which we can build, and how we can make sense of conflicting perspectives and interpretations. The conceptual framework developed throughout the book is further extended to include key issues arising from these explorations. Finally, possible future trends are discussed, including the potential for enhanced teaching and learning as the Web continues to develop.

# Chapter I

# Learning:
## Basic Processes

## Introduction

Learning is the process of acquiring knowledge, which is an active process and operates at both individual and social levels. This book explores both, but this first chapter focuses on the individual in terms of the basic mental processes entailed in transforming information into knowledge—in other words, learning. In doing so, it introduces a number of themes which will recur throughout the book.

These key themes include the notion of *tentative theories* used to generate *themes* by which integrate otherwise fragmented entities become integrated. This process underlies the construction of meaning at all levels—from basic comprehension through critical thinking to creativity. Complex meaning construction can be seen as the generation, testing, and refinement of such tentative theories, *education* being concerned with providing optimal support to learners in engaging in these activities.

A further theme is that of *conversations*. The generation, testing, and refinement of tentative theories may be thought of as essentially a dialogue, or conversation in which ideas are tested out—confirmed, refuted, partially confirmed, or partially refuted in relation to different points of view, or *conceptual systems*. These conversations may take place between a learner and other people (teachers, advisors, friends, or colleagues)—or indeed can take place as an *inner dialogue* within the same person. The notion of conversations introduces another pervasive theme in the book, namely, *conversation theory* devised by the cybernetician Gordon Pask. Pask and his associates worked for over 30 years to develop this theory. It is supported with extensive empirical investigations into learning across a wide range of complex academic subject matter, and it has had wide influence in higher as well as other levels of education.

Educational informatics represents the convergence of education, computing, and library/information science. Traditional, studies of *learning* and *information seeking* have been largely separate enterprises, with relatively little overlap or interaction. Related concepts such as *learning needs* and *information needs* have been considered in very different terms, by researchers populating largely different worlds, even though library/information science and education have long been partners in the enterprise of education.

This chapter first defines the terms *knowledge*, *information*, and *learning*, before going on to explore at the most basic level the biological processes involved in constructing meaning.

## Basic Information Processes

A common concern of education and library/information science is with the processing of information to generate knowledge. Within the context of this book, *knowledge* is defined as a conceptual system that enables its possessor (whether human or machine) to act in the world (e.g., in the form of autonomous activity or response to stimuli). *Information* is defined here as potential knowledge, and *learning* as the process of transforming information into knowledge.

Knowledge may be thought of as existing both within and between individuals. As we will see later in this book, social constructivist views of learning emphasise the notion of knowledge as consisting of interactions between individuals (cooperating processing units) within communities—as opposed to merely the sum of the knowledge states of each individual. Social mores and cultural memes, for example, may be thought of as types of knowledge that transcend the individual.

While acknowledging the role of social processes and interactions in learning and the generation of communal knowledge, we start our exploration at the level of the individual human being. Yet even within each of us, the notion of patterns of interaction between cooperating processing units is central to our thought processes. At a basic level, we can think of knowledge as being stored as links, or associations, between neurons in the brain. Neurons are highly interconnected processing units, and basically send excitory and inhibitory messages to one another. A neuron receives input, from other neurons to which it is connected, via its *dendrites*. If the total amount of input exceeds a certain threshold, then the neuron sends out its own signal via its *axon*. The communication between the axon of one neuron and the dendrite of another neuron takes place via a *synapse*. This is a temporary chemical, rather than a permanent physical link.

Each dendrite can receive input via many synapses, and each axon can provide input to many dendrites, thus achieving massive interconnectivity. Some synapses may excite the dendrite, while others may inhibit it, and learning entails changes in these effects. *Productive* connections can be reinforced—made more excitory by increasing the strength of the signal passed through the synapse from one neuron to the other. Conversely, *nonproductive* connections can be weakened. Strengthening and weakening entail differences in the amount of neurotransmitters released by the axon, and in the number of reciprocal receptors opened in the dendrite. This has the effect of *weighting* the signal transmitted by the axon, and this effect has been simulated in computer-based neural nets via the assignment of numerical weights to connections between artificial neurons.

This process is represented in Figure 1, which shows a simplified model of a neuron as used by computer scientists to create artificial neural networks. The sending and receiving of chemical messages are replaced here with numbers. The neuron shown there has a *firing threshold* of 2. Let us assume that the strength of each signal coming in from the axons of other neurons is 1. The weightings applied to each connection coming into the neuron are different. The first is 0.7, the second 0.5, and the third 1.2. This means that each signal of strength 1 will be multiplied by the weighting before it reaches the neuron. The first two will have the effect of attenuating the input (0.7 and 0.5 respectively), while the third will increase it (1.2). Thus in this case, the total input to the neuron is the sum of all three inputs, multiplied by the weightings—that is, a total of 2.4. This exceeds the threshold value of 2, and so the neuron fires its output signal.

Learning in a neural network is a process by which the network comes to a state of equilibrium in which constraints are maximally satisfied and tensions are minimised. The stabilisation of the network may be thought of as the identification of a high-order pattern of weightings (linking the neurons) which essentially *integrates disparate forces*—that is, balances competing tensions in such a way as to render the network as a whole maximally relaxed.

The following *traffic lights* example associates individual neurons with concepts—one neuron each for *red*, *green*, *stop*, and *go* The neurological reality is very much more

*Figure 1. An artificial neuron*

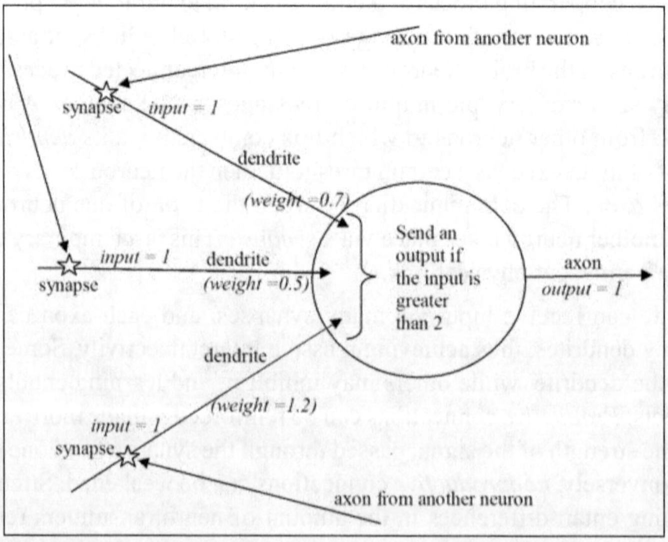


complex than this crude simplification—made for the sake of clear illustration of the basic ideas. In reality, even the simplest concepts are represented by complex patterns of interactions between many interconnected neurons. Bear in mind that it has been estimated that the human brain is made up of something like 10,000,000,000 neurons, each neuron being connected to 10,000 others!

Figure 2 shows a very simple network of such neurons, of the type used in a number of artificial intelligence applications. Each of the circles shown in the figure represents a neuron as depicted in Figure 1. The neurons at the bottom of the figure are assigned to represent input to, and those at the top to represent output from, the neural network. The neurons in the centre represent a hidden layer—hidden in the sense that they are not associated to input or output.

For our traffic lights example, let us associate two of the input neurons with the concepts red and green, and two of the output neurons with stop and go. We want the network to learn to associate red with stop, and green with go. That is, when we excite the neuron associated with red, then the neuron associated with stop should be the one that shows most activation. Similarly, the go neuron should show most activation when we excite the green neuron. Let us also assume that the weights associated with the links between the neurons are initially set *at random*.

If we now *stimulate* one of the input neurons to send an output signal, this signal will be sent to all the other neurons to which it is connected. Since the weights acting on these signals are initially random, the pattern of activation of these other neurons will also be random, as shown in Figure 3. In this figure, the level of activation of each neuron is indicated by its size.

*Figure 2. A simple artificial neural network*

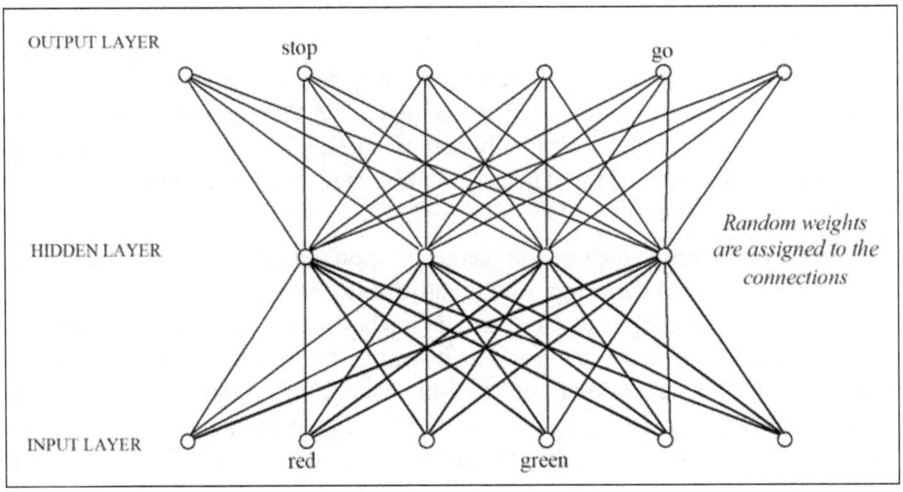


*Figure 3. Stimulation of an input neuron*

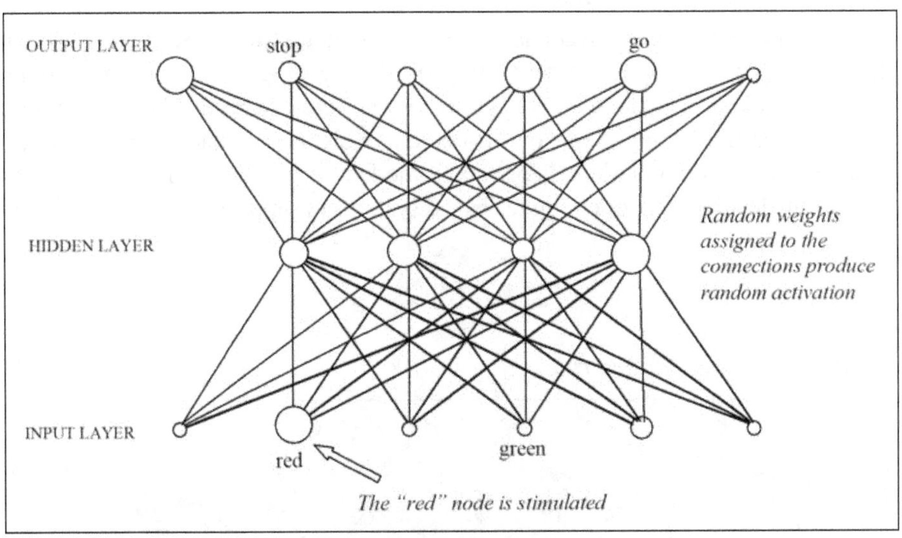


Since the weights acting on the strength of the signal passed via each connection were assigned randomly, the pattern of activation will itself be random. So in its present state, the network is far from associating red with stop. In fact, in Figure 3 it is more strongly associated with go!

The next stage in learning is for the network to make use of a *learning rule* (Figure 4). This rule essentially states: Increase the weights of the productive connections—that is, all those which led to stimulation of the correct output neuron (red), and reduce the weights of all the unproductive connections—that is, those which led to the stimulation of the wrong neurons.

Next time the red neuron is stimulated, the result is not perfect—but it is better. The procedure is repeated, and the weights changed again. After a number of iterations of this procedure, the network finally settles into a stable pattern of weightings whereby each time the red input neuron is stimulated, the stop output neuron is the one most excited (Figure 5).

We can now go through the same procedure to train the network to associate green with go as well as red with stop. Importantly, the same network can learn to make *both* associations. Learning the new association between green and go will interfere with the weights already established as it learned the red/stop association. However, over time the network will find a stable pattern of weightings between all its connections reflecting both associations. Thus when the red node is stimulated, the network will consistently activate the stop neuron, and when the green neuron is stimulated, it will consistently activate the go neuron (Figure 6). At this stage, the network has stabilised and reached a state of equilibrium whereby tensions between competing constraints are minimised.

When the network is given feedback on what constitutes the correct association (in this case, red with stop and green with go) it is engaging in *supervised* learning. However, neural nets can also engage in *unsupervised* learning. This distinction introduces another major theme of this book, namely: a dimension from *mediation* to *autonomy* which underlies theories and models of learning more generally, as well as the development of computer-based systems to support learning. Mediation

*Figure 4. Use of a learning rule*

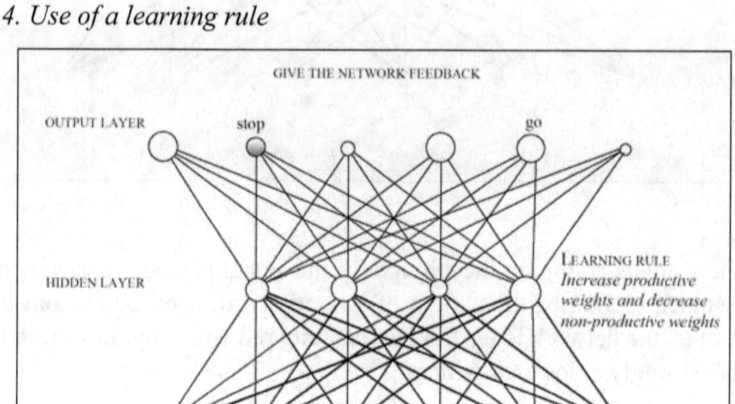

*Figure 5. A learned association*

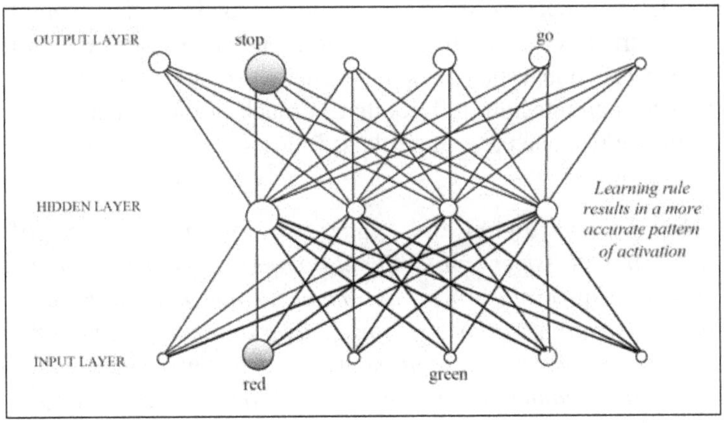


*Figure 6. Two learned associations within the same network*

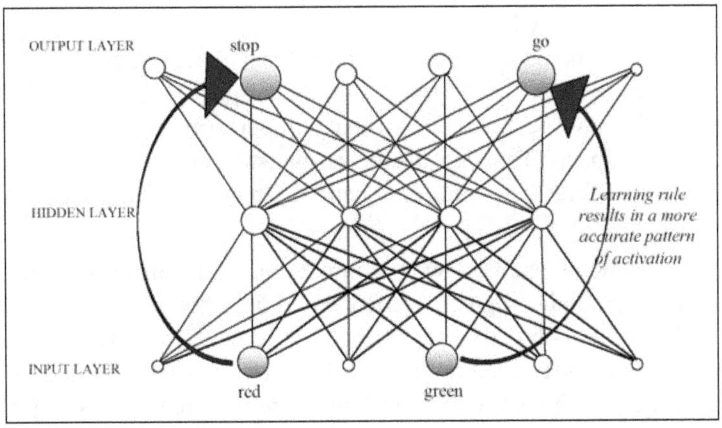


is used here to refer to intervention, intended to help a learner in his or her learning, on the part of another person (for example, a teacher) or machine (for example, a computer-assisted learning package). A learner is autonomous to the extent that he or she is not dependent on such mediation.

Within the context of neural networks, unsupervised learning entails finding patterns in data without being provided with explicit feedback by a *teacher* on what are the *correct* patterns. This assumes that there exists clusters of useful outputs and that the constituents of each cluster will share some common features. One approach, using Kohonen's famous algorithm, is to organise neurons on a flat grid (as opposed to the three-layer model described previously) and to use spatial mapping to model complex data structures internally with vectors. Beale and Jackson (1990) note that it has been suggested that such mapping is what the human brain does, and that the two-dimensional architecture reflects that of much of the human cerebral cortex. They explain the Kohonen learning rule as follows:

*The learning algorithm organises the nodes in the grid into local neighbourhoods that act as feature classifiers on the input data. The topographic map is autonomously organised by a cyclic process of comparing input patterns to vectors 'stored' at each node. No training response is specified for any training input. Where inputs match the node vectors, that area of the map is selectively optimised to represent an average of the training data for that class. From a randomly organised set of nodes the grid settles into a feature map that has local representation and is self-organised. (p. 109)*

Kohonen (1988) used this approach as a major component in the development of his phonetic typewriter, which was able to convert spoken language into typewritten form, using an unlimited vocabulary (Hämäläinen, 2001). Indeed, it is important to note that the simplicity of the traffic lights example belies the fact that artificial neural networks have been developed that can perform very complex and subtle tasks, including aspects of medical diagnosis, industrial process control, stock market modelling, and so forth (for example, Chang & Chung, 2000; Shachmurove, 2005; Ubeyli & Guler, 2005).

A number of artificial neural network computational models have been developed within psychology and computer science, based on some of the basic principles of biological brains. Although they represent an extremely simplified view of biological structures and processes, they are useful in providing a clear and simple picture of some of the principles involved in human information processing of concern to us here. They introduce at a basic level a number of notions that are pervasive throughout this book, namely: the production of new knowledge as the resolution of tensions or incongruities via *integrating themes*, and the generation and testing of tentative theories representing such potential themes.

As we will see later in this book, such incongruities may relate to complex concepts (for example, tension between some thesis and antithesis), and the integrating theme relates to some resolution (synthesis). In the case of neural networks, the *incongruity* is at a much lower level of granularity and relates to tension between the initial output of the network, when stimulated with some input, and the *desired* output—whether specified explicitly (in supervised learning, as in the traffic lights example given previously) or in terms of procedures designed to produce an optimal stable pattern (in unsupervised learning, as in the example of Kohonen's phonetic typewriter). The integrating theme is the stable optimised pattern of weights linking the neurons—optimised to minimise tension or incongruity between the initial and desired outputs of the network. The *generation and testing* of potential integrating themes is brought about by the network's learning rule, which specifies how the pattern of weightings may be modified in order to reduce the tension.

At whatever level we map concepts (e.g., red, green, stop, go) onto such associations, a concept can be thought of as being relatively *deeply* understood in terms of the strength and richness (spread) of these associations. Particular combinations of neurons may be linked more, or less strongly than others. Strength of association will lead to reliability (for example, consistently associating red with stop). The spread of associations—whereby given concepts are richly interconnected with others—also underlies what educationists have long referred to as relatively deep, as opposed to surface knowledge.

Thus, the response stop may be stimulated by exposure to red via rote memorisation. The concepts may, however, be richly linked with other concepts relating to vehicles, safety, law, traffic flow, congestion, commercial infrastructure, and so forth. Such richer associations will enable deeper understanding of the purpose of traffic lights, and the ability to know when and how to respond flexibly—for example when faced with lights stuck on red late at night. As well as relating to the comprehension of how and why traffic lights exist and operate, the concepts may engage with wider conceptual systems relating to attitudes, values, and beliefs.

However, depth of knowledge as defined in terms of the strength and spread of associations does not necessarily imply flexibility and generalisability. Strong and rich interconnections may enable quick and reliable retrieval over time, but the nature of the knowledge so represented may not necessarily be readily generalisable to new (previously unmet) circumstances.

These qualities derive from what Baum (2004) has termed *compression*. This relates to distilling the essence of a phenomenon and representing it more economically than the phenomenon itself. In this, it is akin to the higher order integrating themes introduced earlier in this chapter. Baum notes that:

*We have come to understand that compression of data yields generalization to new, as yet unseen, data, and that compression of data into a computer program implies that the symbols in the program have meaning." (p. 79)*

The effect of compression can be seen in a neural network example. Take a neural network with a hidden layer. A typical shape for the network is an hourglass—the hidden layer being narrower (composed of fewer nodes) than the input and output layers. This enables the network to store generalisable knowledge—knowledge that can be applied to novel input the network has not previously encountered during training.

Too many nodes in the hidden layer (insufficient compression) will result in the network erring on the side of rote learning. In other words, it will tend to memorise each specific case on which it is trained, and while it could successfully produce the desired output when stimulated with that precise input, it would be unable to generalise its knowledge to novel input. That is, it will not have learned the *essence* of the concepts it has learned such that this essence can be applied to similar but not identical stimuli. Too few nodes in the hidden layer (excessive compression), however, and the network may err on the side of overgeneralisation. It is interesting to compare these effects with learning pathologies described by Pask based on his studies of complex learning. As we will see in Chapter II, overgeneralisation is associated with an extreme global learning style, while an extreme analytic learning style may characteristically lead to overly fragmented (undergeneralised) learning.

Baum (2004) develops the notion of compression to explain human development at an altogether more fundamental evolutionary level:

> *the compression, most of the learning, that goes into human understanding of the world was done at the level of evolution.* (p. 156)

> *It is not surprising that the evolved program of mind is much more sophisticated than those in our computational experiments. Biological evolution was a vastly greater calculation than those within our computers' capabilities. Our computational experiments ran for a few million learning trials. But over evolutionary time [...] perhaps 1035 organisms have been created, each coded for by a DNA program. The DNA program was executed and selected preferentially based on how it performed, how effective the phenotype was at reproduction. [...] So the result of 1035 or so learning trials has been compressed into 10 or so megabytes of the human DNA, a fantastic compression, through Occam's razor and through the ability of Occam's razor to exploit structure for computation.* (p. 303)

Self-evidently, the precise make-up of each person's knowledge structure will be unique. However, as we will see in Chapter II, there is evidence of the existence of systematic patterns of difference shared by groups of people in the form of distinctive cognitive and learning styles, motivational orientations, level of criticality, and so forth. A major challenge for education, library/information science, and educational informatics is to enable and facilitate the generation of new knowledge via an appropriate enmeshing, or integration, of new concepts with each person's existing knowledge structure.

*Figure 7. The notion of an integrating theme*

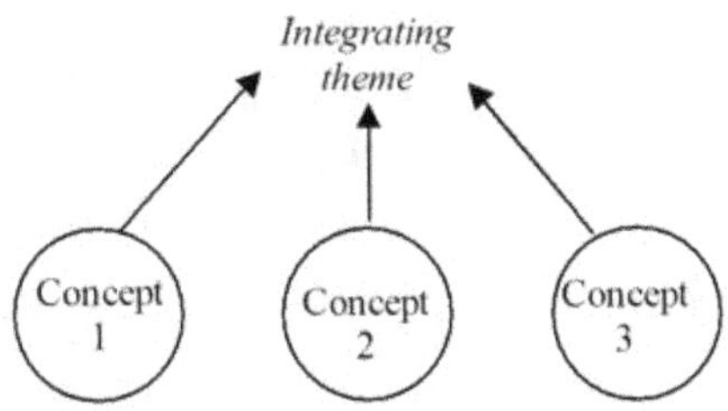


## Integrating Themes

The notions of (a) disparate entities becoming integrated via the identification of some higher-order pattern or integrating theme, and (b) the generation and testing of tentative theories—that is, potential unifying themes—are pervasive in this book. The general idea is illustrated in Figure 7.

Clearly, information (potential knowledge) can be learned and recalled via rote memorisation. A series of numbers such as the following can be thus memorised and recalled without any understanding of what they might signify:

20:10 21:10 22:10

However, we may come to know that, for example, these numbers represent train times from Sheffield to London. In other words, a number of otherwise discrete (unconnected) concepts are coherently brought together via a higher order concept providing an integrating theme (Figure 8). This figure depicts an example of its application to basic understanding at the level of knowing what a particular set of numbers *mean*:

This basic model of some broad integrating concept (theme) unifying what would otherwise be disassociated narrower concepts can be applied at a range of different levels of granularity and complexity. Figures 9 shows the same basic model applied to more complex understanding of how some machine or system works.

The same basic model may be used to conceptualise understanding at a more general abstract level—for example, in relation to the generation of some thesis from conflicting arguments (Figure 10).

Or the identification of some analogy by which to understand some problem through understanding of a similar problem (Figure 11).

*Figure 8. An integrating theme: Example 1*

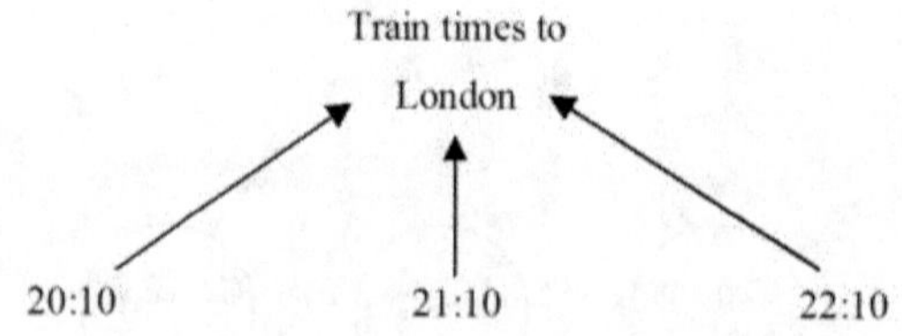


*Figure 9. An integrating theme: Example 2*

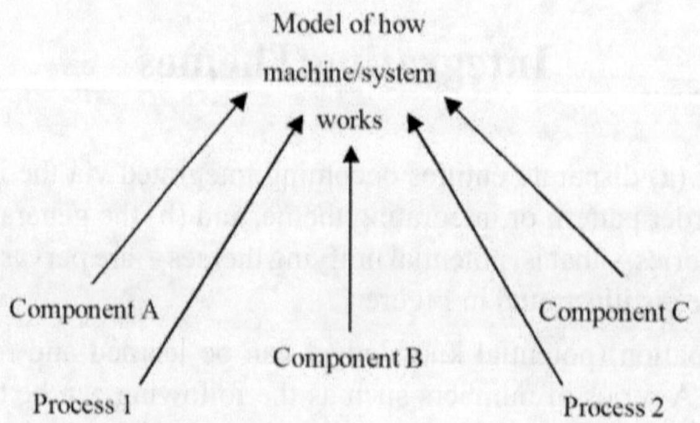


*Figure 10. An integrating theme: Example 3*

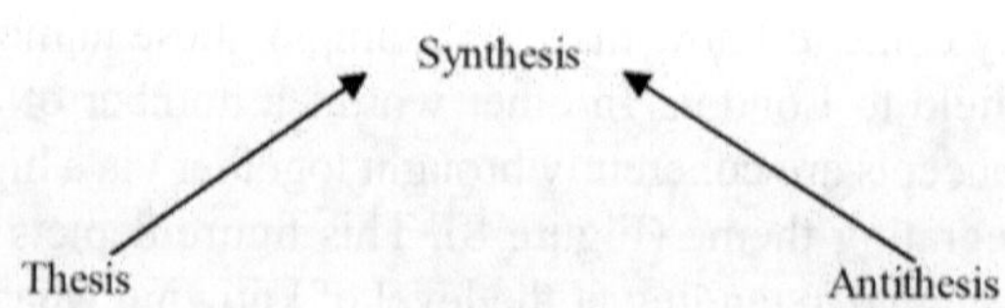


*Figure 11. An integrating theme: Example 4*

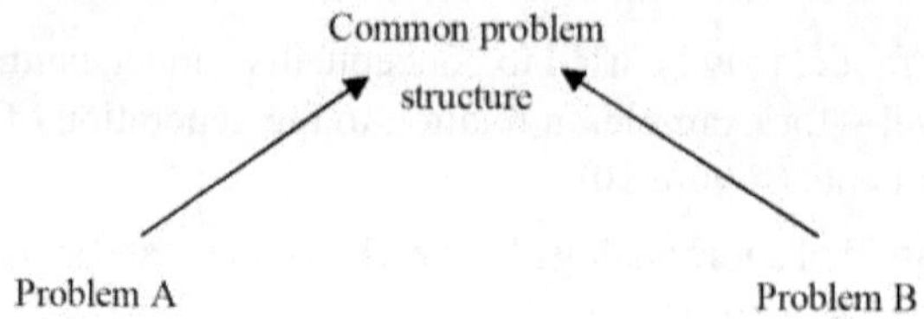

*Table 1. Data relating to the use of keyword search engines or directories*

| Person | Information need | Level of confidence | Level of experience | Choice of search tool |
|---|---|---|---|---|
| Mike | specific | confident | experienced | search engine |
| Jenny | general | confident | novice | directory |
| Bill | specific | unconfident | novice | directory |
| Mary | Specific | unconfident | experienced | search engine |

Before we continue, this short exercise will enable you to get a conscious feel for generating an integrating theme. Let us assume that we want to learn what factors lead people to use keyword search engines as opposed to (browsable) directories. We ask a number of people about what they did last time they needed to find information. The data are recorded in Table 1.

Mike is an experienced searcher, and has a high level of confidence. When he needed to find some specific item of information, he used a search engine. Jenny is a novice with low levels of confidence. She had a more general need for information and searched using a Web directory. Bill is also a novice with low confidence. He needed specific information and, like Jenny, he used a directory. Mary is experienced but with low confidence. When searching for specific information, like Mike, she used a search engine.

Your task is to study the data in Table 1, and try to work out a *rule* that specifies the combination of factors that (from our data) lead to the use of a search engine as opposed to a directory. The rule will be of the form:

IF a person's information need is *X*
AND their level of confidence is *Y*
AND their level of experience is *Z*
THEN they will use a search engine
ELSE they will use a directory

Your task is to replace the variables *X*, *Y*, and *Z* with real data. Make the rule as short as possible—in other words, there is no need to specify all three conditions if only one or two are needed to generate a rule that works.

It will be clear that both Mike and Mary had specific information needs, so you may quickly conclude that the rule should be:

IF a person's information need is *specific*
THEN they will use a search engine
ELSE they will use a directory

Think again! Bill also had a specific information need, but used a directory—so the rule does not work.

Bear in mind, as you try to generate a rule that will explain all the data in the table, what you are trying to do is distil or compress the data to extract its essential meaning—to discover a conceptual *theme* by which the data can become *integrated.* Without such an integrating theme, the data do not tell us anything *as a whole.* They tell us individually about what happened in Mike's search, what happened in Jenny's search, and so forth. But we are looking for a theme that will enable us to understand what the data are telling us as a whole.

A rule that does explain all of the data in the table is the following:

IF a person's level of experience is *high*
THEN they will use a search engine
ELSE they will use a directory

Imagine now that we gather some further data, and add this to our table. This data from two more searchers—Jane and John—is shown in Table 2 along with our original data. Your task is to check whether your rule still works—and if it does not, to modify it so that it does.

An elaboration of the original rule is now required, as follows:

IF a person's information need is *specific*
AND their level of experience is *high*

*Table 2. Data from two new interviews*

| Person | Information need | Level of confidence | Level of experience | Choice of search tool |
|---|---|---|---|---|
| Mike | Specific | confident | experienced | search engine |
| Jenny | General | confident | novice | directory |
| Bill | Specific | unconfident | novice | directory |
| Mary | Specific | unconfident | experienced | search engine |
| Jane | General | confident | experienced | directory |
| John | Specific | unconfident | experienced | search engine |

*Figure 12. Incomplete integration*

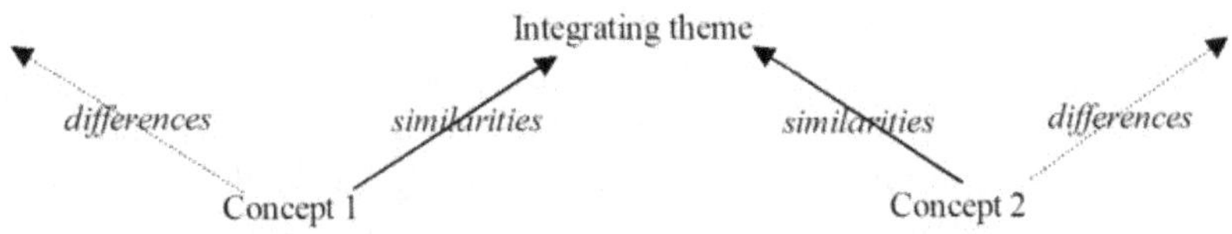


THEN they will use a search engine
ELSE they will use a directory

This is a very simple exercise, but it does give a feel for the process of generating a theme by which otherwise discrete data become integrated.

It is important to note that the identification of some integrating theme may commonly leave other discrete elements that cannot be integrated via that theme, and which must be subsequently dealt with in their own right via some other integrating theme (Figure 12).

Learning occurs via the identification of integrating themes as the learner is exposed to or encounters new conceptual anomalies. However, it is also important to ensure that they are compatible with his or her *existing* knowledge. Recall that in the neural network example presented earlier in this chapter the process of learning the association of green with go did not leave unaffected the weights already established (whereby the association between red and stop had previously been learned). The effects of new learning affected the weights more holistically, requiring new adjustments of the whole pattern of weights across the network in order to accommodate both sets of associations. In a similar way, items of new knowledge may have implications for existing knowledge, and any conflicts between the two must be resolved. This process entails the generation of an appropriate integrating theme at a higher level of abstraction, without which there may be conflict and confusion within the individual's knowledge structure.

As we have seen with these simple examples, the basic elements requiring integration (the *discrete entities*) may vary in complexity, granularity, and type. For example, they may represent complex or simple concepts—facts, ideas, opinions, theories, attitudes, values, and beliefs. They may be already close or widely dispersed within an individual's knowledge structure. The basic *integration* model may be applied across a range of intellectual activity—from basic comprehension through problem solving and critical thinking to creativity. What differs between these activities are the type and nature of the discrete entities to be integrated.

Within an educational context, individuals may be set a variety of tasks by teachers—for example, writing essays, engaging in problem-solving exercises, taking examinations, writing theses, and so forth. Such tasks are often set for learners by educators with the intent that learners will engage in a particular desired type of intellectual activity. These activities may entail very different types and granularity of entity and require integrating themes of varying levels of complexity. Such activity is often expressed in terms of learning objectives. These typically state that as a result of performing the task the learner will have demonstrated possession of the desired ability to engage in the type(s) of thinking specified. As we will see in Chapter III, this represents one particular perspective on teaching and learning, which may be challenged by a number of competing views as to how we might most productively view them.

A number of taxonomies of learning objectives have been developed. Particularly well established are those devised originally some 50 years ago by Bloom and Krathwohl (1956), and subsequently developed to cover three overlapping areas of human activity—cognitive, affective, and psychomotor.

Their cognitive domain objectives (Anderson & Krathwohl, 2001; Bloom & Krathwohl, 1956) consist of abilities to:

- Recognise or recall information.
- Understand information, showing this for example by describing, comparing, or contrasting ideas.
- Apply previously learned knowledge to solve a problem or come to an answer to some question.
- Analyse: for example, to break a problem down into its constituent parts, or to identify causes or reasons.
- Synthesise: to put ideas together or to draw conclusions based on evidence.
- Evaluate: to judge the worth of an idea using explicit criteria.

Anderson and Krathwohl (2001) developed the original scheme including within it metacognition. Metacognition is essentially knowledge of—and consequently the ability to monitor and develop—one's own powers of thought. Metacognition will be discussed in more depth in Chapter III.

Beyond simple recall and recognition, which do not necessarily require any depth of understanding, these activities—understanding, applying, analysing, synthesising, and evaluating—may all be viewed in terms of different types and levels of integration of otherwise disparate entities. The same applies to affective objectives (Anderson & Krathwohl, 2001; Krathwohl, Bloom, & Masia, 1964), which are concerned with interests, opinions, emotions, attitudes, and values. They are aimed at the development of attitudes and behaviour, as opposed to the intellectual abilities forming the focus of the cognitive domain. Affective domain objectives consist of:

- Receiving or paying attention to some stimulus.
- Responding or reacting to a stimulus in some way.
- Valuing particular ideas.
- Organising different values—comparing different values and resolving conflicts between them and beginning to develop a personal value system.
- Commitment to a coherent, internally consistent value system.

Valuing; comparing and contrasting; and resolving conflicts between ideas, as well as integrating them with one's own coherent value system, can all be viewed in terms of the basic integrating theme model previously presented.

Learning objectives in the *psychomotor* domain relate to physical abilities, from basic reflexes to skilled and expressive movement (e.g., Harrow, 1972). These are not included within the focus of this book, which is primarily concerned with cognitive and affective aspects of complex learning.

A number of alternative schemes have also been developed, such as the Structure of Observed Learning Outcomes (SOLO) taxonomy (Biggs, 1999, n.d.; Biggs & Collis, 1982). This consists of five increasingly complex levels of understanding of a subject, from a *prestructural* level, in which unconnected pieces of information are acquired, through *unistructural multistructural*, and *relational* levels to "extended abstract" level, in which connections are made beyond the specific material learned, in terms of generalisation and the transfer of ideas to other contexts. Table 3 shows these different levels.

Beyond the prestructural, all levels entail the development of progressively more complex themes by which disparate entities can become an integrated whole. Other taxonomies exist—for example, that of Zimmer (2001), with eight levels

*Table 3. Biggs' SOLO taxonomy*

| | |
|---|---|
| **Prestructural** | The learner's response is too simple—for example, simply talking about keywords mentioned in the question and failing to understand the question. |
| **Unistructural** | The learner focuses on only one aspect of the question. |
| **Multistructural** | The learner addresses several aspects of the question, but in an unconnected way rather than as a unified whole. |
| **Relational** | The learner pulls together the different aspects of the question into a coherent whole. |
| **Extended abstract** | The learner goes beyond the relational by developing a higher level abstraction of the issues, generalisable to other topics. |

comprising: abstracting, recognising, adducing, applying, defining, exemplifying, generalising, and exploiting. However, although originally published over 50 years ago, the taxonomies of Bloom and Krathwohl (1956) continue to form the basis of more modern formulations and have a widespread influence on educational practice. Saint Edward's University (n.d.), for example, presents a "task oriented question construction wheel" based on the Bloom taxonomy. This scheme extends the taxonomy with over 90 verbs exemplifying the six basic categories, and over 80 examples of associated types of learning task. As will be seen in Chapter IX, Bloom and Krathwohl's taxonomy is also currently being used in the *iHelp Courses* educational informatics system developed at the University of Saskatchewan's Advanced Research in Intelligent Educational Systems (ARIES).

At appropriately high levels of abstraction, such processes may lead to *creativity*. The generation of creative new ideas entails elements of what Hudson (1968) termed "divergent" as opposed to "convergent thinking." Divergent thinking entails generating ideas that diverge from the planned and predictable. Convergent thinking entails following beaten paths, extrapolating existing trends and patterns, and developing the next logical step in chains of knowledge. Convergent thinking has an important role to play in the development of knowledge. However, also vital are the products of the more speculative, unplanned, and genuinely novel forms of thinking. Divergent thinking often entails the questioning of current knowledge and current approaches, and the development of new concepts often via creative analogy. Divergent thinkers are often thought of as excelling at "free association" as opposed to more "logical" forms of thought (Gregory, 1987).

Paradoxically, however, a degree of convergence is required in so-called divergent thinking. Creativity arguably relates to relatively low levels of convergence, but within an essentially convergent process. This is so since so-called divergent thinking does in fact proceed, like other forms of thinking previously discussed, via the identification of integrating themes. Generating or discovering integrating themes essentially entails the identification of similarity relationships. Just as with other less creative forms of thinking, so-called divergent thinking entails generating new ideas by identifying themes by which otherwise discrete entities become integrated. Such integrating themes are essentially similarity relationships between concepts (Holyoak & Thagard, 1996; Keane, 1988; Minsky, 1986; Pask, 1976b, 1976c, 1979).

What distinguishes creative from less creative (or the essentially misnamed *divergent* from *convergent* thinking) is the type and level of dissimilarity which applies to the discrete entities integrated by the similarity relationship. As Ford (1999) notes:

*The identification of themes capable of integrating entities which are relatively similar to one another, and/or between entities which operate at relatively low levels of abstraction, relates to concept formation and learning in general—that is, at levels that do not necessarily entail creativity... It is the extent of dissimilarity*

*Figure 13. Creativity as theme integration (adapted from Ford, 1999)*

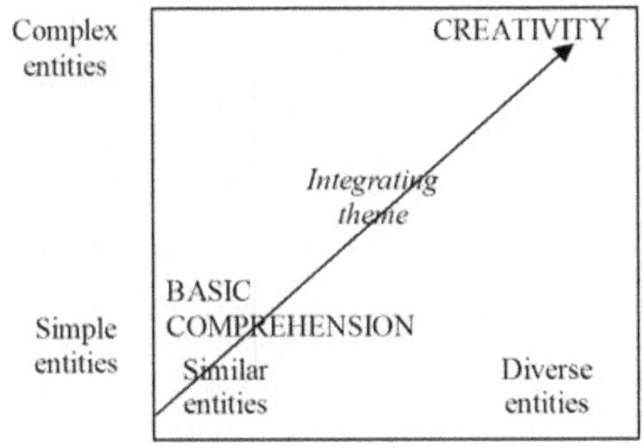


*and the level of abstraction that differentiate creative from less creative forms of thinking.* (p. 529)

Thus, identifying a common problem-solution structure across two complex and apparently very dissimilar problems in very different fields is arguably more creative than solving a relatively simple problem by analogy with another similar problem in the same or closely related field. For example, applying biological evolutionary principles observed in an animal population to the development of computer systems may arguably be considered more creative than applying those principles from one animal species to another. This notion of creativity is depicted in Figure 13.

Creative may thus be differentiated from less creative forms of thinking by the extent of dissimilarity and the level of complexity entailed. The identification of an appropriate integrating theme may enable the identification or generation of a synthesis capable of resolving a thesis and antithesis. Or it may enable a problem structure or solution existing in one context to be integrated with—therefore enabling potential application to—some other context. At appropriately high levels of complexity and dissimilarity of context, this may be regarded as *creative.*

## Where do Integrating Themes come From?

The learning processes that result in the different types and levels of understanding previously described—from basic comprehension through application, analysis, synthesis, and evaluation to creativity—all essentially entail the generation and testing of integrating themes. But where do integrating themes come from? If they

*Figure 14. Popper's problem-solving model (adapted from Popper, 1979)*

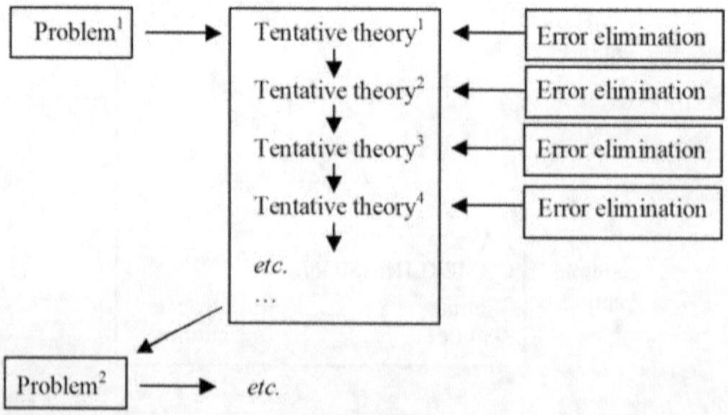


represent what the learner does not yet know, how can he/she generate this new knowledge? Clearly, at one level they may be given to the learner—for example, by a teacher or in a book. This issue will be taken up in Chapter III, when we discuss the notions of autonomy and dependence in learning. However, where a theme is not simply *provided for* the learner, one possible answer is that he/she somehow generates hypothesised integrating themes—or tentative theories. These are then tested out to assess the extent to which they bridge the gap or resolve the anomaly (i.e., successfully integrate the as-yet unconnected concepts). Such a process is described in Popper's (1979) model of interaction between an individual and new information. In this interaction, he/she develops progressively more advanced states of knowledge via iterative theory generation and testing.

As shown in Figure 14, based on his or her initial conceptualisation of a problem requiring solution (problem$^1$), an individual formulates one or more hypotheses (tentative theories) as to how it might be resolved. Such theories are then tested and refined by the weighing of evidence (error elimination). This process results in a modification of the individual's conceptualisation of the problem (problem$^2$).

Thus a tentative theory may be thought of as*: a theme hypothesised as potentially useful in integrating concepts which would otherwise remain unconnected.* By definition, a tentative theory is one which requires further testing, via the weighing of relevant evidence, for its usefulness or otherwise to be established. As such, a *first round theory* (tentative theory$^1$ in a given iteration) may, prior to the gathering and consideration of relevant evidence, be only partially, superficially or incorrectly specified when compared with hindsight to the *second round* theory (tentative theory$^2$). The latter theory would be generated by the learner's modified knowledge state—changed as a result of the testing of the first round theory. Theories may be iteratively refined (confirmed, modified, rejected) as evidence is sought and applied to test them.

However, the question remains: how might integrating themes—the tentative theories described by Popper (1979)—be *generated*? Theory generation may be seen as a natural function of the information processing structures and processes inherent in the brain—which have, to a limited extent, been modelled using artificial neural networks. The notion of unsupervised learning was introduced earlier with Kohonen's (1988) self-organising feature map. In this case, the neural network achieved a stable balance minimising competing tensions (i.e., generated an integrating theme) in the absence of any mediation in the form of feedback from a *teacher* as to what was the *correct* expected output. Another striking example is work by Linsker (1988). Linsker provided evidence that a self-organising neural network, taking as input stimulus random noise, and with no supervised training, can produce as output provisional classifications (tentative theories) that are meaningful and subject to revision in the light of new stimulus data. Linsker's self-organising system in fact generated—as the natural output of its information processing structures and processes—feature-recognition capabilities able to distinguish between dark and light contrast and between different orientations of light/dark edges very similar to orientation-sensitive cells found in the visual cortex of a monkey.

Being in a constant state of such inductive learning and adaptation is central to the human condition. As Scott (2001a) notes:

*The brain/body system is a dynamic self-organising, 'variety eating', adaptive and habituating system... As Pask often put it, 'Man is a system that needs to learn.'* (pp. 27-28)

Even at the most basic level, humans are well equipped to adapt to their environment by generating, testing, and modifying theories (Figure 15). At higher levels, intellectual development resulting from experience and education equips us further with sophisticated organising procedures with which to convert stimuli to more

*Figure 15. Inductive processing of stimuli to produce tentative theories*

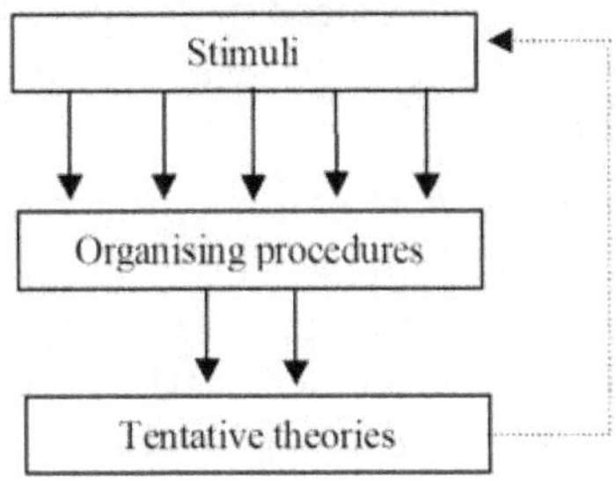

*Figure 16. Inductive processing of stimuli to produce tentative theories*

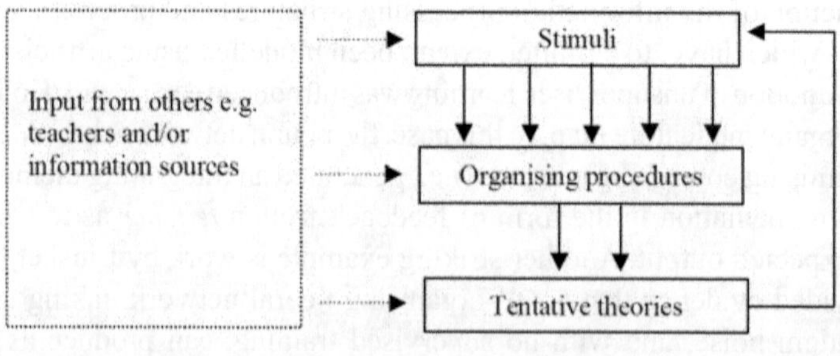


complex tentative theories—for example, logical deduction and the recognition of analogy relations.

There is a sense, then, in which the source of information needs—tentative theories requiring testing, improving, and extending—arise spontaneously from humans' natural processes of adapting to stimuli within their environment.

However, tentative theories are by no means always generated autonomously by learners. It may often be the case that, when aware of some conceptual incongruity and the consequent need to resolve it via an integrating theme, the learner may turn to others—whether person to person, or in the form of recorded information sources—in the hope that they may suggest an appropriate integrating theme. These people and information sources may do so with varying degrees of evidential support, which will affect the extent to which the theme is accepted by the learner as a *tentative* as opposed to relatively secure theory. It may be, for example, that the level of supporting evidence provided by, coupled with the authority of the source, as perceived by the learner, is sufficient for the learner to accept the theory and to integrate it into his or her existing knowledge structure without further examination.

However, in an alternative scenario, a teacher may suggest to learners a tentative theory (or, indeed, several) with the intention that the learners examine the evidence supporting the theory for themselves and come to their own conclusions. The extent to which the learner perceives the need to do this, and possesses the ability to do so, may relate to his or her stage of critical development—an issue discussed in more detail in Chapter II.

Such input from others (or *mediation*) is not restricted to the generation of tentative theories (integrating themes). As shown in Figure 16, it may also relate to exposing learners to the *need* for an integrating theme by exposing them to relevant stimuli in the form of conceptual incongruities of which they may not have been aware. Input from others may also relate to helping the learner to develop his or her own strategies—or organizing procedures—for generating integrating themes. These issues are further discussed in Chapter III.

In complex learning situations, especially those lacking mediation or guidance by knowledgeable others (for example, a teacher or research supervisor), such tentative theories are likely to be imperfect and to require iterations of the theory generation/test cycle to improve over time in response to feedback. During this process, the individual will seek, retrieve, and evaluate information to assess the extent to which it (1) wholly or partially supports the tentative theory in terms of its power satisfactorily to resolve the conceptual anomaly, (2) fails to provide support for, or contradicts the theory, (3) suggests one or more new integrating themes, or (4) raises new anomalies, themselves requiring resolution.

## Theory Generation and Testing

In complex learning situations, then, the testing of a tentative theory entails considering evidence—whether already possessed by the individual in his or her existing knowledge, or deriving from new external information sought or otherwise encountered (from people and/or recorded information sources). External information sources may also, as noted previously, be used in the generation of tentative theories.

The individual may seek, retrieve, and evaluate information to assess the extent to which it may help in the process of generating and testing an integrating theme capable of resolving the conceptual anomaly. Such a process entails asking (and answering) the question: *To what extent does consideration of the evidence enable the incongruity to be resolved?* In terms of the integrating theme model, this entails incongruity resolution via the establishment of similarities shared by discrete entities whereby they can become conceptually integrated. As previously noted, differences between entities may, however remain—indeed new ones may appear as a result of processing new information. These represent further incongruities requiring resolution. But how might these theories be generated and tested, in such a way as to improve their quality over time?

The cybernetician Gordon Pask conceived of the processes whereby tentative theories are generated then tested, via the exploration of evidence, to form new levels of understanding (based on the establishment of similarities and differences) as constituting what he termed "conversations." These ideas are formulated in conversation theory, developed by Pask, Scott, and others over 30 years of theoretical and related empirical work (Ford, 2000; Pangaro, 2001; Pask, 1975a, 1975b, 1976a, 1976b, 1976c, 1979, 1988, 1990, Pask & Gregory, 1986; Pask & Scott, 1972, 1973).

Conversation theory is one of very many learning theories which have been developed over the years. Theories range from early behaviourist, through information processing, to more modern constructivist theories. These include, for example, *andragogy theory* (Knowles, 1984); *Gagne's conditions of learning* (Gagne, 1985; Gagne, Briggs, & Wager, 1992); *constructivist theory* (Bruner, 1973, 1996); *conversation theory* (Pask, 1976a, 1990); *experiential learning* (Rogers & Freiberg, 1994); *information processing theory* (Miller, Galanter, & Pribram, 1960); *levels of processing* (Craik & Lockhart, 1972); *operant conditioning* (Skinner, 1954, 1971); *script theory* (Schank & Abelson, 1977); *situated learning* (Lave & Wenger, 1990; McLellan, 1995); *social learning theory* (Bandura, 1977); *structural learning theory* (Scandura, 1973, 1976); *cognitive dissonance* (Festinger, 1957; Wickland & Brehm, 1976); *genetic epistemology* (Gallagher & Reid, 1981; Piaget, 1970); and so forth.

However, conversation theory is particularly appropriate to the focus of this book since it is applicable to—indeed, was generated from empirical investigations into—the learning of complex educational subject matter. It is a constructivist theory and bridges individual cognitive and social theories of learning (discussed in Chapter II), as well as offering a bridge between autonomous and mediated learning (discussed in Chapter III), and between learning from people and from the results of autonomous information seeking from recorded information sources (discussed in Chapter IV) including those presented and mediated by computers (Chapter V). Its focus and empirical base thus map extremely well onto the central concerns of this book, namely, the integration of aspects of education, information and communications technology (ICT), and library/information science.

Conversation theory is complex, and it redefines commonly used terms such as *conversation, understanding,* and *concept* formally and rigorously. The theory conceives of understanding as resulting from conversations between different conceptual participants (what Pask terms "p-individuals"). A p-individual is a "coherent conceptual system." Thus, for example, a p-individual may be someone's understanding of a particular topic, or a view on a particular issue. Different people (for example, a teacher and a learner) may have different views on the same issue. Two (or more) people could engage in conversation in which ideas are exchanged and discussed and negotiated in order to learn. In this case, each different p-individual is *located* in a different person.

However, an alternative scenario is one in which a single person is aware of, and considering, two (or more) different views of some issue without interacting with any other person. In this case, the two (or more) p-individuals (coherent conceptual systems) are "located" in the same person, and the conversation takes the form of an inner dialogue in which the person considers and discusses the issues autonomously. In Pask's terms, an individual person is a "mechanical participant" or "m-individual." As well as people (biological m-individuals), m-individuals can be nonhuman—for example, computer systems (machine m-individuals). Thus, p-individuals *may or may not* correspond to mechanical participants (m-individuals, including people and machines). As Green (2002) notes:

*the P-individual which is a dynamic productive and incidentally reproductive, adaptive, evolving and learning collection or entailment mesh of concepts. Second the M-individual which is a mechanical or biological medium e.g. a brain or a star, which supports the P-individual and the strains its concepts produce.*

A conversation consists of interactions between p-individuals whereby both agree on the nature and derivation of one or more concepts. Where agreement is reached, the concept can be shared by both in further intellectual activity. Differences may result in new concepts being available to both. A conversational domain is a set of topics making up a coherent subject of study or attention. Theory generation and testing via the exchange, explanation, and justification of mental models is the essence of conversations. Thus, p-individuals engage in conversations with other p-individuals within particular conversational domains, in which they try to form agreements. In relation to a given topic, each p-individual will try to form a model of the other p-individual's model of the topic, and they will exchange and justify theories to each other.

Higher order p-individuals are the result of agreements between lower order p-individuals. A conversation may itself be a p-individual. Agreement about what constitutes a conversational domain is also a p-individual. As noted previously, a particular p-individual may be *housed in* and thus correspond to a particular human being—a biological m-individual. Conversations may thus take place between two p-individuals corresponding to two people—for example, learner and teacher; information seeker and search intermediary; and so forth. However, this is not necessarily the case. An m-individual may possess many p-individuals (conceptual systems), and a p-individual may be shared by many m-individuals.

A *topic* is a set of connected propositions (e.g., a definition, model, or theory) interpreted in terms of a context (e.g., educational, psychological, or social). A *concept* is a mental procedure that recognises or brings about a particular instantiation or modelling of a topic. A *task structure* is the description of a concept—that is, a description of what must be done to bring about the instantiation or modelling of a topic. To take an example from Scott (2001a), instantiating or modelling of the topic *hand* may be achieved by, say, assembling a model of a hand from component parts, or drawing a diagram of a hand. Although this example is simple, it should be noted that Pask and Scott's empirical work extended across a wide range of complex academic topics and subject areas.

A *memory* is a mental procedure for recognising, reproducing, or maintaining relationships between topics—for example, explaining how a topic A derives from subtopics B and C. An *entailment mesh* is a description (usually presented in graphical form as a map of the domain showing topics as nodes, and relationships between topics as arcs) of a memory—that is, of topics and relationships between them. These relationships may be hierarchical, for example, showing that topic A

*Figure 17. Derivations and analogies in related universes of discourse (Thin arrows denote derivations; the broad arrow denotes analogous relationships)*

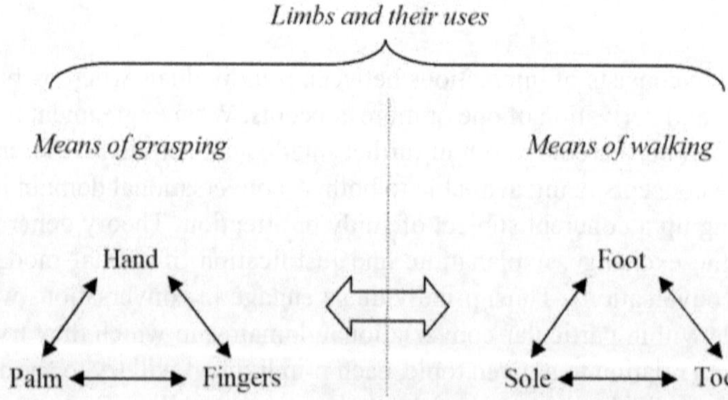


(hand) is defined in terms of topic B (fingers) and topic C (palm)—or hierarchical, showing how topics and topic relationships are analogous to others, for example, how the relationship between hand, fingers and palm (which may relate to a *means of grasping* universe of discourse) is analogous (in a joint analogical universe of *limbs and their uses*) to that between foot, toes, and sole (which may relate to a *means of walking* universe of discourse). Figure 17 shows an example of derivational and analogous relationships.

To understand a topic A is to be able to reconstruct the *concept* of A. To understand subject matter entailing more than one topic (as in all realistically complex learning) the individual must also be able to reconstruct an appropriate *memory* by explaining how relevant topics relate to and are derived from other topics. To demonstrate full understanding, a learner must be able both to provide *why explanations* (for example, verbally or in an essay) and how topics interrelate to form a conceptual whole, and to provide nonverbal *how demonstrations* of each topic *in action* as it were.

A conversational domain is a set of topics making up a coherent subject of study or attention. According to conversation theory, any conversational domain includes *why* relationships and *how* relationships. These not only map onto the nature of understanding (see next paragraph), but also onto the type of interactions engaged in by participants in a conversation. *Why* relationships concern how a topic is related to other topics (memories). *How* relationships concern how to recognise and reconstruct a topic (concepts).

In terms of the nature of understanding, Pask identified two fundamental components of understanding which apply to the learning of any complex subject matter, namely,

*Table 4. Types of conversational interactions (adapted from Scott, 2001a)*

| **Participant 1 may...** | Ask why? | Ask how? | Offer an explanation of why | Offer an explanation of how | Ask for a demonstra-tion | Carry out a demonstra-tion |
|---|---|---|---|---|---|---|
| **Participant 2 may...** | Offer an explanation of why | Offer an explanation of how | Request an explanation of why | Request an explanation of how | Carry out a demonstra-tion | Request a demonstra-tion |

*descriptions* and *procedures*. Both description building and procedure building are necessary to achieve full understanding. Description building entails the construction of an overall conceptual map—a description of what may be known in a subject area. Procedure building relates to mastering operational details—the evidence and logical arguments necessary to support the larger picture. Both components are necessary for full understanding. As noted by Entwistle (1981):

*Pask has likened these two aspects to the way an architect designs a building. He has to build up the overall plan (description building) and also to work out the detailed processes, and the logistics of those processes (...procedure building) whereby the plan can be converted into an actual building.* (p. 93)

Description building maps onto the *why* questions mentioned previously, while procedure building maps onto *how* questions. These map onto the type of interactions engaged in by participants in a conversation (Table 4). In this table, participant 1 may be, for example, a learner or information seeker, and participant 2 may be a teacher or information provider.

Conversation theory thus illuminates the nature of the interactions, and sequences of interactions entailed in the learning process. It describes the types of questions individuals need to (and, based on empirical studies of learning—*do*) pose to an information source (whether teacher, book, or other recorded source, or self in an inner dialogue) in order to achieve understanding. Such interactions between new information and the learner's existing conceptual structure may result in confirmation, extension, challenge, or contradiction—even plain failure to comprehend or accept. Information needs emanate from these interactions, as agreements and disagreements are explored. The nature and types of these information needs will depend on the nature and precise contact point of conflicts and conceptual incongruities between the two p-individuals. At a fine-grained level, this is likely to be highly complex.

In simple terms, *why* relationships (and associated questions posed by learners) relate to a broad conceptual overview of the subject area to be learned. *How* relationships (and associated questions) relate to the detailed evidence supporting the broad overview. Pask likened the difference to that between creating an overall architectural design for a building (what it will look like and what it is designed to achieve) and the detailed operational plan for building it (procedural requirements such as the practical details of the electrical wiring, the plumbing, etc.). In terms of learning a new subject area, *why* questions would relate to establishing a broad overview of what the main topics are, and how they seem to relate to one another. *How* questions would relate to getting to grips with the details of each of the individual topics.

As noted previously, a conversation consists of interactions between p-individuals in which both agree on the nature and derivation (the *why* and the *how*) of one or more concepts. Where agreement is reached, the concept can be shared by both in further intellectual activity. Differences may result in new concepts being available to both. This is the intellectual activity that (1) results in changes in the individual's knowledge structure that we refer to as learning and (2) generates what we refer to as information needs.

In Pask's terms, agreement represents shared understanding of the nature and derivation of topics. The same basic idea drives the notion of understanding as the identification of higher order themes by which otherwise discrete lower order units of information become integrated. In both cases, conceptual incongruities result from the extent to which agreement is not reached, or discrete units of information do not become integrated. Such incongruities may generate further information needs geared to the further exploration of such incongruities.

During this process the learner may need to bring in other information sources to shed light upon aspects of the interaction—for example, to further clarify points made by the author of a book or paper, or to seek evidence for disputed ideas. Such interactions may thus generate further information needs. Further conversations will be initiated that are subsumed by others—that is, the function of a conversation may be to inform a higher level conversation.

A conversation may take place between the two conceptual systems represented by a learner and another person. Thus teacher and learner can interact, negotiating agreements and flagging disagreements as learning goes on. However, although particularly applicable to information processing situations entailing teachers and learners, the theory is also applicable to less formal and mediated information use. Pask (as cited in Scott, 2001a) points out that conversations between different p-individuals can take place within the brain of a single person—representing inner dialogues as people come to understand:

> *Pask argues that the distinctions required to characterise the cognition of an isolated psyche are the same as those made by the external observer of a conversation... In the 'outer conversations' that constitute social institutions, the participants agree and disagree and negotiate shared descriptions, explanations and justifications. In her 'inner conversation', a person explains and justifies herself to herself.* (p. 28)

*Figure 18. Outline model of a Paskian conversation (adapted from Scott, 2006)*

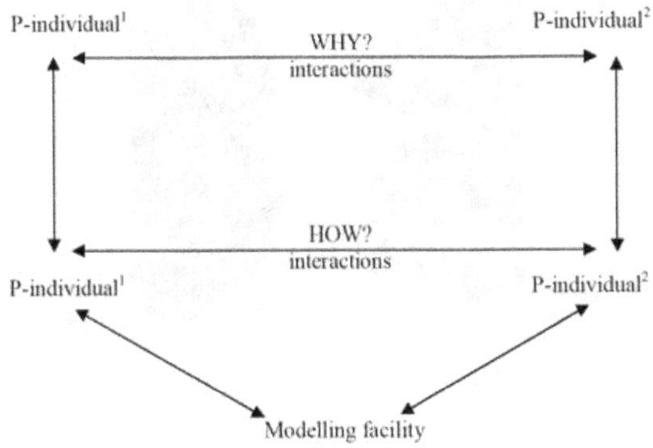


As we will see in Chapter IV, this is interesting from the point of view of library and information science, which has a particular concern with autonomous information seeking and interaction between information seeker and information sources, which is not necessarily mediated by a formal teacher or adviser. In such situations, the notion of an inner dialogue between p-individuals (conceptual systems) existing within a single m-individual (the information seeker) is central.

However, the quality of information possessed by a second p-individual—acting in relation to a first p-individual in the role of teacher and evaluator of theories—is important. This is especially so where both p-individuals are housed within the same person (in Pask's terms, the same biological m-individual). In this case, access to external information may be needed in the iterative process of testing and improving theories. This is interesting from the point of view of library and information science, which has a particular concern with relatively independent information seeking, and interaction between information seeker and information retrieval (IR) system, which does not necessarily include a formal teacher or adviser.

Pask's conversational model (adapted from Scott, 2006) is shown in Figure 18. The model includes a *modelling facility* in which emerging understandings can be tested out in the real world, or as Scott (2006) puts it: "in which the pragmatic consequences of their theorising may be explored" (p. 311). This feature of conversation theory is further explored in Chapter X, where the importance of pragmatic feedback in linking theory and practice, classroom and real world, is discussed.

Scott (2001b) describes conversation theory with reference to the work of Kolb and Rescher. In his experiential learning cycle model, Kolb (1984) also recognises the fundamental difference between abstract conceptualisation and concrete experimentation. Kolb proposes that learning takes place as a cycle of activity moving from:

*Figure 19. An ambiguous image*

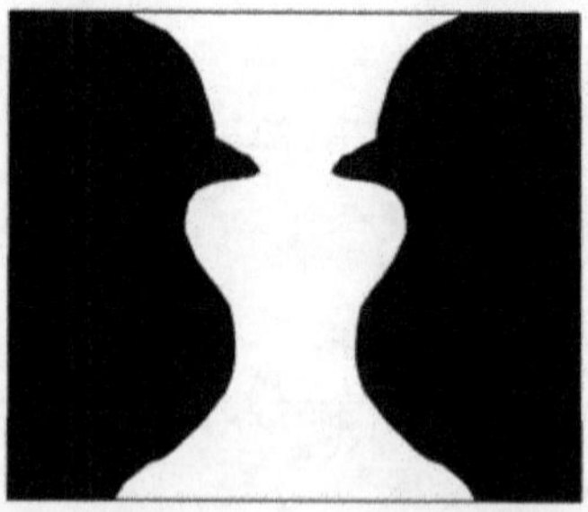

concrete experience of the world; through reflection on that experience; abstract conceptualisation resulting from that reflection, entailing the generation of concepts and theories; to active experimentation, entailing the application and testing of theory in the real world; leading back to the beginning of the cycle—concrete experience. Kolb's learning cycle is explored in the next chapter in relation to learning styles.

Pask flagged the importance of the distinction between the *conceptual* and the *operational/procedural*. Scott goes on to describe Rescher's (1973, 1977) model in which he elaborates this fundamental distinction to show how the two elements work together in complementary ways, with different types of testing/validation, to enable scientific discovery. This link with Rescher's work is further explored in Chapter X.

Theory generation as described so far appears a somewhat logical, sequential process linked to conscious thought. However, theory generation may also result from altogether less consciously controlled, more holistic and intuitive perceptual processing. Such processing is perfectly compatible with Pask's conversation theory, representing essentially an inner *why* dialogue within the same person (m-individual), in which there occurs a sudden perception of a re-configuration of the relationships making up a whole, or gestalt. In the case of creativity, this reconfiguration is particularly novel. Accounts of creativity often describe such forms of processing.

An example may be seen in the classic account of early pioneers of flight who, presumably initially looking to birds for an analogy, attempted to build aircraft with wings that flapped. The breakthrough came when they reconfigured their conception of the problem to one which could be better solved by applying the notion of driving air over a fixed wing. This entailed perceiving a high order similarity shared by these apparently very different configurations of objects and forces, in terms

of their both matching the complex problem requirements and constraints. Reconfiguring the way in which a problem is perceived may entail the type of perceptual *flip* experienced when viewing one of the popular ambiguous figures found in

*Table 5. Wallas' (1926) stage model of the creative process*

| | |
|---|---|
| Preparation | This stage entails focusing on the problem and thinking about its nature and features. |
| Incubation | During the incubation stage, the problem becomes internalised into the unconscious mind. |
| Intimation | This is in some ways similar to the "tip of the tongue" feeling in relation to remembering a word. The person has a feeling that a solution is imminent. |
| Illumination or insight | The flash of insight arrives, and the person is consciously aware of the solution. |
| Verification | The solution is then worked through and if necessary refined and applied. |

psychology texts. A familiar example is the picture which may be seen as either a black vase, or two birds facing each other in profile (Figure 19).

Rarely will both interpretations be equally visible to a person seeing the picture for the first time. He or she is likely to see it in terms of either vase or birds. To shift perception from one interpretation to the other requires a mental flip. However, the point is that this flip tends to be experienced as sudden and holistic. The alternative perception does not gradually emerge from the other, and it is not a question of the logical, step by step working out of feature by feature. Rather, the alternative perception suddenly comes—almost as a surprise. Once held, the perception can at first be quite difficult to reverse. When it is reversed, again, the change comes as a relatively sudden, holistic reconfiguration.

This does not imply that creative thinking is *entirely* holistic, parallel, and perception-based. Rather, these qualities seem to characterise the initial process of similarity recognition—particularly at high levels of complexity. Relatively sequential logic-based processing is of course important. However, this is likely to apply at the stage of verifying and elaborating the initial vision of similarity. Indeed, as long ago as 1926 Wallas (1926) recognised such differences in his model of creative processes. In this model, creativity proceeds in five stages (Table 5).

While it is still necessary to work through the logic of a creative idea in procedural detail before it can be tested, refined, and successfully applied, some flash of recognition is needed initially in order to perceive some key similarity. Such a flash of insight has been described as being more perception-based than logic-based (Hofstadter, 1995; Mitchell, 1993).

In accounts of creativity, it would appear that an important element of creative thinking does entail a relatively unplanned and often sudden recognition of a similarity between disparate entities. Often descriptions by people who have experienced some creative thought talk of some sudden flash of insight—an unexpected realisation in which previously unconnected phenomena come together. This often happens when the person is not concentrating on the particular problem. A classic example is the discovery of the ring structure of benzene by Kekule. He had a dream in which he saw snakes seizing their own tails and "awoke as if by a flash of lightning" (Sternberg & Davidson, 1995). Indeed, according to Strauss and Corbin (1997):

*Only under certain conditions will those insights arise ... [Questions and answers] are raised and sought even if on a subliminal level of consciousness, and sometimes for quite a time, before the vital question or answer breaks through to consciousness. Although knowledgeable about data and theory, the investigator somehow has to escape the very features of his or her work that may otherwise block the new perspective inherent in the sudden hunch, the flash of insight, the brilliant idea, or the profoundly different theoretical formulation. Specific knowledge, alas, is not only necessary but at times constitutes mental baggage that impedes this kind of intellectual creativity.* (p. 29)

Gregory (1987) also comments that mathematicians have often reported that, after worrying a particular problem for some time, it is only when they relax their focus that a solution suddenly comes to them in a flash. As Gregory notes:

*The clear implication is that our brains are at their most efficient when allowed to switch from phases of intense concentration to ones in which we exert no conscious control at all. (p. 171)*

In fact, Pask recognises the difference between relatively logical, step-by-step cumulative processing and more holistic parallel impressionistic processing as characterising distinct styles and strategies of learning—themselves linked to fundamental components of understanding. These issues are elaborated in the next chapter.

However, before going on to Chapter II, let us summarise the main concepts to have emerged from this exploration of basic learning processes in the form of a simple model (Figure 20).

These basic information processes are used with varying types and levels of conceptual incongruities, tentative theories, and evidence supporting theories in order to engage in varying types and levels of intellectual task—including those specified in the learning objectives previously discussed. The latter are labelled *information processing types* in Figure 21, which links basic information processes to such information processing types. The actual list of task-related information processing types (cognitive and affective) shown there is illustrative only.

As previously noted, there are many such lists. However, the types of *cognitive* task-related information processing selected as elements for the model are based on the cognitive objectives of Bloom and Krathwohl's (1956) taxonomy, rather than those of, for example, Biggs or Zimmer (2001). Categories from the Biggs' SOLO taxonomy were considered both too fine-grained and too narrow in focus for the

*Figure 20. The basic information processes entailed in learning*

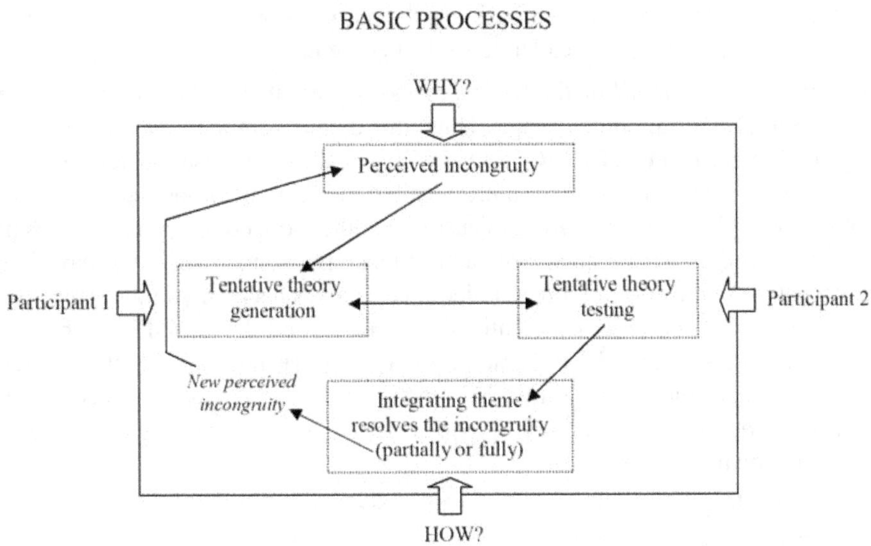


*Figure 21. Basic information processes and information processing types*

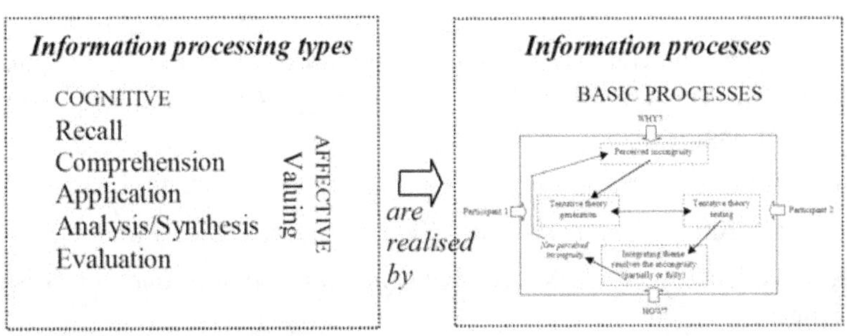


purposes of this holistic model. They do not exhibit the breadth of scope of Bloom's scheme in that they do not explicitly differentiate analysis, synthesis, application or evaluation. Zimmer's scheme is also arguably too fine-grained for the purposes of the model presented here, with its differentiation between such constructs as: abstracting and recognising; adducing, defining, and exemplifying; and applying, generalising, and exploiting.

From Bloom and Krathwohl's (1956) five *affective* objectives, only *valuing* has been used in the model. The first two categories—paying attention and responding to stimuli—were considered too basic for the purposes of the model, which relates to the learning of complex academic subject content.

In Figure 21, the *detail* of the basic processes presented in Figure 20 has been condensed into a thumbnail image. Thus, this detail is implied, or referenced, in Figure 21 by the heading BASIC PROCESSES. Such a condensation device is used elsewhere in this book, where a more detailed model is incorporated into a more holistic one. This is done in order to ensure that the more complex model does not have to reproduce all the details of each of its components, which will have been previously introduced at a more detailed level. This is necessary in the interests of clarity, since the model is systematically expanded and developed in each of the coming chapters. The model will gradually evolve, as we move through the chapters, to form a holistic model of learning. This model will blend key aspects of education, library/information science, and ICT to provide an integrated conceptual framework for educational informatics.

This chapter has explored basic learning processes common to us all. However, each of us may use these basic processes in very different ways, and with differing results in terms of resultant knowledge. The next chapter will explore such differences.

## References


Anderson, L. W., & Krathwohl (Eds.). (2001). *A taxonomy for learning, teaching, and assessing: A revision of Bloom's taxonomy of educational objectives*. New York: Longman.

Bandura, A. (1977). *Social learning theory.* New York: General Learning Press.

Baum, E. B. (2004). *What is thought?* Cambridge, MA: MIT Press.

Beale, R., & Jackson, T. (1990). *Neural computing: An introduction*. Bristol, UK: Hilger.

Biggs, J. (1999). *Teaching for quality learning at university*. Buckingham, UK: SRHE and Open University Press.

Biggs, J. (n.d.). *SOLO*. Retrieved August 1, 2007, from http://www.tedi.uq.edu.au/downloads/Biggs_Solo.pdf

Biggs, J., & Collis, K. (1982). *Evaluating the quality of learning: The SOLO taxonomy*. New York: Academic Press.

Bloom, B. S., & Krathwohl, D. R. (1956). *Taxonomy of educational objectives: The classification of educational goals, by a committee of college and university examiners. Handbook I: Cognitive domain*. New York: Longman.

Bruner, J. (1973). *Going beyond the information given*. New York: Norton.

Bruner, J. (1996). *The culture of education*. Cambridge, MA: Harvard University Press.

Chang, C. Y., & Chung, P. C. (2000). Two-layer competitive based Hopfield neural network for medical image edge detection. *Optical Engineering, 39*(3), 695-703.

Craik, F., & Lockhart, R. (1972). Levels of processing: A framework for memory research. *Journal of Verbal Learning and Verbal Behaviour, 11,* 671-684.

Entwistle, N. J. (1981). *Styles of learning and teaching*. Chichester, UK: Wiley.

Festinger, L. (1957). A *theory of cognitive dissonance*. Stanford, CA: Stanford University Press.

Ford, N. (1999). Information retrieval and creativity: Towards support for the original thinker. *Journal of Documentation, 55*(5), 528-542.

Ford, N. (2000). The increasing relevance of Pask's work to modern information seeking and use. *Kybernetes, 30*(5/6), 603-629.

Gagne, R. (1985). *The conditions of learning* (4th ed.). New York: Holt, Rinehart and Winston.

Gagne, R. M., Briggs, L. J., & Wager, W. (1992). *Principles of instructional design* (4th ed.). Orlando, FL: Harcourt Brace Jovanovich.

Gallagher, J. M., & Reid, D. K. (1981). *The learning theory of Piaget and Inhelder*. Monterey, CA: Brooks/Cole.

Green, N. (2002). *Axioms from interactions of actors theory*. Cardiff, UK: University of Wales, Department of Computer Science, Real Time Study Group.

Gregory, R. L. (Ed.). (1987). *The Oxford companion to the mind*. Oxford, UK: Oxford University Press.

Hämäläinen, T. D. (2001). Parallel implementation of self-organizing maps. In *Self-organizing neural networks: Recent advances and applications archive* (pp. 245-278). New York: Springer-Verlag. (Springer Studies in Fuzziness and Soft Computing Series.)

Harrow, A. (1972). *A taxonomy of the psychomotor domain. A guide for developing behavioural objectives*. New York: McKay.

Hofstadter, D. (1995). *Concepts and creative analogies: Computer models of the fundamental mechanisms of thought*. New York: Basic Books.

Holyoak, K. J., & Thagard, P. (1996). *Mental leaps: Analogy in creative thought*. Cambridge, MA: MIT Press.

Hudson, L. (1968). *Contrary imaginations*. Harmondsworth, UK: Penguin.

Keane, M. T. (1988). *Analogical problem solving*. New York: Ellis Horwood.

Kohonen, T. (1988). The "neural" phonetic typewriter. *Computer, 21*(3), 11-22.

Kolb, D. A. (1984). *Experiential learning*. Englewood Cliffs, NJ: Prentice Hall.

Knowles, M. (1984). *Andragogy in action.* San Francisco: Jossey-Bass.

Krathwohl, D. R., Bloom, B. S., & Masia, B. B. (1964). *Taxonomy of educational objectives: The classification of educational goals. Handbook II: Affective domain.* New York: David McKay.

Lave, J., & Wenger, E. (1990). *Situated learning: Legitimate peripheral participation.* Cambridge, UK: Cambridge University Press.

Linsker, R. (1988). Self-organization in a perceptual network. *Computer, 21*(3), 105-117.

McLellan, H. (1995). *Situated learning perspectives.* Englewood Cliffs, NJ: Educational Technology Publications.

Miller, G. A., Galanter, E., & Pribram, K. H. (1960). *Plans and the structure of behaviour.* New York: Holt, Rinehart & Winston.

Minsky, M. (1986). *The society of mind.* New York: Simon & Schuster.

Mitchell, M. (1993). *Analogy-making as perception: A computer model.* Cambridge, MA: MIT Press.

Pangaro, P. (2001). THOUGHTSTICKER 1986: A personal history of conversation theory in software and its progenitor, Gordon Pask. *Kybernetes, 30*(5/6), 790-806.

Pask, G. (1975a). *Conversation, cognition and learning.* Amsterdam: Elsevier.

Pask, G. (1975b). *The cybernetics of human learning and performance.* London: Hutchinson.

Pask, G. (1976a). *Conversation theory: Applications in education and epistemology.* Amsterdam: Elsevier.

Pask, G. (1976b). Conversational techniques in the study and practice of education. *British Journal of Educational Psychology, 46,* 12-25.

Pask, G. (1976c). Styles and strategies of learning. *British Journal of Educational Psychology, 46,* 128-148.

Pask, G. (1979). *Final report of SSRC Research Programme HR 2708.* Richmond, Surrey: System Research Ltd.

Pask, G. (1988). Learning strategies, teaching strategies, and conceptual or learning style. In R. R. Schmeck (Ed.), *Learning strategies and learning styles* (pp. 83-99). New York: Plenum Press.

Pask, G. (1990). Some formal aspects of conversation theory and Lp. In F. Heylighen, E. Rosseel, & F. Demeyere (Eds.), *Self-steering and cognition in complex systems: Toward a new cybernetics* (pp. 240-247). New York: Gordon and Breach.

Pask, G., & Gregory, D. (1986). Conversational systems. In R. J. Zeidner (Ed.), *Human productivity enhancement. Volume II* (pp. 204-235). New York: Praeger.

Pask, G., & Scott, B. (1972). Learning strategies and individual competence. *International Journal of Man-Machine Studies, 4,* 217-253.

Pask, G., & Scott, B. (1973). CASTE: A system for exhibiting learning strategies and regulating uncertainty. *International Journal of Man-Machine Studies, 5,* 17-52.

Piaget, J. (1970). *The science of education and the psychology of the child.* New York: Grossman.

Popper, K. R. (1979). *Objective knowledge: An evolutionary approach* (Rev. ed.). Oxford, UK: Clarendon Press.

Rescher, N. (1973). *Conceptual idealism.* Oxford, UK: Blackwell.

Rescher, N. (1977). *Methodological pragmatism.* Oxford, UK: Blackwell.

Rogers, C. R., & Freiberg, H. J. (1994). *Freedom to learn* (3rd ed.). Columbus, OH: Merrill/Macmillan.

Saint Edward's University. (n.d.). T*ask oriented question construction wheel based on Bloom's Taxonomy*. Retrieved August 1, 2007, from http://edselect.com/Docs/wheel.pdf

Scandura, J. M. (1973). *Structural learning I: Theory and research.* London: Gordon and Breach.

Scandura, J. M. (1976). *Structural learning II: Issues and approaches.* London: Gordon and Breach.

Schank, R. C., & Abelson, R. (1977). *Scripts, plans, goals, and understanding.* Hillsdale, NJ: Earlbaum.

Scott, B. (2001a). Conversation theory: A constructivist, dialogical approach to educational technology. *Cybernetics & Human Knowing, 8*(4), 25-46.

Scott, B. (2001b). Gordon Pask's conversation theory: A domain independent constructivist model of human knowing. *Foundations of Science, 6*(4), 343-360.

Scott, B. (2006). Reflexivity revisited: The sociocybernetics of belief, meaning, truth and power. *Kybernetes, 35*(3/4), 308-316.

Shachmurove, Y. (2005). Business applications of emulative neural networks. *International Journal of Business, 10*(4), 303-322.

Skinner, B. F. (1954). The science of learning and the art of teaching. *Harvard Educational Review, 24*(2), 86-97.

Skinner, B. F. (1971). *Beyond freedom and dignity.* New York: Knopf.

Sternberg, R. J., & Davidson, J. E. (Eds.). (1995). *The nature of insight.* Cambridge, MA: MIT Press.

Strauss, A. L., & Corbin, J. (Eds.). (1997). *Grounded theory in practice*. London: Sage.

Ubeyli, E. D., & Guler, I. (2005). Improving medical diagnostic accuracy of ultrasound Doppler signals by combining neural network models. *Computers in Biology and Medicine, 35*(6), 533-554.

Wallas, G. (1926). *The art of thought*. New York: Harcourt Brace.

Wickland, R., & Brehm, J. (1976). *Perspectives on cognitive dissonance*. New York: Halsted Press.

Zimmer, R. S. (2001). Variations on a string bag: Using Pask's principles for practical course design. *Kybernetes, 30*(7), 1006-1023.

# Chapter II

# Learning: Individual Differences

## Introduction

The previous chapter sketched some of the basic intellectual processes entailed in learning that are common to us all. However, different individuals may use these same basic processes in very different ways and may bring to them very different types and levels of prior knowledge. Certain stylistic differences in the way people go about learning are relatively value free. That is, adopting one style rather than another is not necessarily better or worse, although qualitatively different types of knowledge may result from relatively strong biases (see, for example, the *global* and *analytic* information processing styles described later on).

However, certain other differences in the way information is processed are more value laden in that they are associated with different types and levels of resultant knowledge. Such types and levels of knowledge may be considered, from certain perspectives, to be of higher or lower quality (see, for example, the *deep* and *surface* approaches to studying described later on).

The outcomes of learning may be affected not only by the learning processes that the individual applies in a learning situation, but also by what he or she brings to the learning situation, in terms of existing types and levels of knowledge. Such differences are also explored in this chapter. This may apply at all levels of learning—from basic concept formation to critical thinking and creativity.

Understanding of a given body of knowledge may be acquired via different routes and with differing emphases. Learning *strategies* are defined here as differences in the way the same information is processed to generate knowledge. Learning *styles* are tendencies and/or preferences consistently used as the same type of strategy across different tasks. Learning styles constitute a subset of a more general class of construct representing characteristic ways of processing information—cognitive styles. Learning styles may be thought of as cognitive styles as they apply and are observed specifically in relation to learning. Many such stylistic differences have been identified (for example, Brumby, 1982; Entwistle, 1981; Honey & Mumford, 1986; Jonassen & Grabowski, 1993; Kolb, 1984; Miller, 1987; Riding & Cheema, 1991; Schmeck, 1988).

The following sections briefly outline some key individual differences that have been the focus of considerable research attention over recent years. Cognitive and learning styles are a subset of human *individual differences*, which have formed the focus of much work in education over the years and which, as we will see in Chapter VII, is informing a number of developments in the emerging field of educational informatics.

Perhaps the most obvious—and influential—individual difference relates to the level of knowledge each person brings to bear on the learning of new material. An obvious if somewhat gross difference is that between *novice* and *expert*—a difference that has formed the focus of many studies. However, much teaching is directed towards classes of students whose level of knowledge is known, or assumed to be relatively homogeneous. For example, knowing that all learners in a class have successfully passed a level 1 course to a recognised standard in a recognised curriculum of, say, mathematics, enables a teacher to design level 2 learning materials and approaches which are appropriate to those learners' existing knowledge level.

However, such standardised descriptions and assumptions of homogeneity relating to what a person knows in a particular subject area can only take us so far. At more intimately detailed levels—and more so in *softer* subjects than the example of mathematics where there may not be such a precise and objective specification of exactly what is and is not known—each person's knowledge structure is much more individual, idiosyncratic, and ultimately, unique.

For effective learning to take place, new information must be *enmeshed* with each person's individually different level of knowledge via the integrating themes introduced in the previous chapter—generated, tested, and refined through the lenses of stylistic individual differences. The present chapter explores individual differences relating to both *styles* of learning and *levels* of learning.

## Styles of Learning

The Coffield Report (Coffield, Moseley, Hall, & Ecclestone, 2004) provides a highly critical view of a number of popular learning style models. The report notes that:

*[S]ome of the most popular models extrapolate from evidence of reliability to strong assertions of generalisability, namely that learners can transfer their styles to other contexts or that measures will produce similar results with other types of student.* (p. 2)

It also draws attention to a degree of conceptual confusion, variation in the quality and value of different models, problems of measurement, and lack of research focus on effect size. Perhaps the main danger is in viewing the research as more mature and less exploratory than it currently is. This can lead to engaging in oversimplistic and uncritical application, particularly of learning style measures, for example, to drive adaptive educational informatics systems.

Having said this, cognitive and learning styles have been the subject of intensive research over many decades, and a number of rich and illuminative models have been derived. The Coffield Report (Coffield et al., 2004) acknowledges that such models may be used in more appropriate ways. These can avoid overly simplistic approaches in which styles may become prescriptive labels, and "a narrow view of 'matching' teaching and learning styles that could be limiting rather than liberating" (p. 3). The report goes on to note that:

[S]*ome theorists promote the idea that learners should develop a repertoire of styles, so that an awareness of their own preferences and abilities should not bar them from working to acquire those styles which they do not yet possess. In particular, as students move from didactic forms of instruction to settings with a mixture of lectures, seminars and problem-based learning, it may become possible for them to use a range of approaches. This can lead to a plan for teachers to develop these styles through different teaching and learning activities, or it can lead to what might be seen as a type of 'pedagogic sheep dip', where teaching strategies aim explicitly to touch upon all styles at some point in a formal programme.*

*Other theorists promote the idea of learning styles instruments as a diagnostic assessment tool that encourages a more self-aware reflection about strengths and weaknesses. For supporters of this idea, the notion of learning styles offers a way for teachers and students to talk more productively about learning, using a more focused vocabulary to do so.*

## Kolb, Honey, and Mumford

It is perhaps unsurprising, granted that there are different processes and stages entailed in learning, that different individuals may display some bias or imbalance in (i.e., be stronger in, and/or have a preference towards) the application of them. In Kolb's (1984) model, learning takes place in a cycle of different stages entailing different types of activity—concrete experience (CE), reflective observation (RO), abstract conceptualisation (AC) and active experimentation (AE) (see Figure 22).

These cyclical *stages* also form the basis for Kolb's (1984) model of learning style*s*. He argued that while ideally all learners would engage in all stages of his cycle, in reality individuals display biases. He proposed a model entailing four such biases, or learning styles, which represent different combinations of the four stages. These styles are:

- *Diverging* (a combination of CE and RO
- *Assimilating* (a combination of AC and RO
- *Converging* (a combination of AC and AE
- *Accommodating* (a combination of CE and AE

Kolb (1984) argued that there is a distinction between how we approach a task, and how we think and feel about it. In terms of *approaching* a task, we may engage in *either* (1) active experimenting (doing) or (2) reflective observation (watching)—but not at the same time. In terms of *thinking/feeling* about the task, we may engage in *either* concrete experience (feeling) or abstract conceptualisation (thinking). These choices may be represented in a matrix as shown in Figure 23.

Kolb (1984) thought of the horizontal dimension in terms of *grasping* experience (doing or watching), and the vertical dimension in terms of *transforming* experience (feeling or thinking). Each of the grasping and transforming dimensions contains its own tension. *Doing* and *watching* are in a dialectical relationship with each other, as are *feeling* and *thinking*—that is, they relate to each other both negatively and at the same time positively. They are negatively related in that they cannot be engaged in simultaneously. Thus, at a particular point in time in relation to a particular task, a choice must be made between doing or watching, and between thinking and feeling.

*Figure 22. Kolb's learning cycle*

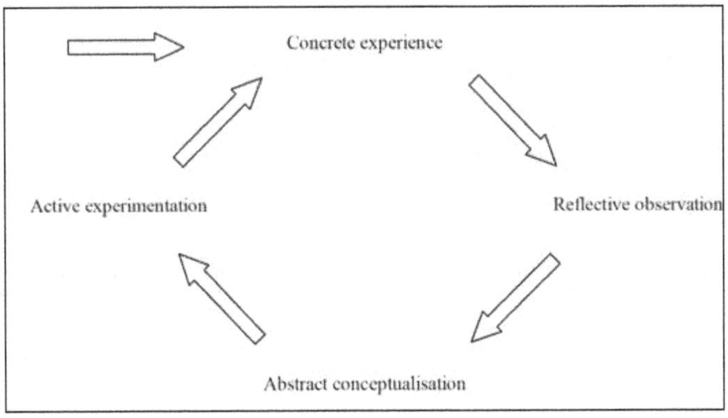


*Figure 23. Kolb's learning styles*

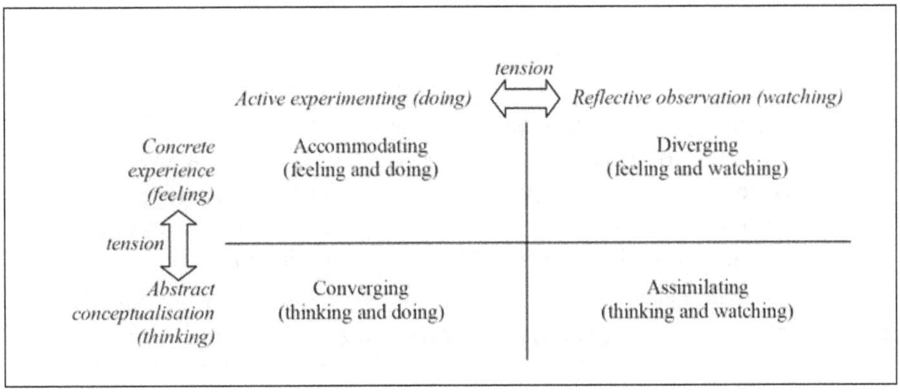


However, as we saw with the learning cycle model, different modes of grasping and transforming experience are complimentary and are all entailed in the full cycle of learning. In the model of learning stages, learning progresses from feeling (transforming) to watching (grasping) to thinking (transforming) to doing (grasping).

Honey and Mumford (1986) built on Kolb's (1984) work and proposed a learning cycle in which four learning styles are aligned directly with four stages. These stages/styles map well onto Kolb's four learning styles. Honey and Mumford's *Activist* is very similar to Kolb's *Accommodating*, *Reflector* to *Diverging*, *Theorist* to *Assimilating*, and *Pragmatist* to *Converging*. Honey and Mumford's learning cycle is shown in Figure 24.

Recall, however, in Kolb's (1984) model, learning styles did not map directly onto learning stages, rather, styles reflected combinations of decisions made by learners in relation to two opposing dimensions (doing *or* watching; feeling *or* thinking) which

*Figure 24. Honey and Mumford's learning cycle*

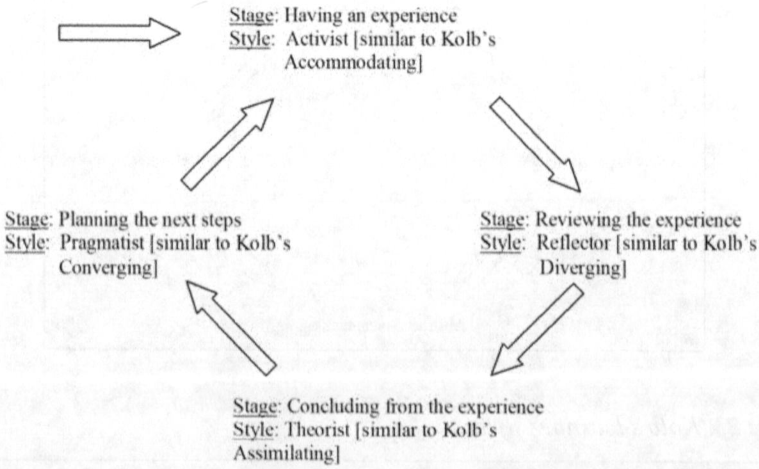


could not be engaged in at the same time. Honey and Mumford (1986) align their four learning styles directly with the four stages of their learning cycle. Although people tend to prefer different approaches to learning characterising the different stages, they do move between the stages in a progressive learning cycle. This cycle is repeated as necessary in order to achieve successful learning.

## Pask's Learning Styles and Strategies

Pask's work on *conversation theory* (briefly introduced in the previous chapter) led him not only to develop learning theory, but also to discover key associated learning styles. In comparison to the styles of Kolb and Honey and Mumford, Pask's styles map onto factors which are arguably more fundamental to the *components* of understanding, and for that reason they are much more directly applicable to the design of teaching materials. Pask's work is also particularly well rooted in empirical studies, relating to the learning of complex subject matter. These studies relate not only to how people actually *go about* learning, but also to the *effects* on learning, in both quantitative and qualitative terms, of the application of different styles. Pask also empirically investigated the effects of matching and mismatching the presentation of educational material with learners' cognitive styles—with dramatic results.

As part of his work developing conversation theory, Pask monitored the routes taken by learners through a range of complex academic topics in a series of experiments (Entwistle, 2001; Pask, 1976a, 1976b, 1976c, 1979, 1988; Pask & Scott, 1972,

1973; Robertson, 1977). In these experiments, learners were found to use one of two basic approaches.

*Holists* tended to adopt a broad approach to learning, examining interrelationships between several topics early in the learning process, and concentrating first on building a broad conceptual overview into which detail could subsequently be fitted. They remembered by relating material to their own experience and found enrichment material, anecdote, and analogies useful. Holists also tended to look further ahead in the hierarchy of topics making up the subject, and to be working on several aspects of the subject at the same time. They soon began to interrelate theoretical and practical aspects of a subject being learned and exhibited higher tolerance of uncertainty, building a tentative descriptive conceptual overview before testing this out with supporting evidence and procedural detail. They tended to work on a number of different parts of the subject map at the same time, testing multi-predicate hypotheses. Pask also found correlations between a holist bias and scores on a test of divergent thinking (Pask, 1979).

*Serialists* tended to use a predominantly narrow learning approach, examining one thing at a time and concentrating on separate topics and the logical sequences linking them. Serialists placed greater emphasis on memory and logical links rather than personal experience, anecdote, and analogy. Serialists kept theoretical and practical aspects of the subject being learned relatively separate and compartmentalised. They built up understanding on a much more secure (less tentative) basis by dealing thoroughly with one *building block* of understanding—carefully examining the detailed evidence supporting it—before sequentially moving on to the next. They adopted a much more *one thing at a time*, as opposed to the holists' *parallel processing* approach, testing out more simple single-predicate hypotheses. The overall picture emerged relatively late in the learning process. To summarise Pask's conclusions:

Serialists prefer an approach which:

- Is step by step, one thing at a time
- Is in a logical sequence
- Gets down to detail early on
- Avoids extraneous *enrichment* content

Holists prefer an approach which:

- Takes a broad focus, concentrating on a number of different aspects at once.
- Gives an early overview.

- Maps rich interrelationships between concepts…before getting down to details.
- Provides lots of *enrichment* content and analogies.

A stereotypical serialist route through subject matter is illustrated in Figure 25. Figure 26 shows a stereotypical holist route. The learning content here is part of that used in Pask and Scott's early experiments, in which learners were asked to learn about a taxonomy of imaginary Martian animals (which attempted to minimise *prior knowledge* effects!). Pask went on to extend his studies to a rich variety of complex *real* topics of study, including the operon, the menstrual cycle, reaction kinetics, spy networks, and the reign of Henry VIII. However, the Martian taxonomy illustrates the basic differences between the two learning approaches.

Figures 25 and 26 map the strategies onto the taxonomy. Within this taxonomy, the *Clobbits* species is made up of Clobs and Bits. There are two types of Clobs—Clob 2a and Clob 2b. Clob 2a has the following features…and so forth. Stereotypically, the serialist would progress in a very ordered and systematic way, working his or her way down to the most detailed level of the hierarchy relatively early. When s/he had mastered (learned all about) Clob2a, he/she would move on to Clob2b. Once the Clobs were mastered, he/she would begin learning about the Bits.

Figure 26 shows a stereotypical holist strategy. Holists tend to skip about much more than serialists, sampling information widely dispersed across the taxonomy. They are essentially trying to establish, early in the learning process, a good overview of what the subject matter is all about—what are its key concepts and how they interrelate—before studying the details. This may be likened to beginning a jigsaw puzzle by putting in occasional pieces of the jigsaw widely distributed across the picture space in order to gain an overall impression of what the hidden picture represents. Such an approach may be contrasted with beginning the jigsaw by concentrating on steadily building up a detailed picture of one part of it, and progressing systematically from there.

Pask subsequently found evidence that holist and serialist approaches were linked to the fundamental components of understanding introduced in the previous chapter, namely, *description building* and *procedure building*. The holist approach is particularly linked to description building, the serialist approach to procedure building. Recall from Chapter I that description building relates to the construction of an overall conceptual map, whereas procedure building entails mastering operational details—the evidence and logical arguments filling out and supporting the broad conceptual overview.

Although both description building and procedure building are necessary to achieve full understanding, Pask argues that individuals may tend generally to prefer, and be better at, one or the other. People displaying a holist-like style emphasise description building. Those displaying a serialist-like style emphasise procedure building.

*Figure 25. A stereotypical serialist learning strategy*

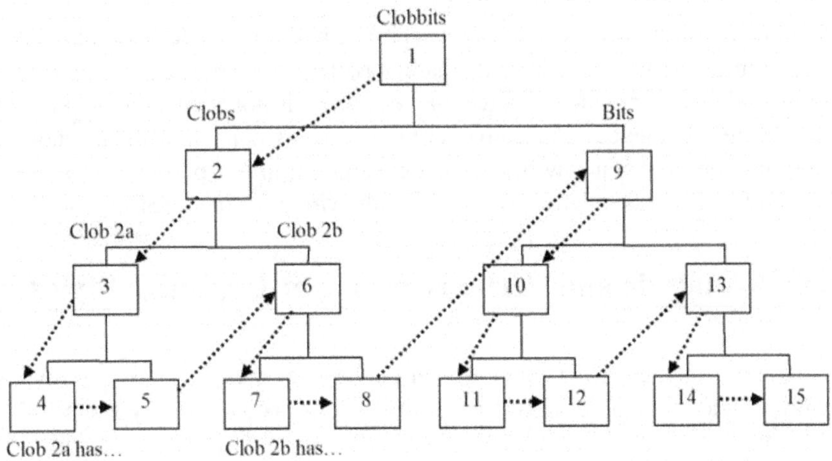


*Figure 26. A stereotypical holist learning strategy*

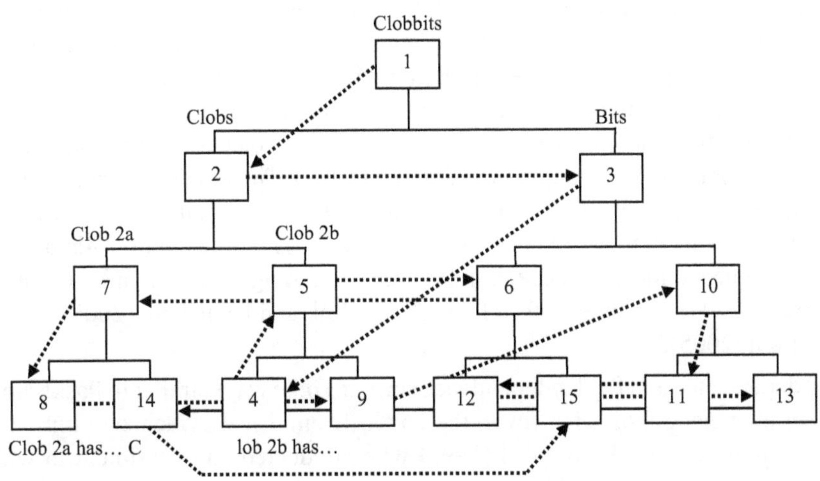


People better at description building and tending to employ a holist strategy Pask termed "comprehension learners." Those better at procedure building and tending to use a serialist strategy he termed "operation learners." Learners who display neither pathology, succeeding in engaging in high levels of both description and procedure building, Pask called "versatile learners."

Individuals with high comprehension learning abilities but low operation learning capabilities tend to display the characteristic pathology of *globetrotting*—or, overgeneralisation in which a conceptual overview is not adequately supported by more detailed evidence. The converse pathology associated with the individual strong in operation- but low in comprehension-learning capabilities Pask termed "improvidence"—essentially, failing to see the wood for the trees.

## Global/Analytic and Verbaliser/Imager Cognitive Styles

Riding and Cheema (1991) conclude, on the basis of their comparative review of cognitive styles, that there are two basic dimensions of cognitive style. One of these is what has been termed *field dependence*. Essentially, *field-independent* individuals (termed *analytic* by Riding and Cheema) tend to experience the components of a structured field analytically, as discrete from their background, and to impose structure on a relatively unstructured field. By contrast, relatively *field-dependent* individuals (termed *global* by Riding and Cheema) tend to be less good at such structuring and analytic activity, and to perceive a complex stimulus globally as a gestalt.

Witkin, Moore, Goodenough, and Cox (1977), in an extensive review of studies into the construct, report links between field dependence and both choice or, and success in, academic subjects and careers in fields with a high social content. Relatively field-independent individuals seem to prefer, and excel in, fields requiring greater analytic powers. The construct continues to receive considerable research attention—see, for example, Tinajero and Paramo (1997); Tinajero and Paramo (1998a, 1998b); and Tinajero, Paramo, Cadaveira, and Rodriguez-Holguin (1993). A number of effects have been found in relatively recent studies into the relationship between field dependence/independence and aspects of learning—for example, Chen and Macredie (2004); DeTure (2004); Lee, Cheng, Rai, and Depickere (2005); and Oh and Limm (2005).

Field dependence and field independence seem in some ways similar to Pask's holist and serialist distinctions. However, there is little empirical evidence to link them. An exception is a study by Ford (1995) who conducted an experiment in which postgraduate university students learned from materials structured to suit holist and serialist learning styles—the former materials being presented in a breadth-first manner, the latter in a depth-first manner. Students were classed as field dependent (global) or field independent (analytic) using Riding's *Cognitive Styles Analysis*. Significant gains in learning were reported for students working in matched relative to mismatched conditions. Matched conditions in the context of this experiment consisted of field-dependent students working with holist learning materials, their field-independent counterparts working with serialist materials.

However, conceptually the constructs have differences. Field-dependent individuals tend not to restructure what they are learning, yet holists are reported to engage in active transformation of learning content. Field-independent learners excel at imposing structure on material being learned, while the serialist will tend to more passive and learn the material as is.

Relatively field-independent individuals thrive in learning situations requiring them to mediate their own learning. They operate with a relatively internal frame of reference, and engage in structuring and analytic activity more than do their field-dependent counterparts. Relatively field-dependent individuals thrive more in situations where learning is structured for them. They tend to prefer a *spectator* approach to learning rather than the hypothesis-testing approach favoured by more field-independent learners. They operate with a relatively external frame of reference. Field-independent individuals are able to engage effectively in analytic and structuring activity with greater autonomy than more field-dependent individuals. As will be seen in the coming chapters, the notions of autonomy and dependence are key themes in this book.

Although Witkin et al. (1977) argues that field dependence/independence is value free and not related to more general ability, there is evidence counteracting this claim, empirically linking field-independence construct with verbal, spatial, and mathematical aptitudes. Tinajero and Paramo (1998b) conclude after a review of related research that since the review by Witkin et al. (1977), all other studies studying field dependence/independence and overall achievement have reported superior performance by field-independent students.

Whether or not independent of ability, interesting other stylistic differences are reported. For example, the Coffield Report (Coffield et al., 2004) refers to studies linking field dependence with greater communicative production in relation to second-language acquisition (Johnson, Prior, & Artuso, 2000), and to greater levels of "hindsight bias" (Davies, 1993), or ability to envisage alternatives after a result is known. The report notes that:

> *Davies' (1993) findings ... are attributed to a 'rigidity in information processing' which reduces FD subjects' ability to 'engage in cognitive restructuring' (1993, 233). This suggests that FD learners might need additional support in tasks requiring imaginative flexibility.* (p. 39)

Hergovitch (2003, also quoted in Coffield et al., 2004) also reports a relationship between field dependence, superstition, and suggestibility, suggesting that:

> *Field independents, who can organise and structure the world by themselves, don't need external references ... Field dependents function less autonomously.* (p. 38)

### *Verbaliser/Imager Styles*

The second main dimension of cognitive style identified by Riding and Cheema (1991) is the verbaliser/imager distinction. As the name of the style suggests, individuals located towards one or other pole of the dimension will tend to perform better in tasks that require the associated form of information representation in memory—visual or verbal. This dimension of cognitive style has received less research attention in relation to learning and information behaviour than has the field-dependent/-independent distinction.

Visual prowess in Japanese students has been linked to memorisation, and possibly as a consequece with the surface approaches to learning discussed earlier in this chapter. As Kawachi (2000) notes:

*This prowess is subsequently reinforced by overload during education and is then utilised for visual memorisation and employed in surface approaches in tertiary education. [...] The risk therefore exists to their drawing upon their prowess in undesirable surface approaches in times of work overload. In this respect, the courseware and tutor should make efforts to initiate intrinsic motivations in Japanese students that induce a deep approach to studying.*

## Convergent and Divergent Thinking

Convergent and divergent thinking (or production) were identified by Guilford (1967). Essentially, convergent thinking entails narrowing down the possibilities to find the correct or best answer to a problem. Divergent thinking entails generating multiple possible answers. Thus a test of divergent thinking may for example ask the individual to think of as many ways as possible to make use of some artefact such as a matchstick or a length of string.

According to Guilford (1967), divergent thinking is characterised by flexibility, fluency, and originality. Flexibility entails a degree of parallel processing in that multiple possibilities can be entertained at the same time. Fluency relates to the ease with which such multiple solutions or perspectives are generated. Originality implies an end product which is genuinely novel. Guilford was of the opinion that most people have a bias towards one or other form of thinking, and associated convergent thinking with scientists and engineers, divergent thinking with artists.

Divergent thinking is also associated with creativity—indeed, the terms are often used synonymously. However, while creative thinking will tend to be divergent, divergent thinking on its own does not guarantee creativity. It is important to note that creativity is a relative rather than absolute concept. That is, what may be regarded by one person or community as novel may be regarded by others as not so. Generating a creative produce in ignorance of the fact that someone else has already created it, for example, undoubtedly entails creative processes on the part of the individual. However, the degree of creativity possessed by the product may be lessened when judged more objectively by others. Thus, creativity may be defined relatively objectively, with reference to the consensus of particular groups. But it may also be defined subjectively, in terms of the novelty of the ideas as perceived by the individual generating them.

Amabile (1983) notes the importance of the end product, which must display the qualities of novelty and value. Such an *endproduct* view is reflected in the second of Boden's (1997) two broad types of creativity, namely: psychological and historical. Psychological creativity entails a definition of creativity in terms of the mental processes it entails. Historical creativity requires that, to be considered creative, an idea or product must be judged to be so relatively objectively by some community.

Boden (1997) differentiates between *exceptional outstanding* levels of historical creativity. Exceptional implies being recognised as creative by experts within a particular knowledge community. Outstanding entails recognition more widely outside that particular community. Gotz (1981) also stresses that creativity must entail some end product and cannot adequately be conceived just in terms of engagement in creative processes. He distinguishes creativity from concepts such as *insight, illumination,* and *discovery.* Creativity must include some form of *concretisation,*—that is, the *making* of something.

Patrick (1937), an early thinker in the area of creativity, identified five stages of creativity: (1) preparation, (2) incubation, (3) insight/discovery, (4) verification, and (5) concretisation. This was echoed in the model of the creative process later proposed by Amabile (1983), which includes problem presentation, preparation, response generation, response validation, and outcome. More recent studies have augmented models of *stages* with the notion of *types* of thinking. Edmonds and Candy (2002), for example, reviewing a number of empirical studies, conclude that creativity tends to entail: breaking away from conventional expectations; total immersion in the activity; taking a holistic view and finding multiple viewpoints; and parallel consideration of such multiple viewpoints and approaches.

## Brain Region Specialisations

As noted in the previous section, recognising complex similarity relationships would seem to entail—at least initially—parallel, intuitive, and perceptual, rather than logical and sequential processing. Although the notion of hemispheric specialisation is by no means straightforward nor devoid of criticism (Efron, 1990), there is evidence of differences in information processing that may conveniently be grouped in terms of characteristics often associated with left and right hemispheric processing.

*Table 6. Characteristics popularly associated with left and right brain hemispheres*

| Left Hemisphere Style | Right Hemisphere Style |
|---|---|
| Rational and logic-based thinking | Intuitive and impressionistic thinking |
| Sequential processing | Parallel/simultaneous processing |
| Analysing a problem into its component parts and tackle them one by one | Viewing a problem as a gestalt and solve via holistic reconfiguration of the whole. Problem solves with hunches, looking for patterns, and configurations |
| Planning and structuring things clearly | Displaying fluidity and spontaneity |
| Low tolerance of uncertainty and ambiguity | High tolerance of uncertainty and ambiguity |
| Good at differentiating (seeing differences) | Good at linking (seeing similarities and analogies) |
| Strong in analytic powers | Strong in terms of social awareness |
| Strong in verbal processing | Strong in visual processing |

However, there is much pseudo science surrounding the function of the different hemispheres of the brain, the *right brain* and *left brain* being popularly associated with very different, and wide-ranging intellectual activities. Indeed, it is tempting to interpret a number of cognitive and learning styles in terms of such hemispheric differences. Table 6 summarizes some of the main features popularly associated with the left and right hemispheres of the brain.

Kawachi (2000) notes links between linguistic and visual prowess and different cerebral hemispheres:

*It is generally well recognized that the dominant cerebral hemisphere for linguistic intelligence is the left cerebral hemisphere for normal right-handed persons, while visuospatial intelligence is in the right cerebral hemisphere.* (Obler & Gjerlow, 1999)

Findings by Riding, Glass, Butler, and Pleydell-Pearce (1997) reinforce the link with cerebral hemispheric dominance in relation to verbaliser/imager and field-dependent/field-independent differences. Ali and Kor (2007) report correlations between hemispheric differences and both sequential/global and sensing/intuitive dimensions of cognitive style.

However, it is important to avoid simplistic *left/right* dichotomies. It is essentially the way in which the two sides of the brain work together that counts (McCrone, 2000). Coffield et al. (2004) also note that:

*We have no satisfactory explanation for individual differences in the personal characteristics associated with right- and left-brain functioning.*

*There does not seem to be any neuroscientific evidence about the stability of hemisphere-based individual differences.*

*A number of theories emphasise functional differences between left and right hemispheres, but few seek to explain the interaction and integration of those functions.*

*Theorists sometimes provide conflicting accounts of brain-based differences.* (p. 14)

Despite the need for caution relating to possible overgeneralising (equivalent to Pask's *globetrotting*) it is also important to avoid failing to see the wood for the trees (Pask's *improvidence*), and there would seem to be evidence supporting the notion that cognitive and learning styles may to some extent reflect differences in regional brain functions.

That the different brain hemispheres have certain specialized functions seems well established. Although more fundamental functions such as reflexes and emotions are not associated with lateral differences, relatively high level brain functions seem to display some lateralization. The main regions associated with language, particularly linear (for example, grammar and word production) are associated particularly with the left hemisphere.

Split-brain patients, although totally exceptional, arguably shed some light on different hemispheric functions. It has been reported that such patients, when an images is shown to them in the left visual field (not the left eye, but rather the left field of both eyes), cannot name what is in the image since the image is processed by the right hemisphere while speech control is in the left. Damage to certain regions in the left hemisphere has been linked to problems with mental arithmetic and applying mathematical concepts. The right hemisphere has also been linked with holistic reasoning, spatial manipulation such as the recognition of faces, and artistic ability.

Also, there is relatively recent evidence of *front/back* brain differences complementing left/right differences, frontal (right) lobes being associated with creativity, coordinating connectivity, multitasking, and shifting attention—other areas being linked with logic, and the working through of details (Flaherty, 2005; Phillips, 2005). There is also evidence of high/low activity in the cortex, inspiration being associated with alpha waves with low cortical arousal—"a relaxed state, as though the conscious mind was quiet while the brain was making connections behind the scenes." Elaboration is associated with increased cortical arousal—"more corralling of activity and more organised thinking." Creativity requires a toggling between the two, and this is particularly noticeable on the right side of the brain. Areas of brain activity may also vary according to the domain of creativity (Phillips, 2005).

Links have also been reported between activity in different brain regions and divergent and convergent thinking. For example, Razoumnikova (2000) reports that in experiments comparing brain activity during convergent and divergent thinking tasks:

*Distinct task-related discrepancies of EEG pattern in the beta2 band between the subjects divided into groups of good and bad performers of divergent thinking are also found. Good performance is related to the special organization of the cerebral areas in the beta2 band: (i) increased functional connectivity of central-parietal areas of both hemispheres; and (ii) greater ipsilateral connections between the cortex regions of the right hemisphere.*

Molle et al. (1996) also report that:

*EEG complexity over the central and posterior cortex was higher while subjects solved tasks of divergent than convergent thinking, and also higher than during mental relaxation. Over the frontal cortex, EEG complexity was comparable during divergent thinking and mental relaxation, but reduced during convergent thinking. Results indicate that the basic process underlying the generation of novel ideas expresses itself in a strong increase in the EEG's complexity, reflecting higher degrees of freedom in the competitive interactions among cortical neuron assemblies. Frontocortical EEG complexity being comparable with that during mental relaxation, speaks for a loosened attentional control during creative thinking.*

In a later experiment, Molle, Marshall, Wolf, Fehm, and Born (1999) again used the EEG to record brain activity of subjects engaging in convergent and divergent thinking, concluding that:

*The dimensional complexity of the EEG was greater during divergent thinking than during convergent thinking. While solving tasks of divergent thinking, subjects with high performance scores had a lower EEG dimension than did subjects with low scores, in particular over frontal cortical areas. The changes were not reflected in single frequency bands of conventional EEG analysis. Based on Hebb's view of neuron assemblies as functional processing units, the higher EEG complexity during divergent than convergent thinking could be the result of the concurrent activation of a greater number of independently oscillating processing units.*

Ultimately, however, evidence of the precise location of such differences is of less relevance to the issue of cognitive styles and learning differences than evidence that systematic differences exist amongst individuals in which particular clusters characterizing broadly different types of information processing exist, can be identified, and have some impact on learning. If there are indeed biological foundations for such differences, this may help to explain the apparent consistency and persistence of these differences within individuals across different tasks.

# Levels of Learning

The stylistic differences discussed so far have been considered by their authors to be value-free in the sense that having a bias toward one or other pole of the dimension is not necessarily either good or bad. Effective (though in some cases different) learning outcomes may be achieved with either bias. As we have seen, however, other researchers have linked certain styles with more general ability and overall superior performance, raising questions about their value-neutrality.

## Deep and Surface Study Approaches

Like learning styles, study approaches are characteristic ways in which different individuals approach the task of learning. They are somewhat broader in focus than learning styles, encompassing features including intentions, motivation, confidence, and time management. They are relatively well established constructs, having been the subject of much investigation in educational research in the past 25 years (e.g., Abouserie, 1995; Biggs, 1987, 1991; Carr, 1997; Cuthbert, 1998; Entwistle, 1981, 1988, 1998, 2000a, 2000b, 2001; Entwistle, Hanley, & Hounsell, 1979; Richardson, 1995; 1997; 1998; Richardson, Mugler, & Landbeck, 1995; Ropo, 1993; Sadler-Smith & Tsang, 1998; Schmeck, 1988; Sutherland, 1995; Waugh, 1999).

One of the most pervasive dimensions of difference in study approaches is that relating to *deep, surface,* and *strategic* approaches. A deep approach consists of: having a meaning orientation (i.e., having an intention to understand, as opposed to memorise and reproduce, material learned); taking an active interest in what is being learned (following up and questioning ideas for oneself); relating ideas (linking ideas together to form an overall picture); and use of evidence (carefully examining the detailed evidence supporting the overall picture).

A surface approach consists of having an intention to reproduce (i.e., to memorise information so that it can be regurgitated, as opposed to extracting its deeper meaning); passive learning (accepting ideas passively without thinking about them for oneself); unrelated memorising (memorising facts and details without fitting them into a broader overall picture—the pathological counterpart to use of evidence); and

*Table 7. Different dimensions of study approach. Adapted from Entwistle (1981, 1988, 2001).*

| Approach | Deep (active or passive) | Surface (active or passive) | Strategic and well-organised |
|---|---|---|---|
| Intention | To understand information | To reproduce information | To be successful via either of the above |
| Process | Relating ideas and using evidence | Unrelated memorising | Any of above as deemed necessary for success |
| Motivation | Intrinsic | Extrinsic (fear of failure) | Extrinsic (intention to excel) |
| Outcome | Deep understanding | Memorisation | Success with or without understanding |

fear of failure. A strategic approach consists of an intention to excel, effective time management, and use of either a meaning or a reproducing orientation as deemed appropriate to achieving academic success. A deep approach has been empirically linked to intrinsic motivation and the achievement of deep understanding. A surface approach is linked to relatively extrinsic motivation in the form of fear of failure, and to memorisation without full understanding. A strategic approach is associated with the relatively confident, but extrinsically oriented motivation of intention to excel, good time management, and academic success via either memorisation or deep understanding.

Research by Entwistle and his colleagues (Entwistle, 1981, 1988, 2001; Entwistle et al., 1979) has resulted in a picture of study approaches in which they are linked with intentions, processes, motivations and outcomes. These links are shown in Table 7.

Further work by Entwistle and his colleagues has focused on refining the model of approaches to learning, linking it with both preferences for teaching approach and academic success (Figure 27).

A factor analyses is reported in the Scoring Key for the Approaches and Study Skills Inventory for Students (ASSIST) ("Scoring Key," n.d.) linking a strategic approach with high first term marks, and a surface apathetic approach with low marks, amongst undergraduate university students. The surface apathetic factor also loads on two items from a section of the inventory asking about preparation for higher education—lack of experience of studying independently, and not having adequate prior knowledge. It also loaded on items detailing students' perceptions of influences on learning, including doing paid work while studying, personal relationships, and difficulties with mathematics. The deep, non-apathetic factor also loaded on choosing a course on the basis of personal interest from the same section. This factor also loaded on items indicating a preference for teaching which encourages understanding, loading negatively on a preference for teaching geared to the

*Figure 27. Approaches to learning (adapted from Scoring Key, n.d.)*

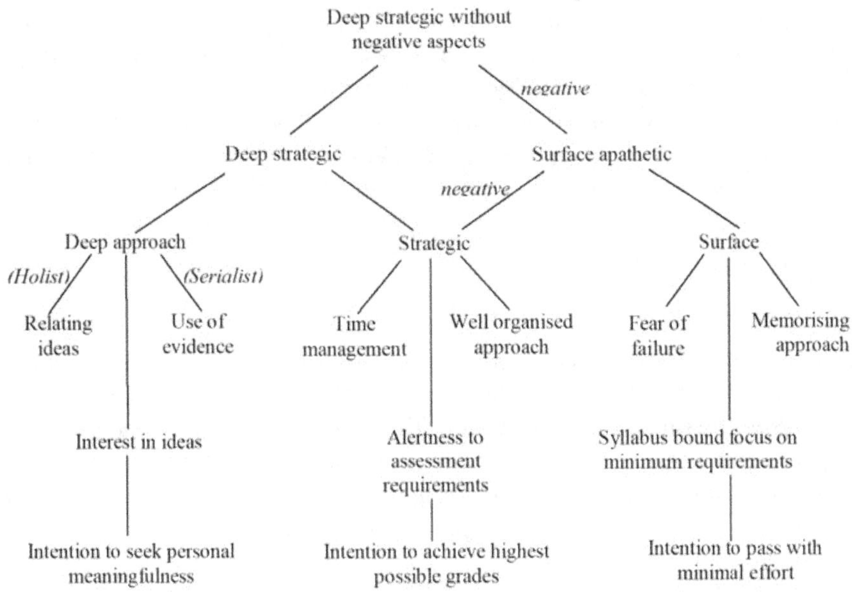


transmission of information. A recent study by Backhaus (2007) using Entwistle's *Revised Approaches to Studying Inventory* (RASI) and the *Cognitive Styles Index* found links between academic performance anmd scores on the deep strategic, metacognitive awareness, and academic self-confidence dimensions. Women scored more highly on the surface strategic dimension and were more likely to display an analytic cognitive style.

A number of studies (Dahlin & Watkins, 2000; Kember, 1996; Kember & Gow, 1990; Marton, Witkins, & Tang, 1997; Meyer, 2000) have suggested that there may be cultural differences in the adoption of, and attitudes to, surface approaches to studying. Research with Chinese learners, for example, has indicated that surface level memorisation may be viewed less pejoratively than is the case in Western educational cultures. Rather, it may be considered a useful stage in developing understanding, both deep and surface approaches being employed in close strategic alliance.

Ramsden and Entwistle (1981) mapped adoption by students of a deep approach onto features of the teaching/learning environment including being allowed to exercise freedom in learning; well-paced learning; real-life illustrations and lively explanations; enthusiastic teaching; and an empathetic approach to student problems. A surface approach was liked to a heavy workload, summative assessments and spoon feeding by lecturers. Coffield et al. (2004) note that:

*Entwistle and his colleagues have explored how to create 'powerful learning environments' in order to change students' conceptions of learning. Referring to work by Perry on progression through different conceptions of knowledge [...] and work by Vermunt and colleagues, Entwistle and Peterson (2003) argue that universities should encourage 'constructive friction' between the curriculum and teachers' and students' conceptions of knowledge. Drawing on constructivist and cognitive apprenticeship ideas about learning, they offer guidelines for promoting a deep approach to learning and more sophisticated conceptions of knowledge.* (p. 99)

Entwistle (2000b) notes that:

*Research findings have indicated, for example, that while level, pace, structure and clarity all contribute to the effectiveness of lecturing, it is generally explanation, enthusiasm, and empathy which are most likely to evoke a deep approach. Similarly, it appears that assessment which encourages students to think for themselves – such as essay questions, applications to new contexts, and problem-based questions – shifts students in a class towards a deep approach. In contrast, procedures perceived by students as requiring no more than the accurate reproduction of information lead to a predominance of surface approaches.* (Thomas & Bain, 1984; Scouller, 1998)

Fear of failure and intention to excel—features of the approaches to learning identified by Entwistle—may to some extent be linked conceptually with the notion of self-efficacy, which Savolainen (2002) defines as:

*a person's judgement of his or her ability to organize and execute action, such as finding information on the Web* (p. 211)

According to Bandura (1986), it is concerned:

*not with the skills one has but with judgements of what one can do with whatever skills one possesses* (p. 391)

Poor self-efficacy has been considered as a combination of anxiety and low levels of experience that is linked to poor performance (Bandura, 1977, 1986; Schunk, 1981)—a proposition supported by studies into computer anxiety (e.g., Meier, 1985) and experience (e.g., McInerney, McInerney, & Sinclair, 1994). Compeau and Higgins (1995) note that:

*Individuals with a weak sense of self-efficacy will be frustrated more easily by obstacles to their performance and will respond by lowering their perceptions of their capability* (p. 192)

## Critical Thinking

Critical thinking entails the ability to make reasoned evaluative judgements when making sense of information sources that contain different (potentially conflicting) findings, perspectives, and interpretations of a given topic or phenomenon. It has been defined as:

*the careful and deliberate determination of whether to accept, reject, or suspend judgment about a claim.* (Moore & Parker, 2001)

*the process of evaluating propositions or hypotheses and making judgments about them on the basis of well-supported evidence.* (Bernstein, Penner, Clarke-Stewart, & Roy, 2003)

The development of critical thinking is a key learning objective in education—particularly higher education (Lipman, 1991; McPack, 1981). Much research has been carried out into critical thinking, particularly in the U.S. and Australia, for example, recent Delphi studies resulting in definitions and detailed taxonomies of skills and subskills making up critical thinking (American Philosophical Association, 1990). Researchers have developed a number of measures of critical thinking, including Likert-based inventories (Facione & Facione, 1992), multiple-choice tests (Facione, 1992) and short-answer essays (Ennis & Weir, 1985) and rubrics (Facione & Facione, 1994). A number of studies have also developed recommendations for approaches to teaching critical thinking (Hannel & Hannel, 1998; Murray & Graham, 1996).

The exercise of critical thinking is generally considered to be affected by a combination of cognitive (skill) and affective (dispositional) elements—that is, competence in being able to exercise critical thinking and disposition actually to exercise it in a given context. It may be defined in terms of the extent to which students (1) perceive that there is scope for competing views or interpretations of a given phenomenon (antithesis as well as thesis); (2) engage in reasoned consideration of evidence supporting such different interpretations; and (3) go on (a) to develop personal commitment to one or other interpretation—that is, integrate it with their existing knowledge and belief systems, or (b) to identify an underlying theme capable of integrating the competing interpretations (synthesis).

A key enabling factor affecting the degree to which an individual is able to engage in critical thinking is cognitive complexity. This represents a construct studied particularly in psychology, relating to the degree of differentiation with which an individual views the world. At one extreme, the cognitively simple individual will view the world in dualistic, black/white, right/wrong terms. More cognitively complex individuals, however, are able to engage in relativistic reasoning in which contrasting views may be equally valid in different circumstances and from different points of view. These differences were studied in a seminal piece of research by Perry (1970, 1981), who devised a theory in which individuals move through the stages shown in Table 8.

King and Kitchener' (1994: quoted in Maclellan & Soden, 2004) proposed seven stages of critical development, grouped into the three broader categories (Table 9) which to an extent map onto Perry's (see Table 8) stages.

Other researchers (Belenky, Clinchy, Goldberger, & Tarule, 1986) have investigated gender differences in relation to Perry's stage theory (Perry's subjects being male college students), and concluded that women experience different styles of critical thinking, as depicted in Table 10.

This work suggests that students do indeed differ in relation to their capacity to make sense of diverse and potentially incongruent findings, perspectives, and interpretations. Ford (1984) identified similar categories in a review of research into critical thinking across a wide range of disciplines, and went on to develop a model, based on empirical evidence, of different levels and types of critical thinking (Table 11). This research identified *sub, surface,* and *deep* levels of critical thinking, each with information behavioural implications (Ford, 1979).

The middle *surface critical* category is particularly worrying for educators and information providers. Many students were happy to "go through the motions" of critical thinking as a clinical academic exercise with little personal engagement with new information. This was to the direct detriment of personal engagement, and the potential acceptance and valuing, and consequent likely subsequent use and application, of new ideas successfully comprehended (but not evaluated and

*Table 8. Perry's critical thinking stages*

| | |
|---|---|
| **Dualism** | in which the world is seen in terms of right or wrong, black or white. Knowledge is passed from authority figures who tell us "how it is." |
| **Multiplicity** | in which diversity of opinions are perceived—but accounted for by thinking that the experts "haven't got the answer yet." |
| **Relativism** | in which the individual perceives that there are multiple valid points of view. Everyone has a right to an opinion and could be equally right. |
| **Commitment** | in which the individual develops a personal commitment to certain viewpoints within a recognition of a relativistic world. |

*Table 9. King and Kitchener' (1994) stages of development in reasoning. Adapted from Maclellan and Soden (2004)*

| Category | Implies that... |
|---|---|
| Pre-reflective thinking... | knowledge is either absolute or is temporarily uncertain—but will become certain when enough data are available;<br>knowledge from "good" authorities is "right";<br>others will not have different views of the same issue;<br>justification is about showing that one's own beliefs are right, by stating them;<br>evidence is unnecessary. |
| Quasi-reflective thinking... | knowledge is not absolute and uncertainty is not just temporary;<br>knowing is idiosyncratic to an individual—thus judgement is idiosyncratic to the person making it;<br>evidence is necessary but need not be evaluated and is chosen to fit own beliefs;<br>rules of inquiry for the context have been invoked. |
| Reflective thinking... | knowledge is not a given but must be actively constructed—the spectator view of the knower that characterised earlier stages will no longer suffice;<br>knowledge is uncertain and claims of knowledge must be understood in relation to the context in which they were generated;<br>beliefs are justified probabilistically on the basis of a variety of interpretative considerations, such as the weight of the evidence, the explanatory value of the interpretations, the risk of erroneous conclusions, the consequences of alternative judgments, and the interrelationships of these factors;<br>conclusions should remain open to re-evaluation. |

*Table 10. Gender differences in critical thinking stages*

| **Silence** | Women perceive themselves to be "subject to whims of external authority" without voice. |
|---|---|
| **Received knowledge** | The individual feels able to receive but not create knowledge. |
| **Subjective knowledge** | Truth and knowledge are "private and subjectively known or intuited." |
| **Procedural knowledge** | Knowledge can be obtained and communicated via the application of objective procedures. |
| **Constructed knowledge** | Knowledge is contextual and may be objective or subjective. |

accepted—or indeed rejected) within the context of an assessed course of study. Indeed, research by Ford both theoretically (Ford, 1979) and empirically (Ford, 1980) identified links between engagement in the critical evaluation of information sources and such personal acceptance and valuing of new ideas.

*Table 11. Subcritical, surface critical, and deep critical levels of thinking (adapted from Ford, 1979)*

| Types of critical thinking | Subtypes |
|---|---|
| *Subcritical*<br>Student does not engage critically with information. | *Unconscious*<br>Student is unaware of alternative possible viewpoints. Information from "authority" sources perceived as largely factual/true.<br><br>*Conscious*<br>Student is aware of alternative viewpoints but does not critically evaluate them. Describes (rather than engages with) viewpoints in essays. |
| *Surface critical*<br>Student "evaluates" different view-points clinically, without personal involvement. May use criteria which s/he perceived will impress her/his assessors. | |
| *Deep critical*<br>Student critically evaluates different viewpoints to a personally satisfying level (whether accepted as valuable or rejected) | *Authority criteria*<br>Criteria based on authority sources rather than personal experi-ence/knowledge.<br><br>*Experience criteria*<br>Criteria based on personal experience/knowledge.<br><br>*Interaction*<br>Criteria based on an interaction between the two, in which, for example, experience and research interact to modify the student's personal viewpoint. |

## Existing Knowledge and Expertise

One of the most influential individual differences relating to levels of thinking that affects learning and teaching is prior knowledge on the part of the learner. Indeed, level of knowledge in a particular topic or subject area is perhaps the most fundamental *individual difference* of concern to educators.

At a general level, we can talk of different people possessing broadly comparable levels and types of knowledge. We may often refer to people as having novice-level or expert-level knowledge in a particular field, and we assume at least a minimum level of comparable knowledge shared by all individuals who have successfully passed a particular academic or professional examination, or have been awarded a particular qualification, where these are widely recognised and subject to appropriate quality control. *Expert/novice* studies have been conducted in a range of subject areas, for example: chess (Chiesi, Spilich, & Voss, 1979); baseball (Spilich, Vesonder, Chiesi, & Voss, 1979); medical diagnosis (Johnson, Hassebrock, Duran, & Moller, 1982) as well as information systems (Bajaj, 1998; Huff & Prybutok, 1998) and information seeking (Chen, Houston, Sewell, & Schatz, 1998).

The notion of possessing different levels of expertise in particular areas of knowledge was extended by Gardner (1993, 1999) in his theory of *multiple intelligences*. Gardner's theory stands between the notion of specific subject domain expertise and that of general intelligence. He considers general intelligence to be too crude way of thinking about ability, and proposed eight different broad types of intelligence. Armstrong (n.d.) lists these as:

*Linguistic intelligence ('word smart')*
*Logical-mathematical intelligence ('number/reasoning smart')*
*Spatial intelligence ('picture smart')*
*Bodily-Kinaesthetic intelligence ('body smart')*
*Musical intelligence ('music smart')*
*Interpersonal intelligence ('people smart')*
*Intrapersonal intelligence ('self smart')*
*Naturalist intelligence ('nature smart')*

However, at a finer-grained level, the precise make-up of each person's knowledge structure is entirely unique. This is potentially problematic in view of the widely acknowledged importance in learning and teaching of enabling and facilitating the enmeshing and integration of new information with existing concepts in the learner's mind. However, different possibilities exist even at the simplest level of concept formation, since individuals' existing knowledge will differ. Within this context, Roschelle (1995) notes that:

*research has shown that a learner's prior knowledge often confounds an educator's best efforts to deliver ideas accurately. A large body of findings shows that learning proceeds primarily from prior knowledge, and only secondarily from the presented materials. Prior knowledge can be at odds with the presented material, and consequently, learners will distort presented material. Neglect of prior knowledge can result in the audience learning something opposed to the educator's intentions, no matter how well those intentions are executed in an exhibit, book, or lecture.*

At the level of the basic learning processes discussed in Chapter I, the precise make-up of each learner's existing knowledge may intimately affect his or her perception of the nature and extent of a particular conceptual incongruity—the need for some integration of otherwise disparate concepts (i.e., the identification of the need to know something). It will also affect the nature of the tentative theories he/she generates in an attempt to resolve the incongruity—to provide an acceptable integrating theme.

Marton and Booth (1997, quoted in Entwistle, 2000b) notes the important influence not only of a learner's prior knowledge and experience, but also of those of his or her teacher—and of the interaction between the two. They consider teaching to be:

*dependent on the object of study created by the teacher, and note that teachers can present their classes with very different objects of study even from the same syllabus. Effective teaching, in their view, depends on 'meetings of awareness' between the teacher and the class, with the teacher shaping the knowledge in ways designed to help students to understand it. That ability depends on an empathetic awareness of what students already know and how they learn. [...]*

*The content of an external syllabus is the result of a consultation process (and political will) which arrives at a certain content appropriate for a particular age and ability group. That represents the formal target understanding. The syllabus, however, has then to be interpreted by the teacher, and that interpretation depends on the teacher's prior knowledge and experience, not just of the subject matter, but also of pedagogy. [...]*

*The pupils experience a presentation of the teacher's understanding of the syllabus—the teacher's target understanding, rather than the syllabus itself—but that is then interpreted in terms of their own personal history and their current knowledge and initial understanding. This personal understanding is not just formed from content knowledge; it also includes beliefs and feelings about the educational context based on past experience. [...]*

*When the teacher examines the evidence of this personal understanding, it is judged in terms of the teacher's own understanding. Thus, when a teacher refers to a pupil 'having understood', that is actually the extent of the match between the pupil's personal understanding and the target understanding set by the teacher.*

At one level, conceptual incongruities requiring resolution via some integrating theme ultimately have to be perceived by the learner him or herself, in terms of his or her existing knowledge structure. However, the role of the educator is to attempt to intervene in some way to attempt to enable and/or facilitate these processes. Such intervention is termed here *mediation*, and may be contrasted with *autonomy* on the learner's part. The balance between these two processes may differ considerably not only between the different theories of *how* we learn introduced in Chapters I and II, but also between different learning philosophies (relating to what learning is *for*) and learning design perspectives (relating to how learning may best be *brought about*). The question of mediation and autonomy will be explored in more detail in Chapter III.

Figure 28 represents an extension of the model originally presented in Figure 21 at the end of Chapter I. The original model consisted of the *Information processing types* and *Information processes* boxes, which now appear at the top left of the new model. The *Information processes* box appears here in abbreviated form, the detail shown in Figure 21 having been suppressed in order to make Figure 28 less cluttered.

The original model is extended here to integrate key concepts presented in the present chapter. In this model, mental *states* are differentiated from mental *processes*. A goal such as the development of increasing levels of autonomy is broad in the sense that it may accrue from multiple tasks over time. Similarly broad goals may also include, for example, increases in self-efficacy, intrinsic motivation, general level of knowledge in a particular subject domain, and development of critical thinking ability. These goals are generally broader than those specific to a particular learning

*Figure 28. Mental processes and mental states (adapted from Ford, 2004)*

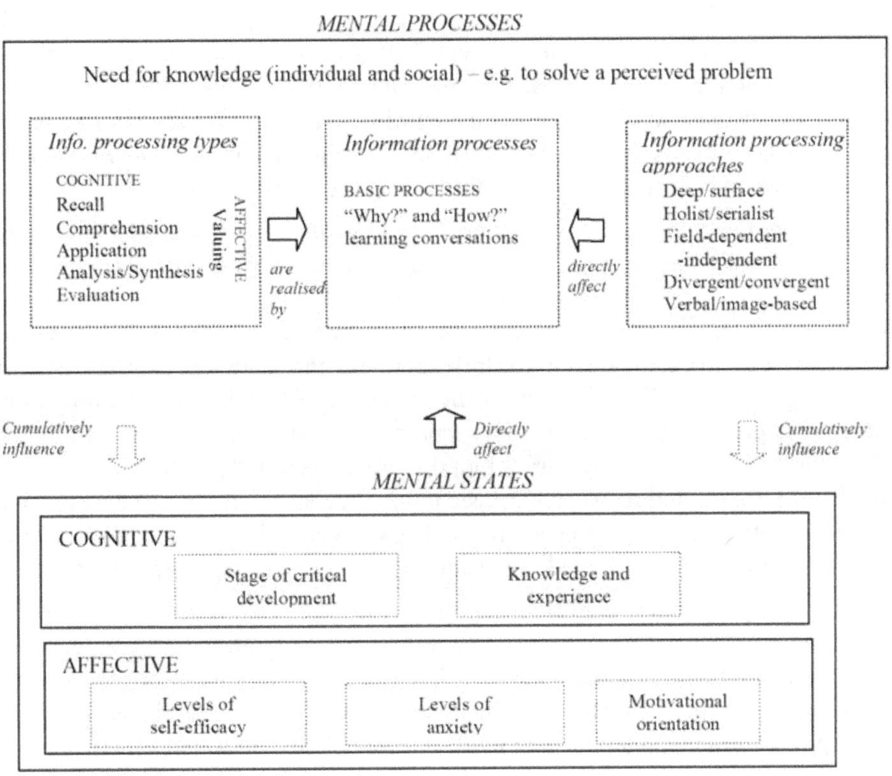

task. Such more general goals may be thought of in terms of mental *states* rather than mental *processes*, since they represent relatively generalised, consistent and persistent states (abilities, attitudes, and feelings).

Mental states may be affective (relating to feelings and emotions) and/or cognitive (relating to knowledge and reasoning). They may affect both perceptions of which information processing goals and styles are appropriate to address particular learning tasks, and learners' ability to execute them. For example, while comprehension may be perceived to be required for a particular task, memory-based recall with minimal understanding may be the reality. This may be due to anxiety, feelings of low self-efficacy, or possibly difficulty in enmeshing new information, as it is presented in those information sources to which the learner has access, with a particular person's existing knowledge structure. Mental processes may be affected by mental states—for example, the ability to apply evaluative processes in relation to a particular task may be affected by the individual's more generalised level of criticality.

However, as well as affecting perceptions of what constitute appropriate information processing goals and styles, and ability to engage in appropriate information processing behaviour, mental states may themselves be less immediately, but nevertheless cumulatively affected by information processing behaviour. Thus, for example, self-efficacy may be adversely affected in the medium and long term by constant or repeated inability to engage in deep level processing despite realisation that such an approach is required. Knowledge levels will also cumulatively increase with the successful completion of each learning task. The different components of the *mental states* element of Figure 28 may also interact with each other. For example, increases in knowledge are likely cumulatively to assist the process of more generalised intellectual development including the ability to engage in critical thinking.

Levels of motivation are also important. For one learner a particular course of study or series of tasks may be enthusiastically embraced as mapping onto his or her own intrinsic subject interests and needs. However, a different individual may pursued the same tasks in a relatively clinical, less personally involved fashion—as an *academic exercise* to be engaged in for little more that the relatively extrinsic goal of obtaining a paper qualification. Such differences may affect the type of information processing perceived by learners to be appropriate—which may not necessarily be the same as those desired by curriculum designers. As noted previously, empirical links have been found between extrinsic motivation and a surface level approach, intrinsic motivation, and a deep approach. High levels of anxiety in the form of *fear of failure* have also been linked to the adoption of a surface level approach.

The relatively stable and persistent cognitive and affective *states* shown at the bottom of Figure 28, as well as representing the desired outcomes of the designers of learning tasks, and thus being *affected by* learning and information seeking, also act as *influences on* the nature of such behaviour displayed by individuals. Thus, for example, while an increase in an individual's broad knowledge and experience of a subject area may be a valid learning goal, the nature of this existing knowledge and experience may significantly influence the way in which learning and information seeking is conducted.

The human individual differences discussed in this chapter form a key factor influencing effective teaching, which is designed to take learners from where they currently are (their existing knowledge state) to somewhere else (a desired knowledge state). The desired destination must be one which they can reach, via a route which they can follow. It is no use starting where they are not—or traveling via a route they are incapable of following. Designing, delivering, and assessing such journeys—in other words, teaching—forms the focus of the next chapter.

## References


Abouserie, R. (1995). Self-esteem and achievement motivation as determinants of students' approaches to studying. *Studies in Higher Education, 20*(1), 19-26.

Ali, R. M., & Kor, L. K. (2007). Association between brain hemisphericity, learning styles and confidence in using graphics calculator for mathematics. *Eurasia Journal of Mathematics, Science and Technology Education, 3*(2), 127-131.

Amabile, T. M. (1983). *The social psychology of creativity*. New York: Springer-Verlag.

American Philosophical Association. (1990). *Critical thinking: A statement of expert consensus for purposes of educational assessment and instruction*. ERIC document ED315-423.

Armstrong, T. (n.d.). *Multiple intelligences*. Retrieved August 1, 2007, from http://www.thomasarmstrong.com/multiple_intelligences.htm

Backhaus, K. (2007). Cognitive styles and approaches to studying in management education. *Journal of Management Education, 31*(4), 445-466.

Bajaj, A. (1998, August). *A comparison of expert and novice judgements in selecting computing architectures for organizational use*. Paper presented at the Association of Information Systems (AIS) Americas Conference on Information Systems, Baltimore, MD.

Bandura, A. (1977). *Social learning theory*. New York: General Learning Press.

Bandura, A. (1986). *Social foundations of thought and action: A social cognitive theory*. Englewood Cliffs, NJ: Prentice Hall.

Belenky, M. F., Clinchy, B. M., Goldberger, N. R., & Tarule, J. M. (1986). *Women's ways of knowing: The development of self, voice and mind*. New York: Basic Books.

Bernstein, D. A., Penner, L. A., Clarke-Stewart, A., & Roy, E. J. (2003). *Psychology* (6th ed.). Retrieved August 1, 2007, from http://college.hmco.com/psychology/bernstein/psychology/6e/students/key_terms/ ch02.html

Biggs, J. B. (1987). *Students' approaches to learning and studying*. Melbourne: Australian Council for Educational Research.

Biggs, J. B. (1991). Approaches to learning in secondary and tertiary students in Hong Kong: Some comparative studies. *Educational Research Journal, 6,* 27-39.

Boden, M. A. (1997). *The creative mind: Myths and mechanisms*. London: Weidenfield & Nicolson.

Brumby, M. N. (1982). Consistent differences in cognitive styles shown for qualitative biological problem-solving. *British Journal of Educational Psychology, 52,* 244-257.

Carr, S. C. (1997). The approaches to study inventory in Malawi: A lesson for educational testing? *Psychology Teaching Review, 6*(2) 157-169.

Chen, H., Houston, A. L., Sewell, R. R., & Schatz, B. R. (1998). Internet browsing and searching: User evaluations of category map and concept space techniques. *Journal of the American Society for Library and information science, 49*(7), 582-603.

Chen, S. Y., & Macredie, R. D. (2004). Cognitive modelling of student learning in Web-based instructional programmes. *International Journal of Human-Computer Interaction, 17*(3), 375-402.

Chiesi, H., Spilich, G., & Voss, J. (1979). Acquisition of domain-related information in relation to high and low domain knowledge. *Journal of Verbal Learning and Verbal Behavior, 18,* 257-273.

Coffield, F., Moseley, D., Hall, E., & Ecclestone, K. (2004). *Learning styles and pedagogy in post-16 learning. A systematic and critical review*. London: Learning and Skills Research Centre.

Compeau, D. R., & Higgins, C. A. (1995). Computer self-efficacy: Development of a measure and initial test. *MIS Quarterly,* 189-211.

Cuthbert, K. (1998). Course perceptions and approaches to studying of psychology students in two degree programmes: Does project work have an influence? *Psychology Teaching Review, 7*(1), 3-13.

Dahlin, B., & Watkins, D. (2000). The role of repetition in the processes of memorizing and understanding: A comparison of the views of German and Chinese secondary school students in Hong Kong. *British Journal of Educational Psychology, 70,* 65-84.

Davies, M. F. (1993). Field-dependence and hindsight bias: Output interference in the generation of reasons. *Journal of Research in Personality, 27*(3), 222-237.

DeTure, M. L. (2004). Cognitive style and self-efficacy: Predicting student success in online distance education. *American Journal of Distance Education, 18*(1), 21-38.

Edmonds, E., & Candy, L. (2002). Creativity, art practice, and knowledge. *Communications of the ACM, 45*(10), 91-95.

Efron, R. (1990). *The decline and fall of hemispheric specialization*. Hillsdale, NJ: Erlbaum.

Ennis, R. H., & Weir, E. (1985). *The Ennis-Weir CT essay test: An instrument for testing and teaching*. Pacific Grove, CA: Midwest Publications.

Entwistle, N. J. (1981). *Styles of learning and teaching*. Chichester, UK: Wiley.

Entwistle, N. J. (1988). Motivational factors in students' approaches to learning. In R. R. Schmeck (Ed.), *Learning strategies and learning styles* (pp. 21-51). New York: Plenum.

Entwistle, N. J. (1998). Approaches to learning and forms of understanding. In B. Dart & G. Boulton-Lewis (Eds.), *Teaching and learning in higher education* (pp. 72-101). Melbourne: Australian Council for Educational Research.

Entwistle, N. J. (2000a). Approaches to studying and levels of understanding: The influences of teaching and assessment. In J. C. Smart (Ed.), *Higher education: Handbook of theory and research, Vol. XV* (pp. 156-218). New York: Agathon Press.

Entwistle, N. J. (2000b, November). *Promoting deep learning through teaching and assessment: Conceptual frameworks and educational contexts*. Paper presented at the TLRP Conference, Leicester, UK.

Entwistle, N. J. (2001). Styles of learning and approaches to studying in higher education. *Kybernetes, 30*(5/6), 593-602.

Entwistle, N. J., Hanley, M., & Hounsell, D. (1979). Identifying distinctive approaches to studying. *Higher Education, 8,* 365-380.

Entwistle, N. J., & Peterson, E. (2003, May). *Conceptions of learning and knowledge in higher education: Relationships with study behaviour and influences of learning environments*. Paper presented to Workshop on Powerful Learning Environments, Antwerp, Blegium.

Facione, P. A. (1992). *The California critical thinking skills test*. Millbrae, CA: California Academic Press.

Facione, P. A., & Facione, N. C. (1992). *The California critical thinking disposition inventory*. Millbrae, CA: California Academic Press.

Facione, P. A., & Facione, N. C. (1994). *The holistic critical thinking scoring rubric*. Millbrae, CA: California Academic Press.

Flaherty, A. (2005). The neurologist: All in my brain. *New Scientist,* 49.

Ford, N. (1979). Study strategies, orientations and "personal meaningfulness" in higher education. *British Journal of Educational Technology, 10,* 143-160.

Ford, N. (1980). Levels of understanding and the personal acceptance of information in higher education. *Studies in Higher Education, 5*(1), 63-70.

Ford, N. (1984). Intellectual development and the organisation of knowledge. *Education for Librarianship, 24,* 157-173.

Ford, N. (1995). Levels and types of mediation in instructional systems: An individual differences approach. *International Journal of Human-Computer Studies, 43*(2), 241-259.

Ford, N. (2004) Towards a model of learning for educational informatics. *Journal of Documentation, 60*(2), 183-225.

Gardner, H. (1993) *Multiple intelligences: The theory into practice.* New York: Basic Books.

Gardner, H. (1999) *Intelligence reframed: Multiple intelligences for the 21st century.* New York: Basic Books.

Gotz, I. L. (1981). On defining creativity. *Journal of Aesthetics and Art Criticism, 39*(3), 297-301.

Guilford, J. P. (1967). *The nature of human intelligence.* New York: McGraw-Hill.

Hannel, G. I., & Hannel, L. (1998). The seven steps to critical thinking: A practical application of critical thinking skills. *NASSP Bulletin, 82*(598), 87-93.

Hergovitch, A. (2003). Field dependence, suggestibility and belief in paranormal phenomena. *Personality and Individual Differences, 34,* 195-209.

Honey, P., & Mumford, A. (1986). *Using your learning styles.* Maidenhead, UK: Honey Publications.

Huff, R. A., & Prybutok, V. R. (1998, August). *Expert/novice differences in IS project management decision making.* Paper presented at the Association of Information Systems (AIS) Americas Conference on Information Systems, Baltimore, MD.

Johnson, J., Prior, S., & Artuso, M. (2000). Field dependence as a factor in second language communicative production. *Language Learning, 50*(3), 529-567.

Johnson, P. E., Hassebrock, F., Duran, A. S., & Moller, J. H. (1982). Multimethod study of clinical judgement. *Organizational Behavior and Human Performance, 30,* 201-230.

Jonassen, D. H., & Grabowski, B. (1993). *Individual differences and instruction.* New York: Allen and Bacon.

Kawachi, P. (2000, October 25-27). *Democratisation of access to learning opportunities: Opening up global education to Japanese learners.* Paper presented at the 14th Annual Conference of the Asian Association of Open Universities,

Philippines. Retrieved 1 August, 2007, from http://www.ouhk.edu.hk/cridal/gdenet/Teaching/Design/EATL11A.html

Kember, D. (1996). The intention to both memorise and understand: Another approach to learning? *Higher Education, 31,* 341-354.

Kember, D., & Gow, L. (1990). Cultural specificity of approaches to study. *British Journal of Educational Psychology, 60,* 356-363.

King, P., & Kitchener, K. (1994). *Developing reflective judgement.* San Francisco: Jossey-Bass.

Kolb, D. A. (1984). *Experiential learning.* Englewood Cliffs, NJ: Prentice Hall.

Lee, C., Cheng, Y. W., Rai, S., & Depickere, A. (2005). What affect student cognitive style in the development of hypermedia learning system? *Computers and Education, 45*(1), 1-19.

Lipman, M. (1991). *Thinking in education.* Cambridge: Cambridge University Press.

Maclellan, E., & Soden, R. (2004). The importance of epistemic cognition in student-centred learning. *Instructional Science, 32,* 253-268.

Marton, F., & Booth, S. (1997). *Learning and awareness.* Mahwah, NJ: Lawrence Erlbaum.

Marton, F., Witkins, D., & Tang, C. (1997). Discontinuities and continuities in the experience of learning: An interview study of high school students in Hong Kong. *Learning and Instruction, 7,* 21-48.

McCrone, J. (2000). "Right brain" or "left brain"—Myth or reality? *New Scientist.* Retrieved August 1, 2007, from http://www.rbiproduction.co.uk

McInerney, V., McInerney, D. M., & Sinclair, K. E. (1994). Student teachers, computer anxiety and computer experience. *Journal of Educational Computing Research, 11*(1), 177-189.

McPack, J. (1981). *Critical thinking and education.* New York: St. Martin's Press.

Meier, S. (1985). Computer aversion. *Computers in Human Behaviour, 1*(1), 171-179.

Meyer, J. H. F. (2000). Variation in contrasting forms of "memorising" and associated observables. *British Journal of Educational Psychology, 70,* 163-176.

Miller, A. (1987). Cognitive styles: An integrated model. *Educational Psychology, 7,* 251-268.

Molle, M., Marshall, L., Lutzenberger, W., Pietrowsky, R., Fehm, H. L., & Born, J. (1996). Enhanced dynamic complexity in the human EEG during creative thinking. *Neuroscience Letters, 208*(1), 61-64.

Molle, M., Marshall, L., Wolf, B., Fehm, H. L., & Born, J. (1999). EEG complexity and performance measures of creative thinking. *Psychophysiology, 36*(1), 95-104.

Moore, B. N., & Parker, R. (2001). *Critical thinking. Chapter 1. Glossary* (6th ed.). Retrieved August 1, 2007, from http://www.mhhe.com/mayfieldpub/ct/ch01/glossary.htm

Murray, D. R., & Graham, T. (1996). *Teaching systematic thinking and problem solving through database searching, synthesis and analysis*. ERIC document ED399-251.

Obler, L. K., & Gjerlow, K. (1999). *Language and the brain*. Cambridge: Cambridge University Press.

Oh, E., & Limm, D. (2005). Cross relationships between cognitive styles and learner variables in online learning environment. *Journal of Interactive Online Learning, 4*(1), 53-66.

Pask, G. (1976a). *Conversation theory: Applications in education and epistemology*. Amsterdam: Elsevier.

Pask, G. (1976b). Conversational techniques in the study and practice of education. *British Journal of Educational Psychology, 46,* 12-25.

Pask, G. (1976c). Styles and strategies of learning. *British Journal of Educational Psychology, 46,* 128-148.

Pask, G. (1979). *Final report of SSRC Research Programme HR 2708*. Richmond, Surrey, UK: System Research Ltd.

Pask, G. (1988). Learning strategies, teaching strategies, and conceptual or learning style. In R. R. Schmeck (Ed.), *Learning strategies and learning styles* (pp. 83-99). New York: Plenum Press.

Pask, G., & Scott, B. (1972). Learning strategies and individual competence. *International Journal of Man-Machine Studies, 4,* 217-253.

Pask, G., & Scott, B. (1973). CASTE: A system for exhibiting learning strategies and regulating uncertainty. *International Journal of Man-Machine Studies, 5,* 17-52.

Patrick, C. (1937). Creative thought in artists. *Journal of Psychology, 4,* 35-73.

Perry, W. (1970). *Forms of intellectual and ethical development in the college years: A scheme*. New York: Holt, Rinehart, and Winston.

Perry, W. G. (1981). Cognitive and ethical growth: The making of meaning. In Arthur W. Chickering and Associates (Eds.), *The modern American college* (pp. 76-116). San Francisco: Jossey-Bass.

Phillips, H. (2005). Looking for inspiration. *New Scientist,* 40-42.

Ramsden, P., & Entwistle, N. J. (1981). Effects of academic departments on students' approaches to studying. *British Journal of Educational Psychology, 51,* 368-383.

Razoumnikova, O. M. (2000). Functional organization of different brain areas during convergent and divergent thinking: An EEG investigation. *Cognitive Brain Research, 10*(1-2), 11-18.

Richardson, J. T. E. (1995). Mature students in higher education: II: An investigation of approaches to studying and academic performance. *Studies in Higher Education, 20*(1), 5-17.

Richardson, J. T. E. (1997). Meaning orientation and reproducing orientation: A typology of approaches to studying in higher education. *Educational Psychology, 17*(3), 301-311.

Richardson, J. T. E. (1998). Approaches to studying in undergraduate and postgraduate students. *Studies in Higher Education, 23(*2), 217-220.

Richardson, J. T. E., Mugler, F., & Landbeck, R. (1995). Approaches to studying in higher education: A comparative study in the South Pacific. *Educational Psychology, 15*(4), 417-432.

Riding, R. J., & Cheema, I. (1991). Cognitive styles: An overview and integration. *Educational Psychology, 11,* 193-215.

Riding, R. J., Glass, A., Butler, S. R., & Pleydell-Pearce, C. W. (1997). Cognitive style and individual differences in EEG alpha during information processing. *Educational Psychology, 17*(1/2), 219-234.

Robertson, I. T. (1977). *An investigation of some relationships between learning and personality*, Unpublished PhD, Open University, Milton Keynes, UK.

Ropo, E. (1993). Studying technology: An investigation of approaches to studying and perceptions of teaching in a Finnish university of technology. *Higher Education, 25*(2), 111-132.

Roschelle, J. (1995). Learning in interactive environments: Prior knowledge and new experience. In J. H. Falk & L. D. Dierking (Eds.), *Public institutions for personal learning: Establishing a research agenda* (pp. 37-51). Washington, DC: American Association of Museums. Retrieved 1 August, 2007, from http://www.exploratorium.edu/ifi/resources/museumeducation/priorknowledge.html

Sadler-Smith, E., & Tsang, F. (1998). A comparative study of approaches to studying in Hong Kong and the United Kingdom. *British Journal of Educational Psychology, 68(*1), 81-93.

Savolainen, R. (2002). Network competence and information seeking on the internet: From definitions towards a social cognitive model. *Journal of Documentation, 58*(2), 211-26.

Schmeck, R. R. (1988). Strategies and styles of learning: An integration of varied perspectives. In R. R. Schmeck (Ed.), *Learning strategies and learning styles* (pp. 317-347). New York: Plenum.

Schunk, D. (1981). Modeling and attributional effects on children's achievement: A self-efficacy analysis. *Journal of Educational Psychology, 73*(1), 93-105.

*Scoring key for the approaches and study skills inventory for students (ASSIST).* (n.d.). Retrieved August 1, 2007, from http://www.tla.ed.ac.uk/etl/questionnaires/ASSIST.pdf

Scouller, K. (1998). The influence of assessment method on students' learning approaches: Multiple choice question examination versus assignment essay. *Higher Education, 35,* 453-452.

Spilich, G., Vesonder, G., Chiesi, H., & Voss, J. (1979). Test processing of domain-related information for individuals with high and low domain knowledge. *Journal of Verbal Learning and Verbal Behavior, 18,* 275-290.

Sutherland, P. (1995). An investigation into Entwistlean adult learning styles in mature students. *Educational Psychology, 15*(3), 257-270.

Thomas, P. R., & Bain, J. D. (1984). Contextual dependence of learning approaches: The effect of assessments. *Human Learning, 3,* 227-240.

Tinajero, C., & Paramo, M. F. (1997). Field dependence-independence and academic achievement: A re-examination of their relationship. *British Journal of Educational Psychology, 67*(2), 199-213.

Tinajero, C., & Paramo, M. F. (1998a). Field dependence-independence and strategic learning. *International Journal of Educational Research, 29*(3), 251-262.

Tinajero, C., & Paramo, M. F. (1998b). Field dependence-independence cognitive style and academic achievement: A review of research and theory. *European Journal of Psychology of Education, 13*(2), 227-251.

Tinajero, C., Paramo, M. F., Cadaveira, F., & Rodriguez-Holguin, S. (1993). Field dependence-independence and brain organization: The confluence of two different ways of describing general forms of cognitive functioning? A theoretical review. *Perceptual and Motor Skills, 77,* 787-802.

Waugh, R. F. (1999). Approaches to studying for students in higher education: A Rasch measurement model analysis. *British Journal of Educational Psychology, 69*(1), 63-79.

Witkin, H. A., Moore, C. A., Goodenough, D. R., & Cox, P. W. (1977). Field-dependent and field-independent cognitive styles and their educational research. *Review of Educational Research, 47*(1), 1-64.

# Chapter III

# Education

## Introduction

We have examined the basic processes underlying learning, and differences in the way in which these basic processes may be deployed by different individuals. We have also explored differences in the knowledge structures of different individuals, in terms of the prior types and levels of knowledge that they bring to bear on a given learning situation. This chapter explores the art and science of learning design and teaching. These represent the reverse side of the learning coin, and entail designing, delivering, and assessing learning activities and experiences in response to individual learners' needs for knowledge, taking into account differences in their styles and levels of learning as discussed in the previous chapter.

Learning design and teaching entail helping learners move from their current knowledge state to some new *desired* state. However, the notion of desired is problematic, in that what is deemed desirable may differ according to the perspectives of different stakeholders in the learning process. To continue the travel analogy, different stakeholders may entertain very different views of what are desirable destinations—and routes. These differences may be substantially influenced by different views of what education is for, how people learn, and how learning may best be brought about.

Chapters I and II discussed how people learn. This chapter explores educational philosophies (which focus on what learning is for), and learning design (the goal of which is to bring about effective learning). This chapter also introduces another theme which recurs throughout the book, namely: the balance between pedagogical mediation (reliance by the learner on educators and/or educational systems) and learner autonomy (independence and self-regulation in learning). The chapter ends by further developing the model originally presented in Chapter I, and extended in Chapter II, by integrating key concepts relating to educational philosophies and learning design.

## Educational Philosophies and Learning Design

Educational philosophies relate to views on *what learning is for* (for example, vocational preparation or self-actualisation). Such views, coupled with those on *how* people learn as discussed in the previous chapter, may influence educationists in specifying pedagogic approaches, which represent views on *how learning may best be brought about*—how teaching and learning should be designed, organised, and delivered (e.g., via lectures or independent study), and how learning can and should be assessed (for example, by providing evidence that *learning objectives* have been achieved). Such differences are characterised by a tension between mediation and autonomy (discussed later in this chapter).

There are a number of *mainstream* philosophies, each with its own distinctive view of what education is for. For example, the *liberal* tradition associated with Aristotle and Rousseau (Bamborough, 1963; Hutchins, 1968) emphasises the development of the intellect via a broad *well-rounded* education. *Realism* also emphasises intellectual development, reality being considered primarily in terms of empirically proven facts (Chisholm, 1961; Whitehead, 1933). The *progressive* tradition (Bergevin, 1967; Dewey, 1938; Lindeman, 1928) stresses links between education and society via the development of community-relevant practical and vocational skills. *Behavioural* educational philosophy (Skinner, 1971; Thorndike, 1927; Tyler, 1949) is predicated on the notions of control, behaviour modification, and compliance with standards, while *humanistic* education (Maslow, 1976; Rogers, 1969; Tough, 1979) places emphasis on freedom and autonomy, personal growth, and self-actualisation. The *radical* tradition (Adams & Horton, 1975; Freire, 1970; Illich, 1970) views the role of education as an agent for fundamental societal, cultural, political, and economic change. Each of these traditions also has implications for particular types of pedagogic approaches and learning goals that are desirable.

Such perspectives on the purpose of education, along with associated views on how learning occurs and associated implications for learning design and teaching, are often broadly categorised into behaviourist, cognitive, humanist, and social categories. To an extent, these broad divisions embrace theories of how people learn, of the purpose of learning, and of how it may effectively be brought about and assessed. Such differences have implications for the nature of learning behaviour deemed desirable and encouraged by educators in their learning designs and teaching approaches. They are briefly summarised next.

A *behaviourist* view considers the intellectual processes involved in learning to be largely a *black box*, not seeking to understand the inner workings of the learner's mind. Rather, learning is viewed in terms of some observable change in the learner's behaviour due to some equally observable external stimulus. The emphasis is on learning through repetition coupled with reinforcement of correct responses. The main goal of education is to help the learner develop measurable knowledge and competencies, often defined in terms of clear behavioural objectives.

A *cognitive* view focuses on precisely those intellectual processes largely ignored by the behaviourist perspective. The learner is viewed much more as a conscious active agent in the learning process, during which he/she engages in the construction of his or her own mental representations and structures. The emphasis is much more on processes and strategies, and individual differences in both learning processes and the resultant learning are recognised. Valid learning outcomes include *learning to learn* and metacognitive knowledge and skills. Teaching emphasises clear structure and presentation of subject content, taking into account each learner's prior knowledge and other individual differences such as learning style. This perspective is essentially constructivist in an individual sense—that is, each individual constructs his or her own internal knowledge structures and representations.

From a *humanistic* perspective, the goal of learning is self-actualisation, entailing personal fulfilment at both cognitive and affective levels. Cognitive relates to intellectual processes; affective to the individual's feelings and emotions. The emphasis is on learning that is driven by each learner's intrinsic motivation and on maximising learner autonomy in determining what is to be learned, how it is to be learned—and how it is assessed.

*A social/situated* perspective places strong emphasis on learning as interaction between people, and in authentic real-world contexts. As the previous perspectives focused on the individual, this view emphasises knowledge not so much as the possession of individuals but more as distributed among the members of communities. It is socially constructivist in that communities construct their own realities through interactions between the individuals of which they are comprised.

A more recent categorisation has been provided Sfard (1998), who distinguished between what she terms the "acquisition metaphor" and the "participation metaphor" of learning. These map to some extent onto the behaviourist, cognitive, and social groups described previously. The acquisition metaphor emphasises learning in terms of the individual cumulatively accruing chunks of knowledge and maps particularly closely onto behaviourist and cognitive perspectives. The participation metaphor emphasises learning as participating in shared social activity. The goal of learning is that learners should become increasingly integrated into communities of practice, moving from the edges towards the centre as leading participants. This maps particularly closely onto the social/situated perspective previously described. Knowledge is essentially distributed within, and to a large extent consists of the activation of processes and interactions shared within, communities—as opposed to chunks of knowledge possessed by individuals.

A third broad perspective—the "knowledge creation metaphor"—has also been introduced (Hakkarainen, Palonen, Paavola, & Lehtinen, 2004; Paavola & Hakkarainen 2005; Paavola, Lipponen, & Hakkarainen, 2002, 2004). This perspective emphasises learning in terms of responding to genuine needs and problems via the development of new shared *objects of activity*—knowledge, perspectives, approaches, and artefacts, which genuinely advance and transform social and organisational practices. Wikipedia provides an example of such activity, its articles representing shared objects produced via community interactions. Paavola et al. (2004) quote, as illustrative examples of this perspective, Bereiter's knowledge building, Nonaka and Takeuchi's organizational knowledge creation theory, and Engeström's expansive learning theory.

The latter theory involves interlinked *activity systems*. Tensions and conflicts build up between these, and new ways forward are found through *expansive cycles* entailing the questioning of norms and the redefinition of objects of activity (Engeström, 1999). Learning and its associated assessment, from *participation* and *knowledge creation* perspectives, entail much higher levels of openendedness and unpredictability. The precise prespecification of learning objectives, and of tightly controlled learning activity sequences, may be anathema to the proponent of these approaches.

Outside those categories, which relate to formal education entailing a strong element of mediation on the part of educators (seeking to establish conditions whereby learners can learn effectively), is the notion of truly autonomous self-directed learning, or autodidacticism. In reality, the autodidact may choose to consult other people, for example, family and friends, in which case the term *autodidact* is, strictly speaking, incorrect. Nevertheless, the self-directed learner who learns essentially outside the context of formal education may be distinguished from the learner who engages in self-direction in relation to certain aspects of his or her learning within the context of formal education. This will happen, for example, in the case of inquiry-based learning, which is increasingly being used within mediated formal education.

Autodidacticism is associated particularly with adult learning which, of course, may also take place within more formal accredited contexts. However, even within such relatively mediated environments, writers have stressed what they consider to be essential characteristics of adult learners. In his work on "andragogy"—or pedagogy for adults—Knowles (1990) characterised adult learners in terms of the desire to be self-directed in their learning, a particular readiness for learning in terms of its potential usefulness to their personal and professional development, the appropriateness of experiential learning in which they can draw upon their personal experience, intrinsic motivation, and the desire to apply what they are learning in meaningful areas of their lives. These are echoed in later work by, for example, Merriam and Caffarella (1999); Argote, McEvily, and Reagans (2003); Garvin (1993); and Yi (2005).

A number of themes and emphases associated particularly strongly with adult learning theory are becoming increasingly relevant to the learning of younger people. In particular, adult learning theory has stressed the need to take account of each learner's existing experience and knowledge and to use it to good effect. Learning should build on each learner's individually different existing knowledge and experience and avoid the requirement for them to cover material with which they are already familiar. Learners should also be offered personal choice in, and control over, their own learning in terms of what is to be learned and how it should be learned.

Adult learning theory stresses the need to avoid a divide between theory and real world, taking into account the learner's work situation and life context. Learning must be authentic—validated against real-life experience. Self-regulation and autonomy are of key importance—but adult learners are often able to appreciate the need to choose dependence as well as independence where appropriate. Adult learning should be a partnership, learners having involvement in the design of learning goals, means, and assessment. Key aspects of adult learning theory are now being taken on board at undergraduate as well as postgraduate levels, for example in the form of inquiry-based learning approaches.

Postmodern learning theories derive from much broader postmodernist ideas and philosophy. Postmodernism may be seen as a reaction against modernist optimism in relation to the power of logic, rationality, and scientific method to solve the problems of the world, and as the basis for education. By contrast, postmodernism entertains multiple valid truths, illusion, incongruity, and inconsistency. It rejects the view that via scientific method, with its emphasis on the isolation of variables, accurate measurement, objectivity and reliability, we are gradually "homing in" on objective reality. Science is not value-free, and we cannot assume the accuracy and validity of any claims to "correct" interpretations no matter how well established they appear to be. Progress does not only take place via logic and rationality. There are multiple realities coexisting within different sociocultural contexts.

Modernism has led to the widespread propagation and acceptance of sweeping norms and assumptions. Postmodernism opens all of this up to fundamental questioning. It also emphasises the importance of context—different truths existing for different people at different times and in different contexts. Postmodernism is often linked with social critical theory to the extent that assumed knowledge and truth build up power and momentum, which may have the effect of dominating and suppressing other voices. Such domination and suppression may work to the disadvantage of particular groups in society relative to others. Social critical theory has a concern to break such dominations and emancipate the oppressed. The role of learning is to expose to question and critical scrutiny any hegemonic claims to *truth*.

In terms of implications for education, postmodernist learning theory stresses the importance of multiple diverse perspectives, the importance of preserving context, the need to deconstruct, and critically question what appear to be apparently well-established knowledge and truth. Knowledge is always tentative and subject to constant review, challenge, and revision. As Kilgore (2001, quoted in Wonacott, 2001) notes:

*Learning is a process of continuous deconstruction of knowledge, of playing with contradictions, and of creatively and productively opening the discourse of a field to an eclectic mosaic of many truths.* (pp. 59-60)

From the perspective of social critical theory, education and learning should have the function of empowering people to free themselves from views of knowledge and truth, which serve others to their detriment. In keeping with such a perspective are views of the goal of knowledge generation and research as bringing about positive change, as opposed to impersonal objective observation and thought.

As noted previously, educational philosophies relate to questions of what should be learned and why—in terms of content and process and the broad aims of education. Learning theories relate to how people learn. Learning design theory relates to how learning might best be brought about (and assessed). As Reigeluth (1999, quoted in Der-Thanq, Hung, & Wang, 2007) noted, learning theory is descriptive, whereas learning design theory is prescriptive in that it seeks to specify principles and guidelines which should be followed in order to bring about effective learning.

Much work has been published that is categorised as *instructional design*. However, it is important not to restrict the notion of learning design to *instruction*, which maps more closely onto behaviourist and cognitive theories of the *why?* and *how?* of learning than constructivist theories.

Stolovitch and Keeps (2002, quoted in Crosby, 2002) distinguishes between training, instruction and education. Training has the goal of enabling people to reproduce what has been taught accurately and reliably. Instruction entails a degree of generalisation in which the learner is able to apply the essence of what has been learned to new situations. Education has longer-term and more holistic goals, namely: the development of general mental models and value systems. Crosby (2002) provides a useful example of these differences:

*In the realm of safety in the workplace: Through training, we build specific safety behaviors (actions), such as set off an alarm, activate a fire extinguisher, or select the right emergency number to call. Through instruction, we acquire the skills to identify new safety hazards or to act when an emergency occurs that we have not encountered before. Through education, we adopt a safety outlook on life. We automatically take precautions and proactively apply measures to avoid accidents. We foresee possible dangers, and we advocate safety working conditions and behaviors.*

The term *learning design* is used in this book to encompass the design of training, instructional, and education. Learning design entails mapping desired learning outcomes onto learning activities and experiences, taking into account psychological, pedagogical, and technological factors.

Principles and guidelines range from the general (affecting every learner) to the individually different (varying according to the individual's learning needs, capabilities, and styles, such as those discussed in Chapter II). As noted previously, learning designers may embrace behaviourist, cognitive, constructivist, or social constructivist perspectives, and many learning design theories are reflective of the broad perspective in the ascendancy at the time of their creation. Classic general theories include those of, for example, Ausubel, Bruner and Gagne. These are presented here as merely illustrative of the diverse range of theories with generalised applicability to learning.

Based on his theory of subsumption, whereby new information is integrated into the learner's existing knowledge structured in a substantive, as opposed to verbatim way, Ausubel (1978) proposed the use in teaching of "advance organisers." This instructional mechanism entails giving the learner, in advance of learning, information designed to facilitate the integration of content which is about to be presented. However, this is more than a mere overview, abstract or summary. As Kearsley (2007) notes:

*Ausubel emphasizes that advance organizers are different from overviews and summaries which simply emphasize key ideas and are presented at the same level of abstraction and generality as the rest of the material. Organizers act as a subsuming bridge between new learning material and existing related ideas.*

Barron and Calandra (2005) further explain that:

*The purpose of an advance organizer is to provide context rather than content—to provide conceptual scaffolding rather than specific detail from a body of to-be-learned information. Ausubel (1978) describes two types of advance organizers: (a) Expository advance organizers are used when learning material is completely unfamiliar—they help provide inclusive subsumers [concepts and principles under which new information is subsumed]; (b) Comparative organizers are used when the learning material is more familiar—they provide ideational scaffolding as well as pointing out explicitly the principal similarities and differences between new and previously learned ideas.*

Advance organisers remain the focus of pedagogical research studies (e.g., Barron & Calandra, 2005; Hung & Chao, 2007; Shapiro, 2000).

Bruner (1974) was concerned with how best to structure and sequence learning material. He also focused on learners' existing cognitive structures which provide meaning and organisation to new information, allowing the learner to select, question and transform new information and "go beyond the information given". Teachers should focus on learners' *readiness for learning,* and on allowing them to engage in discovery. Teachers should engage in active (Socratic) dialog with learners. Bruner (1975) also devised what he termed the "spiral curriculum":

*I was struck by the fact that successful efforts to teach highly structured bodies of knowledge [...] often took the form of metaphoric spiral in which at some simple level a set of ideas or operations were introduced in a rather intuitive way and, once mastered in that spirit, were then revisited and reconstrued in a more formal or operational way, then being connected with other knowledge, the mastery at this stage then being carried one step higher to a new level of formal or operational rigour and to a broader level of abstraction and comprehensiveness. The end stage of this process was eventual mastery of the connexity and structure of a large body of knowledge.* (pp. 3-4)

Early learning should entail an intuitive grasping of basic ideas, which are then revisited in a *spiral* fashion adding detail and depth each time. Bruner (1990, 1996) went on more recently to take account of sociocultural aspects of learning.

Gagné Briggs, and Wager (1992) devised nine instructional events (and associated cognitive activities) designed to provide the necessary conditions for learning to occur. These principles were also intended to guide the design of learning activities and experiences, as well as the selection of appropriate media. They consist of the following:

- Gain the learner's attention (reception)
- Make the learner aware of the objective of the learning activity (expectancy)
- Stimulate recall of the learner's relevant prior learning (retrieval)

- Present the learning stimulus (selective perception)
- Provide the learner with appropriate guidance (semantic encoding)
- Elicit performance on the part of the learner (responding)
- Give the learner feedback (reinforcement)
- Assess the learner's performance (retrieval)
- Enhance the learner's retention and transfer of what is learned (generalization).

Recall from the previous chapter that in Pask's experiments learners displayed a holist or a serialist approach to learning. Pask went on to explore the implications for learning design, by developing teaching materials structured according to these different learning approaches. The following is an example of material designed to suit a serialist:

> Clobbits are divided into 2 subspecies – Clobs and Bits
>
> Clobs have 1 head. Bits have 2 heads.
>
> There are 2 subdivisions of Clobs: Clob-2a and Clob-2b
>
> Clob-2a has 2 heads the same size. Clob-2b has a front one smaller than the rear
>
> Bits are subdivided into those with 3 legs and those with 4
>
> There are 2 kinds of 4-legged Bit: Bit-Q and Bit-L
>
> There are 3 kinds of Bit-Q
>
> *etc.*

Here is essentially the same taxonomy written in a style to suit a holist.

> Clobs are distinguished by the number of heads (1 or 2); Bits by the number of legs (3 or 4). Bits are further subdivided by the way they walk and their tails.
>
> There are 2 types of Clob, and 8 types of Bit. Clob-2a has 2 heads the same size, whereas Clob-2b's front head is smaller than the rear. Scientists think that these differences developed due to ……

> These differences between Clobs have a greater impact on their life styles than the differences between the various Bits. Bits are distinguished by number of legs, position of legs and type of tail….. etc.
>
> The word "Clobbit" is Martian for "night eater". Clobbits live in damp, dark caves and are active only at night.
>
> *etc.*

The serialist material is devoid of *enrichment* information, which is strictly speaking nonessential for learning the taxonomy. It is also presented in a linear, sequential manner, adopting a *depth first* approach as shown in Figure 25 in Chapter II. The holist material is presented in a way that focuses on the overall framework of the taxonomy—for example, by comparing and contrasting relatively high order characteristics of the creatures making up the taxonomy, and spending time providing enrichment details to help the holist learner establish rich mental connections to make the material more meaningful.

Pask and Scott investigated what would happen if holists and serialists were taught in *matched* and *mismatched* conditions. Matched conditions entailed serialists learning from serialist materials and holists learning from holist materials. Mismatched conditions consisted of serialists learning from holist material and holists learning from serialist material. The effects were dramatic. Learning in matched conditions was far superior to that in mismatched conditions, mismatched learning being severely disrupted. However, it must be noted that the investigation entailed strict experimental conditions uncharacteristic of normal study contexts. This issue, and other problems and limitations surrounding work on cognitive and learning styles, is explored in Chapter X.

Building on this type of work relating to individual differences, *aptitude-treatment interaction,* emerged in the 1970s as an approach to designing learning (Cronbach & Snow, 1977; Snow, 1990). *Aptitudes* were interpreted broadly, and the approach entailed matching teaching to a wide variety of learner characteristics including ability, personality variables, and learning styles. As we will see in Chapter VII, such an approach is adopted by a number of educational informatics systems, which attempt to adapt resource discovery to learner characteristics (including learning preferences and learning styles). However, while the notion of matching may seem attractive as a means of attempting to optimise learning, it does raise certain problematic issues. These are discussed in Chapter X.

More recently Merrill (2002) has reviewed a wide range of instructional design theories, and has abstracted five "first principles of instruction." Theories reviewed include McCarthy's 4-MAT model (McCarthy, 1996), Gardner's (1999) performance-based approach, Schanks' learning by doing problem-centred model (Schank, Berman, & Macperson, 1999), Van Merriënboer's (1997) Four Component

Instructional Design (4C/ID), Nelson's (1999) collaborative problem solving, and Jonassen's (1999) constructivist learning environments approach.

Merrill's (2002) purpose was to abstract general principles regardless of pedagogic (behaviourist, cognitive or constructivist) perspective:

> *The premise of this paper is that there is a set of principles that can be found in most instructional design theories and models and even though the terms used to state these principles might differ between theorists, the authors of these theories would agree that these principles are necessary for effective and efficient instruction. The premise also assumes that these design principles apply regardless of the instructional program or practices prescribed by a given theory or model.* (p. 44)

He goes on to conclude that:

> *This survey of instructional theories and models demonstrates that these theories do include first principles of instruction that are similar, regardless of theory or philosophical orientation.* (p. 58)

Merrill's (2002) "first principles" suggest that learning is enhanced when:

- It is *task-based,* entailing tasks which are meaningful to the learner. Complex tasks should be analysed into subtasks, and there should be a progression of task complexity over time as learners develop their knowledge and skills.
- The learner's existing relevant knowledge and experience are *activated,* in order to facilitate the building of new knowledge structures using existing mental framework. Where lacking, the learner should be provided with appropriate experience and knowledge—possibly via the activation of models which are analogous in structure to what is to be learned.
- Learners are provided with a *demonstration* of the principles or essence of what is being taught. Demonstrations may include, for example, visualisations, models, and simulations.
- Learners are given opportunities to *apply* what is learned. As they do so, they should be provided with feedback and guidance. Such mediation should be progressively withdrawn as their performance improves.
- Learners are given the opportunity to *integrate* their new knowledge by applying and testing it in different meaningful contexts, typically via reflection and discussion with others.

However, the theories reviewed, and Merrill's (2002) abstracted principles (indeed, he refers to them as principles of *instruction*), while they map well onto cognitive and constructivist perspectives, fall short of more radical social constructivist and knowledge creation perspectives. Jonassen (1999, quoted in Merrill, 2002), for example, is quoted in relation to constructivist learning environments as conceding that:

*you must provide interesting, relevant, and engaging problems to solve [...] The problem should not be overly circumscribed [...] so that some aspects of the problem are emergent and definable by the learners* (p. 219)

This still largely directed approach may be contrasted with social constructivist approaches to collaboration that locate the essence of problem generation and ownership much more firmly within the learning community and learners themselves than with an orchestrating teacher. Indeed, Merrill (2002) acknowledges that:

*I agree that collaboration is a very important implementation of activation and integration but I am not yet convinced that collaboration is a first principle.* (p. 57)

Compare this somewhat limited approach to collaboration and open-ended enquiry to inquiry-based learning (IBL) as embraced, for example, by the Centre for Inquiry-based Learning in the Arts and Social Sciences (CILASS) at the University of Sheffield. This is a Centre for Excellence in Teaching and Learning (CETL) funded by the Higher Education Funding Council for England (HEFCE). According to CILASS ("Inquiry-based learning," n.d.), IBL entails:

*approaches to learning that are based on a process of self-directed inquiry or research. Students conduct small or large-scale inquiries that enable them to engage actively and creatively with the questions and problems of their discipline, often in collaboration with others. IBL approaches include case-study and problem-based learning (PBL) methods as well as research projects of different kinds. It is a key characteristic of IBL that inquiry tasks facilitate exploration and investigation of issues or scenarios that are open-ended enough for different responses and solutions to be possible (Khan and O'Rourke, 2005).*

There is currently much interest in inquiry-based learning, particularly in higher education. This follows on a rich tradition in higher education, as well as education at other levels, of approaches to learning that emphasise the exercise and development of autonomy on the part of learners. It is related to, but not identical to problem-based learning in that, as Khan and O´Rourke (2005) go on to note:

*By contrast, EBL advocates a wider use of project work or research activity, emphasising the use of project-work to master a given body of knowledge itself, and not simply to make connections within an existing body of knowledge. Toohey (1999) indicates that this kind of approach is a key factor that distinguishes an enquiry-based approach from a more traditional use of projects.* (p. 5)

It is distinct from the more traditional use of problem solving within education in which solutions, as well as appropriate information sources, are known in advance by teachers. By contrast, IBL is much more open-ended and maps well onto the participation and knowledge creation learning metaphors described earlier in this chapter. Khan and O´Rourke (2005) note that in IBL:

*...students pursue their own lines of enquiry, draw on their existing knowledge and identify the consequent learning needs. They seek evidence to support their ideas and take responsibility for analysing and presenting this appropriately, either as part of a group or as an individual supported by others. They are thus engaged as partners in the learning process.* (p. 1)

According to CILASS, IBL has:

*[...] the potential to further strengthen the relationship between teaching and research in universities (Jenkins and Healey, 2005). This is because IBL makes the links between research and learning explicit, and encourages forms of learning and teaching that enable students to participate more fully in the research practices and communities of their discipline. [...] Collaboration with peers on inquiry tasks, and with more experienced learners and researchers in the discipline, can facilitate the development of students' identity as members of a learning or research community and the development of their group-work skills. Collaboration across disciplinary boundaries enables students to recognise both the distinctiveness and transferability of their own knowledge, practices and capabilities, and to contribute to the learning of their peers in other disciplines.*

Collaboration is at the centre of *learning communities* as championed by the Center for the Integration of Research, Teaching and Learning—a network of universities funded by the U.S. National Science Foundation. Learning communities represent one of the central pillars of this network (along with the notion of *teaching as research* and *learning through diversity*). Learning communities (Basic Learning community Principles and Guidelines, 2006):

*bring people together for shared learning, discovery, and the generation of knowledge. Within a learning community (LC), all participants take responsibility for achieving the learning goals. Importantly, learning communities are the process by which individuals come together to achieve learning goals. These learning goals can be specific to individual courses and activities, or can be those that guide an entire teaching and learning enterprise.*

They are founded on the following principles:

*Shared discovery and learning. Collaborative learning activities where participants share responsibility for the learning that takes place help the development of a learning community. Rather than relying on traditional "expert centered" lecture formats, practitioners should include collaborative learning techniques so learners can see their contribution to the learning goals.*

*Functional connections among learners. Learning communities develop when the interactions among learners are meaningful, functional and necessary for the accomplishment of the "work" within the courses or learning activities (rather than serving as "window dressing" or simply as a "feel good" activities). Moreover, meaningful connections must extend throughout the entire learning community—for example, among students, post-docs, faculty, and staff-rather than simply among cohort- or role-related peers.*

*Connections to other related learning and life experiences. Learning communities flourish when implicit and explicit connections are made to experiences and activities beyond the course or program in which one participates. These connections help situate one's learning in a larger context by solidifying one's place in the broader campus community of learners and life experiences. These connections decrease one's sense of curricular and personal isolation.*

*Inclusive learning environment. Learning communities succeed when the diverse backgrounds and experiences of learners are welcomed in such a way that they help inform the group's collective learning. Whenever possible, activities should be sought that help participants reach out and connect with others from backgrounds different from their own.*

As is the case with IBL, this approach can relate to individual activities, courses, or entire programmes of study. A recent study by Cho, Gay, Davidson, and Ingraffea

(2007) using social network analysis suggests that the behaviour and effectiveness of performance of individuals within a learning community may be affected by both personality features and their relative position within the community. Learners with high levels of willingness to communicate, or who were initially peripheral players within the community, tended more to explore new network linkages, while learners who played central roles in the community tended to achieve higher grades.

As with learning theories, learning design theories may be grouped in terms of the broad perspective they assume. Behaviourist theories emphasise the learning of skills and knowledge via the design of appropriate learning stimuli and reinforcements. Learning outcomes entail well–specified, predetermined, and objectively measurable skills and knowledge. Cognitive theories imply a focus on the mental processes entailed in learning (largely ignored in behaviourist theories). Learning outcomes focus on explicit and objectively measurable skills and knowledge, and learning design entails designing conditions and activities to enable knowledge transmission via carefully analysed learning objectives mapped onto appropriate learning tasks. The emphasis is on controlling the learner's cognitive processes via the analysis of the content to be learned, and the design of instructional events that will bring about these processes in order to produce the desired learning outcomes.

Constructivist approaches place more emphasis on learners developing their own cognitive processes in order to construct their own meanings. Der-Thanq et al. (2007) associate this approach with learning goals emphasising reflective action and metacognition. Learning design entails creating appropriate constructivist learning environments (CLEs) in which authentic problems can be posed:

*CLEs are open-ended platforms with the goal of solving authentic issues and problems, and which offer tools that allow learners to explore a problem space and interact with others in order to discover meanings and relationships. The design process should then be an iterative process of situating and contextualising problems appropriate to the level of abilities of learners.*

Constructivist learning design also emphasises giving learners the opportunity to engage in and develop their powers of reflective thought and metacognition.

Social constructivist approaches emphasise facilitating interactions between learners and both social and technological aspects of communities, focusing not only on the rules that govern interactions and the roles of the various players in the community, but also the tools used within the community to accomplish its various tasks. Social constructivist approaches engage with learners' belief systems (epistemic cognition). As noted by Maclellan and Soden (2004):

*It was King and Kitchener's (1994) thesis that one's epistemic cognition will be more or less sophisticated depending on the stage of reasoning that has been achieved; with the reasoning being dependent on how problematic a phenomenon is perceived to be. Further, perceiving a phenomenon to be problematic is predicated on assumptions about the nature of knowledge and how it is acquired.* (p. 256)

This echoes the discussion of levels of critical thinking discussed in Chapter II. Der-Thanq et al. (2007) distinguish constructivism from social constructivism in that the latter:

*... enables belief enculturation. Beliefs and values are enculturated through experiencing meaning (possibly through problem solving) within rich contexts where social interactions abound. In the process of these interactions—both with problems and with persons—hidden tacit knowledge comprised of beliefs is manifested and understood.*

They go on to draw attention to the danger of what they call "lethal mutations," which may occur when perspectives on what should be learned, and how it may best be brought about and assessed, do not match actual learning designs. This may occur all too easily where even well-meaning, learning designers stray into a situation in which there is an unintended incongruence between the two.

Laurillard's (2002) *Conversational Framework* is based on the notion of conversations as propounded by Pask, and discussed in Chapter I. There is a useful chart describing the framework (see http://www2.smumn.edu/deptpages/~instructTech/lol/laurillard/index.htm). It represents a learning design theory in that it recommends 12 stages through which teaching should progress in order to facilitate effective learning. These include a number of conversational dialogues between teacher and learner. The stages are as follows (adapted from Heinze, Procter, & Scott, 2007):

- The teacher communicates theory/ideas to the student.
- The student communicates his or her conceptions of these to the teacher.
- The teacher redescribes them to the student in the light of this communication.
- The student redescribes his or her conceptions to the teacher.
- The teacher adapts the task goal in the light of the student's description.
- The teacher establishes goals and communicates these to the student.

- The student engages in learning actions.
- The teacher provides the student with feedback on these actions.
- The student modifies his or her actions in the light of this feedback.
- The student adapts his or her activities in the light of theory, goal and feedback.
- The student reflects on his or her conceptions in the light of experience.
- The teacher reflects on the student's actions in order to modify his or her descriptions of his or her conceptions.

Student action in relation to the tasks set by teachers take place within a learning environment constructed by the teacher. Four types of activity should take place in iterative cycles. The following should take place:

*Discussion* entailing both teacher and learner agreeing on learning goals. Teachers' and students' conceptions should be accessible to both parties.

*Adaptation* on the part of both teacher and learner. The teacher should adapt the learning environment, including goals, to take account of learner's actual conceptions. Students should adapt their conceptions and actions in the light of feedback from the teacher.

*Interaction* between the student and the learning environment constructed by the teacher. The teacher must provide a learning environment appropriate to the student's learning task. The teacher must provide appropriate support to the student in performing the learning task, and appropriate feedback on his or her performance.

*Reflection* by the student and the teacher. The teacher should reflect on the student's actions and modify goals and learning environment as appropriate. The student should reflect on his or her learning—conceptions, actions, and feedback.

As Heinze et al. (2007) note:

*The iterative learning cycles highlight the dialogic nature of the model. These require at least three engagements with one topic. Thus a student will have an opportunity to learn from theory, action and feedback [...] Laurillard suggests that there is no one right medium for the conversation; each medium has its own drawbacks and hence it is important to maintain the various dialogic aspects all the time. These are some of the reasons that make the Conversational Framework an attractive option for Blended learning.* (p. 112)

As we will see in Chapter IX, Heinze, Procter, and Scott go on to evaluate the *Conversational Framework* in an action research study of its applicability to a real world blended learning context. Blended learning entails the use of a mix of pedagogical approaches (media and/or modes). It is often used to refer to a mix of e-learning and more traditional delivery approaches including face-to-face. Heinze and Procter (2004) define it as:

*learning that is facilitated by the effective combination of different modes of delivery, models of teaching and styles of learning, and is founded on transparent communication amongst all parties involved with a course.* (p. 12)

Bonk, Kim, and Zeng (2006) provide a more expansive description:

*Blended learning is seen in the linkages between instructors, learners, and classrooms located in two or states, provinces, regions, countries, or continents. Blended learning occurs in those exciting opportunities where students debate and discuss scholarly ideas in an asynchronous forum and then bring in the authors for a synchronous chat or videoconference. Blended learning happens when some course meetings or training events are conducted virtually rather than face-to-face. Such classes or training experiences can blend students located at various remote regions or perhaps instructors collaboratively teaching a class at two or more locations. Of course, blended learning might simply supplement course readings and activities with online articles, simulations, events, and other resources.* (p. 550)

However, the lack of clarity of many working definitions of blended learning is noted by Oliver and Trigwell (2005). They review possible blendings, including those between:

- E-learning and traditional learning.
- Online with face-to-face learning; different learning media.
- Different contexts in which learning takes place.
- Different theories of learning.
- Different learning objectives.
- Different pedagogies.

Oliver and Trigwell (2005) argue that educational benefits often attributed by educators to "blended learning" in reality derive from the experience of variation:

*According to variation theory, it is necessary to experience certain patterns of variation in order to develop certain ways of seeing. This is true regardless of the particular method of instruction used, and regardless of the particular way in which educational resources are organised. It is therefore possible that certain patterns of variation may be experienced in reading a book, in watching a video, or in participating in a field trip.* (pp. 22-23)

However, they acknowledge that mixes of media and modes characterising *blended learning* may be an effective form of enabling learners to experience variation, and that new technologies may offer enhanced opportunities for learners to experience variation and provide forms of variation that were not previously possible.

Chatti, Klamma, Jarke, and Naeve (2007) present an extended model of blended learning which in which Web 2.0 concepts offer a vehicle for an integration of Nonaka's knowledge transformation model and knowledge management to facilitate a mix of formal and informal, personal and social collaborative learning. Web 2.0 concepts and their implications for learning will be introduced in Chapter VI.

## Autonomy and Mediation

A broad distinction may be drawn between different contexts in which autonomy is exercised by learners. Those engaged in project-, problem-, or inquiry-based learning within a formal educational setting may be given considerable degrees of autonomy in seeking information to satisfy goals set by teachers. However, they may also be accorded considerable autonomy in setting learning goals for themselves. Autonomous learning may also take place outside the context of any formal educational establishment—by independent, self-directed learners. Such learners may be seeking to answer questions, solve problems, inform, and educate themselves in relation to their personal and working lives.

Mediation and autonomy are key issues underlying, and differentiating, different conceptions of what education and learning—both formal and informal—are for, how learning should and does take place, and how people can be most effectively be helped to learn. This theme is particularly relevant to the focus of this book in that it seeks to provide an integrated conceptual framework for both mediated and autonomous self-directed learning.

Some level of autonomy is ultimately the goal of all education, insofar as it implies an ability to do something or think something *for oneself*. But this may be at the level of a learning goal or learning approach designed to reach some other goal. The goals of particular tasks may relate to the types of intellectual activity described in Chapter I (for example, comprehension, analysis, synthesis, critical evaluation, etc.). However, the ability to engage in these types of information processing autonomously—that is, without requiring high levels of interaction with and support from others—may represent a higher order goal, which may be achieved through engagement in a number of specific tasks over time.

Thus autonomy may thus be both a goal and a means to achieve a goal. As a goal, it consists of having acquired the ability to execute a particular function autonomously—and one of the ways in which a person may achieve this goal is by engaging in (possibly progressively increasing levels of) autonomy. Within the theories of learning presented earlier in this chapter, a broad distinction may be made in relation to the degree of autonomy accorded to the learner, from the stimulus-response and reinforcement notions of behaviourist theories to the negotiation of shared meanings emphasised by their constructivists counterparts.

Within formal education, a desire to increase levels of autonomy accorded to learners has driven successive vogues in pedagogic approach, such as discovery learning; self-directed and project-based study; individualised instruction; resource-based learning and, more recently, inquiry-based learning; and the design of constructivist learning environments (e.g., Baptista Nunes & McPherson, 2003; Barrilleaux, 1965; Brookfield, 1985; Clarke, 1982; Colliver, 2000; Cull, 1991; Evenson & Hmelo, 2000; Hiemstra & Brockett, 1994; Jonassen, 1991; Jonassen & Rohrer-Murphy, 1999; Matthews, 2002; Reigeluth, 1999; Tam, 2000; Terhart, 2003; Tough, 1979). Such approaches have direct implications for the types of learning goals and associated tasks that are set for learners.

Within highly mediated learning contexts, teachers take responsibility for selecting and presenting learning content to learners in their charge. As we will see in Chapters VII and VIII, educational informatics systems can help teachers in the discovery of appropriate learning content and resources for use in such highly mediated educational contexts. They can do so by helping them in the task of discovering appropriate resources. Educational informatics systems can also support learners engaged in more autonomous forms of learning, from project- and inquiry-based learning in formal educational settings. Educational informatics systems are also capable of supporting independent self-directed learning outside any formal educational institution, where learners need to engage in resource discovery for themselves.

Figure 29 extends the model of basic information processes entailed in learning, originally presented in Figure 20 in Chapter I, to include the notions of mediation and autonomy. The model applies to both formal mediated and informal, autonomous self-directed learning. The various stages of learning include:

- Awareness of a set of concepts which contain some conceptual anomaly.
- Perception of such an anomaly requiring some integrating theme.

- Generation of some potential integrating theme—or tentative theory—whereby the anomaly might be resolved
- The testing of such a tentative theory. .

New ideas may be fed into this process at any stage, as the learner thinks of, encounters, or is presented with them during the course of learning. At each of these stages, what the learner requires may be:

- Given to him or her (for example, by a teacher).
- Discovered by the learner via some pedagogical intervention which encourages or facilitates such discovery.
- Autonomously discovered by the learner without such pedagogical intervention (whether by active searching or serendipitous encountering).

Any particular tentative theory may be judged to be:

- A failed attempt at a solution
- A partial solution
- An uncertain solution
- A complete solution

This judgement may also be provided entirely by the learner, by some mediator, and/or as a result of interaction between them. The judgement may be made in relation to the learner's own knowledge (narrowly defined in terms of comprehending, or broadly defined in terms of enmeshing with beliefs and values), and/or the knowledge of others. Such others may include, for example, friends and work colleagues, organisations, communities, and society. Indeed, as we have seen in Chapter III, a number of mainstream prevailing educational perspectives emphasise learning in terms of increasing integration of the individual within communities, and of learning goals and tasks as responding to genuine needs within such organisations and communities.

Approaches entailing relatively high levels of autonomy in seeking and processing information to generate new knowledge are particularly appropriate to the goal of developing learning to learn metacognitive skills (Kuiper, 2002; Metcalfe & Shimamura, 1994; Schraw, 1998; Sternberg, 1998). Such goals also map onto learning models that view the learner as actively engaged in the construction of personal meaning, as opposed to a relatively passive recipient of *accepted* (that is, other people's) meanings.

*Figure 29. Autonomy and mediation in the basic information processes entailed in learning*

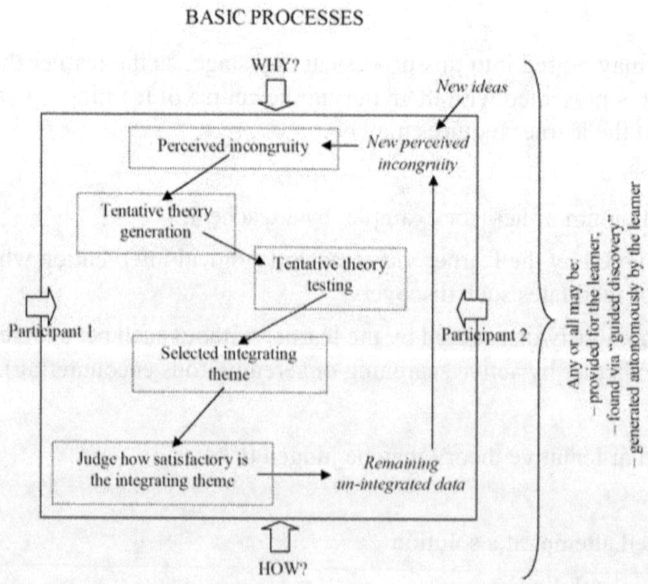


Metacognition refers to reasoning about one's own thinking—an ability which may be used to regulate one's own cognition and maximize one's potential to engage in effective learning and problem solving. Livingston (1997) describes metacognition thus:

*Metacognition refers to higher order thinking which involves active control over the cognitive processes engaged in learning. ... Because metacognition plays a critical role in successful learning, it is important to study metacognitive activity and development to determine how students can be taught to better apply their cognitive resources through metacognitive control.*

Metacognition may be contrasted with *supplantation,* which is associated with high levels of mediation. Supplantation entails the performing of cognitive processes *on behalf of*, rather than *by* the learner. They may be performed for the learner by someone, or something external to the learner. Levels of supplantation are inherent in the development of intelligent computer systems, which are designed to perform some cognitive process or processes for their users. This may be at the level of saving them the drudgery of some low level routine information processing such as trawling Web sites looking for the cheapest price for a particular product. However, it may also be at the level of enabling them to punch above their intellectual weight and perform some task at an expert level even though they are not expert. Many so-called *expert systems* were built particularly in the 1980s, precisely to do this, examples being found in a great variety of applications from medical diagnosis through the control of complex industrial processes to education.

Much research has focused on building "smartness" into computer-based systems to support learning and information seeking. However, the specification and satisfaction of an individual's learning and information needs—beyond a certain level of complexity—are not always sufficiently simple to be effectively handled by machine intelligence (Ford, 2005). Attempting to maximise the level of smartness of the human information seeker and user to compensate for the limitations of computer systems has for long been a focus of information literacy research and development (Johnston & Webber, 2003).

Clearly, the effectiveness of learning and information seeking may be affected by many factors specific to topic, task, and individual—for example, level of subject knowledge. However, there has been growing interest in the potential role of metacognition in this process. Individuals' knowledge and awareness of their own cognitive processes potentially enables them to maximise their self-regulation and executive control. Well-developed metacognitive skills may enable learners to manage their learning and to react to information system behaviour and output, in a way that provides a much finer-grained more intimate response to the subtleties, intricacies, and on-going development of their particular learning and associated information needs than could be provided by other people or machine systems.

Metacognition consists of metacognitive knowledge and metacognitive regulation (Flavell, 1979; McCormick, 2003). Metacognitive teaching is generic to the extent that it does not entail the acquisition of specific subject domain knowledge. Rather, it is designed to empower individuals to better align their knowledge and skills to the task in hand. However, its effect is potentially also to improve domain-specific intellectual activity. Indeed, there is evidence that the use of metacognitive knowledge and skills can compensate for a lack of subject matter knowledge (Land & Greene, 2000).

Significant levels of metacognition may be possessed in tacit form by the individual. Thus, arguably much of the smartness required to engage in effective learning and related information seeking may be possessed by individuals but latent—inaccessible and unrealised. Although the teaching of metacognition may entail the teaching of new knowledge (but generic rather than domain specific), it also entails helping individuals to make explicit and accessible such latent knowledge.

Much research has been conducted into developing metacognition in relation to learning—*deep* learning being associated with the use of metacognitive strategies (e.g., Chin & Brown, 2000). More recently work has focused on the application of metacognitive teaching to inquiry-based learning and information seeking (Aþkar & Yalçýnalp, 2000; Brush, Saye, & Wolf, 2003; Tsai, 2004). Quintana, Zhang, and Krajcik (2005), for example, have developed a metacognitive *scaffolding* framework. Williams and Conlan's (2007) report proposes the use within e-learning systems of facilities that enable learners to visualise the conceptual space in which they are learning, in order to support the development of metacognitive awareness of their own learning styles. Bull, Dimitrova, and McCalla (2007) stress the potential value of *open learner models* in helping learners to develop metacognition. Open learner models are models used, for example, to drive adaptive systems, which can be inspected and in some cases changed by learners themselves. Bull et al. note that:

*... not only can the learner contribute information to help increase the accuracy and therefore the utility of their learner model for adaptation purposes, but the model can also become a learning resource for the student in its own right. Such an open learner model (i.e. a learner model accessible to the learner modelled) offers the learner a perspective on their understanding that is not usually available to them, which can facilitate reflection on their knowledge and on the learning process more generally, as students must carefully consider their knowledge state before suggesting changes to their model. Furthermore, even non-interactive open learner models (that is, learner models that are inspectable but not changeable by the user) have the potential to prompt learner reflection and metacognition in a similar manner, as they confront the learner with information about their understanding which is likely to provoke some kind of cognitive reaction from them. (p. 83)*

We will also see in Chapter VII an example of an educational informatics system that attempts to help learners leverage their metacognitive abilities in order to improve the information-seeking skills they need to support their learning (Cole, Beheshti, Leide, & Large, 2005; Cole, Cantero, & Ungar, 2000). This system applies experimental metacognitive devices designed to enhance information searching by better aligning individuals' existing search knowledge to the particular academic task on which they are engaged.

Autonomy, metacognition, versatility, and learning to learn are linked. Versatility is used here in a broader sense than Pask's. Recall from Chapter II that Pask used the term to describe learners equally able to engage in global holist-like "comprehension learning" *and* analytic serialist-like "operation learning." The term is used here, rather, to indicate the ability effectively to apply different approaches to learning as required by different learning tasks and conditions—including but not restricted to learning styles.

*Versatility*, as defined previously, is a necessary, though not sufficient condition for autonomy in that, if a learner is not able to adapt his or her approach to different strategic requirements of different tasks, or to learn from informational materials not matched with his or her particular style, then assistance and support from others (such as courseware designers and teachers) will be required—reducing autonomy.

*Autonomy* without versatility may not necessarily be effective. For example, a learner may find him/herself in a situation where he/she is working with a considerable degree of autonomy. But he/she may be unable to utilise this autonomy effectively and may require high levels of mediation by a teacher. In one sense, versatility may be thought of as effectively applied autonomy.

*Metacognition* is a key contributor to the development of both autonomy and versatility. However, it does not necessarily imply either. That is, metacognition may include awareness of one's own limitations—for example, of one's own lack of versatility, and/or of one's own need for dependence rather than autonomy. Avoiding learning materials structured in ways not well matched to one's own preferred learning style, and avoiding situations in which autonomy is required, may both be evidence of the effective use of metacognition to learn more effectively.

Metacognition as used here necessarily implies self-awareness on the part of the learner. Cognition on the part of a person about the cognition of other people represents knowledge about how people learn. It does not represent metacognition, even though it is *cognition about cognition*. Metacognition as used here entails cognition about one's own cognition—knowledge of ones own learning processes. For example, cognitive scaffolding may be used as a teaching device. Only when the learner becomes aware of the scaffolding as separate from the content, and as something that can be generalised to the learning of other content, can the devise be thought of as metacognitive.

To explore further the previous example, learners may be taught to recall a list of items using visual associations. This cognitive scaffolding is a teaching device. Only when the learners become aware of visual association as a technique separate from the specific content taught (the list of items they can now recall) and which may be applied to memorising other content can it be thought of as a metacognitive device. Thus the term *metacognitive* is to a degree fuzzy, since if a teacher intends that the learner should become aware of, and be able to generalise such a teaching device, we may refer to that teacher as applying a metacognitive device. We will see in Chapter VII an example of an educational informatics system that employs metacognitive devices in this sense to help learners become more effective information seekers. However, if the teacher's intentions are not realised, and the learner learns only to recall the list of items taught, then we can arguably think of the cognitive scaffolding as a *failed metacognitive device*. Metacognition itself—that is, awareness on the part of the learner in relation to his or her own learning processes—has not been achieved. The achievement of metacognition is a necessary, but not sufficient, condition for learning to learn.

Learning to learn implies the presence of metacognition, autonomy, *and* versatility. However, it implies more than just metacognition (which as noted previously can result in avoidance of learning contexts mismatched with one's own preferred style). It implies more than just being versatile, in that one may develop versatility without active awareness or control over the process (in which case one will have simply *learned* rather than having learned to learn. And it implies more than autonomy, since as noted previously, autonomy may be exercised (1) ineffectively, and/or (2) without any conscious improvement over time.

To have learned to learn implies:

a. Having developed the ability to learn effectively in conditions not necessarily optimally suited to one's own learning style and capability—that is, to have developed versatility.
b. Thus minimising dependence on the pedagogical mediation of others (in the form of, for example, structuring of learning for the learner by teachers)—that is, to be able to exercise autonomy effectively.
c. having developed conscious strategies to improve (a) and (b) over time—requiring metacognition.

Pask's conversational model of learning, introduced in Chapter I, has been extended (Laurillard, 2002; Thomas & Harri-Augstein, 2001) also to embrace learning to learn. Figure 30 shows this extended model. The original model (Figure 18 in Chapter I) is condensed into the bottom line which represents a conversation between participants concerning the *why* and *how* of the particular topic being learned. However, at a more abstract level, conversations also take place relating to the *why* and *how* of learning itself.

Figure 31 represents the further development of the ongoing model, last presented in Figure 28 at the end of Chapter II. The extended version now integrates key concepts from the present chapter, including metacognition, autonomy, versatility, and learning to learn. In Figure 31, metacognition now appears in the *Information processing types* box. Learning to learn appears in the *Information processes* box. The learning to learn concepts shown in detail Figure 30 are integrated into the extended model Figure 31 but in abbreviated form. That is, the detail shown in Figure 30 is collapsed and represented simply by the text "conversations about learning conversations (learning to learn)."

As previously noted, autonomy and versatility are particularly closely linked, versatility representing the effective application of autonomy. They are grouped together in a new box at the bottom right of Figure 31. The *Autonomy and versatility* box represents differences between individuals in terms of the extent to which they are "locked into" a particular information processing approach—that is, cannot unaided adopt flexibility in their approach as required by different tasks and situations. This difference in mental state may be applied to any of the strategies listed in the *Infor-*

*Figure 30. Conversational model of learning to learn (adapted from Harri-Augstein & Thomas, 1991)*

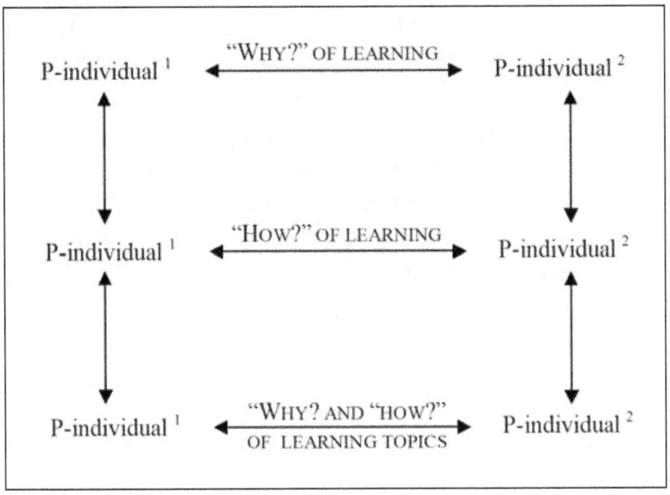


*mation processing approaches* box. This enables differentiation between learning strategies and learning styles.

It is important to be able to distinguish between strategies and styles. Some individuals may be more locked into the consistent use of a particular information processing strategy than others. An individual strongly predisposed in this way to apply a particular *strategy* consistently regardless of task is said to display a particular *style*. By contrast, versatile learners are able more flexibly to switch between different strategies as appropriate to different tasks or situations. Similar levels of versatility (as defined here, rather than in Pask's more specific sense, restricted to comprehension and operation learning) may be observed in relation to imager/verbaliser, and deep/surface approaches.

No distinction between strategy and style is made in the *Information processing approaches* box of the figure. Rather, this distinction is represented by the application of the *Autonomy and versatility* mental state box to the *Information processing approaches* box. Relatively *low* levels of versatility (i.e., the effective application of autonomy) applied to a deep or surface approach implies that the learner is relatively locked into that approach, which indicates a *stylistic* bias. The same can be said in the case of versatility apply to holist or serialist strategies, or indeed any of the approaches listed.

Compared to the version of the model presented in Chapter II, the version shown in Figure 31 has a number of other features in addition to those already introduced. The new box at the top of the figure indicates the influence of the educational philosophies and learning design theories introduced in this chapter. In a formal educational context knowledge needs are often represented by tasks linked to learning goals or objectives set by others. The nature of such goals/objectives, and consequently of related learning behaviour, may depend to a significant degree on the different educational philosophies and learning design theories of those who set them. The nature of individuals' responses to such tasks may depend on a range of psychological factors that constitute the main part of the model presented here.

The outermost box in Figure 31 represents the social context within which the individual operates. This context includes other people, organisations, communities, and society. It is characterised by multiple perspectives among such organisations and communities. The next innermost box represents the individual learner and encloses the two boxes representing mental processes and mental states, which were previously described in Chapter II.

This chapter has explored different perspectives concerning what education is for, and how learning can best be designed. A key theme in thinking about both the purposes

*Figure 31. Mental processes and mental states in context (adapted from Ford, 2004)*

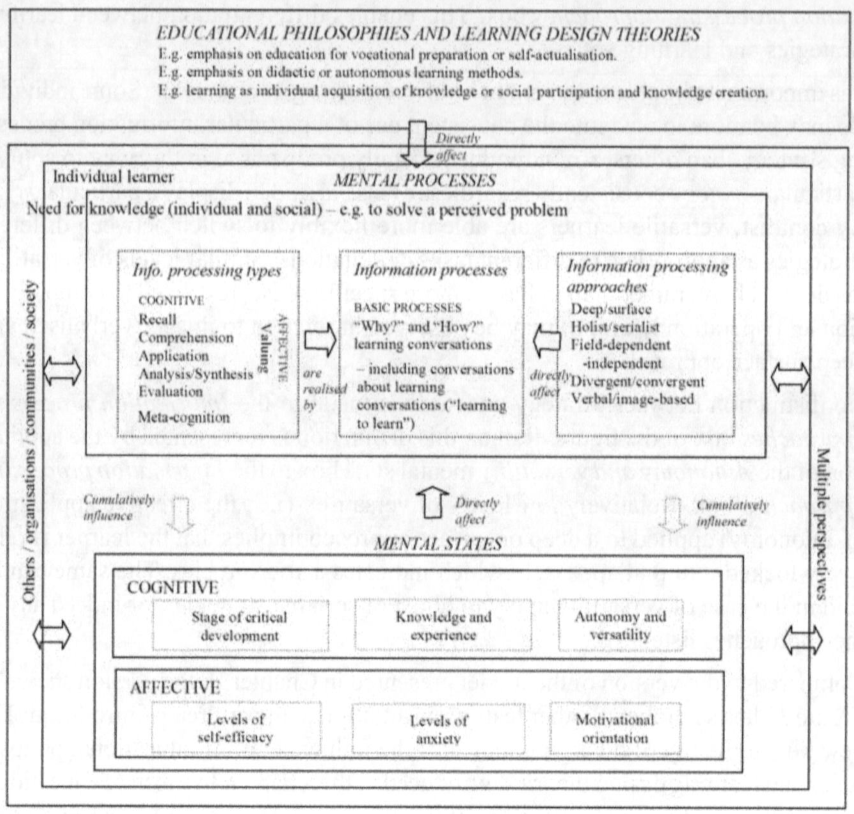

and the methods of education is that of mediation and autonomy. Learners engaged in formal education may be given varying types and levels of autonomy, and this may depend on their level of study, their competencies as perceived by—and the particular approach to learning design espoused by—their educators.

The ability to seek out information and resources for oneself—as opposed to having them provided (prescribed or recommended) by teachers—is a key element in such learning. This activity is also central to the sort of autonomous self-directed learning in which people and communities engage when seeking to learn—to answer questions, to solve problems, or to educate themselves—outside the context of any formal course or educational institution. Information seeking and resource discovery form the focus of the next chapter, which explores approaches to these issues that have been developed within library and information science.

## References


Adams, F., & Horton, M. (1975). *Unearthing seeds of fire.* Winston-Salem, NC: John F. Blair.

Aþkar, P., & Yalçýnalp, S. (2000). Understanding of adults' metacognitive knowledge about information seeking skills via Internet. In P. Kommers & G. Richards (Eds.), *Proceedings of World Conference on Educational Multimedia, Hypermedia and Telecommunications 2000* (pp. 1245-1246). Chesapeake, VA: AACE.

Argote, L., McEvily, B., & Reagans, R. (2003). Managing knowledge in organizations: An integrative framework and review of emerging trends. *Management Science, 49*(4), 571-582.

Ausubel, D. (1978). In defense of advance organizers: A reply to the critics. *Review of Educational Research, 48,* 251-257.

Bamborough, R. (1963). *The philosophy of Aristotle* (Signet Classics). New York: New American Library. Baptista Nunes, J. M., & McPherson, M. A. (2003, July 9-11). Constructivism vs. objectivism: Where is the difference for designers of elearning environments? In V. Devedzic, J. Spector, D. Sampson, & Kinshuk (Eds.), *Proceedings of the 3rd IEEE International Conference on Advanced Learning Technologies (ICALT 2003),* Athens, Greece (pp. 496-500). Los Alamitos, CA: IEEE Computer Society.

Barrilleaux, L. E. (1965). *An experimental investigation of the effects of multiple library sources as compared to the use of basic textbook on student achievement and learning activities in junior high school science.* Unpublished PhD dissertation, University of Iowa, Iowa City.

Barron, A. E., & Calandra, B. (2005). A preliminary investigation of advance organizers for a complex educational website. *Journal of Educational Multimedia and Hypermedia, 14,* 5-23.

*Basic Learning Community Principles and Guidelines.* (2006). Retrieved August 1, 2007, from Center for the Integration of Research, Teaching and Learning Web site: http://cirtl.wceruw.org/pillars_LC.html

Bergevin, P. (1967). *A philosophy for adult education.* New York: Seabury.

Bonk, C. J., Kim, K. J., & Zeng, T. (2006). Future directions of blended learning in higher education and workplace learning settings. In C. J. Bonk & C. R. Graham (Eds.), *Handbook of blended learning: Global perspectives, local designs* (pp. 550-568). San Francisco, CA: Pfeiffer Publishing. Retrieved August 1, 2007, from http://www.publicationshare.com/c083_bonk_future.pdf

Brookfield, S. (Ed.). (1985). *Self-directed learning: From theory to practice* (New directions for continuing education, Number 25). San Francisco: Jossey-Bass.

Bruner, J. (1974). *Going beyond the information given.* New York: Norton.

Bruner, J. S. (1975). *Entry into early language: A spiral curriculum.* The Charles Gittins Memorial Lecture, University College of Swansea.

Bruner, J. (1990). *Acts of meaning.* Cambridge, MA: Harvard University Press.

Bruner, J. (1996). *The culture of education.* Cambridge, MA: Harvard University Press.

Brush, T., Saye, J., & Wolf, S. (2003). Using information problem-solving model as a metacognitive scaffold for multimedia-supported information-based problems. *Journal of Research on Technology in Education, 35*(3). Retrieved August 1, 2007, from http://www.iste.org/jrte/

Bull, S., Dimitrova, V., & McCalla, G. (2007). Open learner models: Research questions (Preface to Special Issue of the IJAIED Part 1). *International Journal of Artificial Intelligence in Education, 17*(2), 83-87.

Chatti, M., Klamma, R., Jarke, M., & Naeve, A. (2007, July 18-20). The Web 2.0 driven SECI model based learning process. In *Proceedings of the Seventh IEEE International Conference on Advanced Learning Technologies (ICALT 2007),* Niigata, Japan (pp. 780-782). Retrieved August 1, 2007, from http://doi.ieeecomputersociety.org/10.1109/ICALT.2007.256

Chin, C., & Brown, D. E. (2000). Learning in science: A comparison of deep and surface approaches. *Journal of Research in Science Teaching, 37,* 109-138.

Chisholm, R. M. (1961). *Realism and the background of phenomenology.* Glencoe, IL: Free Press.

Cho, H., Gay, G., Davidson, B., & Ingraffea, A. (2007). Social networks, communication styles, and learning performance in a CSCL community. *Computers and Education, 49*(2), 309-329.

Clarke, J. (1982). *Resource-based learning for higher and continuing education.* Chichester, UK: Wiley.

Cole, C., Beheshti, J., Leide, J. E., & Large, A. (2005). Interactive information retrieval: Bringing the user to a selection state. In A. Spink & C. Cole (Eds.), *New directions in cognitive information retrieval* (pp. 13-41). Dordrecht, Netherlands: Springer.

Cole, C., Cantero, P., & Ungar, A. (2000). The development of a diagnostic-prescriptive tool for undergraduates seeking information for a social science/humanities assignment: Part III. Enabling devices. *Information Processing and Management, 36,* 481-500.

Colliver, J. (2000). Effectiveness of problem-based learning curricula: Research and theory. *Academic Medicine, 75(*3), 259-266.

Cronbach, L., & Snow, R. (1977). *Aptitudes and instructional methods: A handbook for research on interactions*. New York: Irvington.

Crosby, D. (2002). *The difference between training, instruction, education and learning*. Posting to the Listserv Safety list (3 Aug 2002). Retrieved August 1, 2007, from http://list.uvm.edu/cgi-bin/wa?A2=ind0208A&L=safety&P=7134

Cull, P. (1991), *Resource-based learning: A strategy for rejuvenating Canadian history at the intermediate school level* (ERIC Document ED 343 829).

Der-Thanq, C., Hung, D., & Wang, Y.-M. (2007). Educational design as a quest for congruence: The need for alternative learning design tools. *British Journal of Educational Technology* (OnlineEarly Articles). doi:10.1111/j.1467-8535.2006.00675.x

Dewey, J. ( 1938). *Democracy and education*. New York: Macmillan.

Engeström, Y. (1999, December). *Expansive learning at work: Toward an activity-theoretical reconceptualization.* Keynote address at Changing practice through research. 7th Annual International Conference on Post-Compulsory Education and Training, Centre for Learning and Work Research, Griffith University, Brisbane, Australia.

Evenson, D., & Hmelo, C. (2000). Introduction to problem based learning: Gaining insights on learning interactions through multiple methods of enquiry. In D. Evenson & C. Hmelo (Eds), *Problem based learning: A research perspective on learning interactions* (pp. 1-16). Mahwah, NJ: Erlbaum.

Flavell, J. (1979). Metacognition and cognitive monitoring: A new area of cognitive-developmental inquiry. *American Psychologist, 34,* 906-911.

Ford, N. (2004). Towards a model of learning for educational informatics. *Journal of Documentation, 60*(2), 183-225.

Ford, N. (2005). New cognitive directions. In A. Spink & C. Cole (Eds.), *New directions in cognitive information retrieva*l (pp. 81-96). Dordrecht, Netherlands: Springer.

Freire, P. (1970). *Pedagogy of the oppressed.* New York: Herder & Herder.

Gagne, R. M., Briggs, L. J., & Wager, W. (1992). *Principles of instructional design* (4th ed.). Orlando, FL: Harcourt Brace Jovanovich.

Gardner, H. (1999). Multiple approaches to understanding. In C. M. Reigeluth (Ed.), *Instructional design theories and models: A new paradigm of instructional theory, Volume II* (pp. 69-89). Mahwah, NJ: Lawrence Erlbaum Associates.

Garvin, D. A. (1993). Building a learning organization. *Harvard Business Review, 71*(4), 78-91.

Hakkarainen, K., Palonen, T., Paavola, S., & Lehtinen, E. (2004). *Communities of networked expertise: Professional and educational perspectives.* Amsterdam: Elsevier.

Harri-Augstein, S., & Thomas, L. F. (1991). *Learning conversations*. London: Routledge.

Hiemstra, R., & Brockett, R. G. (1994). From behaviorism to humanism: Incorporating self-direction in learning concepts into the instructional design process. In H. B. Long and Associates (Eds.), *New ideas about self-directed learning*. Norman, OK: University of Oklahoma, Oklahoma Research Center for Continuing Professional and Higher Education.

Heinze, A., & Procter, C. (2004). Reflections on the use of blended learning. In *Proceedings of the Education in a Changing Environment Conference, University of Salford.* Retrieved August 1, 2007, from http://www.ece.salford.ac.uk/proceedings/papers/ah_04.rtf

Heinze, A., Procter, C., & Scott, B. (2007). Use of conversation theory to underpin blended learning. *International Journal of Teaching and Case Studies, 1*(1/2), 108-120.

Hung, W.-C., & Chao, C.-A. (2007). Integrating advance organizers and multidimensional information display in electronic performance support systems. *Innovations in Education and Teaching International, 44*(2), 181-198.

Hutchins, R. M. (1968). *The learning society.* New York: Frederick A. Praeger.

Illich, I. (1970). *Deschooling society*. New York: Harper and Row.

*Inquiry-based learning (IBL)* (n.d.). Retrieved August 1, 2007, from the University of Sheffield, Centre for Inquiry-based Learning in the Arts and Social Sciences Web site: http://www.shef.ac.uk/cilass/ibl.html

Johnston, B., & Webber, S. (2003). Information literacy in higher education: A review and case study. *Studies in Higher Education, 28*(3), 335-352.

Jonassen, D. (1991). Objectivism vs. constructivism. *Educational Technology Research and Development, 39*(3), 5-14.

Jonassen, D. (1999). Designing constructivist learning environments. In C. M. Reigeluth (Ed.), *Instructional design theories and models: A new paradigm of instructional theory, Volume II* (pp. 215-239). Mahwah, NJ: Lawrence Erlbaum Associates.

Jonassen, D., & Rohrer-Murphy, L. (1999). Activity theory as a framework for designing constructivist learning environments. *Educational Technology Research and Development, 47*(1), 61-79.

Kearsley, G. (2007). *Subsumption theory* (D. Ausubel). Retrieved August 1, 2007, from Explorations in Learning & Instruction: The Theory into Practice Database Web site: http://tip.psychology.org/ausubel.html

Khan, P., & O'Rourke, K. (2005). Understanding enquiry-based learning. In T. Barrett, I. Mac Labhrainn, & H. Fallon (Eds), *Handbook of enquiry and problem based learning*. Galway: CELT. Retrieved August 1, 2007, from http://www.aishe.org/readings/2005-2/contents.html

Kilgore, D. W. (2001). Critical and postmodern perspectives on adult learning. *New Directions for Adult and Continuing Education, 89,* 53-61.

King, P., & Kitchener, K. (1994). *Developing reflective judgement.* San Francisco: Jossey-Bass.

Knowles, M. S. (1990). *The adult learner: A neglected species*. Houston: Gulf Publishing Company.

Kuiper, R. (2002). Enhancing metacognition through the reflective use of self-regulated learning strategies. *Journal of Continuing Education in Nursing, 33*(2), 78-87.

Land, S. M., & Greene, B. A. (2000). Project-based learning with the World Wide Web: A qualitative study of resource integration. *Educational Technology, Research and Development, 48*(1), 45-68.

Laurillard, D. (2002). *Rethinking university teaching: A conversational framework for the effective use of learning technologies.* London: Routledge Farmer.

Lindeman, E. C. (1928). *The meaning of adult education.* New York: New Republic.

Livingston, J. (1997). Metacognition: An overview. Retrieved August 1, 2007, from http://www.gse.buffalo.edu/fas/shuell/cep564/Metacog.htm

Maclellan, E., & Soden, R. (2004). The importance of epistemic cognition in student-centred learning. *Instructional Science, 32,* 253-268.

Maslow, A. (1976). Education and peak experience. In C. D. Schlosser (Ed.), *The person in education: A humanistic approach*. New York: Macmillan.

Matthews, M. R. (2002). Constructivism and science education: A further appraisal. *Journal of Science Education and Technology, 11*(2), 121-134.

McCarthy, B. (1996). *About learning*. Barrington, IL: Excell Inc.

McCormick, C. B. (2003). Metacognition and learning. In W. M. Reynolds & G. E. Miller (Eds.*), Handbook of psychology volume 7: Educational Psychology* (pp. 79-102). Hoboken, NJ: Wiley.

Merriam, S. B., & Caffarella, R. S. (1999). *Learning in adulthood: A comprehensive guide* (2nd ed.). San Francisco: Jossey-Bass.

Merrill, M. D. (2002). First principles of instructions. *Educational Technology Research and Development, 50*(3), 43-59.

Metcalfe, J., & Shimamura, P. (Eds). (1994). *Metacognition: K-nowing about knowing*. Cambridge, MA: MIT Press.

Nelson, L. M. (1999). Collaborative problem solving. In C. M. Reigeluth (Ed.), *Instructional design theories and models: A new paradigm of instructional theory*, Vol. II (pp. 241-267). Mahwah, NJ: Lawrence Erlbaum Associates.

Oliver, M., & Trigwell, K. (2005). Can "blended learning" be redeemed? *E-learning, 2*(1), 17-26.

Paavola, S., & Hakkarainen, K. (2005). The knowledge creation metaphor—An emergent epistemological approach to learning. *Science & Education, 14*(6), 535-557.

Paavola, S., Lipponen, L., & Hakkarainen, K. (2002, January 7-11). Epistemological foundations for CSCL: A comparison of three models of innovative knowledge communities. In G. Stahl (Ed.), *Computer support for collaborative learning: Foundations for a CSCL community*. Proceedings of CSCL 2002, Boulder, Colorado (pp. 24-32). Hilldale, NJ: Lawrence Erlbaum Associates.

Paavola, S., Lipponen, L., & Hakkarainen, K. (2004). Models of innovative knowledge communities and three metaphors of learning. *Review of Educational Research, 74*(4), 557-576.

Quintana, C., Zhang, M., & Krajcik, J. (2005). A framework for supporting metacognitive aspects of online inquiry through software-based scaffolding. *Educational Psychologist, 40*(4), 235-244.

Reigeluth, C. (1999). Instructional design: *Theories and models. Volume 2*. Hillsdale, NJ: Erlbaum.

Rogers, C. R. (1969). *Freedom to learn*. Columbus, OH: Merrill.

Schank, R. C., Berman, T. R., & Macperson, K. A. (1999). Learning by doing. In C. M. Reigeluth (Ed.), *Instructional design theories and models: A new paradigm of instructional theory, Volume II* (pp. 161-181). Mahwah, NJ: Lawrence Erlbaum Associates.

Schraw, G. (1998). Promoting general metacognitive awareness. *Instructional Science, 26*(1-2), 113-125.

Sfard, A. (1998). On two metaphors for learning and the dangers of choosing just one. *Educational Researcher, 27*(2), 4-13.

Shapiro, A. M. (2000). The effect of interactive overviews on the development of conceptual structure in novices learning from hypermedia. *Journal of Educational Multimedia and Hypermedia, 9*(1), 57-78.

Skinner, B. F. (1971). *Beyond freedom and dignity*. New York: Knopf.

Snow, R. (1990). Aptitude-treatment interaction as a framework for research on individual difference in learning. In P. Ackerman, R. Sternberg, & R. Glaser (Eds.), *Learning and individual differences* (pp. 13-59). New York: Freeman.

Sternberg, R. (1998). Metacognition, abilities, and developing expertise: What makes an expert student? *Instructional Science, 26*(1-2), 127-140.

Stolovitch, H. D., & Keeps, E. J. (2002). *Telling ain't training*. Alexandria, VA: American Society for Training and Development.

Tam, M. (2000). Constructivism, instructional design, and technology: Implications for transforming distance learning. *Educational Technology & Society, 3*(2), 50-60.

Terhart, E. (2003). Constructivism and teaching: A new paradigm in general didactics? *Journal of Curriculum Studies, 35*(11), 25-44.

Thomas, L., & Harri-Augstein, S. (2001). Conversational science and advanced learning technologies (ALT): Tools for conversational pedagogy. *Kybernetes, 30*(7/8), 921-954.

Thorndike, E. L. (1927). The Law of Effect. *American Journal of Psychology, 39,* 212-222.

Tough, A. M. (1979). *The adult's learning projects* (2nd ed.). Austin, TX: Learning Concepts.

Tsai, C.-C. (2004). Beyond cognitive and metacognitive tools: The use of the Internet as an "epistemological" tool for instruction. *British Journal of Educational Technology, 35*(5), 525-536.

Tyler, R. (1949). *Basic principles of curriculum and instruction*. Chicago: University of Chicago Press.

Van Merriënboer, J. J. G. (1997). *Training complex cognitive skills*. Englewood Cliffs, NJ: Educational Technology Publications.

Whitehead, A. N. (1933). *Adventure of ideas.* New York: Macmillan.

Williams, F., & Conlan, O. (2007, July 18-20). Visualizing narrative structures and learning style information in personalized e-learning systems. In *Proceedings of the Seventh IEEE International Conference on Advanced Learning Technologies (ICALT 2007),* Niigata, Japan (pp. 872-876). Retrieved August 1, 2007, from http://doi.ieeecomputersociety.org/10.1109/ICALT.2007.282

Wonacott, M. E. (2001). *Postmodernism: Yes, no, or maybe? Myths and realities 15.* Retrieved August 1, 2007, from http://www.calpro-online.org/eric/docs/mr00030.pdf

Yi, J. (2005). Effective ways to foster learning. *Performance Improvement, 44,* 34-38.

# Chapter VI

# Library and Information Science

## Introduction

A key theme of Chapter III was the need to be able to seek out information and resources for oneself. Learners require this ability whether working in formal education (especially if engaged in project- or inquiry-based learning) or as autonomous learners outside any formal educational context. However, teachers and learning designers are themselves learners. They also need to be able to find information and resources to help them teach and design the learning resources, activities, and experiences of others.

Library/information science has always been linked with education in relation to:

a. Supporting the organisation of, and access to, learning resources to support mediated learning—for example, via educational libraries, resource centres, and repositories of learning resources.
b. Supporting relatively autonomous information seeking within the context of project-, problem-, and inquiry-based learning designs within formal education.
c. Supporting the information seeking of autonomous self-directed learners working outside the context of formal education.

Indeed, the integration of key aspects of education and library/information science, with information and communication technology (ICT), is the central driving force behind the field of *educational informatics*.

This chapter begins by introducing some of the key techniques, approaches, and standards developed within library/information science to enable and facilitate information seeking and resource discovery. These focus on ways of describing information and learning resources in such a way as to enable their effective discovery. The chapter goes on to explore the psychological processes entailed in information seeking. These processes are interpreted in terms of the *integrating themes* model introduced in Chapter I and its incorporation within a *conversation theory* framework. These concepts are then integrated into the developing model introduced with increasing complexity in the three previous chapters.

## Standards for Supporting Resource Discovery

Cataloguing, indexing, and classifying information sources is the stock-in-trade of library science. These processes entail generating descriptions of information sources (metadata) that can act as surrogates, enabling large, diverse, and remotely located collections of information sources such as libraries, databases, and repositories to be searched relatively quickly and easily. Traditional library catalogues are based on such descriptions, and a number of standards have been developed in the library world to facilitate consistency in producing them and to promote interoperability. Such standards relate to describing a resource—whether an information source, a learning package, artwork, music, and so forth—in terms of, for example, *bibliographic* aspects including the person intellectually or artistically responsible for its content (author, composer, etc.); title; details such as pagination for books, running time and format for audiovisual materials, and so forth; publishing details; subject content; rights; and location and access details.

A number of international standards have been developed that are now well established and widely used. The Anglo-American Cataloguing Code (AACR), now in its second edition (AACR2) with a third in preparation (see below), concentrates on specifying how information sources should be described in terms of their bibliographic, as described previously. AACR2 provides guidance on how, for example, to choose the *correct* form of a name and to describe the details of a source in a standard way, with standard punctuation.

A variety of approaches may also be taken to generating descriptions of the *subject* content of information sources. A number of standards address the need to provide vocabulary control relating to how concepts are described and to indicate relationships between concepts—typically for a given concept indicating broader, narrower, and related concepts.

Such standards include lists of subject headings such as the Sears List of Subject Headings and the Library of Congress Subject Headings (LCSH). Take the following extract from an LCSH entry:

Models and modelmaking
UF Model-making
Modelmaking
BT Handicraft
Miniature objects
RT modelmaking industry
SA *subdivisions* Models *under types of objects e.g.* Automobiles – Models
NT Archeological models
Engineering models
*etc.*

The example indicates that when an indexer is indexing an information source about *model-making*, he or she should use the term *Models and modelmaking*—and *not* other terms such as *Model-making* or *Modelmaking*. The code UF means *use for*, and refers the user to the approved form of a subject heading from its variants.

The entry also indicates that a person searching for information on models and modelmaking may *also* find relevant material that is indexed under some other topic with Models as a subdivision. Thus, for example, Automobiles—Models is an approved subject heading that appears elsewhere in the LCSH scheme. SA means *see also*.

The information seeker may wish to narrow or broaden his or her search. BT indicates terms that are broader than (i.e., up a level in the subject hierarchy from) Models and modelmaking. NT indicates narrower terms. Thus, as well as providing vocabulary control—funnelling variant ways of describing a given concept into one preferred way—this scheme also enables a degree of concept navigation, allowing the searcher to move up, down, and horizontally in the subject hierarchy via broader, narrower, and related terms.

Library classification schemes also enable such concept navigation. But in addition, they provide a subject notation that can be used to organize the information sources in subject order, progressing from the general to the specific. For example, the Dewey Decimal Classification Scheme (DDC) assigns numbers to subjects. Dewey numbers are widely used to shelve books in libraries, the appropriate subject number being put on the spine of each book, which is then slotted into its numerical sequence on the library shelves.

Within the Dewey system, knowledge is divided into 10 main sections (Figure 32). Each section is itself divided into 10 subsections, which are themselves divided into 10. After the third digit, the numbers are divided decimally. Each subject therefore is assigned a number. When an information source is classified, the number assigned to its subject matter is added to the description of that information source. In the

*Figure 32. Overview of the Dewey decimal classification*

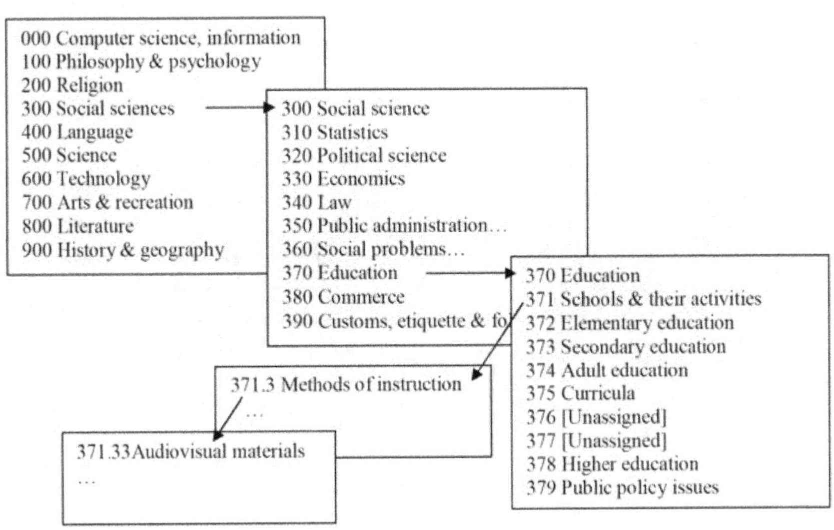

case of books in a library using the Dewey system, this number can be marked on the spine of the book, and the book shelved according to this number.

A number such as 371.33 thus indicates not only a particular subject (in this case, Audiovisual materials), but also the context of this subject—its place in the subject hierarchy:

| | |
|---|---|
| 3 | Social Sciences |
| 37 | Education |
| 371 | Schools and their activities |
| 371.3 | Methods of instruction |
| 371.33 | Audiovisual materials |

Thus the number 371.33 signifies that the subject is within the social sciences (3). Within the social sciences, it relates specifically to education (37). Within education, it relates to school activities (371), and within that, to teaching methods (371.3), of which audiovisual materials (371.33) is a subdivision. What this means is that, if books are shelved according to these numbers, the library user can browse the shelves moving to the right to find narrower topics, and to the left to find broader

*Figure 33. The Dewey decimal classification as used on the BUBL Web site*

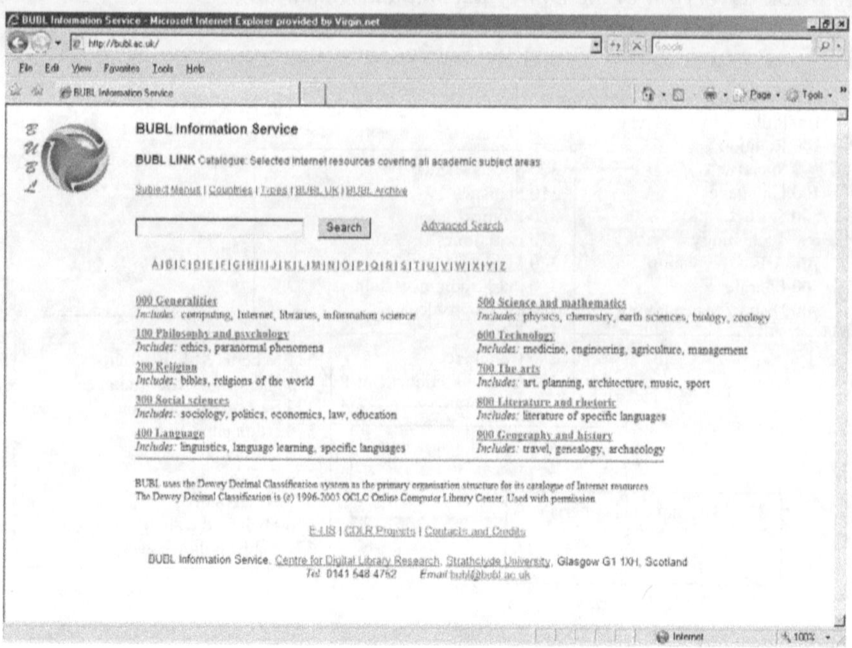

topics. The same is true if such a system is used to organise virtual resources, searchers being able to explore narrower topics by moving to more detailed numbers, and vice versa.

A number of Web sites (for example, the BUBL Information Service: http://bubl.ac.uk/) use the Dewey and other classifications to organize their materials. Figure 33 shows the BUBL Web site. The subject categories presented there resemble the broad alphabetical topics found on directory sites such as the Yahoo (http://dir.yahoo.com/) and Google directories (http://www.google.com/Top/). The difference is that the numbers assigned to the BUBL categories link it in to the Dewey classification.

The screen shown in Figure 33 presents the top level of the classification scheme—the 10 main Dewey numbers from 100 to 900. Clicking on any of these main numbers will reveal its subdivisions. Thus if we click, for example, 300 Social sciences, we will be presented with the screen shown in Figure 34.

Figure 34 displays the 10 main subdivisions within the 300 Social sciences area. Again, if we click on 370 Education, we will be presented with the next more detailed level of subdivisions (Figure 35).

This process enables the searcher to drill down, eventually being presented with lists of information sources that have been classified by the particular Dewey number. The screen in Figure 36 shows, for example, entries classified at 371.3 Educational technology.

Note that the information sources listed to the right of the screen shown in Figure 36 are not organised according to the AACR2 previously mentioned. Indeed, Web-based information sources rarely are. However, there are moves to increase the use, in Web-based contexts, of cataloguing standards similar to or based on AACR2—and to increase the applicability of library-based cataloguing standards to Web-based documents. Examples, in the form of work on the Resource Description and Access (RDA) code, and the Functional Requirements for Bibliographic Records (FRBR) model are described next.

Machine Readable Cataloging (MARC) is a library-based protocol that specifies how the descriptions of information sources constructed in accordance with AACR2 and classification schemes like Dewey can be interpreted and exchanged by computers. A full cataloguing record may include a bibliographic description generated in accordance with AACR2, plus one or more indications of the subject content of the information source, using subject headings (such as those provided by LCSH) and/or classification numbers (such as those provided by DDC). Figure 37 shows an example catalogue record.

Parts of the MARC version of this record are shown next. These are written in accordance with MARC21—currently used by the U.S., Canada, and the UK, and representing a blend of previous U.S. and Canadian versions of MARC. There are various other versions of MARC including AUSMARC (Australia), CMARC

*Figure 34. The social sciences Dewey divisions on the BUBL Web site*

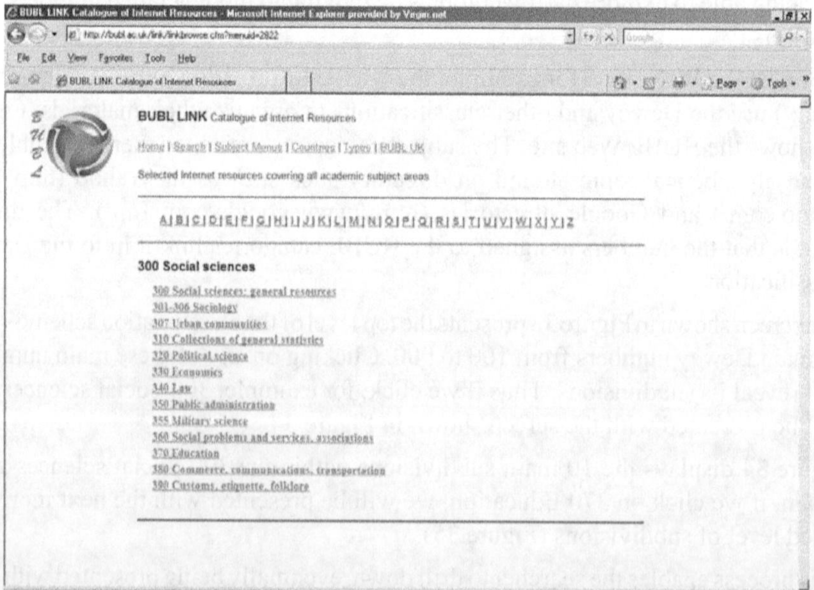


*Figure 35. The education Dewey divisions on the BUBL Web site*

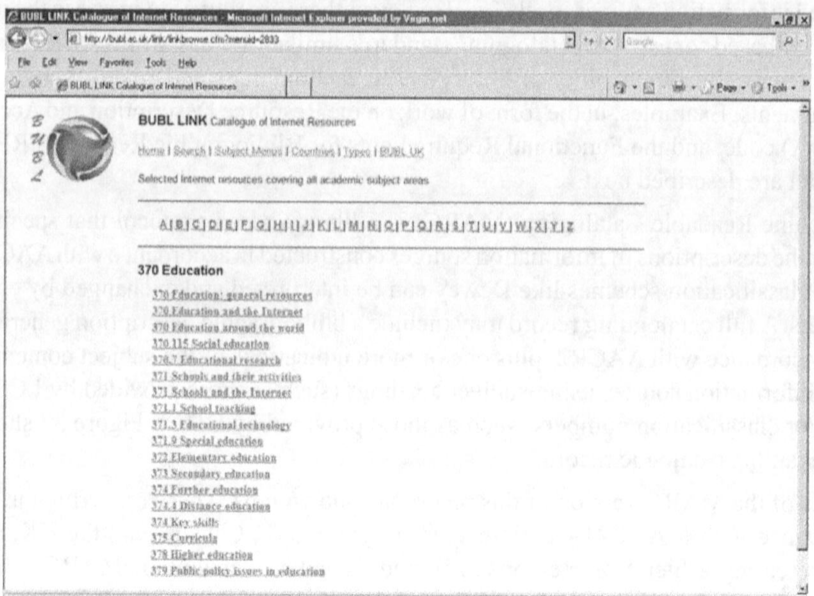

*Figure 36. Resources classified at the Dewey number 371.3 on the BUBL Web site*

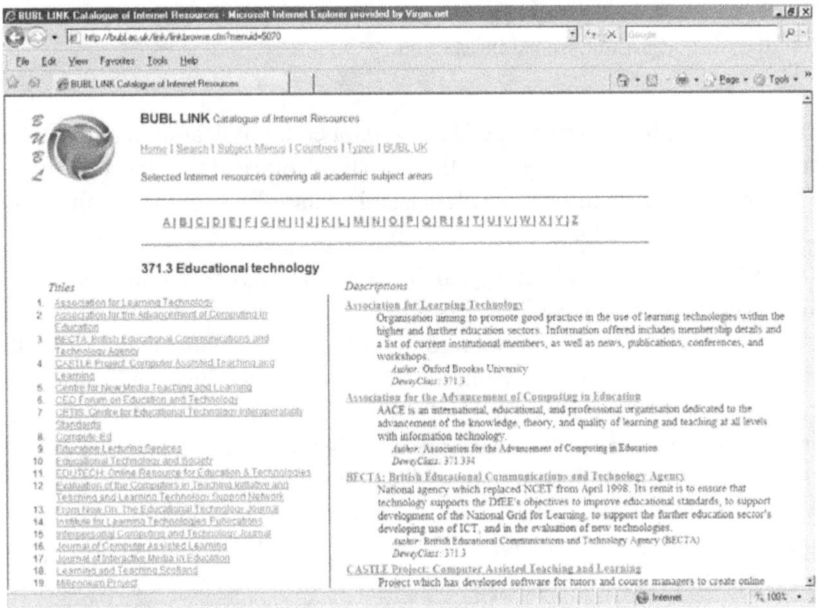


*Figure 37. An example cataloguing record*

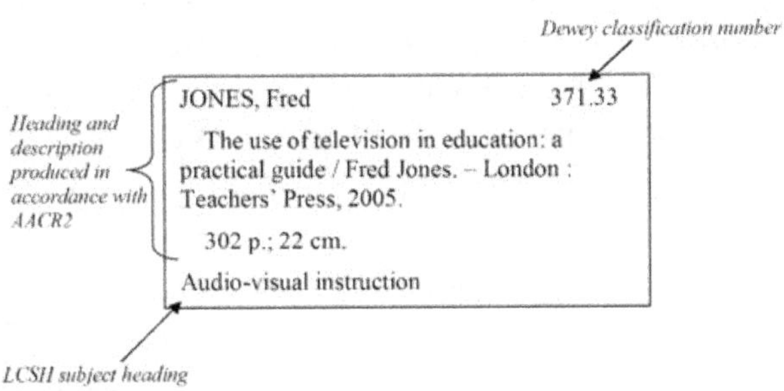


(Republic of China), danMARC2 (Denmark), NORMARC (Norway), UNIMARC (France), and so forth.

| | | |
|---|---|---|
| 082 | 04 | $a371.33$221 |
| 100 | 1# | $aJones, Fred |
| 245 | 14 | $aThe use of television in education:$ba practical guide. |
| 260 | ## | $aLondon :$bTeachers' Press,$c2005. |

300 ## $a302 p. ;$c22 cm.

500 ## $aIncludes index.

650 #0 $aAudio-visual instruction.

On the first line, 082 signifies the Dewey number, 04 indicating that the catalogue record was produced by an agency other than the Library of Congress. $a introduces the Dewey number (in this case, 371.33), and $2 the edition of Dewey that was used (in this case, edition 21).

100 signifies author, 1# indicating that the name consists of a surname and forename in inverted order (as opposed, for example, to a family name or a given name such as Sting or Madonna). 245 introduces the title, the following 1 indicating that an additional entry under title is required for the catalogue. The 4 indicates the number of characters to be ignored in filing—thus the record will not be filed under the word The (three letters plus a space are to be ignored). 260 represents publication details ($a place of publication, $b publisher's name, and $c date). 300 introduces physical details including pagination ($a) and size ($c). 500 indicates notes, while 650 indicates any subject headings. The 0 indicates that the subject headings come from the LCSH.

MARC21 can also be used to represent authority records covering subjects and names, such as the Medical Subject Heasings (MeSH), the Library of Congress Name Authority File (LCNAF) as well as the LCSH. A name authority file gives guidance on the form of a name to be preferred in cataloguing. Cataloguers and information seekers can then be referred to the preferred form if they search under variants of the name. The following examples (taken from Library of Congress, 2006) refer people to the preferred name of Tchaikovsky:

Tchaikovsky, Piotr Ilitch, 1840-1893
*See*: Tchaikovsky, Peter Ilich, 1840-1893

and the correct entry for Lewis Carroll's *Alice in Wonderland*:

Carroll, Lewis, 1832-1898. Alice in Wonderland
*See*: Carroll, Lewis, 1832-1898. Alice's adventures in Wonderland

Since, for example, Charles Dodgson wrote mathematical texts using his real name, but fiction using the pseudonym Lewis Carroll, AACR2 will specify that mathematical texts should be catalogues under Dodgson, fiction under Carroll. *See also* references inform information seekers that they will find books by the same person catalogued under both his names:

Carroll, Lewis, 1832-1898
*See Also*: Dodgson, Charles Lutwidge, 1832-1898

Dodgson, Charles Lutwidge, 1832-1898
*See Also*: Carroll, Lewis, 1832-1898

The example that follows (Library of Congress, 2005) combines both elements, referring information seekers to books catalogued under both names of Mark Twain (born Samuel Langhorne), and referring them *to* the preferred form of his real name Samuel Langhorne *from* the pseudonym Sieur Louis de Conte:

Twain, Mark, 1835-1910
*see also*: Clements, Samuel Langhorne, 1835-1910
Clemens, Samuel Langhorne, 1835-1910
*see also*: Twain, Mark, 1835-1910
Conte, Louis de, 1835-1910
*see*: Twain, Mark, 1835-1910

This authority record would be represented in MARC as:

100 1# $a Twain, Mark, $d 1835-1910
400 1# $a Conte, Louis de, $d 1835-1910
500 1# $a Clemens, Samuel Langhorne, $d 1835-1910

The AACR is currently in its second edition (AACR2), and is being revised for a third edition with the working title Resource Description and Access (RDA). This new edition will be informed by the FRBR conceptual model developed by the International Federation of Library Associations and Institutions (IFLA). This is an entity relationship model of the *bibliographic universe,* which takes a more analytical and relational view of "works of intellectual and artistic endeavour" than was embodied in previous cataloguing codes (IFLA, 1998). It was devised in order better to reflect relationships within and between "families" of bibliographic items. Items within a bibliographic family are related to one another. For example, a particular document may be a translation, adaptation, summary, commentary, evaluation, critical review, parody, or so on of another. The model recognizes that works may be up to a point equivalent, derivative, or descriptive of other works, representing a *new* work at a particular point on such a dimension. The model is outlined in Figure 38.

*Figure 38. Outline of the FRBR conceptual model (adapted from IFLA, 1998)*

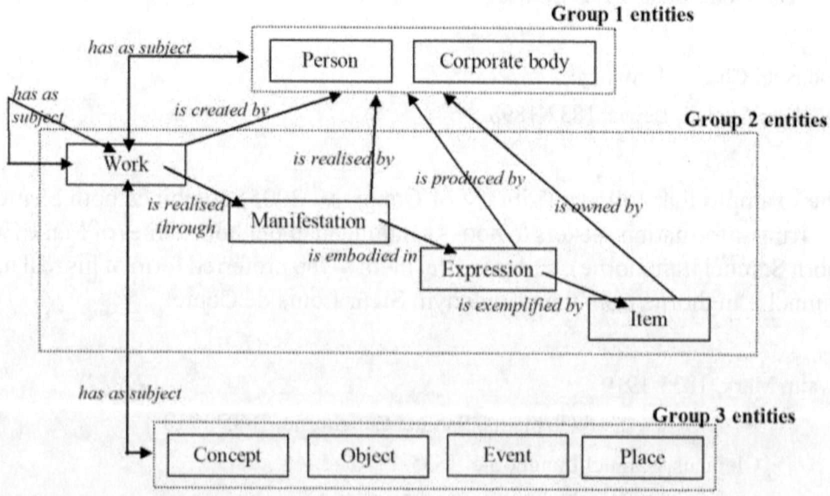


*Table 12. Examples of FRBR group 2 entities*

| **Work** | Jean-Jacques Rousseau's *Émile.* |
|---|---|
| **Expressions** | 1. Rousseau's original text.<br>2. English translation by Barbara Foxley. |
| **Manifestations** | 1. *Émile.* First Lyon Edition.<br>2. *Émile.* Everyman's Library Edition. |
| **Items** | 1. Mary Jones' copy of the Everyman's Library (Paperback) edition of *Émile.*<br>2. Fred Smith's copy of the Everyman's Library (Paperback) edition of *Émile.* |

The model proposes three groups of entities. Group 2 consists of work, expression, manifestation, and item. A *work* is a distinct intellectual or artistic product, which may be *realized* through one or more different *expressions*. An *expression* may be physically *embodied* in one or more *manifestations*, which may be *exemplified* in one or more specific physical *items*. Examples are shown in Table 12.

A *work* can have attributes including, for example: title, form, date, other distinguishing characteristic, intended audience, context for the work, and so forth. An expression may have: title, form, date, language, other distinguishing characteristic, extensibility of expression, revisability of expression, extent of the expression, summarization of content, context for the expression, critical response to the expression, use restrictions on the expression, sequencing pattern, and so forth.

A *manifestation* may have: title, statement of responsibility, edition/issue designation, place of publication/distribution, publisher/distributor, date of publication/distribution, fabricator/manufacturer, series statement, physical medium, capture mode, dimensions of the carrier, manifestation identifier, source for acquisition/access authorization, terms of availability, access restrictions on the manifestation, typeface (printed book), type size (printed book), playing speed (sound recording), colour (image), file characteristics (electronic resource), mode of access (remote access electronic resource), access address (remote access electronic resource), and so forth.

An *item* may have: identifier, fingerprint, provenance, marks/inscriptions, exhibition history, condition of the item, treatment history, access restrictions on the item, and so forth. A *person* or *corporate body* may have: name, dates associated with the person or body, of person, other designation associated with the person, and so forth. The items concept, object, event, and place have the attribute: term (IFLA, 1998).

Also emanating from the library world is the Open Archives Initiative Protocol for Metadata Harvesting (OAI-PMH) standard. This is a protocol designed to facilitate the collection of descriptions of information sources (metadata) from digital libraries and other information source repositories. As Lynch (2001) notes, the metadata harvesting protocol:

> *is simply an interface that a networked server ... can employ to make metadata describing objects housed at that server available to external applications that wish to collect this metadata.*

Widely adopted by libraries, museums, and other repositories, this protocol is also used by search engines including Google and Yahoo for harvesting metadata.

Concern to facilitate searching across multiple databases was the basis for the development of Z39.50. Z39.50 is a client server protocol enabling searching across remote heterogeneous databases, including individual library catalogues, union catalogues, museums, archives, and so forth without needing to know about—or formulate different searches to accommodate—the structure of the target databases. Z39.50 is widely used in library systems and personal bibliographic reference software.

A search is formulated on a client computer and sent to servers hosting the targeted databases. Each server will then map the search requirements onto the structure of the database in question. Results can be variable since widely differing database structures may not always map directly, or in the same way, onto the requirements of a given search. This situation is being addressed by the Bath Profile, which is defining a core set of functionality and specifications intended to increase levels of semantic interoperability between heterogeneous systems.

In a Web environment, the Z39.50 International: Next Generation (ZING) project is being developed to replace Z39.50 with an HTTP protocol, enabling search requests to be sent in URLs and retrieved results returned as XML. ZING uses the Search/Retrieve Operation (SRU) and Search/Retrieve Web services (SRW) protocols. SRU uses the Common Query Language (CQL), which is designed to combine the benefits of a query language such as SQL which is powerful but difficult for the nonspecialist, and easier languages which lack expressive power.

The codes and standards described previously are designed to enable and facilitate the discovery and management of resources—that is, what IFLA (1998) terms "the products of intellectual and artistic endeavour" (p. 12). Clearly, resource discovery is an activity engaged in by information professionals, and by computer systems operating on their behalf. However, resource discovery is also conducted by end users including learners, learning designers, and teachers as they seek information and learning materials to help them in the process of designing, teaching, and learning. The next section focuses on resource discovery by such end users. It explores in particular the intellectual processes entailed in information seeking and further extends the model introduced in previous chapters by integrating *information behaviour* and *learning* within an overall framework of *knowledge behaviour*.

## Information Seeking and Autonomous Learning

As noted previously, one of the functions of the various codes and standards described in the previous section is to enable and facilitate information seeking on the part of end users wishing to discover information resources which may help them generate integrating themes whereby conceptual incongruities may be resolved. Within an educational setting, such information seeking may be engaged in by both educators, seeking to discover resources that may help them in their teaching, and learners seeking resources to assist them in their learning.

As discussed in Chapter III, a concern to promote autonomous learning has for long been a prominent concern in education, being manifested in a number of vogues including *resource-based, independent, project-based,* and *inquiry-based* learning. Such forms of learning have emphasised the type of relatively autonomous information seeking that is a central concern of library/information science, which is essentially concerned with information behaviour, and with systems and techniques designed to support it. *Information behaviour* (defined later on) takes place within the context of—and as a response to—a realisation of some *need for knowledge* (also defined later on).

As stated in Chapter I, *knowledge* is defined here as a conceptual system that enables its possessor to act in the world. *Information* is potential knowledge, and *learning* is the process of transforming information into knowledge. Perceiving a need for knowledge represents the realization that one is in a situation for which one's existing knowledge is not adequate. Information is needed to generate, via learning, appropriate new knowledge.

However, the *need for knowledge* is broader than the *information need* in that the former entails defining the nature of the sought-for knowledge, as opposed to the type and nature of the information that may be used to generate it. Importantly in this context, functionally the same knowledge may be generated via the processing of alternative items of information. The realization and specification of the knowledge need, along with the evaluation of information behaviour in terms of its contribution to satisfying the knowledge need, are termed here *knowledge behaviour*.

Information behaviour comprises those activities entailed in the acquisition of information that may be transformed into knowledge. It subsumes *information encountering* and *information seeking*, the latter subsuming *searching* and *retrieval*. Figure 39 shows the relationships between the various components of knowledge behaviour. It also lists within each component of knowledge behaviour the main processes it entails.

As discussed in Chapter III, when engaged in learning, an individual may be *provided with* an appropriate integrating theme by another person (e.g., teacher or research

*Figure 39. Knowledge and information behaviour*

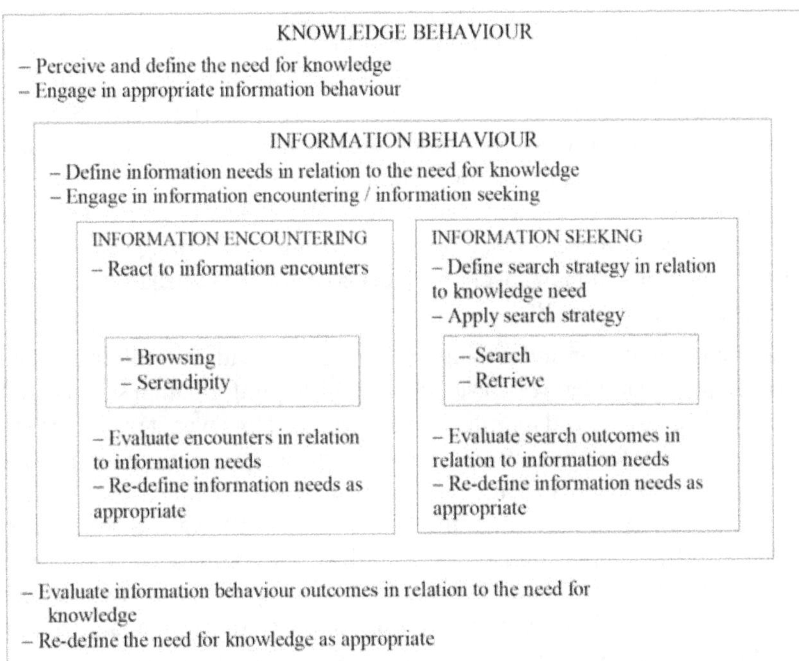

*Figure 40. Results from a simple keyword search*

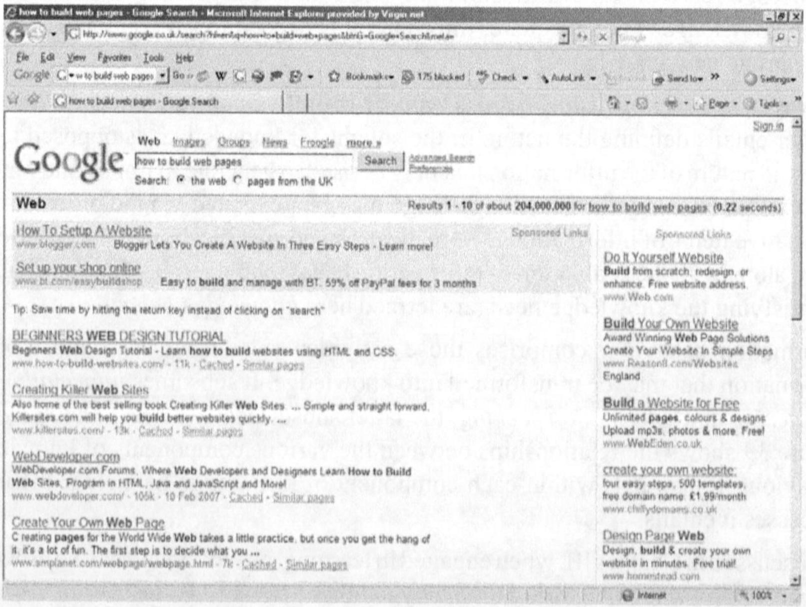


supervisor) or by a recorded information source given to or encountered by the individual—in which case he or she has only to recognise it rather than generate it. This may be the case with, for example, a lecture or teaching text. However, an integrating theme may also be *generated by* the individual—a procedure particularly encouraged within formal educational contexts by educationists who adopt pedagogic perspectives favouring active and inquiry-based learning, and who embrace learning goals geared to the acquisition of metacognitive (*learning to learn*) skills in addition to the acquisition of specific subject content. These pedagogic viewpoints were discussed in Chapter III.

The situation in which an integrating theme is not provided for an individual is a scenario of particular interest to researchers in library/information science in that it is likely to generate the need for information seeking. However, it may seem strange that there is a need for research and theory in the study of information needs and how they might be satisfied. Surely needing some information and seeking it, for example, in a library or using a Web search engine, is basically a straightforward procedure. And indeed it is up to a certain level of complexity. If we need, for example, to learn how to build Web pages, then simply tapping into Google the keywords *how to build Web pages* will result in the retrieval of a large number of hits, including some excellent tutorials on the subject (Figure 40).

However, beyond a certain level, these apparently very simple issues become rather more complex. Much depends on how we define the purpose of information seeking. If we think of it in terms of how the discovery of information can be optimised in order to help, say:

- A university student to be a more effective learner
- A PhD researchers to produce a more informed and useful thesis
- A doctor better to treat his or her patient
- A citizen to become a more effective participant in society
- Problem solvers in diverse roles generate more effective solutions

then our knowledge of information needs and how they might be most effectively satisfied has to be more sophisticated. These are complex goals, the achievement of which is not always particularly easy to measure.

Thus, a Google search using fairly obvious search terms would be likely to retrieve relevant information for a very simple search which may go a long way to satisfying that particular information need. However, much learning and research entails less clear-cut problems, and beyond a certain level of complexity difficult issues arise. Indeed, the study of complex information needs and information seeking has been a focus of library and information science reach for many years.

Preceded by work such as that of Taylor (1968), a number of early models conceived of information needs as deriving from some gap or anomaly in people's knowledge. Dervin's (1983) *sense making* theory, for example, assumes that:

*reality is neither complete nor constant but rather filled with fundamental and pervasive discontinuities or gaps (p. 4)*

—such gaps requiring *bridging*. Key universal components of the sense-making model are: *situations*, that is, the context in which problem situations arise; *gaps*, that is, questions that people have that may require information to resolve; and *uses* to which the outcomes of the sense-making process are put in the situational context.

Belkin, Oddy, and Brooks (1982) termed the sort of anomalies giving rise to information needs "anomalous states of knowledge" (ASKs). He hypothesised that:

*an information need arises from a recognized anomaly in the user's state of knowledge concerning some topic or situation and that, in general, the user is unable to specify precisely what is needed to resolve that anomaly. (p. 62)Belkin queried how the person can accurately describe to an information retrieval (IR) system what it is that s/he needs to know—that is, the nature of some appropriate integrating theme—since this is precisely what he/she does not yet know. He went on to propose a methodology for the design of IR systems which attempted to infer information needs from statements expressing the problem along with its perceived anomaly. However, this theoretical advance in how we might conceive of information needs was not matched by success in terms of the practical implementation of a more effective IR system (Toum, 1993), and the fundamental problem raised by Belkin's second hypothesis—that is, that an information seeker may often be unable to specify precisely what it is that he or she does not know but needs to know—still remains.*

The problem raised by Belkin's hypothesis, is essentially:

*How can an information seeker specify a request to an IR system describing what it is s/he does not know—and therefore needs to retrieve?*

This problem derives from a more fundamental question:

*How can awareness of what integrating theme is required to resolve the anomaly—which is precisely what the individual does* **not** *possess at this stage—be generated?*

This "kicks in" particularly beyond a certain level of complexity—that is, relating to complex *information needs* mapping onto a substantial *problem* to be solved (e.g., researching an essay or thesis rather than a request for, say, a train timetable!). As someone with a complex information need, expressing what you *do* know—as opposed to what you do *not* know—means that the information need may require further definition and interpretation. These may be—indeed often are—inferred by

*Figure 41. A health-related anomaly requiring resolution*

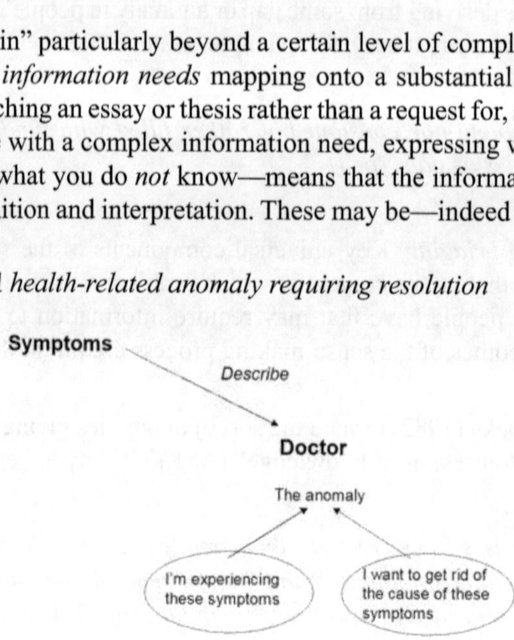

*Figure 42. A solution, or integrating theme*

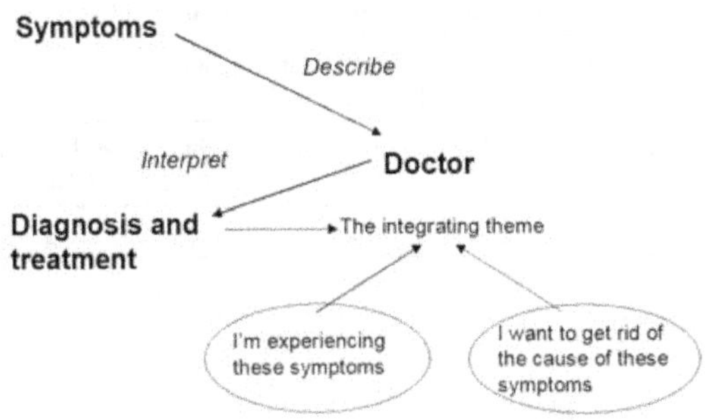


human search intermediaries. An analogy may be drawn between an information and a health need. In Figure 41, a patient may present to the doctor with a set of symptoms. The anomy requiring resolution is that the patient is not feeling as he would like to feel, and seeks a way of restoring health. The patient expresses to the doctor what he *does* know—namely, his symptoms.

As shown in Figure 42, the doctor then interprets what the patient says to him/her, and all being well supplies an appropriate integrating theme—a diagnosis and treatment.

"I have a headache" could indicate many things to the doctor, who needs to know something about the person and the context. The headache may be due to stress at work, problems at home, or a range of medical problems. An appropriate treatment may vary accordingly, from aspirin through stress counselling, diet, fitness regime to carbon monoxide monitoring, and so forth.

Within library/information science, there is an increasing recognition that we also need to consider information needs and their satisfaction within the broader context of people's lives. Information professionals and researchers have been developing ways of "teasing out" implicit (hidden) parameters of an information need, often by investigating the precise context for a query (equivalent to the doctor's in-depth investigation of what a particular patient's headache *really* signifies). They have attempted better to understand information needs in terms of the broader problem-solving contexts that give rise to them.

Medical researchers and professionals need some *model* of the patient, in order to be able to treat people, to advise and educate people to keep themselves healthy (with appropriate diet, exercise, lifestyle, etc.), and to design medical products. Similarly, information researchers and professionals need some model of the information seeker, in order to find information for people (in the case of information professionals); advise and educate people to be able to find, use, and handle information for themselves; and to design information products (for example, IR systems). These analogous functions of user models are summarised in Table 13.

*Table 13. The uses of models*

| In the medical world, patient models help us to... | In the information world user models help us to... |
|---|---|
| Treat people ( in the case of medical professionals) | Find information for people (in the case of information professionals) |
| Advise/educate people to keep themselves healthy (diet, exercise, lifestyle) | Advise/educate people to be able to find, use, and handle information for themselves |
| Design medical products | Design information products (e.g., IR systems) |

We have the technological capability to access, retrieve, describe, and present information in many possible different ways, and we have the capacity to build systems that can adapt to individual users. We also have the capacity to build systems that can learn about their users as they interact with them and adapt their behaviour appropriately. However, the problem is: *what is appropriately*?

To discover this, we need to consider information needs and information seeking within a broad context. We need to study information seekers in context and holistically. We need research into the human side of information (i.e., information and knowledge behaviour) in order to know what people want and need, and how we can build systems that behave *appropriately* in terms of helping them search for, use, and handle information more effectively. However, within the context of this endeavour, two fundamental questions persist:

*To what extent can we build systems that can choose, for a given person and information need, the most appropriate information seeking and search strategy (i.e., "smart" systems)?*

*To what extent do the complexities of information needs and information seeking mean that information seekers must be helped to improve their ability to devise and execute effective information seeking strategies for themselves (i.e., become "smart" users)?*

Clearly, work to develop both smarter systems and smarter searchers is desirable. However, there is some tension between the perspectives of different stakeholders in research, development, and education in relation to the relative importance, and likely payoff, of efforts designed to attack one or other of these goals. An additional problem, taken up in Chapter IX, is that interaction between investigators and developers engaged in these two different aspects of information science research, whereby each may benefit from engagement with the other, is arguably sparse.

Part of the problem is, as suggested by the second question, that information needs and the information-seeking strategies required to satisfy them, may be complex and subtle. These issues have been the subject of much research, and to an extent research approaches designed to address them have diverged in emphasis away from those characterising much mainstream IR and systems development research. Indeed, since the 1980s, there has been a great deal of user-related research that has utilised what Dervin and Nilan (1986) termed at the time an *alternative paradigm*. The picture of human information processing deriving from such studies seems far removed from the *traditional* information systems view of information processing as characterised by order, sequence, analysis, objectivity, and control.

Problem solving and decision making can be complex, multifaceted, and highly context-dependent, as can be the task of seeking information to support them. Researchers such as Ellis (1989) and Kuhlthau (1991) have drawn attention to different stages through which information seeking in relation to a given problem may develop. Search specifications during such stages can be dependent on dynamically changing conceptions of what is and is not *relevant* to a user's query as documents are retrieved and evaluated. Spink (1996) and Bates (1989) have also drawn attention to the successive nature of much information seeking, which develops dynamically over time.

Information needs can vary across many dimensions. Florance (1992), for example, distinguished between procedural and declarative aspects of need. She argued that the object of retrieving information in an evidence-based context is largely procedural (to know what to do) rather than declarative (to know that something is so), and that procedural information is generally less well handled by IR systems, and consequently can be relatively difficult to retrieve. In an analysis of queries by physicians, she found that although clinical problem solving requires both declarative and procedural knowledge, treatment decisions require more procedural knowledge relative to diagnosis. She argued that it is difficult for physicians to articulate the difference between these forms of knowledge in their requests for literature searches relating to patient care decisions.

Richardson and Wilson (1997) differentiated between *foreground* and *background* needs. A given problem or decision may entail different types of need at different times, or indeed combinations of such needs. They argued that a major determinant of whether questions are background or foreground seems to be one's level of prior experience with the condition or situation one is facing. Thus, although all information seekers would have both background and foreground information needs, the proportion of each will differ between, say, a medical student, a junior doctor, and a consultant or between a student, a teacher, and an educationist.

Indeed, the complexity of information needs is reflected in the reverse side of the information-seeking coin—namely the notion of *relevance* as judged by the person seeking information. Recent models have attempted to reflect more of the complexity of relevance. Spink, Greisdorf, and Bateman (1998), for example, proposed a three-dimensional model that differentiates aspects of relevance including *level* and *region* as well as *time*. Ford (1995; Ford & Ford, 2002) provided evidence that the same problem may be solved in different ways and in different sequences by individuals with different learning styles, such as the holist- and serialist-like styles introduced in Chapter II.

The global holist problem solver, for example, is more likely to tackle a problem demanding complex understanding by first building up declarative knowledge to form a broad conceptual overview into which procedural details are subsequently fitted. The more analytic serialist problem solver, by contrast, is likely first to concentrate on building up chains of procedural detail, the overall declarative view emerging later in the problem-solving process. Fine detail may not be relevant during the initial stages of a holist learner's information seeking and relevance judging, but may be highly relevant to the serialist learner at the same chronological stage of his or her project.

Complexity lies at the very root of the IR process in that, as Bates (1998) has pointed out, echoing Belkin et al.'s (1982) previously mentioned concept of *anomalous states of knowledge*:

> *The user's experience is phenomenologically different from the indexer's experience [...] The user's task is to describe something that, by definition, he or she does not know [...] The user, in effect, describes the fringes of a gap in knowledge, and can only guess what the "filler" for the gap would look like.*

Complexity may also characterise types of information need. In a review of reference interview questions, White (1998) found evidence of 16 of 20 types of questions proposed by Graesser (1994). Examples of these categories included: verification (e.g., checking that factual information is correct); disjunctive (ascertaining which of alternatives is true); comparison (discovering how constructs are the same or different from others); causal antecedent (discovering states or events that followed from others); causal consequence (discovering states or events that led to others); enablement (what allows an action to be performed); and so forth. Within this context, the notion of one-stop, authority-approved information sources and access mechanisms to support evidence-based information seeking is limited. While such approaches have a role to play and may provide satisfactory solutions to many information needs, they cannot address all such needs.

Increasingly, studies are bringing into question the ecological validity of models that characterise human information behaviour in terms of a relatively ordered sequence of well-structured activities. Foster (2004), for example, in his doctoral study of interdisciplinary researchers, notes the nonlinear nature of the interactions between the processes entailed in information seeking. In his model, processes and contexts shift and interact in complex, dynamic and subtle ways. The nonlinear and holistic uses of, and interactions between these processes are:

*analogous to an information seeker holding a palette of information behaviour opportunities, with the whole palette available at any given moment.*

Even such an apparently discrete stage as *problem definition* was not clear cut, problems being constantly redefined throughout information seeking.

Based on a review of the educational and cognitive research literature, Ford (2004) presents a model of information needs and relevance judgments that echoes aspects of Foster's (2004) model. It views these aspects of information behaviour as sometimes characterised less by discrete sequences than by the relatively holistic processing of many interacting factors. Ford notes that information needs and relevance judgments are influenced not only by the nature of the task, but by a range of factors such as motivation, anxiety, and levels of existing knowledge and experience. The profiles of information seekers in terms of these factors may be thought of as individually different, and time-dependent, templates through which the individual information seeker perceives his or her information needs. He or she judges relevance dynamically throughout the information-seeking process. The templates change with the acquisition of new information, and relevance may be viewed very differently via changed templates as information seeking progresses.

Aspects of this picture relating to the dynamic, shifting nature of relevance judgments are echoed in an in-depth longitudinal ethnographic study of academic researchers reported by Anderson (2005), who also stresses the context-dependency of, and the role of intuition in, the making of such judgments:

*Observed experiences were varied, dynamic, and shifting. Judgments of relevance were ongoing activities, embedded in the search and research processes in which the informants were engaged. ... The informants applied experience, prior knowledge (e.g., key figures, critical issues) and intuition in these situations to personalize their judgments. ... understanding judgements of relevance requires understanding the contexts in which they occur.*

The ongoing assessment of information needs and the relevance of retrieved information may at least sometimes be characterized more in terms of the holistic processing entailed in the reconfiguring of a gestalt, than the more analytic step-by-step working through of logical procedures. Such processing, linked with the notion of intuition as noted by Anderson, (2005) is reminiscent of the *flash of insight* often reported as characterizing divergent (creative) as opposed to more convergent thinking (Ford, 1999):

*It would also appear that to a significant degree, creativity often depends on the relatively unplanned and often sudden recognition of a similarity between disparate entities – as opposed to the more progressive, controlled jettisoning of dissimilarity. This is characteristic of ... perceptual, holistic, parallel information processing discussed above. Often descriptions of instances of creative thought suggest a sudden perception or realisation – a flash of insight when things come together – occurring when the person is not intensely focused on the particular problem. (p. 532)*

Convergent information processing is an essential aspect of IR. Indeed, at one level, it seems eminently sensible to try to establish maximum convergence between concepts specified by an information seeker in a query to a retrieval system and concepts contained in documents retrieved. Interestingly, however, Spink and Greisdorf (1997) found an *inverse* relationship between high levels of relevance—defined in terms of the extent to which retrieved documents matched user queries—and the generation of new ideas and directions by researchers engaged in online searches:

*'highly' relevant items do not change the users' cognitive or information space in relation to their information problem ... Highly relevant items may not relate to a shift in a user's information problem towards resolution but reinforce the current state of the user's information problem and knowledge state ... Items retrieved that are not 'highly' relevant, but partially relevant, are related to shifts in the users' thinking about their information problem by providing new information that leads the users in new directions ... (p. 276)*

*Highly relevant* items contributed to relatively convergent thinking—helping users confirm what they already knew and to maintain existing directions, as opposed to relatively divergent or creative thinking—generating new ideas and directions. This is perhaps not surprising in that IR systems work essentially via convergent processing to achieve as close a match as possible between queries and documents. However, the complementary role of divergent information processing has a complementary role to play. Recall from Chapter I how creativity depends on the type and level of *dissimilarity* applying to the context and/or the nature of the discrete entities brought together and integrated by a similarity relationship. It was argued there that it is the extent of dissimilarity, in addition to the level of complexity, that differentiates creative from less creative forms of thinking.

Divergent information processing entails a relaxation in the specification of precisely what information is required when searching. Indeed, Strauss and Corbin (1997) note how insights often occur when people switch off from conscious focused analysis of a problem—which can actually hinder the process of realizing "the sudden hunch, the flash of insight, the brilliant idea, or the profoundly different theoretical formulation."

Such relaxation and implicit openness to new ideas can sometimes be well served by serendipitous encounters with what may turn out to be useful—though unanticipated—information. Foster (2004) found evidence of serendipity as a widely experienced, and valued, aspect of information behaviour among his sample of interdisciplinary researchers. Serendipity itself has often been associated with the flash of insight, previously referred to in relation to accounts of creativity. Foster and Ford (2003) note the difficulties entailed in researching such an essentially *fuzzy* concept as serendipity, since it is by definition not particularly susceptible to systematic control and prediction. Nevertheless, serendipity did emerge in Foster's (2004) study as an important aspect of researchers' information behaviour and their generation of new ideas.

Foster and Ford (2003) went on to develop a model of serendipitous information encountering, in which serendipity could have the effect of reinforcing the researcher's existing problem conception, or taking the researcher in some new direction, in which the problem conception is reconfigured in some way. A number of different types of such information encounters were identified. For example, the nature of information required to solve a particular problem may be anticipated, but acquisition of such information happened serendipitously. Alternatively, information was encountered serendipitously and was to be valuable in progressing the researcher's problem in ways which had not been anticipated.

They concluded that, in the particular sample of interdisciplinary researchers studied, serendipity was widely experienced, and certain attitudes and strategic decisions were perceived to be effective in exploiting serendipity when it occurred. There were mixed attitudes towards the question of whether serendipity could be induced. It was felt that some element of control could be exercised to attract *chance encounters*. However, there was a perception that such chance encounters might often be due less to pure chance, than to the hidden effects of, for example, library classification schemes.

Such serendipity is close to what Erdelez (1996a, 1996b, 1999) describes as *information encountering*, claiming that it has long been identified, although little investigated. She found that it was an integral element of information seeking, and she classified information seekers as non-encounterers, occasional encounterers, encounterers, and super-encounterers, noting that (Erdelez, 1996a):

> *[S]uper-encounterers [...] appeared to share a common excitement for information encountering. They believed in creating situations conducive to information encountering and in that way finding useful and important information. (p. 418)*

## Information Seeking as Conversations

The generation and testing of tentative theories by individuals in relation to learning was discussed in Chapter I. However, the same basic processes may apply to the problem of the anomalous state of knowledge proposed by Belkin et al. (1982) and discussed previously. This centres around an information seeker having to specify to a retrieval system what it is that he or she needs to—but does not yet—know. In terms of the integrating themes model proposed in Chapter I, such an anomalous state of knowledge entails the information seeker having a perception that a set of concepts requires some integration via some as yet unknown theme—in other words, a knowledge need. The search strategy and keywords that he or she uses to interrogate an IR system—as he or she translates the *knowledge* need into the specification of an *information* need—represent tentative theories. Figure 43 shows a simplified view of the information seeker's problem in terms of the need to generate an integrating theme, which will reconcile the need to use keywords which: (1) describe the information need—itself a theory tentatively proposed to solve the knowledge need, as opposed to the information need; and (2) satisfy the requirements of the indexing system used by the retrieval system. If search terms do not match terms used to index the information being searched for, the tentative integrating theory (a particular set of keywords to be input into the retrieval system) will not be appropriate.

*Figure 43. An integrating theme view of an information search*

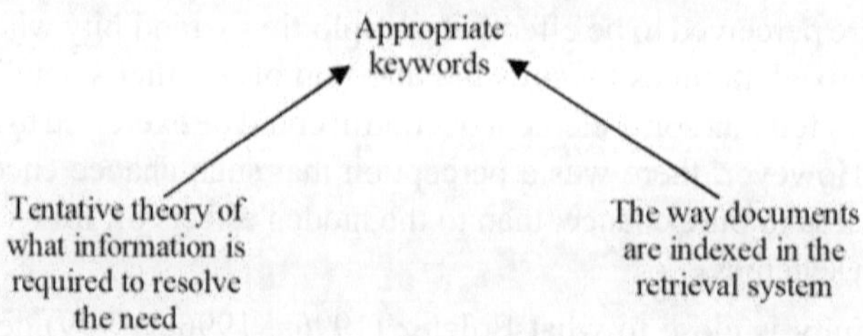


*Figure 44. A partially successful search strategy*

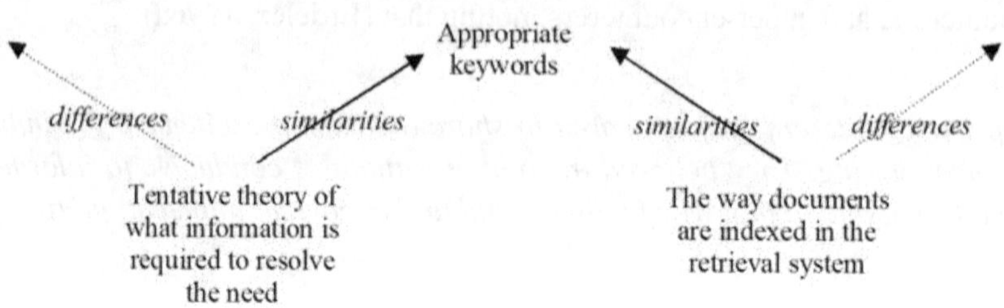

In the case of complex searches, this process may be iterative—as show in Popper's model of the development and testing of tentative theories in Chapter I. This would entail the sort of process again first proposed in that chapter in relation to learning. Figure 44 shows this process, whereby an initial attempt at a tentative theory only partially integrates the to-be-integrated concepts, leaving a need to refine the theory—in this case, by modifying the search query, for example with extra keywords or the use of Boolean operators, and so forth.

Such a process is described by Cole (1999) who combines Popper's (1979) model with Shannon's classic theory, adapting it to include two-way communication in which the receiver also acts as a sender of information. Figure 45 shows this process. Cole thus models the interaction between an individual and new information in which he or she develops progressively more advanced states of knowledge via iterative theory generation and testing.

*Figure 45. Problem solving via interaction with an IR system (adapted from Cole, 1999)*

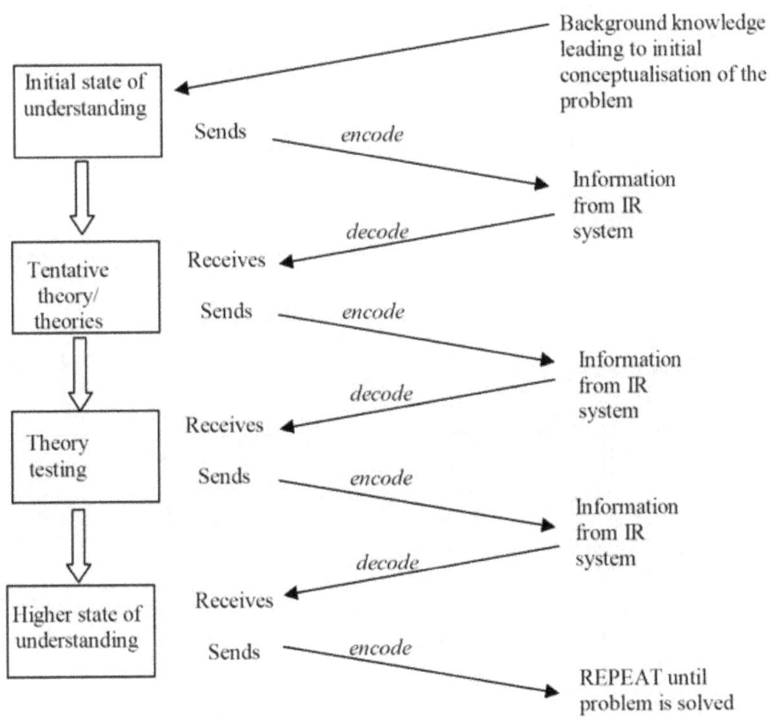

In this model, an initial understanding of the problem situation is derived from the processing of background information. An information need is then encoded as a request to an IR system. The response from the IR system—that is, retrieved information—is decoded and fed into the process of making sense of the problem situation. This process modified the information seeker's state of understanding of the problem situation, which results in the generation of a tentative theory. Further information may then be sought to help in the process of testing and weighing evidence about this theory, the result being that the information seeker potentially reaches a higher state of understanding. The process is iterated until the problem is solved to the user's satisfaction.

Figure 46 represents a fusion of aspects of the models of Pask and Cole (1999), depicting the inner dialogues through which tentative theories are tested and refined in terms of Pask's conversation theory—that is, via conversations between two p-individuals housed within one m-individual, as well as an external IR system and associated information sources.

*Figure 46. The inner dialogue of the information seeker. Fusion of aspects of Pask's conversation theory and Cole's (1999) model (adapted from Ford, 2004)*

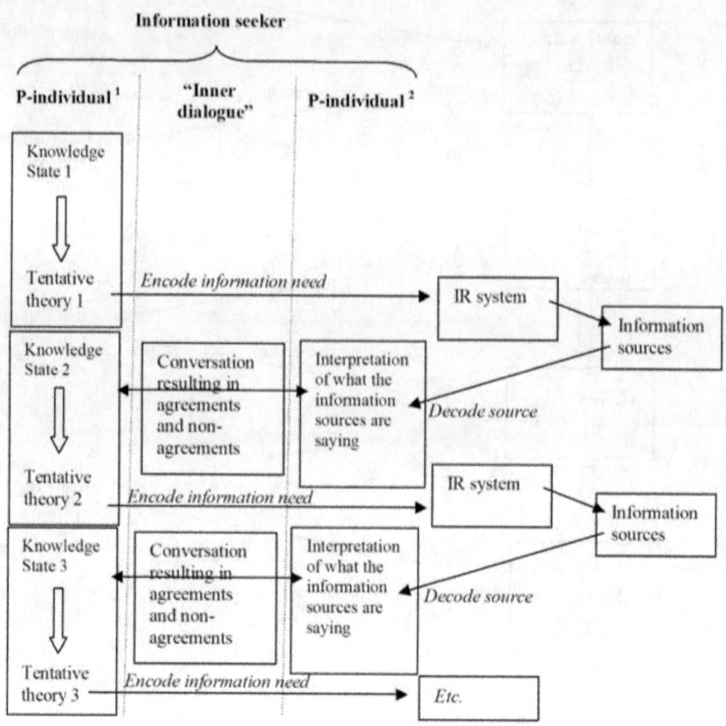

Figure 46 depicts processes whereby knowledge states change as a result of the generation and testing of tentative theories. Some anomaly in a knowledge state gives rise to a tentative theory, which in turn gives rise to an information need. Information is sought to explore and test out the theory via what Cole (1999) terms an *enabling* IR system. Retrieved information is fed into the conversation representing the inner dialogue of the information seeker as he or she attempts to resolve the conceptual anomaly. The initial knowledge state is changed as a result, and a new or modified tentative theory is generated—giving rise to the next information need.

Agreements negotiated in the inner dialogue represent resolutions to anomalies—that is, understood concepts. Non-agreements may represent further anomalies within the new higher order state of knowledge, for which integrating themes must be found and which give rise—at least in part—to the next round of information needs. Once there are no further disagreements resulting from the conversation (Pask)—or, in other words, gaps requiring bridging (Dervin), anomalies in the new state of knowledge (Belkin), tentative theories requiring support or refutation (Popper), or disparate entities requiring integration (Ford)—then *coming to understand* is complete, and associated information needs are satisfied. In reality, complete closure is unlikely, and arguably undesirable, since coming to understand at any given level is likely to open up further needs for understanding at higher and related levels.

Conversation theory may be applied recursively. As Scott (2001) notes:

> *... conversations may, by recursive 'laddering', have many logical levels above the basic 'how' and 'why' levels: levels at which conceptual justifications are themselves justified and where there is 'commentary about commentary'. Indeed, reflexively the conversation may itself become a topic of conversation. (p. 31)*

The conversational framework may be applied recursively to components of a conversation taking place at a particular level. In this way, we can also represent the information seeker's interaction with an IR system in terms of a Paskian conversation, as shown in Figure 46. Whereas Figure 46 showed the *inner dialogue* between p-individual[1] and p-individual[2] within the same person (the information seeker, or in Pask's terms, m-individual1), Figure 47 drills down to show more detail in relation to the interaction between this individual and the IR system. In this case, there are two distinct m-individuals: (a) the information seeker (m-individual[1]), and (b) the IR system (m-individual[2]).

The conversation in this case is between the information seeker and the IR system, and takes place via the system interface. The tentative theories developed by the information seeker represent the search strategy—for example, the particular keywords chosen to try to retrieve relevant information. In the case of complex searches, such a tentative first attempt at defining keywords—that will successfully retrieve information which will successfully resolve the information need—may well be imperfect. The extent to which it does, and does not, satisfy the need is the subject of the Paskian conversations shown in Figure 47.

Thus the *encode information need* interaction shown in Figure 46 itself entails a conversation (shown in detail in Figure 47) between p-individual[1] and a new p-individual[3] in the form of the conceptual system represented by the interface of the IR system. P-individual[1] (the information seeker) is the prime source of intelligence and must attempt to build a model of p-individual's[3] *understanding* of his or her information need as expressed in the request. P-individual[3] (the IR system interface), insofar

*Figure 47. The encode information need conversation between information seeker and IR system interface (adapted from Ford, 2004)*

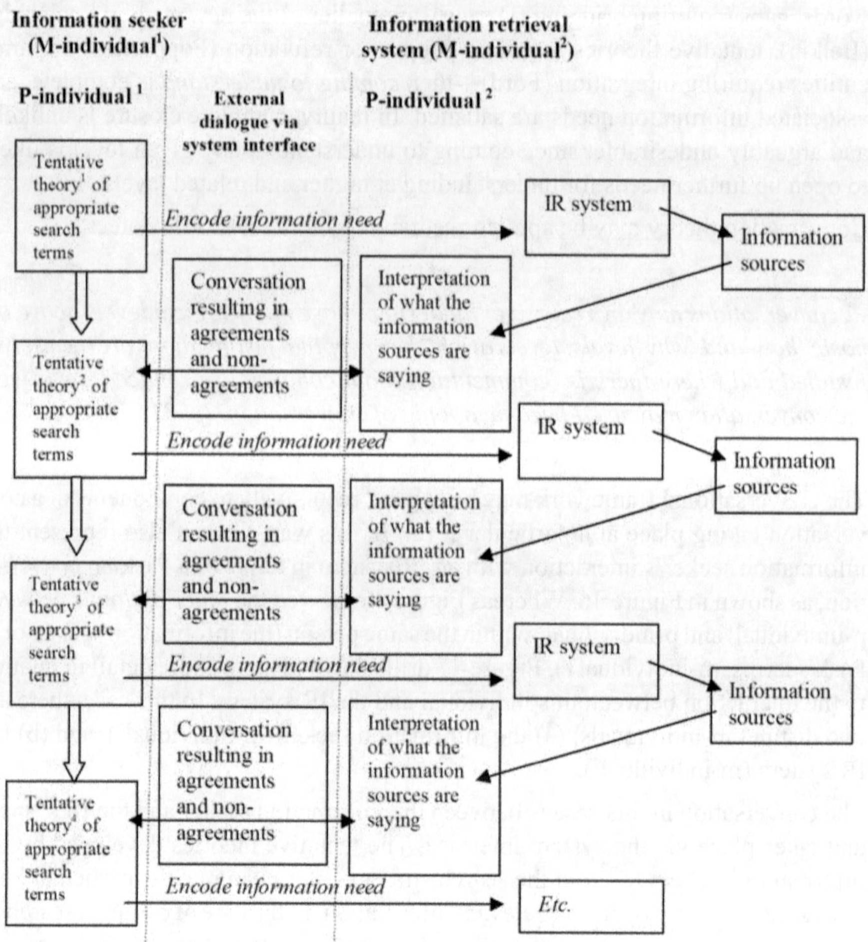

as it is intelligent, may also attempt to build a model of the information seeker's information need from his or her request. Thus both participants attempt to build, evaluate, and modify as appropriate their models of the other's model in relation to the information need. In Figure 47, the *tentative theory* is the information seeker's theory of what will constitute an effective query to submit to the IR system.

Note that this conversation is only part of the wider (Figure 46) conversation in which information sources retrieved are decoded, interpreted, and evaluated. The results of the latter (Figure 47) processes are fed back as input to the lower level (Figure 46) conversation in order progressively to inform theory testing and modification.

An information need may often be expressed in the form of keywords describing topics, for example: *"I need information on **business models** appropriate to **e-commerce.**"* However, an information need requires further parameters which may be—indeed often are—inferred by human search intermediaries. But if we infer them, we must ignore neither their importance, nor the possibility that our inferences may be incorrect. Notably within medicine, techniques have been developed to make explicit certain parameters of information that may otherwise remain unexpressed (e.g., Snowball, 1997). However, such parameters as developed in medicine are essentially problem based—that is, referenced objectively to the problem, and external to the user—as opposed to parameters referenced to subjective learner differences. The parameters discussed here are different in that they relate intimately to aspects of the individual learner's mental processing and mental states.

The nature of information needs, and the reverse side of that coin, of relevance judgments, is affected by differences in the types of information processing in which individuals are engaged, and by differences in the strategic and stylistic approaches they adopt in relation to particular tasks. These may be influenced not only by the nature of the task, but by mental states relating, for example, to motivation, anxiety, and levels of existing knowledge and experience. As previously suggested, differences in the characteristics of different individuals in relation to these variables may be thought of as constituting templates—different for each individual, and subject to development over time—through which different learners perceive their *information needs* and judge *relevance* as they seek, select, and use information.

Such templates change as learning develops with the acquisition of new information. The same information may be viewed very differently via changed templates as learning progresses. Information not relevant at one point in time may become so at another. Information may also be relevant in different ways at different points in time. Indeed, a number of researchers have explored information seeking in terms of changes in knowledge states over time and have utilised relatively sophisticated conceptions of relevance as multifaceted and dynamically changing across successive searches (e.g., Cole, 1999; Kekäläinen & Järvelin, 2002; Spink & Greisdorf, 2001; Spink et al., 1998).

The basic processes of learning entail the successful enmeshing of new information with existing knowledge and the building of new concepts on the basis of other, already understood concepts. Thus, an essential parameter of information need is that new information be presented in a cognitively ergonomic way (Ford, 1995). This means that the learner possesses, or is readily able to acquire understanding of the basic concepts an author or educator assumes to be already understood. It is onto this assumed knowledge that the author or educator builds, as he or she introduces new ideas.

In relation to the critical evaluation and personal valuing of information, the equivalent parameters of information needs require that new information should not only be cognitively ergonomic in relation to comprehensibility, but also cognitively ergonomic in relation to *criticality*, and *affectively* ergonomic. For the personal acceptance and valuing of information to take place, new information must enmesh with the learner's existing attitudes, values and critical capacity—or extend them by virtue of arguments, evidence, and persuasion that bring about such enmeshing.

The importance of including such additional parameters scales up rapidly when long-term, complex topics are being studied in which relatively large numbers of information items are searched for by someone working in a relatively autonomous learning mode—for example, in the development of a dissertation or doctoral thesis. The problem may be relatively trivial when viewed from the perspective of writing an introductory essay in the context of a heavily guided course. In such a content, most of the information required may be contained in very few sources, these being recommended by teachers as opposed to having to be searched for within a mass of relevant, partially relevant, and nonrelevant information sources.

Figure 48 integrates the model of knowledge and information behaviour, introduced in Figure 39 earlier in this chapter, with the mental processes and states, and educational context presented in Figure 31 in Chapter III. The conversational models of interaction between the information seeker and IR system presented in Figures 45-47 in this chapter are subsumed within the *why* and *how* learning conversations within the *Information processes* box in Figure 48.

This chapter has introduced techniques, approaches, and standards devised within library and information science to enable and facilitate information seeking and resource discovery. It also further extended the model, which has been progressively developed in each chapter so far, to integrate the concepts of knowledge and information behaviour from the perspective of library/information science. As we will see in Chapters VII and VIII, it is the integration of pedagogical and library/information science perspectives and approaches—offering a blend of pedagogical mediation and autonomous resource discovery—that forms the major foundation for the development of educational informatics. It is via the application of developments in digital ICT that it has become feasible to operationalise and deliver this integration automatically to large numbers of learners. These ICT developments—and others impacting teaching and learning—are the focus of the next two chapters.

*Figure 48. Knowledge and information behaviour in context*

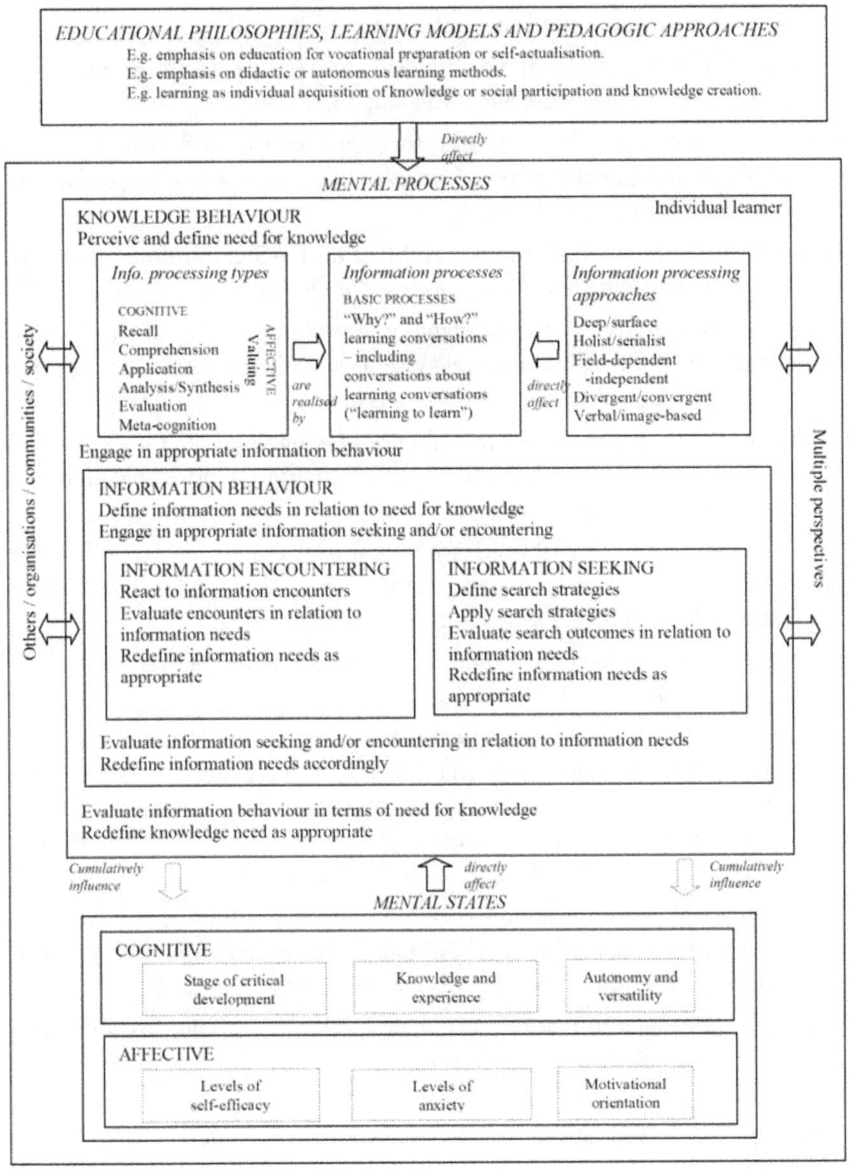

# References

Anderson, T. D. (2005). Relevance as process: Judgements in the context of scholarly research. *Information Research, 10*(2) paper 226. Retrieved August 1, 2007, from http://InformationR.net/ir/10-2/paper226.html

Bates, M. J. (1989). The design of browsing and berrypicking techniques for the online search interface. *Online Review, 13,* 407-424.

Bates, M. J. (1998). Indexing and access for digital libraries and the Internet: Human, database, and domain factors. *Journal of the American Society for Information Science, 49*(13), 1185-1205.

Belkin, N. J., Oddy, R. N., & Brooks, H. M. (1982). ASK for information retrieval: Part I. Background and theory. *Journal of Documentation, 38*(2), 61-71.

Cole, C. (1999). Activity of understanding a problem during interaction with an "enabling" information retrieval system: Modeling information flow. *Journal of the American Society for Information Science, 50*(6), 544-552.

Dervin, B. (1983, April). *An overview of sense-making research: Concepts, methods, and results to date.* Paper presented at International Communication Association Annual Meeting, Dallas, TX.

Dervin, B., & Nilan, M. (1986). Information needs and uses. *Annual Review of Information Science and Technology (ARIST) 21,* 3-33. White Plains, NY: Knowledge Industry Publications.

Ellis, D. (1989). A behavioural approach to information retrieval design. *Journal of Documentation, 45*(3), 171-212.

Erdelez, S. (1996a). Information encountering: A conceptual framework for accidental information discovery. In P. Vakkari, R. Savolainen, & B. Dervin (Eds), *Information seeking in context: Proceedings of an International Conference on Research in Information Needs, Seeking, and Use in Different Contexts, Tampere, Finland.* Los Angeles, CA: Taylor Graham.

Erdelez, S. (1996b). Information encountering on the Internet. In M. Williams (Ed.), *Proceedings of the 17th National Online Meeting, Information Today* (pp. 101-107). Medford, NJ: Information Today.

Erdelez, S. (1999). Information encountering: It's more than just bumping into information. *Bulletin of the American Society for Information Science, 25*(3), 25-29.

Florance, V. (1992). Medical knowledge for clinical problem solving: Structural analysis of clinical questions. *Bulletin of the Medical Library Association, 80,* 140-149.

Ford, N. (1995). Levels and types of mediation in instructional systems: An individual differences approach. *International Journal of Human-Computer Studies, 43,* 241-259.

Ford, N. (1999). Information retrieval and creativity: Towards support for the original thinker. *Journal of Documentation, 55*(5), 528-542.

Ford, N. (2004). Modeling cognitive processes in information seeking: From Popper to Pask. *Journal of the American Society for Information Science and Technology, 55*(9), 769-782.

Ford, N., & Ford, R. (1992). Learning strategies in an ideal computer assisted learning environment. *British Journal of Educational Technology, 23,* 195-211.

Foster A. E. (2004). A nonlinear model of information seeking behavior. *Journal of the American Society for Information Science and Technology, 55*(3), 228-237.

Foster, A., & Ford, N. (2003). Serendipity and information seeking: An empirical study. *Journal of Documentation, 59*(3), 321-340.

Graesser, A. C. (1994). Question asking and answering. In M. A. Gernsbacher (Ed.), *Handbook of psycholinguistics* (pp. 517-538). San Diego, CA: Academic Press.

International Federation of Library Associations and Institutions (IFLA). (1998). *Functional requirements for bibliographic records : Final report.* IFLA Study Group on the Functional Requirements for Bibliographic Records. München, Germany: K. G. Saur. Retrieved August 1, 2007 from http://www.ifla.org/VII/s13/frbr/frbr.pdf

Kekäläinen, J., & Järvelin, K. (2002). Using graded relevance assessments in IR evaluation. *Journal of the American Society for Information Science and Technology, 53*(13), 1120-1129.

Kuhlthau, C. C. (1991). Inside the search process: Information seeking from the user's perspective. *Journal of the American Society for Information Science, 42,* 361-371.

Library of Congress. (2005). *What is a MARC record, and why is it important?* Retrieved August 1, 2007, from http://www.loc.gov/marc/uma/pt1-7.html#pt4

Library of Congress. (2006). *Library of Congress authorities.* Retrieved August 1, 2007, from http://authorities.loc.gov/

Lynch, C. (2001, August). Metadata harvesting and the Open Archives Initiative. *ARL Bimonthly Report 217,* 1-9. Retrieved August 1, 2007, from http://www.arl.org/resources/pubs/br/br217/br217mhp.shtml

Popper, K. R. (1979). *Objective knowledge: An evolutionary approach* (Rev. ed.). Oxford, UK: Clarendon Press.

Richardson, W. S., & Wilson, M. C. (1997). On questions, background and foreground. *Clinical Epidemiology and Biostatistics,* 6-7.

Scott, B. (2001). Conversation theory: A constructivist, dialogical approach to educational technology. *Cybernetics & Human Knowing, 8*(4), 25-46.

Snowball, R. (1997). Using the clinical question to teach search strategy: Fostering transferable conceptual skills in user education by active learning. *Health Libraries Review, 14*(3), 169-72.

Spink, A. (1996). A multiple search session model of end-user behavior: An exploratory study. *Journal of the American Society for Information Science, 46,* 603-609.

Spink, A., & Greisdorf, H. (1997). Users' partial relevance judgements during online searching. *Online and CDROM Review, 21*(5), 271-280.

Spink, A., & Greisdorf, H. (2001). Regions and levels: Mapping and measuring users' relevance judgments. *Journal of the American Society for Information Science, 52*(2), 161-173.

Spink, A., Greisdorf, H., & Bateman, J. (1998). From highly relevant to not relevant: Examining different regions of relevance. *Information Processing and Management, 34*(5), 599-621.

Strauss, A. L., & Corbin, J. (Eds.). (1997). *Grounded theory in practice.* London: Sage.

Taylor, R. S. (1968). Question-negotiation and information seeking in libraries. *College and Research Libraries, 29,* 178-194.

Toum, T. (1993). *The ASK information retrieval methodology.* Unpublished doctoral dissertation, University of Sheffield, UK.

White, M. D. (1998). Questions in reference interviews. *Journal of Documentation, 54*(4), 9443-465.

# Chapter V

# ICT Developments: Resource Discovery

## Introduction

Information seeking and resource discovery, for which library/information science researchers and developers have devised the techniques and approaches introduced in the previous chapter, may be engaged in by teachers seeking information and learning resources that they can reuse or reconfigure in their own teaching. Resource discovery may also be engaged in by learners themselves—either within the context of a formal course of study in which they are given the opportunity to seek out information and resources for themselves, or as autonomous self-regulated learners operating outside the context of any formal course. Library/information science is concerned with the seeking and discovery of information and resources in both of these contexts. As educationists have developed information and computer technology (ICT)-based approaches to learning design and teaching (which will be introduced in Chapter VI), so library and information scientists have developed ICT-based approaches to enabling and facilitating effective information seeking and resource discovery. These approaches—including ICT-based standards—form the focus of the present chapter.

# Tools and Techniques to Support Information Seeking and Resource Discovery

Relative to the concerns of library and information science, computer assisted learning systems have tended to focus predominantly on the deep analysis and representation of small volumes of homogeneous subject content, providing high levels of pedagogical mediation. Early systems were not particularly concerned with either interoperability or resource discovery, although as we will see in chapters VII and VIII, this is changing with the development of educational informatics systems.

Compared to the ICT-based educational systems introduced in the next chapter, those developed within library/information science have traditionally entailed less semantically deep and less sophisticatedly structured knowledge representations. They have also tended to be less geared to attempting to provide supplantation (in which the system engages in cognitive processing on behalf of the user) compared, that is, with ICT-based intelligent tutoring systems. Library/information science has typically been concerned with developing and utilizing relatively shallow representations of a relatively large volume of more heterogeneous subject content. Its concerns have been centred on controlling vocabulary used to describe concepts, and on indicating hierarchical relationships between concepts, and the resource discovery systems developed have not sought to provide any significant level of pedagogical mediation.

A principal focus of library/information science is on cataloguing, indexing, and classifying information sources to aid their discovery and retrieval on the part of relatively autonomous information seekers, and on the information behaviour of people engaged in information seeking and resource discovery. Thus, the concern of educational computing with pedagogical mediation in selecting and presenting information is countered in library and information science with a concern for autonomous information seeking and resource discovery. This has entailed an emphasis on standards for interoperability, cross searching of multiple heterogeneous databases, and the international exchange of metadata between libraries and other organizations.

This complexity of information needs combines with the complexity of both the information environment and the tools available to search it. Information may be sought via a range of channels, from libraries and bookshops to databases and the Web. There is also a wide range of digital tools designed to enable people to search for information within and sometimes across these channels. These information seeking and resource discovery tools vary considerably in terms of the techniques they use and the facilities they offer—from *best match* and Boolean searching, through query expansion and recommender systems to retrieval tools that learn to improve their own performance via machine learning mechanisms.

Some retrieval tools operate on large indexes compiled automatically by *spiders* trawling the Web while others offer the fruits of human labour in the form of selection and editing. Some enable browsing across hierarchically structured directories, while others offer the raw power of searching for keywords that occur in the text of indexed documents. Agent-based information retrieval systems can trawl the Web searching autonomously on behalf of their owners and reporting back the products of their labour—improving their performance over time in the light of feedback from their owners.

A great range of information retrieval systems have been developed to facilitate the discovery of information and resources on the Web. Indeed, Web searchers have available to them an increasingly rich range of search techniques and tools. Two broad stands may be seen in this development.

One approach entails scanning information sources and extracting keywords for input into an index. The index contains a list of keywords and links to information sources that contain them. Search engines, such as Google and AltaVista, have *spiders* or *crawlers* that constantly patrol the Web looking for new documents and gathering the words used in the documents into indexes. When a Web searcher types a search query into an engine's search box, it matches these search terms with words in its index and retrieves the documents that contain those words. The process is altogether more sophisticated than this brief description belies, and much research focuses on how to improve the matching process in order to maximise the effectiveness of the retrieval process from the searcher's point of view.

There are many complex, some proprietary, algorithms that attempt to list documents retrieved in order of relevance and quality. Higher weighting may be given, for example, to words that appear in the title and early paragraphs of a document, and documents that have links coming in to them from other documents known to be of high quality and authority (as judged by patterns of links) are accorded higher priority than others.

Such best match search facilities (so called because they attempt to list first the information sources which best match the user's query) are complemented by techniques including Boolean searching. In Boolean searching, the user can use the operators AND, OR, and NOT. Search engines vary in the extent to which they allow the use of such operators. Yahoo, for example, allows AND, OR, NOT, or AND NOT and the use of brackets, for example:

(learning OR cognitive) AND (strategies OR styles)

whereas Google does not permit the use of brackets or NOT (though the NOT function is allowed via the minus sign -). Various advanced search options are offerered in the different search engines. Google, for example, would allow the following search:

allintitle: "learning styles" -strategies filetype:pdf

which specifies "find me all pdf files that contain the exact phrase *learning styles,* and do *not* also contain the word *strategies.*" Google offers a friendly interface allowing complex queries, including Boolean, to be specified via the filling in of a form, as shown in Figure 49.

Search engines may also offer a range of other advanced search features. In addition to the features shown in Figure 49, Google, for example, offers the following:

- Stemming, which finds variants of the actual word types in by a searcher. Stemming entails replacing a word with its root. So, for example, if a user enters *computing,* the system may search for any word beginning with *comput* thus retrieving documents containing the words *computer, computers, computing, computation,* and so forth.
- define:[keyword]—*define:learning* will find definitions of the word *learning,* retrieved from various online dictionaries and other sources.

*Figure 49. Google's Advanced Search screen*

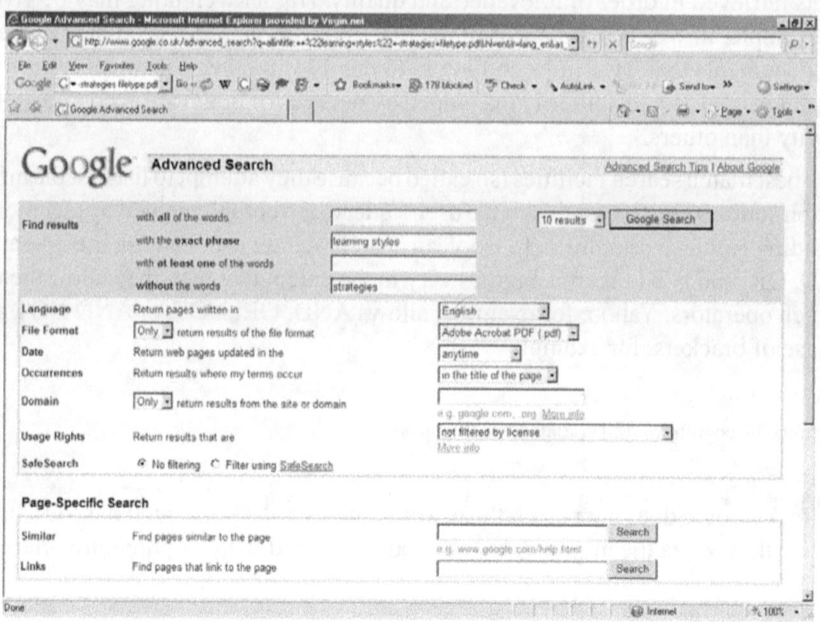

- stocks:[stock ticker symbol]—*stocks:SCIL* will retrieve stock information relating to Scientific Learning Corp. Lists linking companies to their stock ticker symbols exist, for example that of Spredgar Software (2007).
- intitle:[keyword] and allintitle:[keywords]—*intitle:learning* will retrieve documents containing the word *learning* on their title. To specify that more than one word should be contained within the title of retrieved documents, *allintitle* should be used, as in *allintitle:learning styles.*
- inurl:[keyword] and allinurl[keywords]: *inurl:cognitive* will retrieve documents with *cognitive* in their URL. *allinurl:cognitive style* will retrieve documents with the words *cognitive* and *style* in their URL.

Google also allows the use of the asterisk (*) as a wildcard standing for one or more unspecified words. This must be used within a phrase, indicated by quotation marks. For example, the query:

"to * or * to *"

would retrieve documents as shown in Figure 50.

*Figure 50. Use of the wildcard (*) in Google*

*Table 14. Comparison of Yahoo and Google search syntax*

| Yahoo | Google |
|---|---|
| learning AND styles | learning styles |
| teaching OR pedagogy | teaching OR pedagogy |
| learning AND (styles OR strategies) | learning styles OR strategies |
| (styles OR strategies) AND (learning OR teaching) | styles OR strategies learning OR teaching |
| learning AND (strategies OR styles OR approaches) | learning strategies OR styles OR approaches |

*Figure 51. Proximity searching in Google*

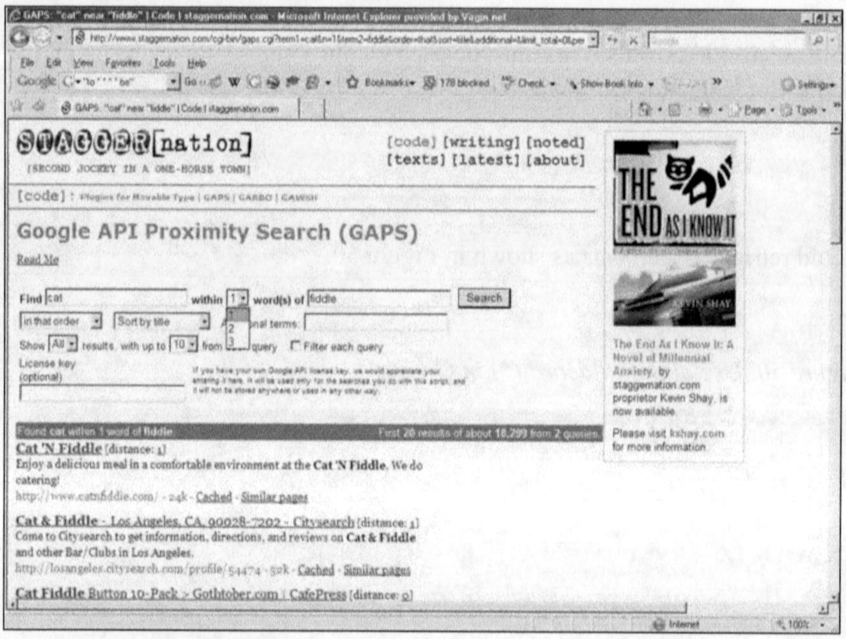


Search engines differ in the search commands they allow. Yahoo, for example, allows the use of brackets to group together elements of a Boolean query. Google has automatic AND-ing (that is, linking search terms together, where no relationship has been specified by the searcher, using the AND operator) whereas Yahoo does not. Table 14 shows examples of these differences, with Yahoo syntax to the left, and the equivalent Google syntax to the right.

A query with the form:

*Figure 52. Automatic query expansion in the Clusty search engine*

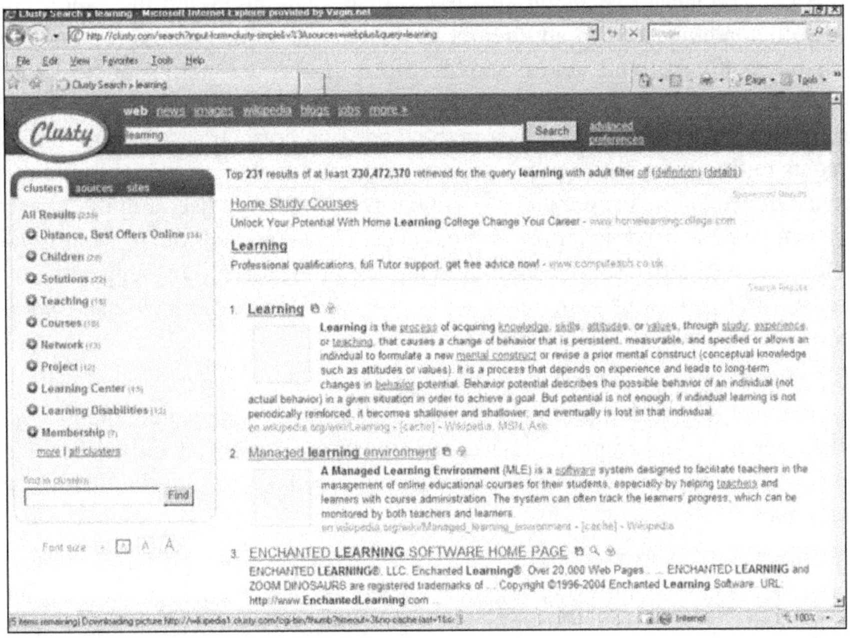


(learning AND teaching) OR (learning AND pedagogy)

which is valid in Yahoo is not allowed in Google. Unfortunately attempting to perform the search in Google using the query:

learning teaching OR learning pedagogy

would be the equivalent in Yahoo of:

learning and (teaching OR learning) and pedagogy

Google does not offer the command NEAR, which enables the searcher to specify that, for example, *cognitive* should occur within a certain number of words of *style.* However, conducting such searches in Google is enabled by a third party tool—the Google API Proximity Search (http://www.staggernation.com/cgi-bin/gaps.cgi) shown in Figure 51.

A number of search tools offer automatic *query expansion* such as Clusty (http://clusty.com/). Query expansion entails the search engine taking the user's initial query, then adding to it in an attempt to improve its effectiveness. To do so, the system may, for example, add synonyms of the user's query terms, or stem a word (recall the example of stemming given in the section describing Google's advanced search features). Other techniques involve spelling correction, applying different weights to the terms in the user's search query, and including words found to co-occur frequently in documents with the terms input by the user. Figure 52 shows an example of a search in Clusty. Here, the user has searched for *learning,* and the system has responded (in the column to the left of the screen) by suggesting other terms the user may wish to include, such as *Distance, Best Offers Online, Children, Solutions, Teaching, Courses,* and so forth.

Many other approaches have been developed including those that entail the use of machine learning techniques in order to develop intelligent search agents, which learn over time and improve their search performance based on the searcher's feedback, and the use of natural language, multimedia, and multilingual retrieval techniques.

Compared to the type of computer-based systems developed within education (discussed in the next chapter), systems developed within library/information science are typically characterised by offering access to relatively wide ranging subject areas. Whereas a computer-assisted learning or intelligent tutoring system may be designed to teach a particular topic or set of topics within a particular subject domain, typically information retrieval systems will allow users to search for information across a wide diversity of topics. Even in the context of subject-specific information retrieval tools, the scope of coverage is relatively broad and compared to more highly pedagogically mediated systems, the semantic depth and complexity of the knowledge representations used are less.

However, moves to allow and encourage greater levels of autonomy among learners at all levels of formal education have been greatly facilitated by the availability of well-developed information retrieval and other resource discovery tools developed by librarians and information scientists. Until the development and wide availability of the Web, school students could support project work and resource-based learning via access to the catalogues of their school libraries and resource centres, and of locally available libraries. Higher education students, as well as being able to access their college and university libraries, could also to a limited extent access remote catalogues and bibliographic databases. The advent of the Web has meant that vast quantities of remotely accessible material are now available to students and staff at all levels. As well as general search engines, various specialist education search engines are also available, as are subject- and discipline-specific search engines and portals (see, for example: http://www.searchengineguide.com/pages/Education/ and http://allsearchengines.com/education.html). Google Scholar (http://scholar.google.

*Figure 53. Google's Directory*

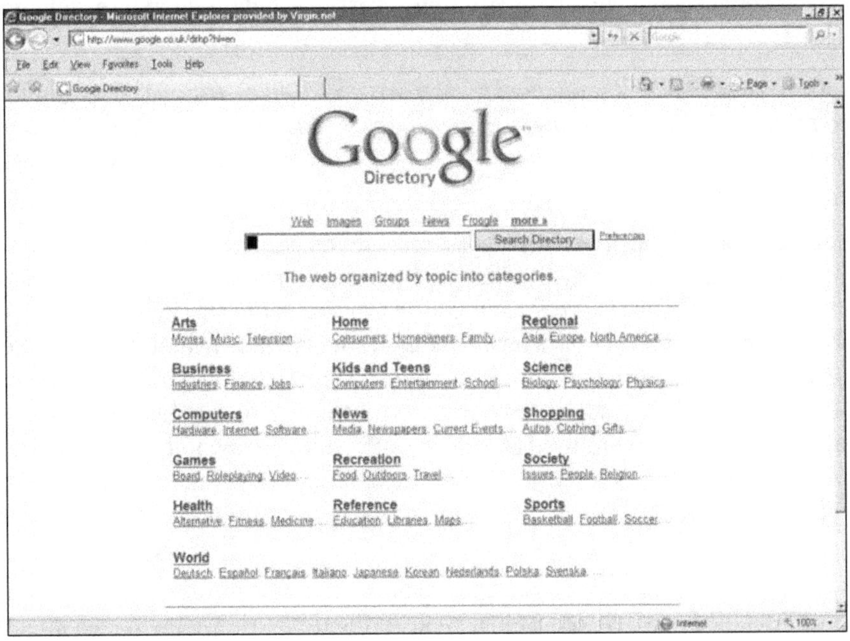


*Figure 54. Browsing to more specific topics in Google's Directory*

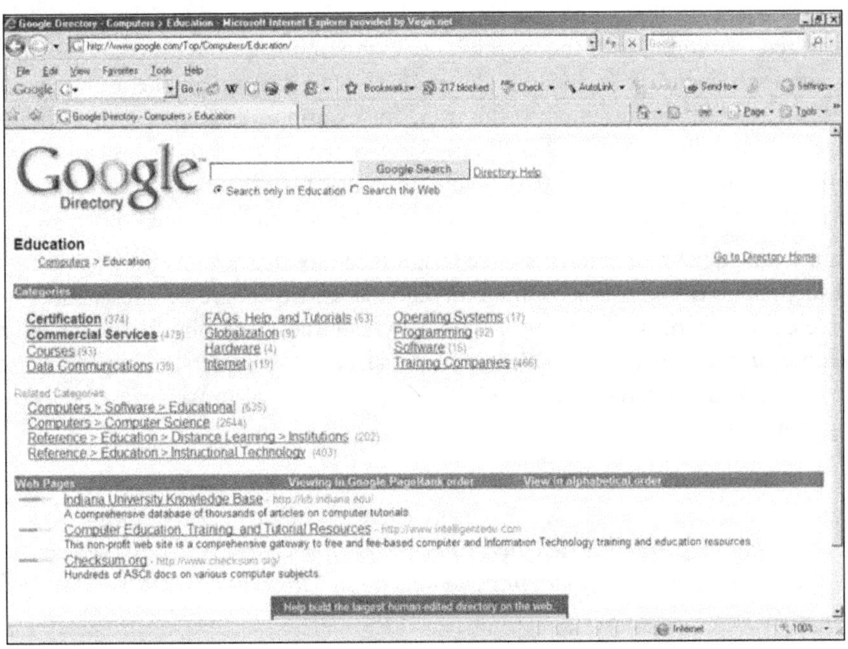

com/intl/en/scholar/about.html) combines the general search engine approach with the need for academic quality by offering access to scholarly literature including:

*peer-reviewed papers, theses, books, abstracts and articles, from academic publishers, professional societies, preprint repositories, universities and other scholarly organizations*

The other broad strand of development in resource discovery tools entails developing conceptual maps of subject areas that describe the relationships between topics and subtopics. These maps support navigation from general to specific and vice versa, and provide vocabulary control by *funnelling* variant terms to a preferred term. Such maps may take the form of thesauri, classifications, taxonomies, and more recently, ontologies. A number of such approaches were introduced in Chapter IV. These maps may also be seen in the form of *directories* offered by many of the search engines. Directories allow users to browse subject headings, and within a particular topic to navigate both to narrower, more specific topics, and from specific topics to the more general. Figure 53 shows the *top level* of Google's directory.

By clicking on one of the broad categories of information, the user can "drill down" to more detailed subdivisions of that subject. Figure 54 shows the screen after the user has selected *Computers,* then, from the subdivisions presented to him or her at the next level down, *Education.*

Further subdivisions are then presented to the user as shown in Figure 54. However, the user is able to further narrow the search by clicking on one of the subdivisions presented—or to broaden the search by clicking on the link below the *Google Directory* logo (in this case, the link *Computers*) to go back up the hierarchy. Related categories are also presented to the user, for example, Reference > Education > Distance Learning > Institutions. By clicking on the *Distance Learning* component of this link, the user can be taken to another area of the directory. Again, he or she may browse by narrowing and/or broadening the search from that point.

Maintaining a team of editors, whose task it is to monitor new Web sites and evaluate them prior to inclusion within a directory is an expensive business. Also, with the relentless increase in the number of Web resources becoming available daily, it becomes increasingly impossible for even a large team to keep up. For this reason, the Dmoz Open Directory Project was developed. The project Web site (http://dmoz.org/about.html) explains:

*The web continues to grow at staggering rates. Automated search engines are increasingly unable to turn up useful results to search queries. The small paid editorial staffs at commercial directory sites can't keep up with submissions, and the quality and comprehensiveness of their directories has suffered. Link rot is setting in and they can't keep pace with the growth of the Internet.*

*Instead of fighting the explosive growth of the Internet, the Open Directory provides the means for the Internet to organize itself. As the Internet grows, so do the number of net-citizens. These citizens can each organize a small portion of the web and present it back to the rest of the population, culling out the bad and useless and keeping only the best content.*

The project thus invites interested Web users to volunteer to monitor a particular area of knowledge on the Web and to contribute to the ever-growing Open Directory.

Such Web-based tools build on a rich tradition of approaches, techniques, and standards developed within librarianship/library and information science initially to cover printed materials. These are being developed, built upon, and adapted to enable some of the advantages, which can derive from them, to be transferred to the Web environment. We will next look at some of these key ICT-based standards and approaches.

## Metadata

As we will see in Chapters VII and VIII, metadata is a key component of educational informatics systems. Metadata is essentially *data about data*. In the library world, it is used to describe books and other information sources—to act as a surrogate for them that can be easily searched and manipulated. In the context of large and/or remote collections of information sources it is impracticable to examine each source in its entirety until you find what you want. A catalogue, in which each information source is represented as a brief description detailing author, title, publisher, subject keywords, and so forth can be searched rapidly and will reveal the location of the information source should you wish to access it in full.

*Table 15. Limited structure as afforded by HTML*

| | |
|---|---|
| <HTML><br><HEAD><br><TITLE> Human-Computer Interaction</TITLE><br></HEAD><br><BODY><br>**Fred Smith reviews** current research...<br></BODY><br></HTML> | <HTML><br><HEAD><br><TITLE> Human-Computer Interaction</TITLE><br></HEAD><br><BODY><br>A critical appraisal of **research by Fred Smith**...<br></BODY><br></HTML> |

As discussed in Chapter V, a number of codes have been developed in the library world, which offer standard ways to create such descriptions—for example, cataloguing codes such as the Anglo-American Cataloguing Rules (AACR), authoritative lists of subject headings such as the Medical Subject Headings (MeSH) and the Library of Congress Subject Headings (LCSH), classification schemes such as the Dewey Decimal Classification (DDC), the Library of Congress Classification (LCC), and the Universal Decimal Classification (UDC). Many specialist classifications and thesauri have also been created, which offer a degree of vocabulary control and support for concept searching within particular subject domains. However, work is ongoing that attempts to leverage the benefits of such codes within the Web environment. Also, new codes are being developed within the *library world* to take account of the need to achieve integration with the *Internet world.*

The original library codes and standards were developed in order to guide the creation of metadata in the form of catalogue records describing books. However, Web resources also require metadata if opportunities are to be maximised for their effective discovery. Some of the functionality of metadata—for example, the capacity to allow fielded searches—is enabled by the use of XML. Fielded searching refers to the ability to specify in a search that the information being searched for should appear in a particular field of a database—for example, author, title, publisher, or subject description. Thus a library catalogue will allow searching for, say, a book *authored by* Winston Churchill as opposed to one *written about* him, or a book *about* IGI Global Publishers as opposed to one simply *published by* them. A further example is shown in Table 15.

HTML allows differentiation to be made between information found in the title of a document, as opposed to the body, and search engines can perform fielded searches to the extent that they allow the searcher to specify that his or her search terms should appear in the title or body of retrieved documents.

HTML also offers the <META> tag. Not only does this allow metadata including subject keywords to be specified, but it also enables the use of standard metadata schemes such as Dublin Core. The code that follows shows how the <META> tag can be used to supply subject keywords, and also Dublin Core (dc in the code) data relating to the document's title, creator and description.

```
<HTML>
<HEAD>
<META NAME="Keywords" CONTENT="economics, finance, financial markets">
<META NAME="dc.title" CONTENT="Economics">
<META NAME="dc.creator" CONTENT="Fred Jones">
<META NAME="dc.description" CONTENT="An introduction to economics...">
<TITLE>Title</TITLE>
</HEAD>
```

*Table 16. Alternative structures for a common document*

| | |
|---|---|
| <course name = "Information retrieval"><br><lecturer> Nigel Ford </lecturer><br></course> | <lecturer name = "Mary Jones"><br><teaches> Information retrieval </teaches><br></lecturer> |

*Table 17. Object: property: value triples*

| Object | Property | Value |
|---|---|---|
| Document 1 | author | Fred Jones |
| Document 1 | title | *Economics Today* |
| Document 1 | publisher | John Wiley |

```
<BODY>Text...
</BODY>
</HTML>
```

However, <META> tags are not widely used by search engines, and their use for the purpose of supplying metadata is not a particularly effective way forward compared to the use of XML and RDF. XML increases the extent to which structural features of documents can be used to search for information, by basically allowing authors of documents to define their own tags. An example is as follows:

```
<employer-details id="SU2435">
    <name>Sheffield University</name>
    <address>
        <street>211 Portobello Street</street>
        <city>Sheffield</city>
        <county>South Yorkshire</county>
        <postcode>S1 4DP</postcode>
    </address>
</employer-details>
```

XML allows authors to define whatever structure they like for a document and enables fielded searching using these structures. However, XML is so flexible that one can express the structure of a complex document in many different possible ways. Thus different people could structure essentially the same information very differently—as shown in Table 16.

*Figure 55. Diagrammatic representation of object: property: value triples*

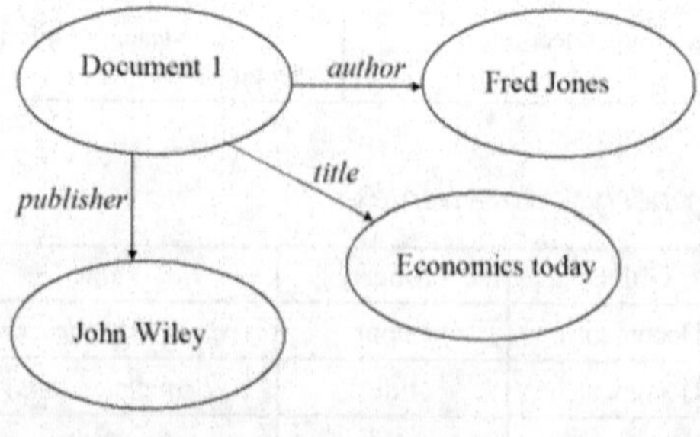


*Table 18. Interlinked object: property: value triples*

| Object | Property | Value |
|---|---|---|
| Document 1 | Author | Fred Jones |
| Fred Jones | Employer | University of Sheffield |
| Fred Jones | Job | lecturer |
| Fred Jones | Email | F.Jones@shef.ac.uk |

*Figure 56. Diagrammatic representation of interlinked object: property: value triples*

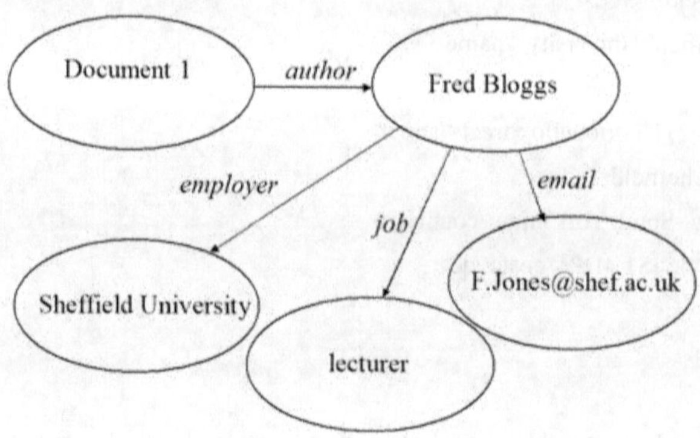


Clearly, searching for the name of lecturers who teach information retrieval on the assumption that the information is structured as in the example on the left would fail to retrieve it if it were structured as on the right. The problem is that XML does not express semantics. It cannot express the fact that it is the same information that is being expressed in different ways. Here is where resource description framework (RDF) can help.

RDF is a simple data model—expressible in XML (and many other syntaxes)—that introduces a standard way of structuring document descriptions. If two people agree to use a common way of describing the same information, then potential confusion arising from different people making different choices can be reduced. RDF is based on *object: property: value* triples, and Table 17 gives some examples:

This can be represented visually as shown in Figure 55.

These representations can be interlinked, for example, as shown in Table 18.

This structure is shown in Figure 56.

RDF is expressible in XML, for example:

```
<RDF:Description about="Document 1">
        <Author> Fred Jones </Author>
        <Title> Economics today </Title>
</RDF:Description>
```

It can describe Web documents, but also any *resource,* that is, an *object* with a unique URI (of which a URL is a subset). Information expressed as RDF can also be queried using, for example, the SPARQL query language (World Wide Web Consortium [W3C], 2007), an example of which will be given later in this chapter.

However, there is still scope for idiosyncrasy—different people and organisations making different decisions in relation to the way in which structural aspects of information sources are described. Figure 57, for example, shows how two record stores might describe the same CD. One store describes the source of the CD as

*Figure 57. Alternative terminology for similar concepts*

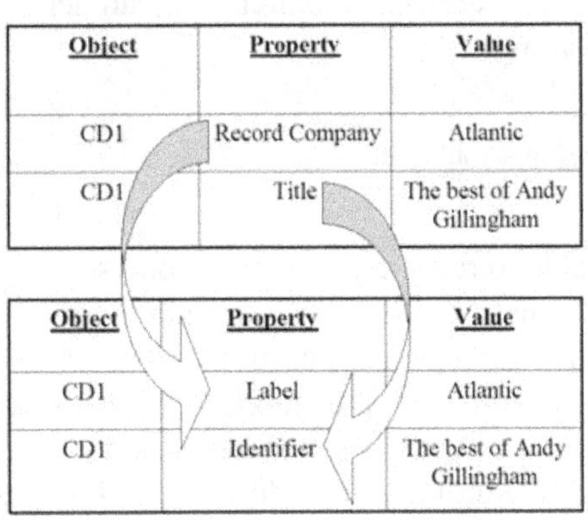

*Figure 58. Mapping between different structures and terminologies*

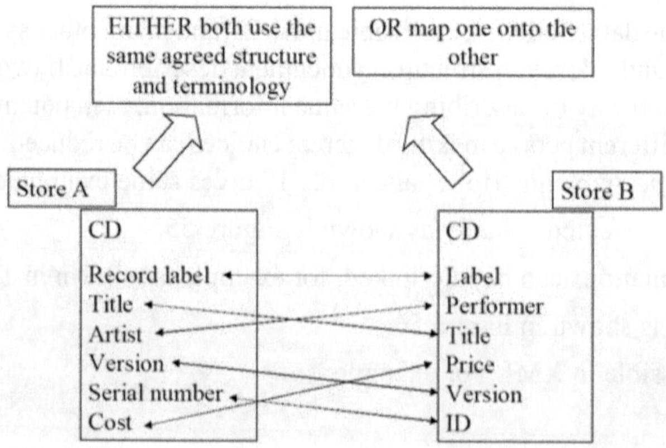


its *record company*, the other as its *label*. What one describes as its *title* the other describes as its *identifier*.

Although RDF specifies the structure in which to describe information in terms of *objects*, *properties,* and *values*, it provides no guidance on which terms (record company, or label; title; or identifier) to use. However, if we wish to be able to search for and use different sources of information, we need either to agree on a standard way of describing them in terms of both structure and vocabulary—or at least, if different standards are used, to know about these different standards and which one is being used by whom so that we can establish a mapping between them (Figure 58).

In the library world, codes like AACR specify how different elements of documents should be labelled and ordered. Thesauri and standardised lists of subject headings, such as the LCSH and the MeSH scheme, specify how we should label particular topics, indicating preferred terms and redirecting searchers and indexers *to* recommended terms *from* variants:

Computers in libraries see Library automation

Such codes are also able to resolve problems of polysemy and synonymy by supplying contextual information. Classifications and thesauri can also help concept navigation by indicating for a given concept broader, narrower, and related terms. Insofar as they represent agreed specifications of concepts making up some subject domain, and relationships between these concepts, cataloguing codes, classifications, and thesauri may be thought of as simple forms of *ontologies*.

*Table 19. Dublin Core's 15 main elements*

| | |
|---|---|
| Contributor | Person or body responsible for contributing to the content |
| Coverage | Description of the extent or scope of the content |
| Creator | Person or body mainly responsible for the content |
| Format | The physical or digital format |
| Date | Date applicable to the resource |
| Description | An description of the content |
| Identifier | An unambiguous identifier for the resource |
| Language | Language of the content |
| Publisher | Person or body making the resource available |
| Relation | Reference to a related resource |
| Rights | Rights relating to the resource |
| Source | A resource from which the present resource is derived |
| Subject | The subject content of the resource |
| Title | Title of the resource |
| Type | Description of the nature or genre of the resource |

Dublin Core is a relatively simple metadata scheme being used increasingly by the authors of Web documents. It can be thought of as a cut-down and simplified form of catalogue code, in that it specifies how to describe a document's structural elements in terms of 15 main elements (Table 19):

The following code shows RDF data for a document represented in HTML:

```
<META NAME = "dc:title" CONTENT = "Economics today">
<META NAME = "dc:description" CONTENT = "An introductory undergraduate text on econom-
ics">
<META NAME = "dc:date" CONTENT = "2007-09-01">
<META NAME = "dc:format" CONTENT = "text/html">
<META NAME = "dc:language" CONTENT = "en">
```

and in XML:

```
<?XML version="1.0"?>
<RDF:RDF
XMLns:RDF="http://www.w3.org/1999/02/22-RDF-syntax-ns#"
XMLns:dc= "http://purl.org/dc/elements/1.1/">
```

*Figure 59. A document classified according to the DCC*

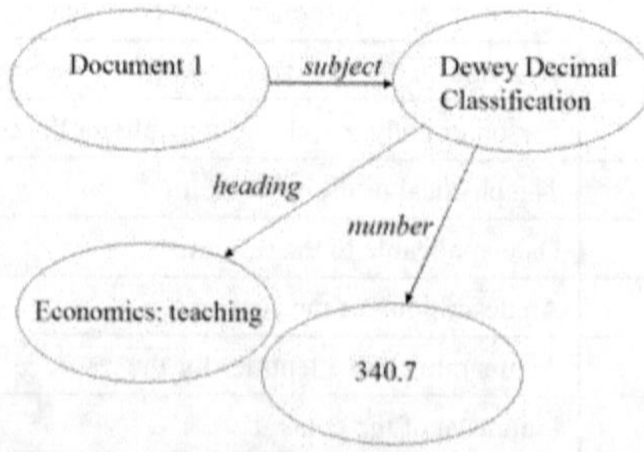


```
<RDF:Description RDF:about="http://www.shef.ac.uk/fred_jones/document_1.htm">
    <dc:title>Economics today</dc:title>
    <dc:description>An introductory undergraduate text on economics</dc:description>
    <dc:date>2007-09-01</dc:date>
    <dc:format>text/html</dc:format>
    <dc:language>en</dc:language>
</RDF:Description>
</RDF:RDF>
```

As previously noted, many lists of subject headings, thesauri, name authority lists, and classification schemes exist. Such external standards may be referenced within Dublin Core as shown in Figures 59 and 60, which depict documents classified according to the DCC and MeSH respectively.

Such referencing may be expressed in HTML as follows:

```
<meta name = "DC.Subject.Classification" scheme = "DDC" content = "158.25">
<meta name = "DC.Subject" scheme = "MeSH" content = "Formate Dehydrogenase">
```

It may be expressed in XML-based RDF as:

```
<?XML version="1.0"?>
<RDF:RDF XMLns:RDF="http://www.w3.org/1999/02/22-RDF-syntax-ns#"
    XMLns:RDFs="http://www.w3.org/2000/01/RDF-schema#"
    XMLns:dc="http://purl.org/dc/elements/1.1/"
    XMLns:dcterms="http://purl.org/dc/terms/">
<RDF:Description>
<dc:subject>
    <dcterms:MESH>
```

*Figure 60. A document classified according to the MeSH scheme*

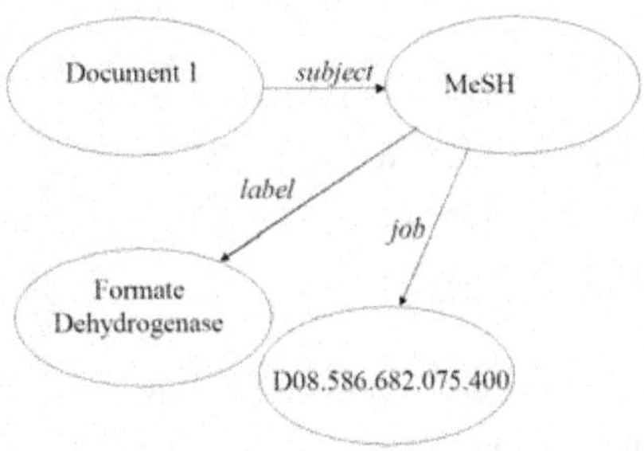


```
        <RDFs:label> Formate Dehydrogenase
        </RDFs:label>
    </dcterms:MESH>
</dc:subject>
</RDF:Description>
</RDF:RDF>
```

Dublin Core is in some ways like a much simplified version of MARC. While MARC is expressively quite powerful but difficult for the non-specialist, Dublin Core is relatively easy to learn and apply—but much less detailed. MARCXML represents some convergence of the previously somewhat separate worlds of the library and the Web. MARCXML is an XML schema in which to represent MARC (Library of Congress, 2002). The following example shows selected parts of a MARCXML instance, with explanatory annotations added in bold:

```
<?XML version="1.0" encoding="UTF-8" ?>
<collection XMLns="http://www.loc.gov/MARC21/slim">
<record>
<datafield tag="082" ind1="0" ind2="0">          Dewey Decimal Classification number
    <subfield code="a">370</subfield>
    <subfield code="2">20</subfield>
    </datafield>
<datafield tag="100" ind1="1" ind2="">           Author
    <subfield code="a">Ford, Nigel,</subfield>
    </datafield>
<datafield tag="245" ind1="1" ind2="0">          Title
    <subfield code="a">Teaching and learning /</subfield>
    <subfield code="c">Nigel Ford and Fred Jones.</subfield>
    </datafield>
```

```
<datafield tag="250" ind1="" ind2="">        Edition details
    <subfield code="a">1st ed.</subfield>
    </datafield>
<datafield tag="260" ind1="" ind2="">        Publication details
    <subfield code="a">London :</subfield>
    <subfield code="b">New Publishers Ltd.,</subfield>
    <subfield code="c">2005.</subfield>
    </datafield>
<datafield tag="300" ind1="" ind2="">        Physical details
    <subfield code="a">300 p. :</subfield>
    <subfield code="c">26 cm.</subfield>
    </datafield>
<datafield tag="520" ind1="" ind2="">        Summary
    <subfield code="a">An introduction to teaching and learning in higher education.</subfield>
    </datafield>
<datafield tag="650" ind1="" ind2="4">           Subject heading
    <subfield code="a">Higher education.</subfield>
    </datafield>
<datafield tag="650" ind1="" ind2="4">
    <subfield code="a">Teaching methods.</subfield>
    </datafield>
<datafield tag="700" ind1="1" ind2="">           Additional author
    <subfield code="a">Jones, Fred,</subfield>
    </datafield>
    </record>
    </collection>
```

Translated into Dublin Core, the entry would be as follows:

```
<?XML version="1.0" ?>
<dc XMLns="http://purl.org/dc/elements/1.1/">
    <title> Teaching and learning /</title>
    <creator>Ford, Nigel.</creator>
    <creator> Jones, Fred </creator>
    <type />
    <publisher>London : New Publishers Ltd.,</publisher>
    <date>2005.</date>
    <language>eng</language>
```

<description> introduction to teaching and learning in higher education .</description>

<subject>Higher education. </subject>

<subject>Teaching methods.</subject>

</dc>

The Metadata Object Description Schema (MODS) is an XML schema designed to represent a simplified version MARC21 (Library of Congress, 2006a). It covers a selection of the fields available in the MARC21 bibliographic format, and language-based tags are used in place of the numerical ones. MODS Lite is a version of MODS restricted to the 15 elements that appear in unqualified Dublin Core (plus an extra field <recordInfo> that provides necessary data relating to managing the record). The Metadata Authority Description Schema (MADS) is also an XML schema, designed to enable the representation in XML of fields from the MARC21 format for *authority* records. It complements MODS, which relates to the MARC21 format for *bibliographic* records. The Metadata Encoding and Transmission Standard (METS) (Library of Congress, 2006b) relates to XML metadata for descriptive, administrative, and structural aspects of digital LIBRARY objects.

## Ontologies and the Semantic Web

The power of RDF has been extended by the use of RDF schemas. These define additional features on top of RDF, including

- *Classes*
- *Inheritance* for classes and properties
- *Domain and range restrictions* for properties

*Figure 61. Classes in RDF schema*

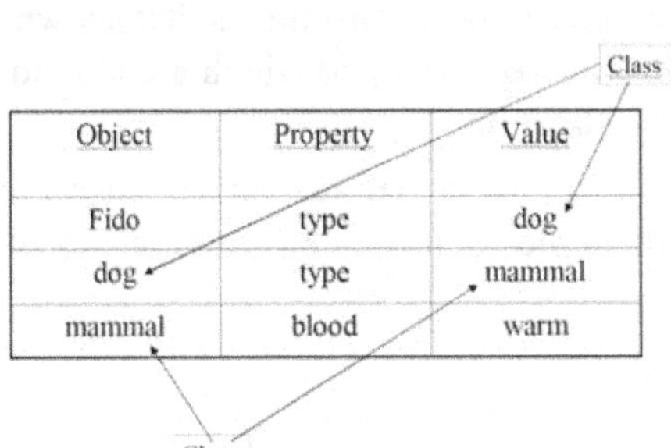

*Figure 62. Scope restrictions for properties and values*

| Object | Property | Value |
|---|---|---|
| Fido | type | dog |
| dog | type | mammal |
| mammal | blood | warm |

May only be used as a property of the "mammal" class

Values for "temperature" are limited to "warm" or "cold"

*Figure 63. Inheritance of class properties by members of a class*

**Is Fido warm blooded?**

**IF Fido is a dog**
**AND a dog is a mammal**
**AND a mammal is warm blooded**
**THEN Fido is warm blooded**

| Object | Property | Value |
|---|---|---|
| Fido | type | dog |
| dog | type | mammal |
| mammal | blood | warm |

Objects can be established as classes. Thus in Figure 61, *Fido* is a member of the class *dog*, which is in turn a member of the class *mammal.*

It is also possible to restrict the scope of properties and values. As shown in Figure 62, we can specify that, for example, *blood* may only be used as a property of the class *mammal*, and that permitted values for *blood* are restricted to *warm* and *cold.*

RDF enables inheritance by members of a class, of class properties. This enables us to ask questions of the type: "Is Fido warm blooded?" Using inference rules such as those shown in Figure 63, we can conclude that Fido is indeed warm blooded.

Inference rules do not have to be so specific as that shown in Figure 63, and powerful generalised rules can be developed which are able to reason across different domains, as we will see later on.

Inference rules basically allow us to draw conclusions from premises. To illustrate a simple example—if people are presented with the two statements:

1. Socrates is a man
2. A man is mortal

… they will have no difficulty concluding that:

3. Socrates is mortal

… even though Statement 3 was not explicitly given to them. One way of representing the knowledge that allows this inference to be made is in the form of a rule.

IF Socrates is a man
AND a man has the property mortal
THEN Socrates has the property mortal

Such inferencing rules may be used in conjunction with some form of knowledge representation. An example of a classic form of knowledge representation used in early intelligent systems is the semantic network—a term first used by Quillian (1968) in his research into human memory. Figure 64 shows such a network.

The words in bold are *nodes*, and they are related to each other by *arcs*. Nodes can represent concepts, while arcs represent relationships between them. Thus, a Mazda 6 is a kind of saloon, which is a kind of car. A Quadzilla X50 is a kind of quad bike, which is a kind of cycle. Both cycles and cars are types of vehicle.

Frames represent an extension of the idea of a semantic network. Frames enable further information to be stored at each node, as shown in Figure 65. This is based on the semantic network shown in Figure 64. The arc labels (*a kind of*) are omitted for clarity.

In Figure 65, we can store additional information about each of the concepts represented in the semantic network in a *frame* with *slots*. For simplicity of illustration,

*Figure 64. A simple semantic network*

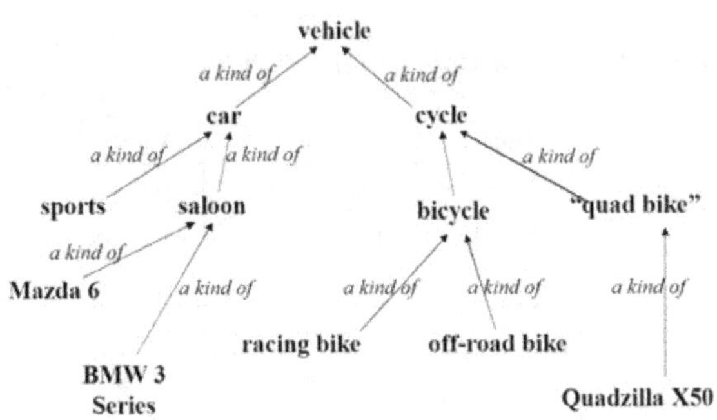

*Figure 65. Simple frames*

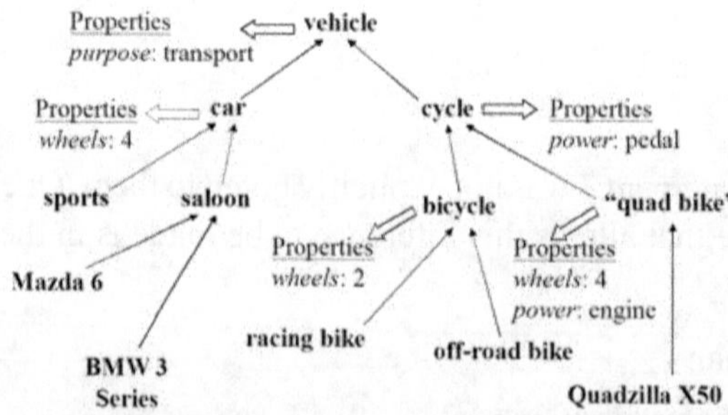


all but one of the frames shown in the figure contain only one slot—*purpose* in the case of vehicle, *wheels* in the case of car, and so forth. Each of these slots has a *value—transport* in the case of the purpose slot, and so forth.

Once we have some sort of knowledge representation, we can devise ways of reasoning using it. In this way, computers can be made to add value to information stored, for example, by answering questions requiring inference rather than simple retrieval of information.

If we return to the vehicles example shown in Figure 65, we can devise rules that the computer can use to deduce the answer to various questions. Clearly, no intelligence is required simply to retrieve directly information that is stored. So, for example, if we have the following information (Table 20) stored in a database.

Questions such as:

"What is the *number of wheels* of a *bicycle*?"

"A cycle is a kind of what?"

can be easily answered using a simple matching procedure. This procedure retrieves the obvious:

*Table 20. Vehicle information stored in a database*

| Object | Property | Value |
|---|---|---|
| off-road bike | is a kind of | bicycle |
| bicycle | number of wheels | 2 |
| bicycle | is a kind of | cycle |
| cycle | is a kind of | vehicle |
| cycle | powered by | pedal |
| vehicle | Purpose | transport |

*Table 21. A statement that must be inferred rather than simply retrieved*

| Object | Property | Value |
|---|---|---|
| off-road bike | number of wheels | 2 |

IF *number of wheels* is one of the properties of *bicycle*, THEN take the value of that property (in this case, "2") as the answer!

However, if we ask:

"What is the *number of wheels* of an *off-road bike*?"

our simple matching procedure will not work. Basically, this information is not literally stored anywhere—that is, nowhere in our database is there any entry like that shown in Table 21.

In fact, a level of intelligence is required to work out the answer from the information that is given. We need to reason that *if* an off-road bike is a kind of bike, *and* a bike has two wheels, *then* an off-road bike has two wheels.

Such knowledge can be represented as a rule:

IF an *off-road bike* is a kind of *bike*
AND a *bike* has *number of wheels* 2
THEN an *off-road bike* has *number of wheels* 2

This may be expressed in different ways, for example:

An *off-road bike* possesses *Property: number of wheels value* = 2
IF an *off-road bike* is a kind of *bike*
AND a *bike* has *Property: number of wheels* value = 2

Clearly, a large number of rules would be required to enable a computer system to do anything useful based on such specific rules. However, rules can be made more general, by substituting variables (place holders whose precise content can change as the rule is applied to different cases). Variables are italicised in the following examples. The power and flexibility of this type of rule increases dramatically if we generalise it to:

*X* possesses Property *Z*
IF *X* is a kind of *Y*
AND *Y* has Property *Z*

This one generalized rule, used in conjunction with the knowledge representation shown in Figure 80, can enable a computer to find the answer to all of the following questions:

"What is the purpose of a bicycle?" (Transport)
"How many wheels has a Quadzilla X50?" (4)
"How is the Quadzilla X50 powered?" (Engine)
"How is a bicycle powered?" (Pedal)

We can ask a question by putting the statement to the computer (in bold in Table 22) using *Z* as a variable of which we do not yet know the value. Lines have been numbered to aid the explanation that follows.
The rule is shown in the column to the left. It is shown in *instantiated* form to the right. This instantiated form shows the rule with the values filled in as it is run for a particular query. In this case, the query gives to the rule values to fill the variables *X* and *Property*. *X* = A racing bike and *Property* = number of wheels (line 1). Since *Z* is unknown, the computer attempts to find a value to fill it. It does so by processing line 2. When it finds the statement that "a racing bike is a kind of bicycle," it now has a value for the variable *Y*, namely: bicycle. It goes on to line 3, knowing that *Y* = bicycle (this information being passed from line 2) and Property = number of wheels (passed from line 1). It thus looks in its database for a statement that matches "bicycle has number of wheels *Z*." If it can find such a statement, it will instantiate the still uninstantiated (unfilled) variable *Z*. Assuming that it finds the statement "bicycle has number of wheels 2," it has found a value for *Z*, namely: 2. Since the value of *Z* is now known to the bottom line of the rule, it is also known by line 1 of the rule. This value is returned as the answer to the query:

*Table 22. A rule and associated query*

| **A racing bike possesses number of wheels = Z** | |
|---|---|
| 1. *X* possesses *Property Z* | *A racing bike* possesses *number of wheels* = *Z* |
| 2. IF *X* is a kind of *Y* | IF *a racing bike* is a kind of *bicycle* |
| 3. AND *Y* has *Property Z* | AND *bicycle* has number of wheels = *Z* |

**A racing bike possesses number of wheels = 2**

However, we need to develop the rules more if we are to be able to answer questions such as:

"How many wheels has a BMW 3 Series?"

"What is the purpose of a BMW 3 Series?"

"How is a racing bike powered?"

Since the rule in its present form can only make inferences from an object to its immediately super-ordinate category—from *off-road bike* to *bicycle* but not from *off-road bike* to *cycle* or *vehicle*; from *BMW 3 Series* to *saloon* but not to *car* or to *vehicle*. Thus if we apply the rule to try to answer the question "How is a racing bike powered," we fail since there is no statement telling us how a bicycle is powered. We need to make the rule recursive so that it can make inferences no matter how many levels up the information is to be found. We can do this by changing the rule as follows:

*X* possesses Property *Z*
IF *X* has Property *Z*

X possesses Property *Z*
IF *X* is a kind of *Y*
AND *Y* possesses Property *Z*

This rule is composed of two parts. The computer will work from the top downwards. If the first part of the rule (the top 2 lines) does not work, it will try the second part. Note that the rule can call itself recursively. Thus, assuming it has not yet found an answer (i.e., has not yet been able to find a value for *Property Y*) when it reaches the bottom line of the rule (i.e., the bottom of its box in Figure 81) it applies itself recursively (as indicated by the downward arrow in the figure). However, the rule applies itself using values passed to it from the first *round*. Thus the first time the rule is applied, the value of *X* in "*X* possesses *Property Y*" is racing bike. However, the rule "calls" itself in its last line (the bottom of its box) giving a new value to *X*. Thus the second round rule uses the value bicycle instead of racing bike in "*X* possesses *Property Y*" (see the first line in the second box down on the right side of the figure). The procedure is shown in Figure 66.

As in the previous example, the rule is shown to the left, and is shown in instantiated form—as it is processed in response to a particular query—to the right. In the instantiated version to the right, those parts of the rule which do not apply to

*Figure 66. A recursive inference rule in action*

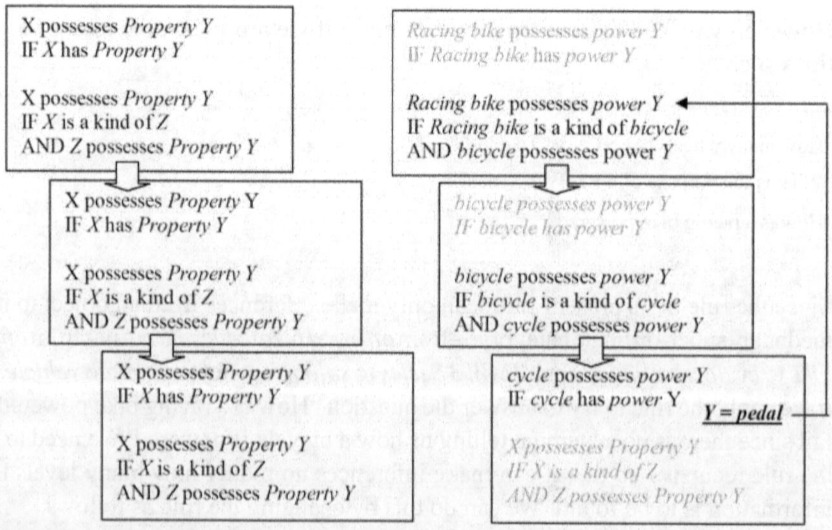


the particular query shown are greyed out. Thus, the first part of the rule does not apply since there is no statement which directly matches its second line "IF racing bike has power *Y*." Since there is no such matching statement, the second part of the rule is applied instead.

The rule will go on calling itself recursively (with a new value in *X* each time) until it finds a matching statement in its database. In this case, it finds it after two rounds of recursion, finally matching the statement "cycle has power pedal." In this final recursive round, the first part of the rule finally *does* apply, since there *is* a statement that "cycle has power pedal." The answer has therefore been found, so there is no need to continue processing the second part of the rule. At this stage, it returns the value *pedal* back through its recursive cycles as the value of *X* to the question that originally called the first rule.

The ability to reason intelligently (e.g., using inference rules) coupled with ontologies is a central component of the Semantic Web. The term *ontology* may be used with varying levels of rigour. At one level, we have referred to library classification schemes, thesauri, and metadata schemes as ontologies. These may be regarded as ontologies if we define the latter simply as schemes that specify concepts and relationships between concepts making up some subject domain.

At another level, ontologies have a more complex structure, and applying a stricter definition would generally require the inclusion of *instances*, *classes*, *attributes*, and *relations*. Ontologies may impose restrictions, as we saw in the RDF schema example that specified that the attribute *blood* cold only apply to the class *mammals*, and the only allowable values for *temperature* were *warm* and *cold*. Ontologies may specify many types of relationship including general ones such as *part of, is a,* and so forth and domain-specific ones—for example, in the case of the vehicles example presented previously, specifying the purpose of a vehicle, the number of wheels a bicycle has, and how cars and bicycles are powered.

A number of formal languages have been developed for creating ontologies. The Web Ontology Language (OWL) is a WWW recommended standard. It extends the vocabulary of RDF schema and offers a formal semantics, thus enabling greater expressive power. This expressive power varies in the three versions of the language: *OWL Lite*, *OWL DL*, and *OWL Full*. It is written in XML.

OWL extends RDF schema in also allowing the expression of, for example, disjoint classes (for example, to specify that while tricycle and bicycle are both subclasses of cycle, they are mutually exclusive). Another limitation of RDF schemas is that they are not able to express the formation of new classes from the combination or intersection of others, or to specify cardinality dictating that a certain property can only have a certain number of values (for example, that a person can only have two natural parents), and so forth. OWL offers these and other facilities. The OWL Web Ontology Language Guide (W3C, 2004) notes the difference between XML Schema and OWL as follows:

> *An ontology differs from an XML schema in that it is a knowledge representation, not a message format. Most industry based Web standards consist of a combination of message formats and protocol specifications. These formats have been given an operational semantics, such as, "Upon receipt of this* `PurchaseOrder` *message, transfer* `Amount` *dollars from* `AccountFrom` *to* `AccountTo` *and ship* `Product`.*" But the specification is not designed to support reasoning outside the transaction context. For example, we won't in general have a mechanism to conclude that because the* `Product` *is a type of Chardonnay it must also be a white wine.*
>
> *One advantage of OWL ontologies will be the availability of tools that can reason about them. Tools will provide generic support that is not specific to the particular subject domain, which would be the case if one were to build a system to reason about a specific industry-standard XML schema.*

The following code shows part of a very simple *vehicles* ontology written in OWL. The code is explained in detail later on.

```
<?XML version="1.0" ?>
<RDF:RDF
XMLns="http://www.myOntologies.com/vehicles.owl#"
XML:base="http://www. myOntologies.com /vehicles.owl">
```

```
XMLns:RDF="http://www.w3.org/1999/02/22-RDF-syntax-ns#"
XMLns:RDFs="http://www.w3.org/2000/01/RDF-schema#"
XMLns:owl="http://www.w3.org/2002/07/owl#"
<owl:imports RDF:resource="http:// myOntologies.com /roads"/>
```

The first two lines of code indicate that the ontology is an XML document, written using RDF:

```
<?XML version="1.0" ?>
<RDF:RDF
```

The RDF declaration will not be closed (</RDF:RDF>) until the end of the ontology. Namespaces are then defined. Namespaces are devices that specify the *context* in which terms are used, thus removing ambiguity. Ambiguity may arise where the same term is used in different ontologies to mean different things—or indeed where different terms are used to mean the same thing. Recall the example of the two music stores, where one used the term Performer and the other Artist to refer to the same person. The same stores may also use the same term to refer to different things—for example, one may use *invoice address* to refer to the address to which an invoice should be sent, while the other may use the same term to refer to the address from which an invoice has been received. A namespace is a statement designed to distinguish a given ontology from other ontologies. Thus, when people or systems wish to make use of the ontology, they will be able to know which meaning of a particular term is appropriate.

The following code specifies that this is the namespace of the current ontology, and should be used as the default namespace (i.e., unprefixed qualified names refer to it), and gives the base URI of the document containing the ontology:

```
XMLns="http://www.myOntologies.com/vehicles.owl#"
XML:base="http://www. myOntologies.com/vehicles.owl">
```

The following code specifies the namespaces of RDF, RDF schema, and OWL—thus indicating that terms and concepts used are from these particular standards:

```
XMLns:RDF="http://www.w3.org/1999/02/22-RDF-syntax-ns#"
XMLns:RDFs="http://www.w3.org/2000/01/RDF-schema#"
XMLns:owl="http://www.w3.org/2002/07/owl#"
```

The *imports* OWL feature enables other ontologies to be brought in and used within the ontology. This means that all terms and concepts in the imported ontology are available for use in the present ontology. In this case, where the current vehicles ontology wishes to refer to aspects relating to *roads,* the author can draw on work already done by someone else—that is, the author of the roads ontology:

```
<owl:imports RDF:resource="http:// myOntologies.com /roads"/>
```

Next follows the ontology itself. The fact that RDF:about is empty simply means that the name of the ontology is the base URI of the owl:Ontology element (see previous example):

```
<owl:Ontology RDF:about="">
<owl:versionInfo>Version 1.0 by Nigel Ford</owl:versionInfo>
</owl:Ontology>
```

The following code sets up the classes and subclasses of the ontology. Figure 67 shows part of the ontology, and the relevant code is reproduced after it. Comments in the ontology explain the semantics being expressed (e.g., "Car is a class").

```
<owl:Class RDF:ID= "car">
<RDFs:comment>Car is a class</RDFs:comment>
</owl:Class>

<owl:Class RDF:ID= "bicycle">
<RDFs:comment>Bicycle is a class that is disjoint from car – i.e. if something is a car it cannot also be a bicycle</RDFs:comment>
</owl:Class>
```

*Figure 67. Part of the vehicles ontology*

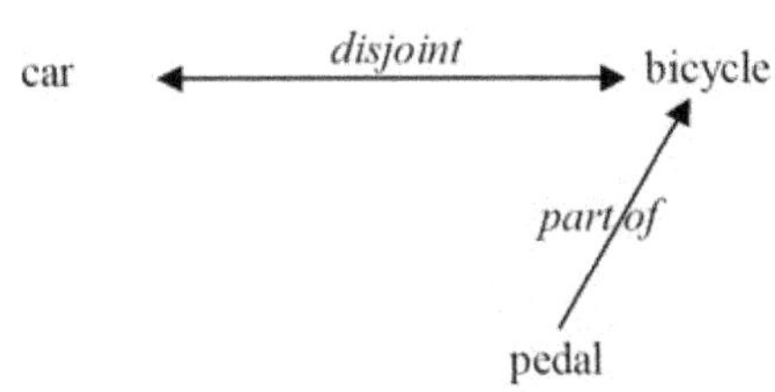

```
<owl:disjointWith RDF:resource="#car"/>
<owl:Class>

<owl:Class RDF:ID="pedal">
<RDFs:comment>Pedal is part of a bicycle</RDFs:comment>
<RDFs:subClassOf>
<owl:Restriction>
<owl:onProperty RDF:resource="is_part_of"/>
<owl:allValuesFrom RDF:resource="#bicycle"/>
</owl:Restriction>
</RDFs:subClassOf>
</owl:Class>
</RDF:RDF>
```

Ontologies can be used to specify RDF queries in the SPARQL query language (W3C, 2007). SPARQL allows queries such as the following, which (assuming a source of appropriate RDF data) will find all African capital cities (example given in Wikipedia, 2007):

```
PREFIX abc: <http://mynamespace.com/exampleOntologie#>
SELECT ?capital ?country
WHERE {
    ?x abc:cityname ?capital.
    ?y abc:countryname ?country.
    ?x abc:isCapitalOf ?y.
    ?y abc:isInContinent abc:africa.
}
```

A number of OWL features allow equivalences to be established between terms used in different ontologies. These include: *equivalentClass* (for example: Car and Automobile); *equivalentProperty* (for example: colour and shade"); *sameAs* and *differentFrom,* which relate to individuals (or instances):

```
<owl:DatatypeProperty RDF:ID="shade">
<owl:equivalentProperty RDF:resource="#colour"/>
<RDFs:domain RDF:resource="#paintwork"/>
<RDFs:range RDF:resource="&xsd;#string"/>
</owl:DatatypeProperty>
```

*Table 23. Examples of OWL expressions*

| | |
|---|---|
| owl:complementOf | owl:maxCardinality |
| owl:differentFrom | owl:minCardinality |
| owl:disjointWith | owl:oneOf |
| owl:equivalentClass | owl:sameAs |
| owl:incompatibleWith | owl:SymmetricProperty |
| owl:intersectionOf | owl:TransitiveProperty |
| owl:InverseFunctionalProperty | owl:unionOf |
| owl:inverseOf | *etc.* |

Table 23 shows examples of other expressions available in OWL.

As the OWL Web Ontology Language Guide (W3C, 2004) notes:

> *In order for ontologies to have the maximum impact, they need to be widely shared. In order to minimize the intellectual effort involved in developing an ontology they need to be re-used. In the best of all possible worlds they need to be composed. For example, you might adopt a date ontology from one source and a physical location ontology from another and then extend the notion of location to include the time period during which it holds.*
>
> *It is important to realize that much of the effort of developing an ontology is devoted to hooking together classes and properties in ways that maximize implications. We want simple assertions about class membership to have broad and useful implications. This is the hardest part of ontology development. If you can find an existing ontology that has already undergone extensive use and refinement, it makes sense to adopt it.*

A simple example of the interuse of ontologies is shown in Figures 68 and 69. Let us assume an ontology for higher education (Figure 68). This specifies that a university is an organization, and that it has staff and students, that a professor is a member of academic staff, and that a head of department is a professor, and so forth.

If we attempt to use this ontology to ask the straightforward question "Does a head of department have a salary?", the answer is unknown. This is because the ontology does not explicitly encode knowledge that would be key in an *organizations* ontology—that is, that members of staff are paid a salary.

However, if we find another ontology that has been developed in the area of organizations, we can import it into our higher education ontology. By doing so we can enable our question to be answered since the concepts specified in the new ontology are now available to ours. Figure 69 shows the line of reasoning which enables our question to be answered.

*Figure 68. Question posed to a higher education ontology*

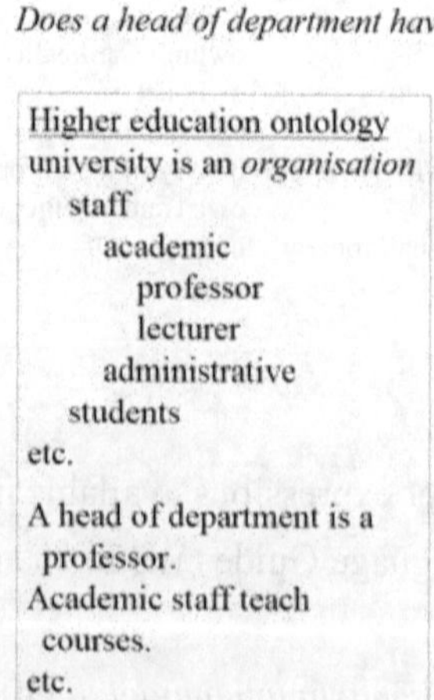


*Figure 69. Inferencing using linked ontologies*

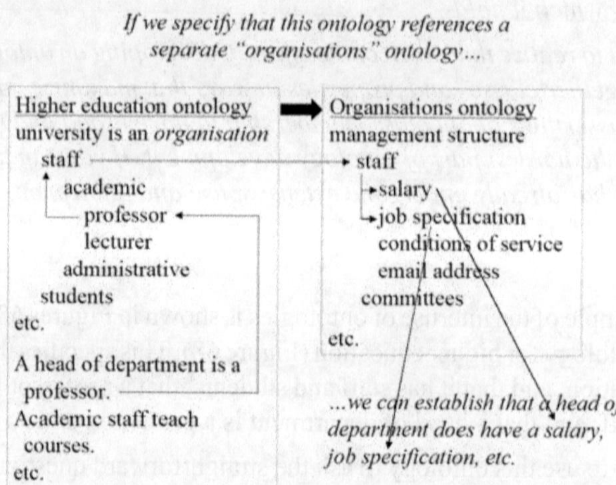


# Educational Metadata and Ontologies

Metadata, ontologies, and inferencing techniques are key tools in the development of ICT-based tools designed to support resource discovery and sharing. In an age of sharing of across digital networks including the Web, learning designers need to be able to able to discover learning resources produced by others, so that they can reuse or reconfigure them for their own teaching. Effective resource discovery is a key enabler in this process and is a central defining component of educational informatics.

If learning resources are to be shared, they must be discoverable. However, if they are to be discovered, then the way in which they are described via metadata must match—or be somehow linked to—the ways in which people search for them. The type of machine inferencing based on ontologies described in the previous section enable such discovery to take place more *intelligently* in the sense that the discovery process is not restricted to a literal matching of search terms with metadata.

Educational computing and library/information science combine insofar as the widespread sharing and reuse of learning objects and other learning resources require tools, techniques, and standards that enable and facilitate resource discovery, whether from specialist learning object repositories or open corpus material available on the Web. Indeed, the very nature of shareability and reusability means that they are essentially linked to the concept of resource discovery.

Such discovery is one of the key functions of metadata. As Godby (2004) states:

*As learning objects grow in number and importance, institutions are faced with the daunting task of managing them. Like familiar items in library collections, learning objects need to be organised by subject and registered in searchable repositories. But they also introduce special problems. As computer files, they are dependent on a particular hardware and software environment. And as materials with a pedagogical intent, they are associated with metrics such as learning objectives, reading levels and methods for evaluating student performance. The conventional wisdom is that a learning object should be accompanied by a metadata record, whose minimal form would contain the information typically found in the description of a book or journal article, such as title, author, subject, and a unique identifier. But a more complete record would describe the technical and educational context required to activate the learning object and connect it with others to create a rich educational experience for an appropriate audience.*

A number of metadata standards have been developed specifically for education. One of the most widely used of these is the learning object metadata (LOM) standard, published by the by the Institute of Electrical and Electronics Engineers (IEEE) Standards Association. This is a leading contender as a worldwide standard for learning object metadata (IEEE, 2002). LOM descriptions include pedagogic knowledge in the form of specifications of a range of learning object characteristics, including level of difficulty, interactivity type and level, semantic density, intended end-user role, typical learning time, educational context, and so forth. Other standards include Dublin Core Education (DC-Ed) from the Dublin Core Metadata Initiative

*Table 24. The main LOM metadata categories (adapted from IEEE, 2002)*

| | |
|---|---|
| 1. **General** | General information describing the learning object as a whole, including title, language, and description. |
| 2.**Lifecycle** | Relates to the history and current state of the learning object and those who have affected it during its development. |
| 3.**Meta-Metadata** | Data about the object's metadata. |
| 4.**Technical** | Technical aspects including location, technical requirements, and duration. |
| 5. **Educational** | Key educational or pedagogic characteristics of the object, including interactivity type, typical learning time, semantic density, and level of difficulty. |
| 6. **Rights** | Intellectual property rights and conditions of use. |
| 7. **Relation** | Relationship between this and other learning objects, including *is part of, is version of, is based on,* and *requires.* |
| 8. **Annotation** | Comments on the educational use of the object (e.g., assessments and suggestions for use), and information on author of the comments. |
| 9. **Classification** | Subject classification of the learning object's content. Existing classification systems can be referenced. |

(DCMI) Education Working Group (DCMI, 2002), and the IMS Global Learning consortium's metadata specification (IMS, 2002). Table 24 shows an overview of the main sections of this standard.

Table 25 expands the LOM categories outlined in Table 24. However, it does so selectively, in order to give a flavour of the scheme.

Where Dublin Core elements (dc) already exist, these can be used in LOM rather than new LOM elements having to be created. Dublin Core Qualifiers (dcq) can also be used. Examples are given in Table 26.

Dublin Core elements within LOM may themselves refer to LOM elements, for example:

```
<dc:creator>
    <LOM:entity>
        (vCard:FN>Fred Jones</vCard:FN>
    </LOM:entity>
</dc:creator>
```

Metadata descriptions can reference existing subject classifications. The following example is adapted from Dolog, Gavriloaie, Nejdl, and Brase (2003). It shows how

*Table 25. Expansion of selected LOM metadata categories (adapted from IEEE, 2002)*

1. General. General information describing the learning object as a whole

| | |
|---|---|
| 1.1.1 **Catalog** | Name or designator of the identification or cataloging scheme for this entry. A namespace scheme. |
| 1.1.2 **Entry** | The value of the identifier within the identification or cataloging scheme. |
| 1.2 **Title** | Title of the learning object. |
| 1.4 **Description** | |
| 1.5 **Keywords** | |
| 1.6 **Coverage** | The extent or scope of the content of the learning object, including the time, culture, geography, or region to which it applies. |
| 1.7 **Structure** | Structure of the learning object. The structure can be:<br>*atomic*: (an object that is indivisible)<br>*collection*: (a set of objects with no specified relationship between them).<br>*networked*: (a set of objects with unspecified relationships between them).<br>*hierarchical*: (the relationships can be represented by a tree structure).<br>*linear*: (a set of objects that are fully ordered). *example*: (connected by *previous* and *next* relationships). |
| 1.8 **Aggregation level** | The granularity of the object.<br>This aggregation level can be:<br>*1*: smallest level, for example, raw media data or fragments;<br>*2*: a collection of level 1 objects (e.g., a lesson);<br>*3*: a collection of level 2 learning objects (e.g., a course).<br>*4*: the largest level (e.g., a set of courses leading to a certificate). |

3. Meta-Metadata. Data about the object's metadata

| | |
|---|---|
| 3.1.1 **Catalog** | The name or designator of the identification or cataloging scheme for this entry. A namespace scheme, for example, URI |
| 3.1.2 **Entry** | The value of the identifier, for example, http://www.ieee.org/descriptions/1234 |
| 3.3 **Metadata schema** | For example, LOMv1.0 |

4. Technical

| | |
|---|---|
| 4.3 **Location** | |
| 4.4. **Requirements** | |
| 4.4.1.1 **Type** | Technology required (e.g., hardware, software, network, etc.). These can relate to:<br>*operating system; browser* |
| 4.4.1.2 **Name** | Name of the required technology. For operating system type, the name can be: *pc-dos; ms-windows; macos; unix; multi-os; none.* For browser type, the name can be: *any; netscape; communicator; ms-internet explorer; opera; amaya* |
| 4.7 **Duration** | Time it takes for the learning object to play |

*Continued on following page*

*Table 25. continued*

5. Educational. Key educational or pedagogic characteristics of the object

| | |
|---|---|
| 5.1 **Interactivity type** | *Active* learning (stimulates productive action on the part of the learner) *Expositive* learning (learner's role is simply to absorb content)<br>Active documents, for example, simulation; exercise (finds a solution); problem statement (writes solution)<br>Expositive documents, for example, Hypertext; video; graphical material; audio<br>Mixed documents, for example, hypermedia with embedded simulation |
| 5.2 **Learning resource type** | These can be: *exercise; simulation; questionnaire; diagram; figure; graph; index; slide; table; narrative text; exam; experiment; problem statement; self assessment; lecture.* |
| 5.3 **Interactivity level** | Interactivity level can be: *very low; low; medium; high; very high* |
| 5.4 **Semantic density** | The degree of conciseness of a learning object. Semantic density can be: *very low; low; medium; high; very high* |
| 5.5 **Intended end user role** | This can be: *teacher; author; learner; manager* |
| 5.6 **Context** | Principal intended environment for use, for example, *school; higher education; training; other* |
| 5.7 **Typical age Range** | |
| 5.8 **Difficulty** | This can be: **very easy; easy; medium; difficult; very difficult**. |
| 5.9 **Typical learning time** | |
| 5.10 **Description** | Comments on how this learning object is to be used. |
| 5.11 **Language** | Language of intended user |

8. Annotation. Comments on the educational use of the object (e.g., assessments and suggestions for use), and information on author of the comments

| | |
|---|---|
| 8.3 **Description** | The content of the annotation |

9. Classification. Any classification system can be referenced, for example, MeSH, LOC, UDC, DDC, and so forth.

| | |
|---|---|
| 9.1 **Purpose** | *Purpose of classifying the learning object.* This can be: *discipline; idea; prerequisite; educational objective; accessibility; restrictions; educational level; skill level; security level; competency.* |
| 9.2 **Taxon path** | A taxonomic path in a specific classification system |
| 9.2.1 **Source** | Name of the classification system, for example, ("en","MESH") |
| 9.2.2 **Taxon** | A particular term within a taxonomy |
| 9.2.2.1 **Id** | The taxon identifier |
| 9.2.2.2 **Entry** | Taxon textual label |
| 9.4 **Keyword** | |

*Table 26. Examples of Dublin Core elements used within LOM*

| | |
|---|---|
| 1. General | dc:title<br>dc:language<br>dc:description |
| 7. Relation | dcq:hasFormat<br>dcq:hasPart<br>dcq:isVersionOf<br>dcq:requires<br>dcq:isRequiredBy |
| 9. Classification | dc:subject |

a learning resource can be tagged with metadata which refers to the Association of Computing Machinery's (ACM) Computer Classification Scheme (ACM CCS) (ACM, 2006). Here is an extract from this scheme:

A. General Literature

B. Hardware

C. Computer Systems Organization

D. Software

D.0 General

D.1 Programming Techniques

…

D.1.3 Concurrent Programming

D.1.4 Sequential Programming

D.1.5 Object-oriented Programming

D.1.6 Logic Programming

D.1.7 Visual Programming

D.1.m Miscellaneous

D.2 Software Engineering

D.3 Programming Languages

D.4 Operating Systems

E. Data

F. Theory of Computation

To annotate our learning resources, we link *dc:subject* to the entry in the classification:

```
<RDF:Description RDF:about= URL.../Logic_programming.pdf >
<dc:subject RDF:resource= URL.../ACM_CCS.RDF#D.1.6 / >
</RDF:Description>
```

Here is an extract from an RDF file (the ACM_CCS.RDF referred to in the second line of the previous code) containing the classification:

```
<dcq:SubjectScheme RDF:ID= ACM_CCS >
<RDFs:label>ACM Computer Classification system
</RDFs:label>
</dcq:SubjectScheme>
<LOM_cls:Taxonomy>
    <LOM_cls:rootTaxon>
    <ACM:ACMCCS RDF:about= URL.../AC_CCS.RDF#D >
    <RDF:value>Software</RDF:value>
        <LOM_cls:taxon>
        <ACM:ACM CCS RDF:about= http://www.kbs.
        uni-hannover.de/Uli/ACM_CCS.RDF#D.1>
        <RDF:value>Programming Techniques
        </RDF:value>
            <LOM_cls:taxon>
            <ACM:ACM CCS RDF:about= URL.../ACM_CCS.RDF #D.1.6>
            <RDF:value>Logic Programming
            </RDF:value>
            </LOM_cls:taxon>
        </LOM_cls:taxon>
    </LOM_cls:rootTaxon>
</LOM_cls:Taxonomy>
```

Different communities engaged in the creation and use of metadata have different needs, and for this reason, make use of different *application profiles,* for example those of SCORM, the Education Network Australia (EdNA), ARIADNE, and the Gateway to Educational Materials (GEM), which are based on Dublin Core, and UK LOM Core and CanCore, based on IEEE LOM. These entail potentially different selections, uses, and interpretations of metadata elements from one or more metadata standards, and are thus not necessarily interoperable. Such application profiles may diverge from—and thus be incompatible with—the generic standards from which they derive elements in that they may interpret existing elements differently, and/or develop their own new elements, to reflect local needs. As pointed out by Godby (2004):

*...two application profiles might use LOM.Classification.Purpose and still fail to interoperate because this element could be used to annotate different facets of the resource, such as pedagogical intent and position within a knowledge hierarchy.*

Godby (2004) goes on to note that agreed controlled vocabularies, and tools to enforce consistent interpretation, are not yet widely available. She reports a comparative survey designed to investigate the degree of overlap between 35 application profiles developed by a range of organizations engaged in the creation and use of learning object metadata. She concludes that there is a trade-off between breadth of interoperability and depth of exposure of technical and pedagogic features of the resources addressed by the metadata. She describes the possibility of deriving an interoperable composite metadata record thus:

*a viable record can be assembled from the most highly recommended LOM elements. It is descriptively similar to an unqualified Dublin Core record and exhibits regional variation. Such a record lacks the elements for describing the educational, social, and technical contexts required for a successful interaction with a learning object. But application profiles designed primarily for the management of locally produced records, such as ENC, include most of these elements and support a rich description. By contrast, meta-profiles such as CanCore, RDN, and UK LOM Core, which are designed to promote interoperability among similar projects, have far fewer recommended fields.*

After observing that organisations tend either to adopt an abbreviated form of a complete scheme, or to mix elements from different schemes, Sun and Fu (2005) go on to propose a LOM-based application profile, which they argue is sufficiently detailed in terms of educational and technical context to enable successful learning interactions, including *personalised content configuration*—a prime feature of current educational informatics developments, which will be described in Chapters VII and VIII. Qin and Hernandez (2006) argue that there is an urgent need to develop an agreed controlled vocabulary for learning objects at a level of detail not catered for in existing metadata schemes. They also propose a learning objects ontology, which they argue is desirable in order to overcome the limitations of metadata standards to express structural components of learning objects.

Standards are also being developed to describe learning competencies, and learners themselves in terms of, for example, their learning goals, existing levels of knowledge and attainment, learning styles, and preferences. Standards developed for the specification of learning competencies include the IEEE LTSC's (Learning Technology Standards Committee) Draft Standard for Competency Definition Data Objects (IEEE, 2005). Specifications also exist for educational levels, such as those of the Metadata for Education Group (MEG, 2002). Learners themselves may be described using schemes such as IMS LIP (Learner Information Package) (IMS, 2001) and the IEEE LTSC's PAPI (Public and Private Information) draft scheme. This standard (IEEE, 2001):

*defines and/or references elements for recording descriptive information about: knowledge acquisition, skills, abilities, personal contact information, learner relationships, security parameters, learner preferences and styles, learner performance, learner-created portfolios, and similar types of information. This Standard permits different views of the learner information (perspectives: learner, teacher, parent, school, employer, etc.) and substantially addresses issues of privacy and security.*

Two of the most widely used metadata schemes in existence for learners are the IEEE LTSC's Public and Private Information (PAPI) and the IMS LIP. The PAPI standard has a number of categories. The *Personal* category includes the learner's name, postal address, telephone number, and so forth. The *Relations* category enables the specification of relations between the learner and others, including *classmate, teacherIs, teacherOf, instructorIs, instructorOf, belongsTo, belongsWith. Security* includes security credentials including passwords, private keys, public keys, biometrics, and so forth. *Preference* indicates the learner's human-computer interaction preferences including, for example, details of any devices which are particularly useful or unusable by the learner, learning styles, physical limitations, and so forth. *Performance* relates to measured performance of the learner, including grades and reports, past learning achievements, current work, and future learning objectives. *Portfolio* contains a representative indication of the learner's various accomplishments and completed work sufficient to illustrate his or her abilities and achievements. These categories can be extended. The IMS LIPS standard contain categories including: *Identification*; *Goal*; *Activity*; *Interest*; *Relationship*; *Competency*; *Accessibility*; *Transcript*; *Affiliation*; and *Security*.

The following example (adapted and simplified from Dolog et al., 2003) shows an RDF-based LOM metadata record that specifies a particular restriction for accessing the learning resource—indicating that it requires as a prerequisite a PAPI performance score on the part of a learner exceeding 50, assuming a grading scale from 1-100. It also records the fact that the subject matter of this learning resource is topic D.1 in the ACM CCS classification scheme (i.e., Programming Techniques) as in the previous example.

```
<LOM-cls:accessibilityRestrictions
RDF:resource="URL…/PAPI#"/>
<PAPI:performance>
<RDF:Description RDF:ID="performance_1">
<PAPI:learning_competency RDF:resource=
"URL…/ACMCCS.RDF/#D.1"/>
<PAPI:granularity>topic</PAPI:granularity>
<PAPI:performance_coding>number
</PAPI:performance_coding>
```

```
<PAPI:performance_metric>1-100
</PAPI:performance_metric>
<PAPI:performance_value>greater_than(50)
</PAPI:performance_value>
</RDF:Description>
</PAPI:performance>
</LOM-cls:accessibilityRestrictions>
```

An extract from a learner's RDF-based PAPI record, specifying that this learner has in fact achieved a score of 60 on a test of this particular topic, is as follows (again, modified and simplified from Dolog et al., 2003):

```
<RDF:RDF
XMLns:RDF=
"http://www.w3.org/1999/02/22-RDF-syntax-ns#"
XMLns:RDFs=
"http://www.w3.org/2000/01/RDF-schema#"
XMLns:PAPI=
"URL…/PAPI#">
<RDF:Description RDF:ID="student1">
<PAPI:performance>
<RDF:Description RDF:ID="performance_1">
<PAPI:issued_from_identifier RDF:resource=
"URL…/Test_D_1"/>
<PAPI:learning_competency RDF:resource=
"URL…/ACM_CCS.RDF/#D.1"/>
<PAPI:learning_experience_identifier
RDF:resource="URL…/Test_D_1.pdf"/>
<PAPI:granularity>topic</PAPI:granularity>
<PAPI:performance_coding>number
</PAPI:performance_coding>
<PAPI:performance_metric>1-100
</PAPI:performance_metric>
<PAPI:performance_value>60
</PAPI:performance_value>
</PAPI:performance>
</RDF:Description>
</RDF:RDF>
```

Such metadata schemes may be underpinned by ontologies specifying concepts, and relationships between them, which make up the particular domains they represent. To this extent ontologies may be considered models of their domain. However, as well as enabling metadata to be derived from them, ontologies may also be used to infer—from the hierarchical subordination of certain concepts within an ontology—pedagogic knowledge relating, for example, to which concepts are prerequisites for the learning of others. Ontologies may also underpin standards for the specification of pedagogical designs, such as the IMS Global Learning Consortium's Learning Design specification (IMS LD) (IMS, 2003).

Ontologies are agreed structural specifications of what they describe. Thus, an ontology describing a learning design will specify the concepts it entails, including their definition and scope, and their interrelationships. Such an ontology enables learning designs to be described with sufficient clarity and consistency to facilitate sharing, reuse, and interoperability. These issues will be explored in the next chapter, which focuses on ICT-based tools and standards developed to enable and facilitate learning design and teaching.

This chapter has focused on ICT-based developments relating to information seeking and resource discovery—central concerns of *library/information science*. Chapter VI will discuss ICT-based developments relating to learning design and teaching—key concerns of *education*. These elements come together in the development of educational informatics, which represents the intersection of education, library/information science, and ICT. Educational informatics systems will be explored in detail in Chapters VII and VIII.

## References

Association of Computing Machinery (ACM). (2006). *The ACM computing classification system*. Retrieved August 1, 2007, from http://www.acm.org/class/1998/

Dublin Core Metadata Initiative (DCMI). (2002). *DCMI education working group*. Retrieved August 1, 2007 from http://dublincore.org/groups/education/

Dolog, P., Gavriloaie, R., Nejdl, W., & Brase, J. (2003, May 20-24). *Integrating adaptive hypermedia techniques and open RDF-based environments*. Paper presented at the 12th International World Wide Web Conference, Budapest, Hungary, International World Wide Web Conference Committee. Retrieved August 1, 2007, from http://www2003.org/cdrom/papers/alternate/P810/p810-dolog.html

Godby, C. J. (2004). What do application profiles reveal about the learning object metadata standard? *Ariadne, 41*. Retrieved August 1, 2007, from http://www.ariadne.ac.uk/issue41/godby/

IEEE. (2001). *IEEE P1484. Draft standard for learning technology—Public and private information (PAPI) for learners (PAPI Learner)—Draft 8 specification core features*. Retrieved August 1, 2007, from http://edutool.com/PAPI/

IEEE. (2002). *Draft standard for learning object metadata. IEEE 1484.12.1-2002*. Retrieved August 1, 2007, from http://ltsc.ieee.org/wg12/files/LOM_1484_12_1_v1_Final_Draft.pdf

IEEE. (2005). *IEEE learning technology standards committee. WG20: Reusable competency definitions*. Retrieved August 1, 2007, from http://ltsc.ieee.org/wg20/index.html

IMS. (2001). *IMS learner information package specification.* Retrieved August 1, 2007, from http://www.imsglobal.org/profiles/index.html

IMS. (2002*). Learning resource meta-data specification. Version 1.3—Final specification—HTML*. Retrieved August 1, 2007, from http://www.imsglobal.org/metadata/index.html

IMS. (2003). *IMS learning design specification.* Retrieved August 1, 2007, from http://www.imsglobal.org/learningdesign/

Library of Congress. (2002). *MARCXML example documents*. Retrieved August 1, 2007, from http://www.loc.gov/standards/marcXML/Sandburg/sandburg.XML

Library of Congress. (2006a). *Library of Congress. MODS*. Retrieved August 1, 2007, from http://www.loc.gov/standards/mods/

Library of Congress. (2006b). *Library of Congress. METS*. Retrieved August 1, 2007, from http://www.loc.gov/standards/mets/

Metadate for Education Group (MEG). (2002). *List of UK educational levels*. Retrieved August 1, 2007, from http://www.ukoln.ac.uk/metadata/education/documents/ed-level.html

Qin, J., & Hernandez, N. (2006). Building interoperable vocabulary and structures for learning objects. *Journal of the American Society for Library and information science and Technology, 57*(2), 280-292.

Quillian, M. R. (1968). Semantic memory. In M. Minsky (Ed.), *Semantic information processing.* Cambridge, MA: MIT Press.

Spredgar Software. (2007). *Ticker list*. Retrieved August 1, 2007, from http://www.spredgar.com/tickers.htm

Sun, L., & Fu, Y. (2005). Interoperability for e-learning services management and provision. *World Wide Web: Internet and Web Information Systems, 8,* 395-412.

Wikipedia. (2007). *SPARQL*. Retrieved August 1, 2007, from http://en.wikipedia.org/wiki/SPARQL

World Wide Web Consortium (W3C). (2004). *OWL Web ontology language guide*. Retrieved August 1, 2007, from http://www.w3.org/TR/owl-guide/

World Wide Web Consortium (W3C). (2007, June 14). *The SPARQL query language for RDF. W3C candidate recommendation*. Retrieved August 1, 2007, from http://www.w3.org/TR/2007/CR-RDF-sparql-query-20070614/

# Chapter VI

# ICT Developments: Learning Design and Teaching

## Introduction

This chapter is the second of two chapters that explore developments in information and communications technology (ICT). This chapter discusses ICT tools and standards developed to support learning design and teaching. Such developments greatly affect the learning media and modes available for deployment by learning designers. These may enable existing learning designs to be delivered in different ways. However, they may also enable the development of new learning designs.

The chapter begins by reviewing developments relating to computer-assisted learning (CAL), with particular emphasis on intelligent and adaptive tutoring systems that incorporate aspects of artificial intelligence and the use of reasoning mechanisms and knowledge representations to support learning. It goes on to discuss learning environments and management systems, and the move to interoperability, sharing, and reuse, which closely interrelates with resource discovery as discussed in the previous chapter.

This chapter also explores a number of more general ICT developments, while not developed specifically for educational purposes, nevertheless offer new educational opportunities for learning. The chapter goes on to discuss these opportunities, and concludes by further developing the on-going model of learning to integrate the educational affordances provided by the ICT developments introduced in both this and the previous chapter.

## Intelligent and Adaptive Tutoring Systems

Within education, there is a long history of attempts to devise CAL systems designed to provide a level of *personalised* learning in order to respond to what is a key theme in this book, namely: individual differences. CAL systems were created in the 1960s, and worked implicitly with a behaviourist/acquisition-based model of learning. These systems essentially presented learners with problems and recorded their responses. Drill and practice systems followed, and these were the first to move away from the *one presentation for all* mode—although the sophistication of their adaptivity was low.

The 1980s saw the development of intelligent tutoring systems (ITS), when attention began to be paid to the development of more complex models of the learner for use in the system (Chabay & Larkin, 1992; Urban-Lurain, 1996). These developments have continued with the more recent emergence of adaptive hypermedia systems (AHS) (Brusilovsky, 2001; Conlan, Hockemeyer, Wade, & Albert, 2003; De Bra, Aroyo, & Chepegin, 2004).

In terms of media and delivery modes, the late 1980s and early 1990s saw the rapid rise of multimedia and CD ROM-based training, largely superseded in the 1990s by Internet-based training, which matured into the e-learning boom of the early 2000s. The convergence of work on intelligent systems; standards for discovering, sharing, and reusing Web-based learning resources; and technologies supporting the emerging Semantic Web are taken up in Chapters VII and VIII, which focus on the development of *educational informatics* systems.

The essence of intelligent adaptive systems has been the creation of (1) a model of the subject domain in terms of parameters relevant to the presentation and sequencing of information (e.g., a representation denoting *prerequisite* concept relationships); (2) a learner model including details of the learner's existing knowledge, history of learning behaviour within the learning session, and so forth; (3) a pedagogical model specifying some interaction between learner and system (e.g., the type of information that should be presented in relation to particular learner responses and/or characteristics); and (4) some reasoning, or inferencing mechanism that will operationalise the pedagogical model. These elements are shown in Figure 70.

*Figure 70. The architecture of an intelligent adaptive system*

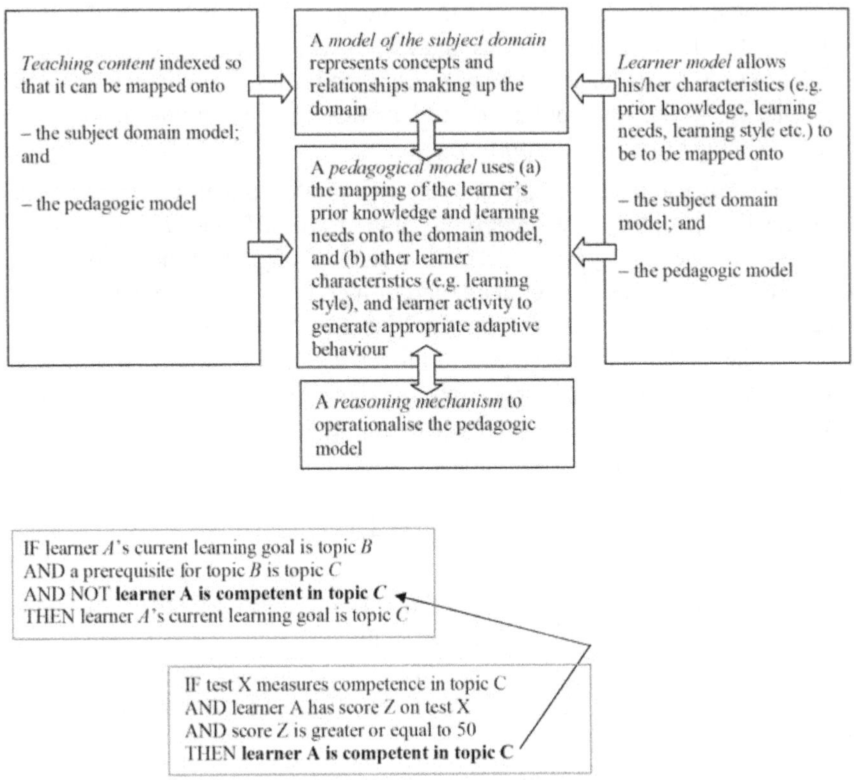


Artificial intelligence displays many facets and strands—philosophical as well as practical—and has a long history of development. For the purposes of this book, it is defined as the science of building computer systems capable of replicating aspects of human expertise. Key concepts include reasoning mechanisms and knowledge representations that enable machines to make inferences. We have already explored the simple use of semantic network-based knowledge representations and rule-based reasoning techniques in the context of the emerging Semantic Web in the previous chapter.

However, before the development of the Web, these and other techniques enabled the development of so-called *expert systems,* which achieved commercial popularity in the 1980s and 1990s. These systems built aspects of human expertise into a system that could utilise it in order to make judgements and decisions comparable with (and in some cases superior to) those made by humans. Systems could routinely explain their lines of reasoning to justify the conclusions they came to.

Many commercial expert system applications were developed in the 1980s and 1990s, designed to function in a wide range of areas of human activity—from industrial plant control through military to medical decision making. Many used explicit and editable inference rules and knowledge representations. Others used techniques such as artificial neural networks (the basics of which were described in Chapter I). These, while not as open to explicit scrutiny, produced a number of systems capable of impressive performance.

However, many useful *drone* applications were produced that were capable of applying relatively routine, low level rules, in the form of *knowledge-based* or *rule-based* rather than expert systems. Yet other systems occupied a middle ground in that they were "smart" rather than either expert or merely drones. Although the type of human expertise that can be built into intelligent systems can include pedagogical expertise, the applications discussed in this book—and characterising most educational informatics development currently—fall more within the smart category than the latter category. Rather than attempting to create educational systems that replicate the high level pedagogical expertise of some super teacher (much as some medical diagnosis systems attempted to replicate the high level expertise of medical experts), many educational systems store and apply often relatively routine rule-based expertise.

However, the end result is smart in that that they do much more than save humans the bother of doing things they could and would do anyway. Rather, they perform and combine routine operations so rapidly, on such a scale, and with networked interactions that would be beyond the scope of what would be possible for humans on their own.

This book does not provide an introduction to the range of reasoning mechanisms and knowledge representations developed over many years within artificial intelligence. For a good introduction to artificial intelligence the reader is referred to the many excellent texts available on the subject. Rather, the present chapter focuses first on a number of education-specific applications that make use of some mechanisms and representations deriving from artificial intelligence.

We explored the simple use of IF... THEN... rules in Chapter V. However, rules may be chained together to form more complex webs of reasoning. Figure 71 shows a very simple single-link chain.

Imagine that the rules that follow are applied to learner John whose current goal is to learn advanced Java programming. In applying these rules to this particular person, we supply the first line with the value $A$ = John. Let us now assume that the system has access to a *learner* database containing information about John. It looks this up and finds that John has indicated that he wants to learn about "advanced Java programming." The variable $B$ is now instantiated with the value "advanced Java programming."

*Figure 71. The simple chaining of rules*

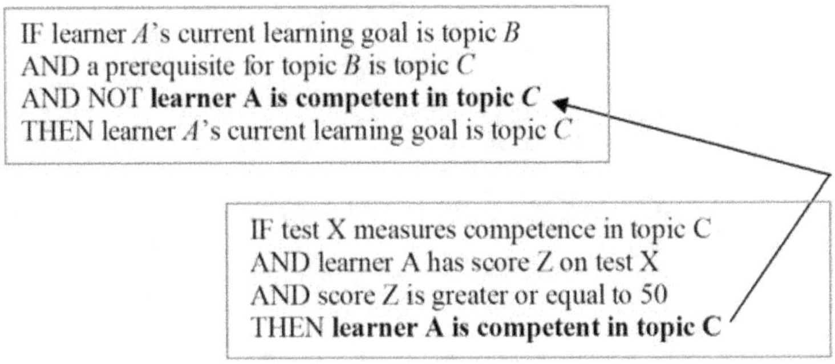


The computer moves on to process the second line of the first rule. It searches to see if it can find a statement that *B* ("advanced Java programming") has some prerequisite (*C*). Typically, a system such as this would have access to an ontology (discussed in Chapter V) or other type of database giving details of topics and their prerequisites. Let us assume that it locates the statement that "Java basics" is a prerequisite for "advanced Java programming." The variable *C* is therefore now instantiated with the value "Java basics."

When the computer processes line 3 of the rule, it tries to establish whether or not John is competent in topic *C* ("Java basics"). However, where the statement that it is trying to establish matches the conclusion of another rule, that rule is applied. Thus the system will apply the second rule. It will pass the values of the variables it has already filled to the new rule, so that when it is applied, the second rule has the values *C* = Java basics and *A* = John.

Line 1 of the second rule will entail looking for information is the system's "tests" database to see if there is a test (*X*) measuring competence in "Java basics." Line 2 of the second rule will cause the system again to search in its learner database to see if there is a statement that John has a score (*Z*) on test *X*. If (1) there is no such statement in the database or (2) John does have a score registered there, but it is below 50, then the system cannot conclude that John is competent in Java basics.

Line 3 of the first rule is therefore true, and therefore all the premises of the rule are satisfied. The system can go on to conclude that John's current learning goal should be changed to "Java basics."

Another key component of such systems is some model of the learner. Such models may take a variety of approaches. A popular approach has been to compare a representation of the learner's knowledge with one of an expert in whatever subject was to be taught. Common approaches were to use the overlay, differential, and

*Figure 72. Overlay model (adapted from Smith, 1998)*

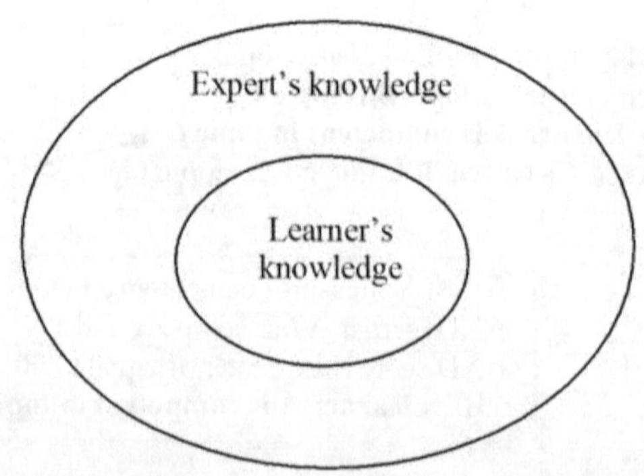


*Figure 73. Differential model (adapted from Smith, 1998)*

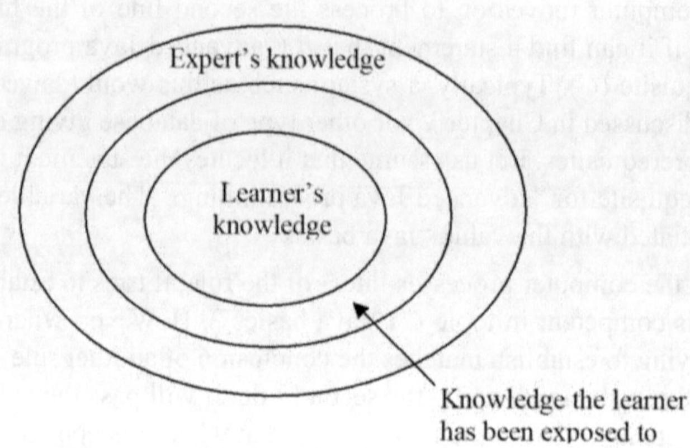


perturbation models. The overlay model limits conceptions of what the learner can know to what the expert knows—other learning on the part of the learner is not allowed for. Figure 72 depicts the simple overlay model.

The differential model (Figure 73) distinguishes between what the learner has been exposed to and can thus be expected to know, and what he/she has not yet been exposed to, and thus cannot be expected to know.

Both the overlay and differential models fail to take into account knowledge that lies outside the expert's knowledge—importantly, errors and misconceptions on the part of the learner. This is addressed by the perturbation model (Figure 74). This model entails the creation of an error library of common or probable mistakes and misconceptions that could be used in the teaching strategy.

*Figure 74. Perturbation model (adapted from Smith, 1998)*

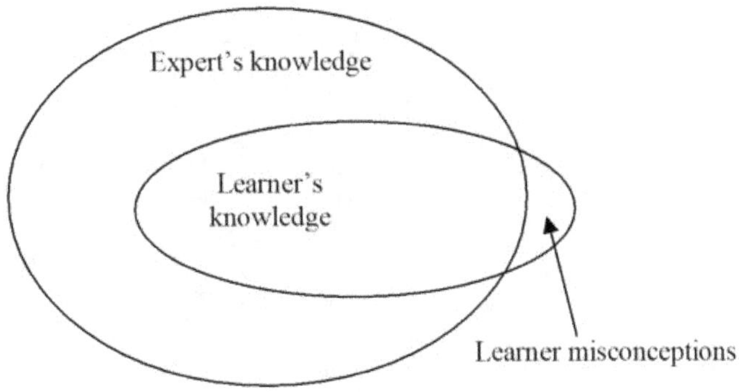


Another key component of such systems is some representation of subject domain knowledge, which may be used to represent both to-be-learned subject content and learners' existing knowledge. Many forms of knowledge representation have been developed over the years for a variety of purposes. As we saw in Chapter V, library classifications and thesauri, for example, may represent hierarchical relationships, and broader, narrower, and related concepts. Devices such as semantic networks and frames have been used in psychology and artificial intelligence to represent a great variety of concept relationships. Aspects of these representations come together in ontologies, which are able to represent not only conceptual components making up a domain, their definitions, and interrelationships, but also rules to enable the intelligent inferencing that forms a vital component in the emerging Semantic Web.

Knowledge representations can be simple or complex, as can the reasoning mechanisms applied to them. The knowledge represented can relate to learners and learning materials as well as subject domains, as in this simple example. The following knowledge can be easily represented in a simple semantic network, shown in Figure 75.

**Learner ID 234**

*Language*: English

*Current learning goal*: Maths level 2

*Subjects completed*: Maths level 1

*Learning style*: visualiser

*etc.*

*Figure 75. Semantic network representation of educational metadata*

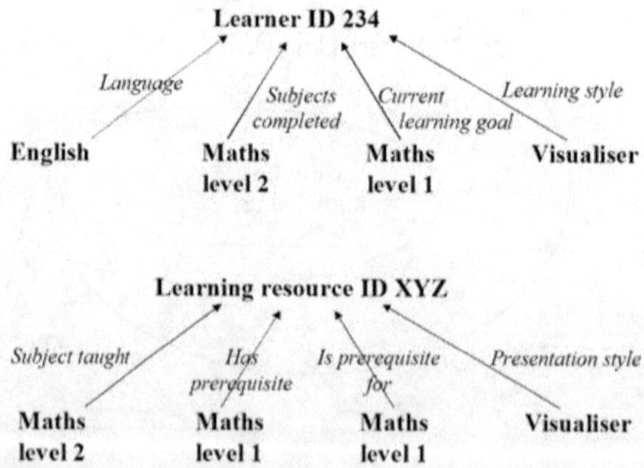


**Learning resource ID XYZ**

> *Subject taught*: Maths:
> *Has prerequisite*: Maths level 1
> *Is prerequisite for*: Maths level 3
> *Presentation style*: visual
> *etc.*

The following rule can be used to find learning materials that are appropriate for a particular learner.

Learning resource *X* is appropriate for Learner *Y*
IF Learner *Y* has Current learning goal *A*
AND Learning resource *X* has Subject taught *A*
AND Learning resource *X* has Prerequisite *B*
AND Learner *Y* has Subjects completed *B*
AND Learner *Y* has Learning style *C*
AND Learning resource *X* has Presentation style *C*

This rule will find learning materials that are (1) designed to teach the learner's current learning goals, (2) at an appropriate level in that the learner has already successfully gained the knowledge required for studying this particular resource, and (3) presented in a style that is compatible with the learner's preferred learning style.

Such knowledge representations are often used to express logical relationships between concepts (*broader, narrower, is-a, part-of, instance-of,* etc.). However, although effective learning depends on the manipulation of *logical* relationships, it also depends on a range of *pedagogical* relationships between concepts. These are not generally—though they are capable of being—expressed in such representations (as opposed to the rules which operate on them). A number of knowledge representations, developed particularly within education, *do* express pedagogical relationships, relating essentially to the *learnability* of the components of a subject domain. For example, a relatively well developed and increasingly widely used form of representation is based on "knowledge space theory" (Albert & Hockemeyer, 1997; Albert & Lukas, 1999; Taagepera, Potter, Miller, & Lakshminarayan, 1997). This maps concept relationships in terms of which concepts must be understood as prerequisites for the understanding of other concepts.

*Figure 76. Inner and outer fringes of knowledge states in knowledge space theory (adapted from ALEKS, n.d.)*

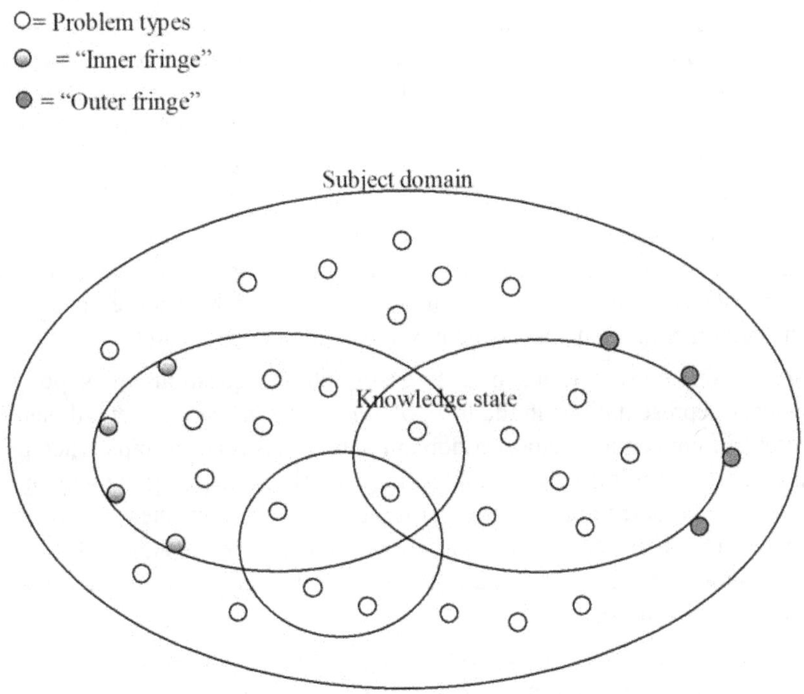

Using knowledge space theory, a subject domain to be learned may be represented as a set of *items*—essentially problems or questions. The ability to solve or answer them constitutes understanding of that domain. Typically, there are many instances (or instantiations) of each item, which can be used to teach and/or demonstrate understanding of the item. A learner's *knowledge state* in relation to a domain at any particular time is the set of items within the domain that are understood. Understanding of a given item implies understanding of any other items that are prerequisites of that item. Since a given item may be a prerequisite of more than one other item, there may be very many alternative—but equally legitimate—pathways to learning within a domain.

From any given knowledge state, there will be certain as-yet-unlearned items that can be learned *immediately,* that is, for which the learner already possesses the prerequisite understanding. Equally, there will be other items that *cannot* be learned immediately, that is, for which the learner does not understand all prerequisite items. Those items that are immediately learnable from a particular knowledge state form the *outer fringe* of that knowledge state. The *inner fringe* of a knowledge state consists of all those items that could legitimately have been the last one learned to bring about that knowledge state, that is, understanding of which brought about the move from a previous knowledge state to the present one (Figure 76).

Knowledge space theory has been used as the basis for a number of intelligent tutoring systems, including Assessment and Learning in Knowledge Spaces (ALEKS) (n.d.), a system for teaching mathematics at college and university levels. In ALEKS, navigation paths are restricted so that new items (problems) offered to learners will always be from the outer fringe of the learner's current knowledge state. If a learner is experiencing difficulties in learning a particular item, however, the system reviews his or her understanding of items in the inner fringe that are prerequisites for the item proving difficult.

Pask and his associates, in their work on *conversation theory*, developed computer-based approaches to (1) the analysis, structuring, and representation of knowledge domains, (2) the monitoring of learning strategies using these representations, and (3) the demonstration and assessment of the resultant understanding.

In Pask's work, conversations, including *why* and *how* questions, are supported by knowledge representations in the form of *entailment meshes*. An entailment mesh represents a conceptual map of a domain and shows relationships whereby topics are defined in terms of other topics. Particularly in mapping the way in which topics are constructed in terms of other topics, entailment meshes provide support for interactions between learners and information sources as they seek to achieve understanding. This support is made possible by the particular qualities possessed by a *well-formed* mesh.

An entailment mesh is essentially a map of topics linked via *coherences*—each topic in a given coherence entailing, and being entailed by, the others. The meaning of

*Figure 77. Topics grouped into three coherences (adapted from Ford, 2005)*

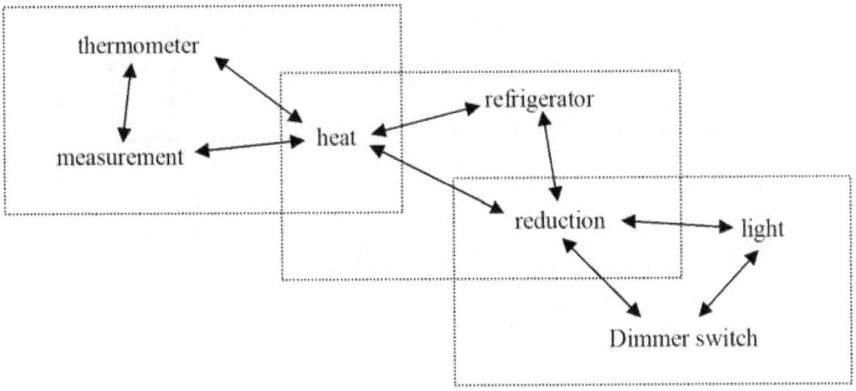


any topic must be unambiguously derivable from the relationship between the other topics in the coherence. For example: the meaning of *thermometer* may be derived from the relationship between *heat* and *measurement*. Heat may be understood as what a thermometer measures, while measurement may be understood as what a thermometer does in relation to heat. As shown in Figure 77, a topic may belong to more than one coherence. Every topic must belong to at least one coherence.

The knowledge representation may be *unfolded* (via a process Pask termed "pruning") from the point of view of any starting topic. Thus an information seeker could enter an entailment structure at any point and be provided with a complete conceptual map of related topics created from that perspective. An example is shown in Figure 78, where a mesh is unfolded from the perspectives of two different entry points. Pruning also enables automatic checking for inconsistencies, ambiguities, gaps, and conflicts in the knowledge representation.

*Figure 78. An entailment mesh unfolded from two starting points (adapted from Ford, 2005)*

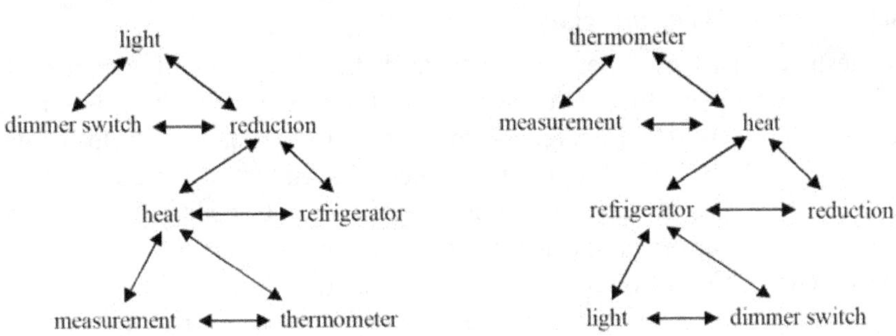

*Figure 79. A more complex entailment mesh (adapted from Ford, 2005)*

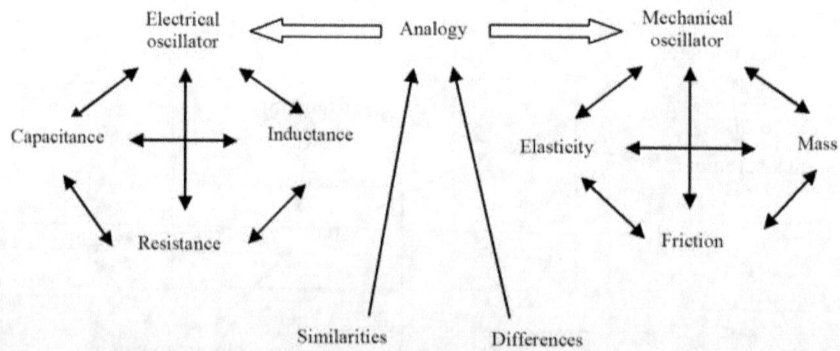


Figure 79 shows an example of a more complex entailment mesh. Double arrows depict analogy relationships and, as shown in the figure, an analogy can itself be a topic.

To an extent, entailment meshes are similar to other knowledge representations such as classifications, thesauri, semantic networks, and ontologies in that they may serve a similar function, that is, to support concept navigation and the establishment of a conceptual overview (description building) on the part of the information seeker. However, entailment meshes are more limited in that they are not expressive of semantic relationships other than *analogous to* and *derived from*; though via the latter relationships they can express the notion of *prerequisite* concepts. This sparseness of logical, as opposed to pedagogical, expression is explored in the penultimate section of this chapter, where work on extending meshes to include such logical relationships is described.

However, importantly, entailment meshes in conversation theory possess certain other characteristics, designed to optimise understanding, that are not necessarily present in other representations. Pask established three defining properties for a well-formed entailment mesh. These properties are designed to render the topic structure formally coherent by removing from it gaps, ambiguities, and contradictions. A well-formed entailment mesh should display *consistency*, *cyclicity,* and what Pask termed "*cognitive glue.*"

The mesh is consistent if there are no contradictions whereby different aspects of meaning of a topic conflict with one another. It possesses cyclicity—or *closure* to use the term preferred by researchers working in this area at the UK Open University (Zimmer, 2001)—if all topics are connected such that, if there is a relational link from topic A to B, there is also one from B to A. Cyclicity militates against the existence of gaps (e.g., the absence of an aspect of meaning of a topic) in the topic structure. "Cognitive glue"—or *connectivity* (Zimmer, 2001)—is the density of interrelationships between topics, whereby a given topic has rich links to (e.g., is used in the explanation of) other topics. This militates against the omission of any important topic relationships in the entailment mesh. These properties ensure the coherence, and thus understandability, of complex bodies of information.

All the concepts making up a classification, thesaurus, semantic network, or knowledge space are ultimately interconnected, and ontologies may include rules stipulating how concepts may be related to each other in a logical fashion. However, an entailment mesh differs from such other forms of knowledge representation in that to a far greater extent it represents a gestalt. All the topics contained in the mesh are interrelated via *entailment* relationships—the mesh *as a whole* being required to display cyclicity, consistency, and rich connectivity. The other knowledge representations discussed previously are not required to display *in their entirety* such properties. In an entailment mesh, topics are interrelated holistically in the sense that a change in the way one is defined has implications affecting others to which it is linked. In this way, the effects of changes permeate through the mesh as a result of the need to maintain consistency, cyclicity, and connectivity.

In representing the analysis of complex bodies of knowledge in terms of their understandability (how topics are defined in terms of each other and how they relate to other topics to form a coherent conceptual system), entailment meshes can:

- Represent the conceptual structures (understandings) of different individuals (e.g., learners, teachers, information source authors).
- Render such conceptual structures susceptible to checking for coherence. Their holistic properties enable the automatic detection of ambiguities, gaps, and contradictions as new knowledge is added.
- Facilitate the *comparison* of different understandings (e.g., those of learner and teacher) and the identification of points of agreement and disagreement, as well as inconsistencies and contradictions within conceptual structures (the essence of Paskian conversations).
- Represent different but *equally valid* understandings constituting different perspectives, and different constructed *realities*—not just different routes to the same ("expert") level of understanding. As noted by Pangaro (1997), entailment meshes can be used to represent the shared understanding of groups and communities as well as the idiosyncratic understanding of particular individuals:

  *... multiple authors, possibly at different sites, can contribute to the same knowledge base without interfering with each other. ... THOUGHTSTICKER keeps individual authors' identities distinct, and so can produce responses of the form, 'A similar statement was made by so-and-so author on such-and-such a date; would you like to see that statement?' ... And this leads into perhaps the most profound contribution of entailment meshes to mental modelling and knowledge acquisition, that of contradiction detection and resolution.*

- Enable individuals flexibly to enter a conceptual structure at any selected point and, via an entailment mesh's unfoldment capability, to be presented with a fully navigable representation of the entire conceptual structure emanating from that starting point. Entailment meshes allow an individualised yet holistically coherent unfoldment from any entry point.
- Facilitate effective learning in that due to their properties (previously discussed) well-formed meshes are, according to Pask's theoretical and related empirical work, supportive of promoting deep, and consequently enduring, understanding.

However, despite its rich pedagogic expressability, the capacity of entailment meshes to specify logical relationships is sparse in comparison with other forms of knowledge representation such as classifications, thesauri, semantic networks, and ontologies. Yet effective learning depends on a range of concept relationships including logical (e.g., *part-of, instance-of*) as well as pedagogic (e.g., *prerequisite, entailment*). It may therefore be desirable to be able to access and move between different types of representation as required to address different learning needs at different times. One approach to this problem would be to explore the extent to which entailment meshes could be integrated with, as opposed simply to communicating with, other knowledge representations. Indeed, interesting work has been conducted in relation to this issue. Heylighen (2001), for example, has developed a knowledge representation formalism that preserves the coherence qualities associated with well-formed entailment meshes while allowing links between topics to be labelled in terms of logical relationships. In a sense, such logical concept relationships may be thought of as a semantic network *overlaid* onto the basic entailment mesh structure. Entailment meshes do not per se possess transitivity, that is, the links between topic nodes are not directed. Nor are the links labelled as they are in semantic networks. However, if we impose a layer on top of an entailment mesh—or, as Heylighen (2001) puts it "choose to focus attention on that part of the entailment relation that is transitive" (p. 704)—then, Heylighen argues, the entailment relation may be interpreted as an if…then relation. Via logical inferences these can in turn be abstracted to represent a range of basic types of node including *class, object, property, situation, change,* and *event*.

Heylighen (2001) notes that:

*If we follow the entailment relation 'upward' between classes we will reach ever more abstract or more general distinctions, e.g. dog –> carnivore –> mammal –> vertebrate –> animal –> organism –> object. The most abstract can be interpreted as the philosopher's 'categories', the most basic or universal distinctions which underlie our understanding of the universe. These fundamental concepts can be said to define an 'ontology', i.e. a theory of the most fundamental categories of existence, such as time, space, matter, truth, cause and effect. These ontological distinctions can be interpreted as basic node types, which allow a classification of other, more concrete nodes.* (p. 705)

Further abstractions can result in a range of basic links including: *a-kind-of, has-part, implies, causes, produces, precedes, involve,* and *instance-of.* Inheritance can also be incorporated, enabling the use of frames. Importantly, such a superstructure is built on—but does not destroy—the entailment integrity of the basic mesh. That is, the mesh still retains its properties of consistency, cyclicity, and connectivity, which enable contradiction, gap, and ambiguity checking. Heylighen (2001) states:

*...the constraints inherent in the ... ontology (and in entailment nets in general) force the user to make implicit – but necessary – distinctions explicit, thus avoiding ambiguities and gaps in the knowledge system.* (p. 709)

More specific, concrete labels can be associated with nodes and links. While handling the associations would be complex and require computer support, it would nevertheless be possible to access the underlying entailments—thus enabling coherence checking and associated authoring support. Thus, this form of representation (Heylighen, 2001):

*...allows us to reduce a complicated set of semantic categories to an extremely simple and flexible formal structure. The disadvantage is that many more links are needed in order to reduce various link types to nodes than if the links could simply be labeled by their types. However, the burden of keeping track of all the links will normally rest on the computer, and not on the user, who could work with a higher level representation using typed links, perhaps mixed with untyped links for those cases where the type may not be clear. All these links will be reduced by the computer to their generic, untyped form in order to test for ambiguity according to the bootstrapping axiom.* (p. 710)

What Heylighen (2001) terms "bootstrapping" in the previous quotation is equivalent to the mutually supportive derivational links inherent in Pask's entailment meshes.

A substantial amount of work has already been accomplished in relation to providing computer-based assistance in such tasks. Pask's THOUGHTSTICKER programme (Pask, 1975, 1976, 1990; Pask & Gregory, 1986) was able to converse with information providers (e.g., subject experts wishing to create an entailment structure for particular topics and domains), applying rules and procedures to establish coherence. This work was taken up by Pangaro (2001), who further developed the system.

*Table 27. Interaction between a subject expert and THOUGHTSTICKER (adapted from Pangaro, 1997)*

| System | User |
|---|---|
| Describe a topic | Flight |
| What is significant about flight? | Flight is achieved via air resistance to a spinning surface |
| Your statement may conflict with another statement made by user X that: "Flight is achieved via air resistance to a flapping surface." Do you wish to keep that statement? | Yes |
| Is flight different in each statement? | Yes |
| The system engages in further dialogue and establishes that this topic coherence relates to the flight of winged seeds, as opposed to the flight of birds forming the focus of the another author who had previously defined flight. It then instantiates an analogy between bird flight and winged seed flight. | |

Table 27 shows a hypothetical interaction with an author using such a system, who wishes to create a knowledge representation relating to *winged seeds*. In this example, another user *X* has already been using the system to generate a knowledge representation relating to bird flight.

ICT-based support has been extended to include not only teaching and resource discovery, but also problem solving and creativity more generally.

Problem solving is a key component in education as well as in the performance of real world work and life tasks. Complex problem solving requires the generation of integrating themes at a relatively high level of abstraction. However, still higher levels of abstraction are required before computer support systems can manipulate and retrieve similarity relationships at the level of problem/solution structures, reasoning strategies, argumentation, and analogy-based reasoning across a wide range of subject domains.

Some work has been conducted, in relatively narrow subject domains, for example into the computation of argumentation (Saeedi & Sillinace, 1999; Sillince, 1995; Vreeswijk, 1993, 1995), case-based reasoning based on analogy representations (Kolodner, 1993), the modelling of analogical reasoning (Mitchell, 1993) and information extraction (Gaizauskas & Wilks, 1998). Such work entails the development of knowledge representations, which operate at relatively high levels of abstraction.

Argumentation systems represent the components and structures of argumentation in such a way to enable the mapping of patterns of argument and counter argument, and the identification of similarities and differences. A number of interactive argumentation systems are available, for example, the InterACtive Argumentation System (IACAS) (Vreeswijk, 1995). A system which maps academic argumentation (Stutt & Motta, 2004) will be described in some detail in Chapter VIII.

A simple example of machine-based argumentation is given in Sillince (1995). Concepts such as *fairness* and *reciprocity* can be encoded into representations able to support machine-based argumentation. Sillince gives the following example of a Prolog-like representation of fairness:

1. exists (current_claim (Arguer), claim (Other))
2. AND equal (current_claim (Arguer), current_claim (Other))
3.1.1 AND (strong (current_claim (Other))
3.1.2 OR accepted (current_claim (Other)))
3.2 AND not_exists (claim (Arguer), claimed (opponent, not_fair (claim (Arguer))))

Sillince (1995) explains that this may be used:

*when arguer's claim is equivalent to other's claim (1 and 2), and the other's claim has been accepted or is likely to be (3.1.1 or 3.1.2) and the other has not claimed that the arguer's claims have been unfair (3.2)* (p. 2)

Many different instances of arguer and claim would match this higher order representation.

Case-based reasoning attempts to discover similarities between stored cases of solved problems in such a way that new problems may be solved by retrieving answers to old but relevant ones. Generally, in relation to a new problem, the most similar case that can be found is retrieved, and if necessary adapted. If used successfully to solve the particular problem, it is stored for possible future application. Research has also been conducted into the modelling of analogical reasoning (French, 2002; Hofstadter, 1995; Mitchell, 1993). Information extraction systems utilise structured knowledge representations, which specify, for example, complex events, situations, or relationships that the system is tasked to find out about or monitor. These specifications are then used to search for information to fill the *slots*. Such systems are often set up to search unstructured natural language text.

A number of systems have also been developed to support the divergent thinking underlying creative thinking as discussed in Chapters I and II, with the aim of promoting creative outputs (Eaglestone, Ford, Brown, & Moore, 2007). As Greene notes (2002):

*Computer tools can facilitate creativity on at least two fairly distinct levels: they can aid in knowledge gathering, knowledge sharing, knowledge integration, and ultimately, idea generation; and they can enable the generation of creative artifacts in a particular domain by providing critical functionality in clear, direct, and useful ways.* (p. 100)

A number of researchers have conducted empirical studies into the effects of ICT-based systems on levels of creativity in problem solving (Elam & Mead, 1987; Marakas & Elam, 1997). Shneiderman (2002) lists a range of techniques which have been used, and Greene (2002) proposes a number of characteristics of software that can facilitate creativity—a number of which match the techniques discussed by Shneiderman. According to Greene, creativity may be facilitated by software which supports activities including: *"pain-free" exploration* (allowing people to backtracking and make u-turns without penalty); *active discovery learning*; *collaboration*; and *support and encouragement for instructive mistakes*. On the basis of observations of use of the Explore Modern Art system, Greene (2002) notes that:

*it became evident just how useful certain kinds of errors could be if they were instructive mistakes. ... As they examined a series of trials one could clearly hear them develop a hypothesis. They would then happen on a trial in which the use of that hypothesis would lead them to choose incorrectly. They would then regroup their thoughts and discover new things.* (p. 104)

## Learning Environments and Interoperability

Early computer-based learning (CAL) systems, although they made use of pedagogic knowledge in their functioning, did not engage in resource discovery in order to search for and integrate learning content from other sources. Early systems were content bound in the sense that content and control were closely linked. Typically, intelligent features were constructed with reference to the particular content that the system was being designed to teach. Knowledge representation schemes were relatively inextricably linked to their control structures.

The advent of ITS did not bring with it any easy ability to slot in alternative content. Later knowledge-based tutoring systems (KBTS) and the availability of software such as expert system *shells* with which they could be built, on the other hand, were characterised by a separation of content and control in that knowledge representations were explicit and editable independently from the inference and other control (e.g., explanation) facilities. Content was represented in agreed formalisms that were supported by standard inference techniques such as backward and forward chaining rule systems.

The content of those rules was obtained via knowledge engineering specific to particular areas of content, and represented in agreed formalisms that were supported by standard inference techniques such as backward and forward chaining rule systems. Knowledge-based and expert system shells were not content bound in that they could be used to generate intelligent systems in different subject and problem areas. Also, Pask's THOUGHTSTICKER system also supported the development of entailment structures across different topic areas. However, the notion of sharing such systems was still relatively limited. Work on intelligent educational systems continues, and with an increasing focus on the integration of resource discovery using educational metadata, it constitutes an important strand in the development of educational informatics, as detailed in Chapters VII and VIII.

At the level of course management, there has been a relatively recent take-up by organisations delivering education and training of computer-based systems that support learning and teaching that are designed to slot in alternative content. Basically these act as a shell into which different subject content can be slotted. Early virtual learning environments (VLEs) and learning management systems (LMSs) were not characterised by interoperability. Courses developed for one system could not necessarily be imported by another. Recent years, however, have seen the development of standards designed to support the sharing and reuse of learning resources, and to promote interoperability between different delivery systems.

Terminology varies, as does usage of the different terms. A learning content management system (LCMS) is sometimes distinguished from a course management system (CMS) or LMS in that the latter does not always offer authoring tools enabling the development and management of learning content, but rather focuses on the presented of such content and the management of learning. VLE is sometimes used more generically to refer to the class of learning support systems.

National usage differs, with CMS and LMS being more commonly used in the USA (LMS being used in corporate training, CMS in educational institutions), VLE and MLE being used in the UK. According to the UK Joint Information Systems Committee Managed Learning Environment Steering Group (JISC) (2007):

*VLE refers to the components in which learners and tutors participate in "online" interactions of various kinds, including online learning.*

An MLE is:

*the whole range of information systems and processes of a college (including its VLE if it has one) that contribute directly, or indirectly, to learning and the management of that learning.*

The main functions provided by a VLE, according to JISC (2007), are:

- Controlled access to curriculum that has been mapped to elements (or "chunks") that can be separately assessed and recorded
- Tracking student activity and achievement against these elements using simple processes for course administration and student tracking that make it possible for tutors to define and set up a course with accompanying materials and activities to direct, guide and monitor learner progress
- Support of online learning, including access to learning resources, assessment and guidance. The learning resources may be self-developed, or professionally authored and purchased materials that can be imported and made available for use by learners
- Communication between the learner, the tutor and other learning support specialists to provide direct support and feedback for learners, as well as peer-group communications that build a sense of group identity and community of interest
- Links to other administrative systems, both inhouse and externally

Basically these act as a shell into which different subject content can be slotted. The types of interaction supported by these systems include information access and presentation (for example, learner or teacher controlled), and the gathering of feedback on student learning via tests of their performance during and/or after learning. Some adaptivity may be built in by which the nature of subsequent interaction with each learner depends on such feedback. To take a simple example, failure to achieve a particular level of success on a test may result in the learner being routed to some remedial instructional content. However, early VLEs and MLEs were not characterised by interoperability. Courses developed for one system could not necessarily be imported by another.

Recent years, however, have seen the development of techniques and standards designed to support the sharing and reuse of learning resources and to promote interoperability between different VLEs and MLEs. There has been much interest in the development of reusable *learning objects*, along with standards for describing, structuring, and utilising them. Many VLEs exist, and they differ according not only to the facilities they offer, but also the learning philosophies behind them. For ease of illustration, we will briefly look at two such systems: WebCT and the Learning Activity Management System (LAMS).

WebCT is a widely used LMS offering a range of facilities to support teachers and learners. It is pedagogically neutral to the extent that it is possible and relatively easy to design WebCT courses entailing individual or group-based learning, using didactic or problem-based exploratory approaches, geared towards the acquisition

*Figure 80. WebCT*

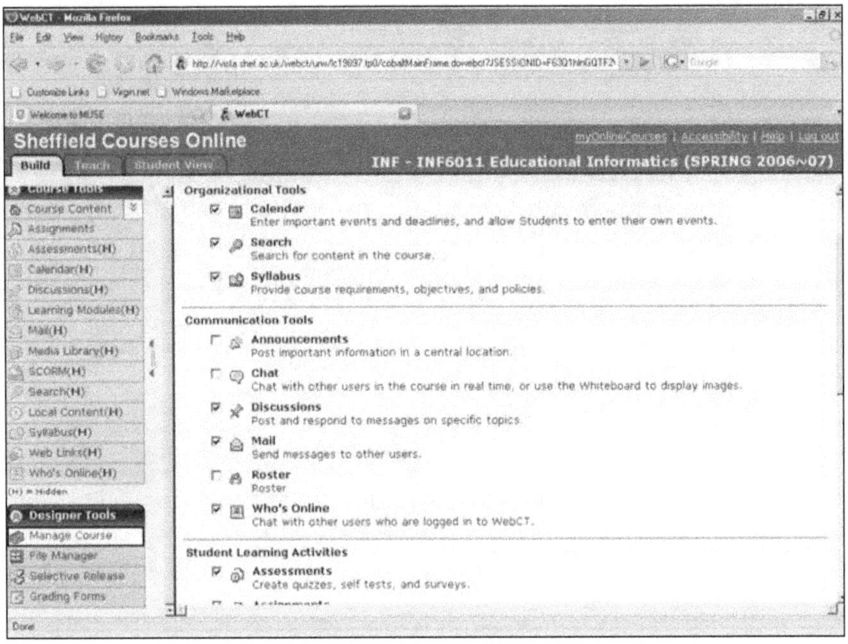


of specified learning content and its assessment, or more open-ended socially participative goals.

As can be seen in Figure 80, as well as content presentation in the form of documents in a variety of formats, WebCT offers discussion boards, e-mail, and chat, as well as a variety of assessment activities including quizzes, surveys, and self-tests. Materials and activities can be scheduled to be made available at particular times.

Laanpere, Põldoja, and Kikkas (2004) argue that the pedagogical neutrality of LMS may serve to inhibit the use of innovative teaching approaches:

*...there is little empirical proof regarding the strength of this link between new learning environments and innovative educational practices. Teachers seem to use up-to-date Learning Management Systems (LMS) in conservative way, mostly for publishing texts and collecting homework. But maybe we should not blame the teachers, maybe the outdated practices are promoted also by the most modern learning environments? [...] [The] trend towards taken-for-granted pedagogical neutrality of LMS is mainly good for marketing purposes. From the viewpoint of pedagogical innovation, the built-in pedagogical neutrality of LMS increases the alienation of theoretical discourse of educational science and technology from the*

*Figure 81. LAMS' drag and drop authoring interface*

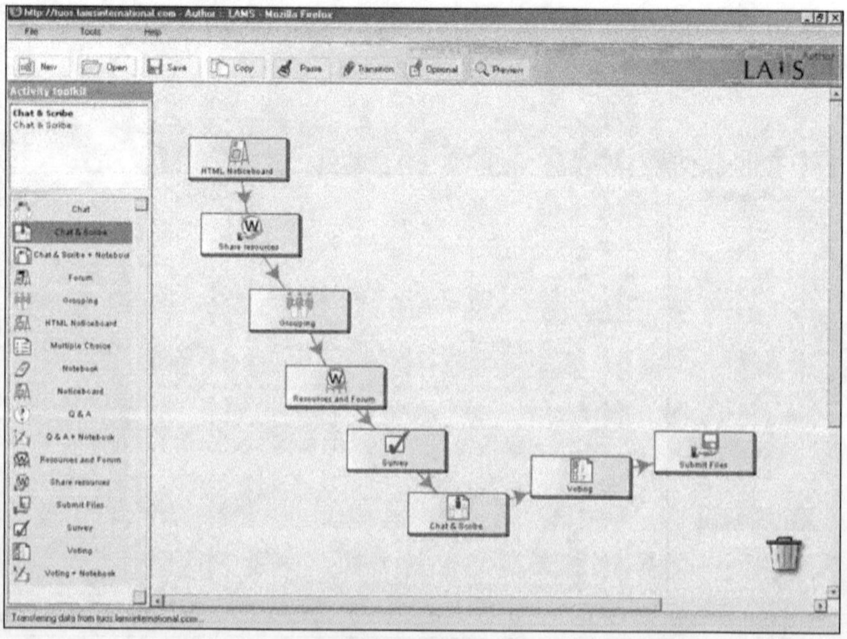

*practice of teaching and learning. One solution would be designing a 'pedagogically biased' LMS ...*

The LAMS LMS is pedagogically biased in that it is built explicitly to support particular models of learning more than others. It is based on, and seeks to provide particular support for, learning designs created in accordance with the Educational Modelling Language (EML).

As Dalziel (2003) notes, LAMS is based on, and inspired by, EML and Instructional Managmenet System Learning Design (IMS LD). In learning design according to IMS LD:

*... the main elements tend to include greater focus on "context" dimensions of e-learning (rather than simply "content"), a more "activity" based view of e-learning (rather than "absorption"), and greater recognition of the role of "multi-learner" (rather than just single learner) environments. While Learning design does not exclude single learner, self-paced modes of elearning, it draws attention to a wider range of collaborative e-learning approaches in addition to single learner approaches. Much of the focus on Learning design arises from a desire for re-use and adaptation at a level above simply re-using and adapting content objects.* (pp. 593-594)

*Figure 82. LAMS' Share resources activity authoring screen*

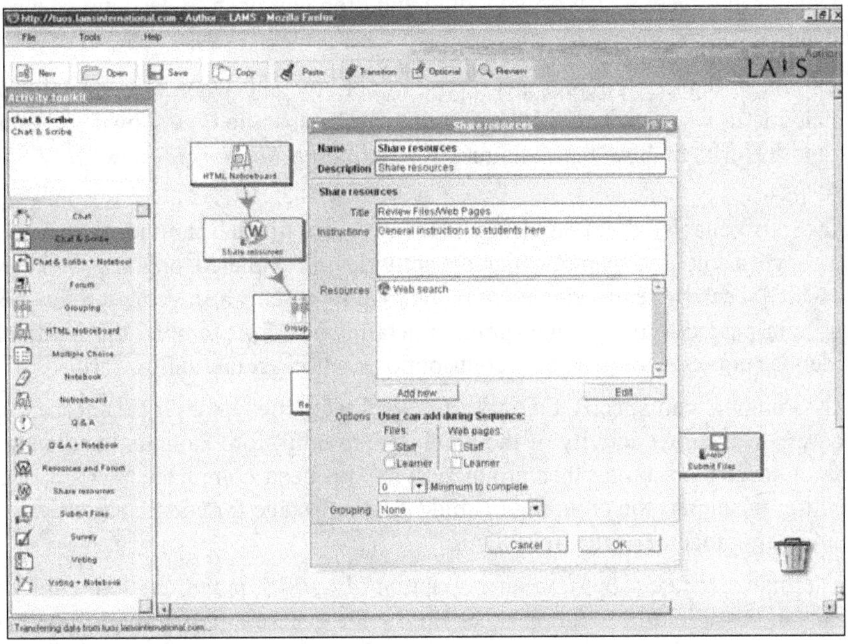


*Figure 83. LAMS' Survey activity authoring screen*

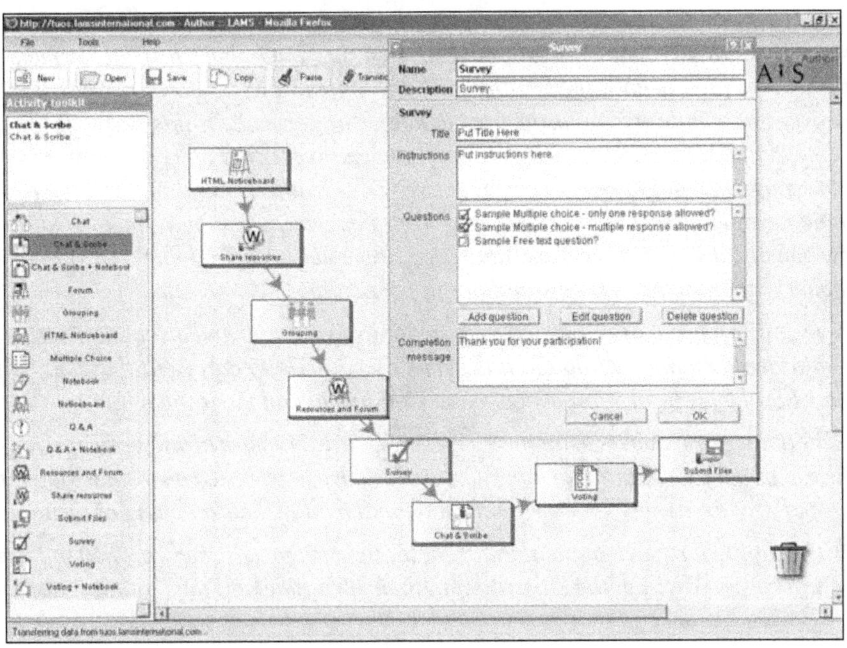

LAMS is based on the notion of sequences of learning activities. Figure 81 shows the author interface, which offers a drag and drop approach to designing such sequences.

Each box in Figure 81 represents a type of activity, and when clicked will open a dialogue in which details of the activity can be specified, as shown in Figures 82 and 83, which show the dialogues for setting up *Share resources* and *Survey activities*.

LAMS also enables the monitoring of the progress of each individual and entire classes via a coloured map in which the activities—completed, ongoing, and as yet untackled—can be seen. Each node in the map represents a student, and this node can be inspected to reveal finer-grained detail about, for example, that particular student's responses to questions, contribution to discussions, and so forth.

LAMS authors can specify the order in which activities take place, and can halt progress to the next activity of the whole group until, for example, results are in from a survey, or some other group activity has been completed. LAMS offers facilities to support the grouping of students at any stage for certain activities, and their coming together again for others.

Masterman and Lee (2005), in an evaluation of LAMS, note that although by no means impossible or difficult in other LMSs, the generation of activity-based and socially participative learning designs is particularly well supported by the facilities in LAMS which enable the easy orchestration and monitoring of learning activities:

*... at least one teacher found that using LAMS had prompted him to shift away from a didactic to a more social-constructivist approach, but this is not something that would have been either "difficult" or "impossible" before, neither had he uncovered a whole new approach to teaching in general. In this respect, the use of LAMS had simply awakened him to an alternative, existing, approach which he then recognised might be more productive. Thus, rather than look for evidence of whole new pedagogies within the data from this trial, we should look for signs of new dimensions to the individual activities, or sequences of activities, that comprise teachers' approaches. Three stand out in particular:*

*i) The ability for teachers to bring together online research and discussion activities in an ordered manner. Although it is perfectly possible to carry out these activities in a VLE, the orchestration aspect is lacking in such an environment.*

*ii) The ability for teachers to analyse, at leisure, the exchanges in online discussions in order to provide feedback that otherwise would have to be based on memory or rough notes of oral exchanges and/or to reflect on and modify their teaching of the topic.*

*iii) The ability for teachers to monitor their students' progress even when the latter are working away from the classroom in their own time and thus to intervene with advice when trouble seems to be looming without having to wait for the student to realise they need help.* (p. 33)

The Modular Object-Oriented Dynamic Learning Environment (MOODLE) is an open source LMS designed to support constructivist and social constructivist approaches to learning design; although is it also capable of providing straightforward knowledge acquisition modes of learning if required. Features that facilitate the reflection, interaction, negotiation, and collaboration that characterise constructivist and social constructivist learning include wikis, blogs, chat, forums, and peer assessment.

MOODLE also enables quizzes; RSS and Atom feeds; and both individual and group coursework submission. It offers content management and enables the importing of courses from other systems including WebCT and LAMS, and MOODLE adheres to a number of widely accepted standards including SCORM, IMS Question and Test Interoperability (QTI), and IMS Content Packaging (these are described later on). As its name states, MOODLE is modular, and many third party plug ins are available.

The developments discussed previously have brought into prominence the role of resource discovery. As discussed in Chapters VII and VIII, an important strand of educational informatics is represented by work integrating course construction with metadata-based resource discovery to provide personalised learning experiences. These developments are closely related to the emergence of the concept of reusable learning objects in which there has been much interest, along with standards for describing, structuring, and utilising them.

According to Casey and McAlpine (n.d.):

*A learning object is any resource or content object that is supplied to a learner by a provider with the intention of meeting the learner's learning objective(s)....and is used by the learner to meet that learning objective(s).*

The Shareable Content Object Reference Model (SCORM), developed by the Advanced Distributed Learning (ADL) initiative of the U.S. Department of Defence and the White House Science and Technology Bureau ("ADL releases SCORM", 2006; "ADL Reaches a Milestone", 2006), details how learning objects should be structured and packaged in order to facilitate reuse and incorporation within different learning environments (Bohl, Schellhase, Sengler, & Winand, 2002). SCORM uses the term "sharable content object" to describe "a learning object that has the appropriate metadata, and is packaged according to the SCORM" (Ploetz, 2004). According to Bohl et al. (2002):

*SCORM denominates the smallest unit which can be administered by an LMS as a Sharable Content Object (SCO). A Sharable Content Object (SCO) represents one or more assets which use the SCORM run- time environment to communicate with different LMSs. An SCO represents the lowest level of content granularity which can be tracked by an LMS. An SCO should be independent of learning context to be reusable in different learning situations. Moreover, several SCOs can be assembled to form learning or exercise units on a super ordinate level. To make a potential reuse practicable, SCOs should be small units. They can be the basis for sharable content repositories which facilitate their exchange.* (p. 950)

SCORM also provides guidelines, in the form of the SCORM content aggregation model (CAM), for the aggregation of SCOs to form learning objects of larger granularity ("ADL SCORM XML controlling document," 2004; "ADL SCORM Content Aggregation Model," n.d.). Other content aggregation schemes include the IMS Simple Sequencing Specification ("IMS Simple Sequencing Specification," n.d.; "IMS Simple Sequencing Best Practice," 2003) and the "IMS Content Packaging Specification" (2007). SCORM has been criticised for imposing a somewhat didactic approach, with a relatively simple and inflexible notion of sequencing built on the simple sequencing standard. Bailey, Zalfan, Davis, Fill, and Conole (2006), for example, comment that:

*SCORM has at its core, an inbuilt sequencing engine based on the earlier Simple Sequencing specification. Simple Sequencing (SS) is an IMS specification which defines a language to express an order or path through a collection of learning activities. The inclusion of SS within SCORM enforces a primarily didactic model of learning, and although pre-defined rules, branches and decisions can be made within the sequenced components, there is a lack of user model which limits the amount of personal adaptability that a SCORM lesson can provide on its own (Abdullah & Davis, 2005).* (p 116)

Interoperability standards also exist relating to the assessment of learning. The IMS QTI standard ("IMS Question & Test Interoperability," 2002), for example, describes how assessment procedures—whether individual test questions or aggregations of them relating to particular learning objects—and procedures for processing the results, should be specified so that they and the learner data they generate can be exchanged and used in different LMS. The IMS Global Learning Consortium ("Technology for E-learning. National Standards and Bodies," n.d.) has also developed standards relating to the tracking of learner progress and the exchange of student records between systems.

The description, discovery, sharing, and reuse of learning designs is greatly facilitated by learning design ontologies, which specify the key concepts, and relationships between them, making up a particular design. The EML was created to support the generation of ontologies. This is a modelling language devised by researchers at the Open University of the Netherlands in order to model learning designs and facilitate the generation of ontologies for particular types of learning design. It was used as the basis for the development of an increasingly widely used standard—the IMS LD. Koper and Manderveld (2004) define the EML as:

*a semantically rich information model and binding, describing the content and process within units of learning from a pedagogical perspective in order to support reuse and interoperability.* (p. 537)

Unlike EML, however, IMS LD enables the integration of other standards where appropriate to perform certain tasks. Thus it allows the use of existing competency; learning resource and learner metadata; and packaging standards.

The concepts and relationships specified by IMS LD allow learning designers to model activities by which learning objectives may be achieved. It does this at a sufficiently generic level to enable the modelling of learning designs, which use a range of pedagogical models, for example, case study, inquiry-based, competency-based learning, and so forth, based on a variety of pedagogical perspectives (behaviourist, cognitive, social constructivist, etc.). Since it allows designers to model different pedagogical models, IMS LD is often described as a pedagogical *meta-model.*

IMS LD uses a "theatre" analogy in that learning designs are described in terms of *plays* consisting of series of *acts*, entailing actors playing different *roles*, engaging in *activities*, within an environment offering *services* (for example, chat rooms, bulletin boards, presentational facilities, etc.) and *learning objects* providing content. Learning designs are geared to the achievement of *learning objectives*, and may entail the specification of *prerequisites.*

Descriptions of learning designs produced using IMS LD can be run (i.e., delivered to learners) by any system (or player) capable of interpreting the language. Such players can be built into virtual learning environments. One such learning environment is LAMS, which is discussed in the next section. If learning designs can be specified using a standard widely accepted modelling language, then (like learning objects) they can be shared, exchanged, and reused. Also, it is important to note that a learning design emphasises learning *processes* not learning *content.* To the extent that it is independent of specific content, a learning design may thus be reused with different content. Conversely, different learning designs may be applied to the same content.

However, as well as enabling the sharing and reuse of learning designs in this way, the separation of learning processes from learning content reflects the predominant emphasis of the learning perspective at the root of IMS LD, namely: learning activities designed to facilitate the achievement of learning goals rather than the accumulation of chunks of content. Focusing predominantly on the use of learning objects for content transmission arguably risks a relative de-emphasis on learning as potentially resulting from collaborative activity and cooperative problem solving in social and work situations.

# General ICT-Based Developments

A range of more general ICT-based developments have had and are having considerable impact on learning design and teaching. They are general in the sense that they are not education- or resource discovery-*specific*, offering opportunities for change and development across a wide variety of human activities—including education. Such developments, which are briefly introduced next, include: *virtual* and *augmented* reality; mobile and ubiquitous computing; intelligent agents; open source applications and open access resources; Web services; and so-called Web 2.0 applications.

## Virtual and Augmented Realities

*Virtual reality* refers to realistic environments, created by a computer, which people can view and with which people can interact. The virtual reality so created may simulate some real environment, or parts of it, or may be entirely imaginary. Virtual realities may vary in sophistication. They range from the type of virtual worlds associated with computer games and/or *Second Life*, viewable on a computer screen with which one may interact via mouse and keyboard, to environments in which the user is more genuinely immersed. The latter type may entail, for example, three-dimensional visual information projected into the user's line of vision via special glasses (allowing users to walk round objects and view them as they would appear were they real), and interacting via hand and body movements translated through wired hand or body gloves—receiving sensory feedback through haptic (force feedback) devices.

*Augmented reality* refers to the blending of virtual reality and real life elements in such a way that our experience of some aspect of the real world is augmented. A simple example is a heads-up display projecting graphics and data onto a driver's windscreen. More sophisticated examples might be the making visible of labels and instructions *attached* to the components of a complex piece of equipment to assist technicians assembling or repairing them in situ—or a museum exhibition composed of a mix of real and virtual artefacts, with virtual explanatory and interactive features attached to them.

## Mobile and Ubiquitous Computing

The widespread use of wireless technology has enabled significant developments in mobile and ambient (or pervasive) computing. *Mobile* computing devices travel with the user and may take many forms including laptops, smart phones, personal digital assistants, wearable computers, and so forth. *Ubiquitous* computing devices, often termed pervasive, ambient, or even "everyware" (Greenfield, 2006), reside in objects in the environment within which the user moves, for example, smart household devices.

Such devices can connect wirelessly to the Internet or other networks and allow users to interact with data, information, people, and programs flexibly in terms of location. These resources can be delivered to users from within the particular environment in which they find themselves (for example, RFID-tagged museum exhibits may communicate information about themselves to visitors), or users may access remotely located resources from wherever they happen to be—including on the move.

## Autonomous Agents

Autonomous agents are a class of computer programs built to act autonomously on behalf of their owner. They are programmed to make decisions as they are needed. They are proactive, working in the background to find and process information before presenting the results of their work to their owners when it is ready. Agents may be built to traverse the Web on behalf of their owners, for example, searching for prices of some particular item among online stores, comparing them to discover the best price, and reporting the results of their research back to their users. Such systems may also, for example, engage in information seeking, or alert their owners to upcoming events that fall within their areas of interest.

Some agents are programmed to learn in the light of feedback from their owners. They use this feedback in order to achieve a better match between what they achieve

*Table 28. Agent applications (source: http://www.botspot.com/)*

| **Search bots**<br>Image bots<br>Meta-search bots<br>Music bots<br>Newsgroup bots | **Shopping bots**<br>Auction bots<br>Shop bots<br>Shopping organizers<br>Stock bots | **Tracking bots**<br>E-mail notification bots<br>News bots<br>Spy bots<br>Weather Bots |
|---|---|---|
| **Web development**<br>Indexing bots<br>Referencing bots<br>Site Management bots | **Surf bots**<br>Form filling bots<br>Pop-up killer bots<br>Privacy protection bots | **Games bots**<br>Bot building<br>Logic bots<br>Simulation games |

and their owners' requirements. Agents can be built not only to act autonomously, but also to interact with other computer systems, including other agents. Agents have been developed in many areas of activity including intelligent interfacing to complex computer systems, data mining, information retrieval, air traffic control, network management, electronic commerce, and so forth. The application of such systems within educational informatics education will be described in Chapter VIII. Many popular applications are listed at http://www.botspot.com/ including those shown in Table 28.

## Open Source and Open Access

Significant developments have also occurred in relation to the "openness" of the Web. The rationale behind open source software is that software should be distributed in such a way that it can be accessed, modified, and developed freely.
According to the Open Source Initiative, open source software should fulfil a number of requirements, including following (Coar, 2007):

- The software must be freely distributable, with no royalties or other fees.
- The source code must be readily accessible if it is not distributed with the compiled version. It should not be deliberately obfuscated to hinder access and modification.
- The generation of modified and derived versions of the software must be permitted, as must distribution of such versions according to the same open source conditions.
- No people, groups or areas of activity must be discriminated against in relation to the availability of the software.
- The software cannot be licensed only to be used with a particular technology or interface.

Complementing the move to open source software has been one towards open access information and resources. The Creative Commons (n.d.) allows the authors of resources—including texts, pictures, videos, music, and so forth—to control how they are used. It defines a range of options between full copyright restriction and no copyright restriction:

*Attribution Non-commercial No Derivatives [...] allows others to download your works and share them with others as long as they mention you and link back to you, but they can't change them in any way or use them commercially. [...]*

*Attribution Non-commercial Share Alike [...] lets others remix, tweak, and build upon your work non-commercially, as long as they credit you and license their new creations under the identical terms. Others can download and redistribute your work just like the [Attribution Non-commercial No Derivatives] license, but they can also translate, make remixes, and produce new stories based on your work. All new work based on yours will carry the same license, so any derivatives will also be non-commercial in nature. [...]*

*Attribution Non-commercial [...] lets others remix, tweak, and build upon your work non-commercially, and although their new works must also acknowledge you and be non-commercial, they don't have to license their derivative works on the same terms. [...]*

*Attribution No Derivatives [...] allows for redistribution, commercial and non-commercial, as long as it is passed along unchanged and in whole, with credit to you. [...]*

*Attribution Share Alike [...] lets others remix, tweak, and build upon your work even for commercial reasons, as long as they credit you and license their new creations under the identical terms. [...] All new works based on yours will carry the same license, so any derivatives will also allow commercial use. [...]*

*Attribution [...] lets others distribute, remix, tweak, and build upon your work, even commercially, as long as they credit you for the original creation..*

Open Access refers to free access to information sources—typically articles published in scholarly journals. Such sources may be published online by their authors as pre-prints or post-prints in repositories provided by themselves or their institutions. Regional open access repositories may also offer open access to such resources, for example, the White Rose Research Online repository shared between the Universities of Leeds, Sheffield, and York (http://eprints.whiterose.ac.uk/).

JISC has also recently launched The Depot (http://depot.edina.ac.uk/), which offers UK academics who do not have access to an institutional repository for their publications to be able to make them available on open access:

*The Depot is a JISC support service, launched in June 2007 with the specific task of ensuring that all in the UK research community can benefit from making their published papers available under Open Access, and helping maximise readership of their work. The Depot is OAI-compliant, allowing deposited e-prints to be 'harvested' by search engines across the world.*

Open Archives Initiative (OAI) compliance refers to interoperability standards promoted by the OAI (http://www.openarchives.org/), which include the Archives Initiative Protocol for Metadata Harvesting (OAI-PMH).

Securing a Hybrid Environment for Research Preservation and Access (SHERPA) was a project established to develop open access e-print repositories in research-led UK universities (http://www.sherpa.ac.uk/projects/sherpa.html). Completed in 2006, it is succeeded by the SHERPA Plus Project (http://www.sherpa.ac.uk/projects/sherpaplus.html), designed further to support repository development. The SHERPA Web site offers lists of repositories (http://www.sherpa.ac.uk/repositories/), and full text search facilities across UK repositories as well as the OpenBOAR Global Search enabling searching the OpenBOAR international list of repositories (http://www.opendoar.org/).

## Web Services

Web services are independently functioning modules accessible over the Web. They may be simple or complex. For example, a Web service may simply translate money from one currency to another. However, complex applications may be built by utilising more complex Web services to create the complex functionality of a digital library (Gardner, 2001):

*[W]eb services are interoperable building blocks for constructing applications. As an example, we can imagine a distributed digital library infrastructure built on Web services providing functionality such as distributed search, authentication, inter-library loan requests, document translation and payment. These Web services would be combined by a particular digital library application to offer an environment for reaching information resources that is tailored to its particular user community.*

As we will see in Chapter VII, Web services may also be used to provide adaptive personalised functionality to educational informatics systems.

Interoperability is the key to the use of Web services, and open XML-based standards have been developed. The Web services Description Language (WSDL) defines how a particular Web service should be described. The description will contain metadata to enable discovery of the service by developers and applications wishing to make use of it. The description will also specify exactly what the Web service does, and how it may be interacted with. Such interaction entails the application "binding" with the service via some interface. Thus the application will send the service a request containing some input information and will receive some output information from the service.

The description will provide sufficient information for a developer to know how to enable this two-way interaction. WSDL allows the actual communication of information between an application and a Web service using a number of different protocols, an example of which is the XML-based Simple Object Access Protocol

(SOAP). However, before it can be discovered and used, a Web service must be entered into a central registry. Universal Description, Discovery, and Integration (UDDI) has been created for this purpose. It is itself a Web service, and it provides a specification for how to create XML-based Web service directories.

## Web 2.0

Much has been written about Web 2.0, and to an extent it is still a fuzzy concept in that it is fraught with different definitions. However, Web 2.0 is often characterised by a number of factors that differentiate it from the current Web (Anderson, 2007).

Tools geared to facilitating easy communication and sharing of ideas and resources, and working collaboratively, are often associated with the concept of Web 2.0. Communicating and sharing ideas are greatly facilitated by the rapid rise of blogs, and facilities such as Google, Yahoo, and MSN Groups, as well as software such as facebook, MySpace, flickr, and del.icio.us. Squidoo lenses and podcasts enable users to communicate and promote their own views on any and every subject to those who encounter or seek them. Collaborative working and conferencing are facilitated by *wikis*, and more sophisticated collaborative group support tools such as Connect Professional (formerly Breeze) (http://www.adobe.com/uk/products/acrobatconnectpro/), Elluminate (http://www.elluminate.com/), and Groove (http://www.groove.net/home/index.cfm).

Web 2.0 is also often used to emphasise the increasing role of Web-based activity that exploits the power of *collective intelligence*. There are different types of collective intelligence. One may be seen in projects such as Wikipedia, which represent the collective contributions of many people. In what is an interesting experiment in trust and notions of "authoritative" information, the hope of many is that quality will prevail—like cream rising to the top of the milk. This certainly works in patches, Wikipedia providing masterful and authoritative overviews of many topics. However, a recent ban on citing Wikipedia articles in academic work by Middlebury College in the U.S. highlights the problematic nature of the enterprise in certain contexts (Cohen, 2007):

> *Middlebury history department notified its students this month that Wikipedia could not be cited in papers or exams, and that students could not 'point to Wikipedia or any similar source that may appear in the future to escape the consequences of errors.'*

A second type of collective intelligence is that deriving from an analysis of collective activity. Wikipedia represents the conscious explicit contribution of different people to create a common artefact—essentially working as multiple contributing authors. By contrast, tools such as Amazon's recommender system, and social tagging systems such as flickr, del.icio.us, and CiteULike utilise—and allow users to benefit from—knowledge that is not possessed by any one individual user of the system, but which is derived from an analysis of the collective activity of all users. Thus, for example, a recommender system such as that of Amazon will discover which *other* books were also bought by customers who bought the particular book you are looking at on screen. *Tag clouds* show the relative frequency of use of particular tags across the user community as a whole; the size of font reflecting level of popularity (Figure 84).

Web 2.0 is also often associated with high levels of two-way interactive participation via networks in which participants provide as well as receive information. Peer-to-peer (P2P) file sharing systems such as Kazaa, Limewire, and BearShare, following in the footsteps of Napster, enable users reciprocally to make resources stored on their computers available to other users. In this situation, the greater the number of users, the more powerful the network becomes since each new user is adding processing power and available resources.

Web 2.0 is also often characterised by a move from a page-based model, in which Web browsers display pages of content put there by a Web site author, to a model in which the Web browser displays the results of interaction with information sources provided remotely by others. The role of the Web author is to orchestrate this interaction—to arrange the accessing, downloading, and processing of information from other Web-based sources. *Processing* in this context may entail combining, filtering, and mixing the incoming information. *Mashups* is a term used to describe Web sites or applications which source information in this way. An example is the BBC News Map, which blends information from Google Maps and BBC News to provide a graphical view of recent news (http://benedictoneill.com/content/ newsmap/). This is shown in Figure 85.

However, whereas creating mashups requires some programming expertise, Yahoo's Pipes system enables users to create multi-sourced Web sites very easily using a simple drag and drop graphical interface. Information feeds from RSS feeds; Yahoo and Yahoo Local Web searches; Google Base; and flickr (see Figures 86 and 87).

Web 2.0 has also been characterised by greater awareness and exploitation of the Long Tail. In commercial terms (Anderson, 2005):

*The Long Tail is the myriad of niche products whose collective market share can rival the blockbusters.*

To take a less commercial example, in an academic library, a relatively small number of titles may be borrowed by a very large number of users. There may be an accompanying pattern in which a relatively high number of titles are borrowed each by a very small number of users (Figure 88).

*Figure 84. An example of tag clouds*

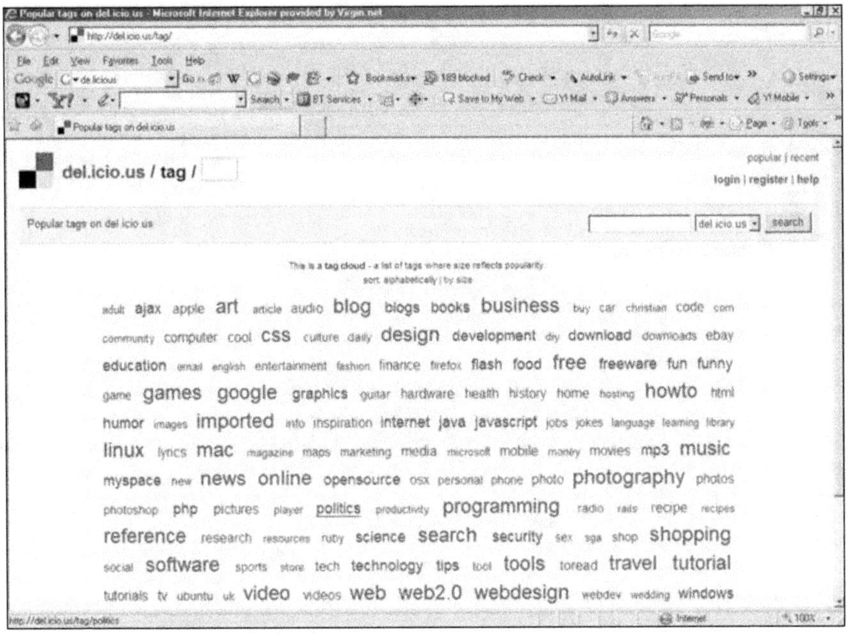


*Figure 85. The BBC News Map mashup*

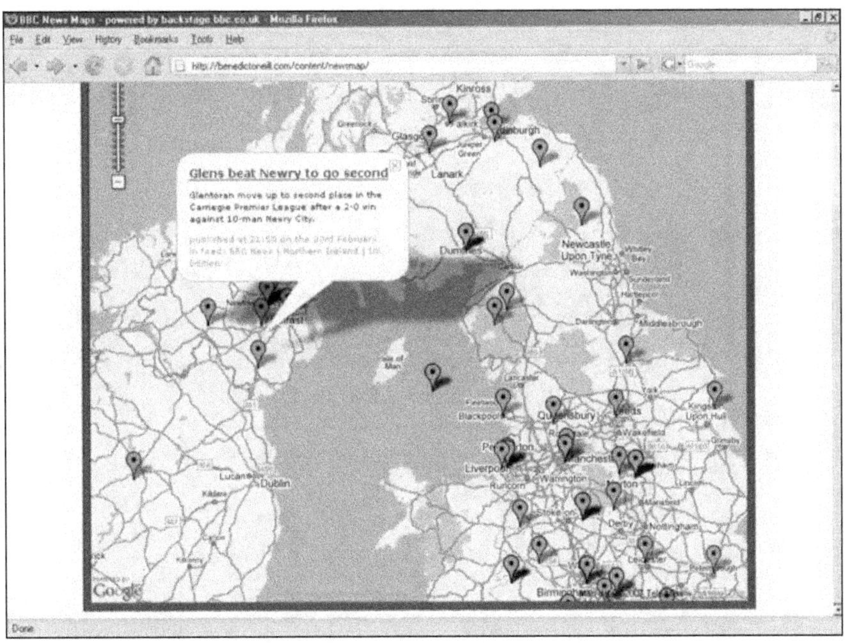

*Figure 86. Authoring screen for the Yahoo's Pipes system*

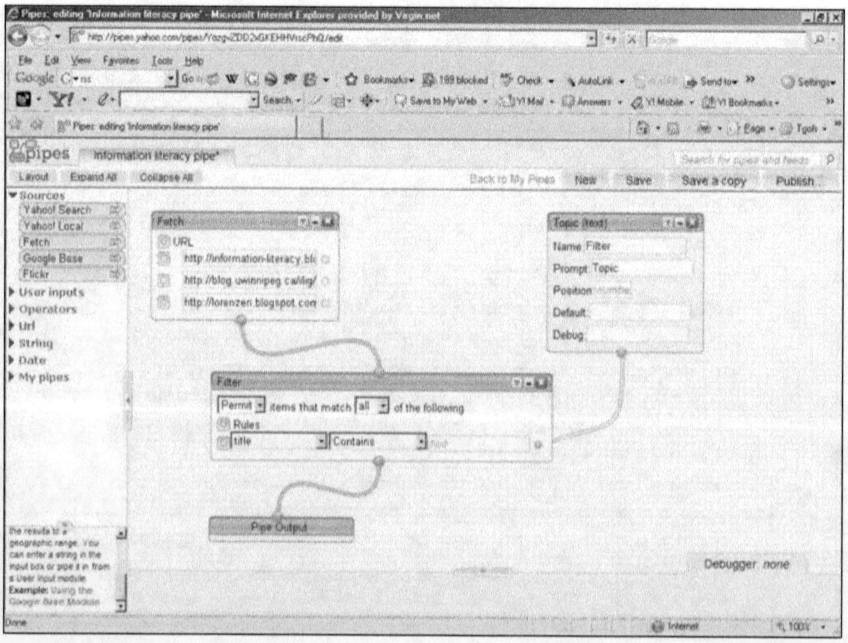

*Figure 87. Searching using a Yahoo Pipe*

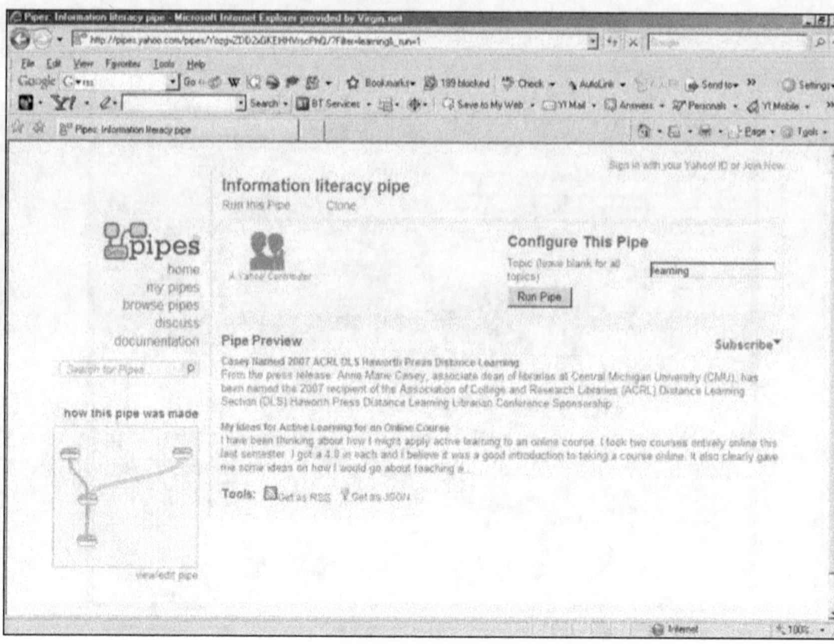

*Figure 88. The Long Tail*

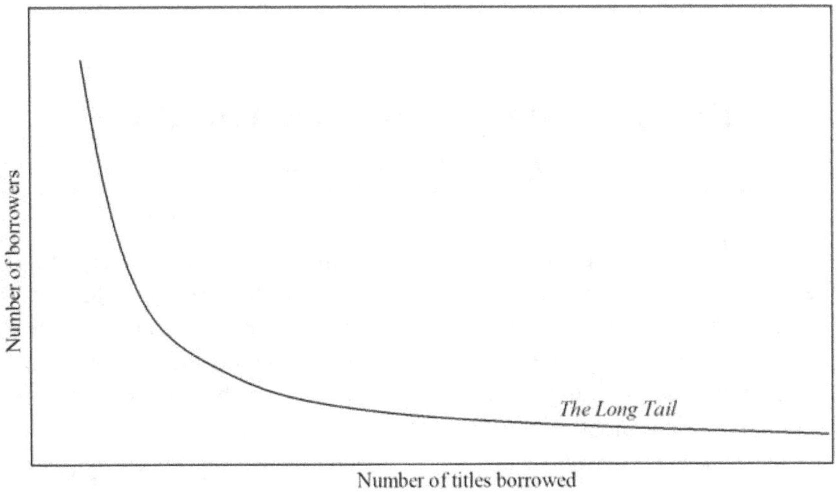


Insofar as relatively high levels of expense, resources and effort must be associated with reaching the Long Tail—satisfying minority interests or selling to small niche markets—business and other enterprises have concentrated on the head rather than the tail.

Much has been written about the relationship of Web 2.0 and postmodernist philosophy. As noted by Byers (2006), this has sometimes been somewhat confused with the notion of collectivism. Essentially, collectivism relates in this context to the harnessing of the collective intelligence of members of particular Web-based communities. Wikipedia would be an example of one type of collectivist activity, while social tagging and recommender systems such as those provided by flickr and Amazon are an example of another type of collective intelligence.

Characteristics of Web 2.0, which to an extent echo themes of postmodernism, however, include radical decentralisation and fragmentation of content and Web services, and the unilateralism inherent in these developments, the relative equality of opportunity for the voicing of multiple, including minority, perspectives for example via blogs and podcasts, and the notion of the Long Tail. Although it can be argued that post-modernist-flavoured, unilateral decentralised development and provision of content and services depend on distinctly non post-modernist notions such as the development of centralised standards for interoperability, such standards operate at the level of agreed pragmatic tools to enable communication—as opposed to agreed "truths" about anything. Just as language represents a centrally agreed centralised convention enabling the expression of post-modernist thought, so Web standards and languages represent a common tool of communication.

## Educational Opportunities Afforded by ICT Developments

This section focuses on the opportunities for learning design and delivery afforded by the ICT-related developments reviewed in this and the previous chapter. The facilitation of blended learning designs is a theme that appears throughout the following subsections. Indeed, they are by no means mutually exclusive, but complement one another in providing a rich range of opportunities both to deliver existing and develop new learning designs.

The pervasive nature of Web infrastructure, whereby Web access using common standards is increasingly available in homes, in the workplace and on the move, as well as schools, colleges, and universities, mean that it is easier than ever before for learning designers to blend modes and media of delivery. There are increasing opportunities to design and deliver learning experiences which flexibly move, as appropriate to different learners and different learning conditions and requirements, between: individual and group; face-to-face and Web-based; text and multimedia; world to desktop and immersive experience; theory and practice; classroom and real world; mediated and autonomous; and experience and reflection.

## Inclusive, Open and Flexible Access to Learning

The Web and associated digital technologies enable access to learning by groups and individuals who otherwise might not have effective access via more traditional routes and methods. Digital learning resources can be accessed 24/7. They can also be accessed more flexibly than ever before in terms of physical location—not only internationally, but at work, at home, or while on the move. The widespread availability of Web infrastructure and basic tools, coupled with interoperability and the impetus towards open access and open educational resources, learning designers are presented with the relatively easy potential to deliver blended as well as single mode learning designs.

Education has not been slow in taking advantage of—indeed, it has been and continues to be a prime mover in—the developments in open access described in the previous section. The volume and range of open educational resources is rapidly increasing, with initiatives such as MIT's OpenCourseWare (http://ocw.mit.edu/ index.html), the UK Open University's OpenLearn (http://www.open.ac.uk/ openlearn/home.

*Figure 89.*

php), the OpenCourseWare Consortium (http://ocwconsortium.org/), and the Open Educational Resources Commons (http://www.oercommons.org/):

*OER Commons provides open educational resources for teaching and learning that are freely available online for everyone to use, whether you are an instructor, student, or self-learner. OER Commons uses Web 2.0 features such as tags, ratings, comments, reviews, and social networking in order to create an online experience that engages educators in sharing their best teaching and learning practices.*

Figure 89 shows a mashup enabling educational podcasts, Webcasts, and open educational resources to be located via a Google map.

## Personalisation

More so than in the past, learners may also expect to engage in learning that is individualised to their particular needs and interests. Developments in learning objects and accompanying standards for discovery and sharing mean that there are growing possibilities for cafeteria style learning entailing the personal configuration of learning elements, components, resources, and delivery modes. Even within formal education, the possibilities of learners co-designing their learning with educators are greatly enhanced by developments in ICT-related learning resources, and standards and approaches to analysing, describing, linking, and reconfiguring them to respond to individual interests, needs, and characteristics.

The Web offers a way of reaching the Long Tail without incurring prohibitive cost and effort. In learning terms, arguably we are all in some ways minority groups. Large numbers of us may all wish to learn about a particular subject area, but learning theory suggests that ideally we may all need to do it with a high degree of *personalisation*. Universities require large numbers of students to select particular courses, or money may be lost or courses may not run since it is not economical to do so. Providing personalised learning experiences that enmesh with each individual student's needs, preferences, styles, and prior knowledge—reaching the long tail of learning needs—is beyond a certain level of individualisation (for example, via the use of individual project work) prohibitively uneconomic unless we can devise cost-effective ways of deliver it. Within this context, as we will see in Chapters VII and VIII, educational informatics may enable us to provide higher levels of personalisation in learning provision—reaching the long tail in terms of learning needs.

Digital technologies offer the prospect of increased levels of, and sophistication in, adaptation of teaching and learning better to match individual learners' personal needs, preferences, and identities. They can also enable high levels of interactivity combined with personalisation. The expertise that it is possible to build into a computer system includes pedagogical expertise. The automation of pedagogical expertise via the application of artificial intelligence techniques enables a level of mediation and interaction also to be available without time or geographical restriction to learners able to access intelligent resources. Building interactive pedagogical expertise into copyable and sharable resources enables a degree of personalisation of learning in terms of allowing learners to learn at a pace and place of their choosing. As the production and availability of a wide range of such resources reaches a critical mass, personalisation is also facilitated in terms of enabling learners to choose not only *how* but also *what* they would like to learn.

At the same time, the potential is enhanced for different types of interactivity with other individuals, groups, and teams both in real time and asynchronously. Where learning is relatively content-centric, and the teacher's role is one of emphasising the transmission of essential content; proliferation of the topics being studied by a class of learners poses considerable logistic problems for the teacher. Where learning is geared more towards the development of generic critical thinking and *learning to learn* skills, there is more scope for variation in the content being studied by individual learners, since the teacher's role is more focused on the processes whereby evidence is gathered, evaluated, analysed, and used. The vast source of potential evidence that is the Web has a great role to play in enabling high levels of personalised research-based learning of the type promoted, for example, in inquiry-based learning. However, new skills are required in any shift to engaging learners in Web-based evidence seeking. With high quality sources of evidence come vast and often obfuscating volumes of low quality, irrelevant, and inappropriate information, and learners need to develop appropriately critical information seeking and evaluation skills.

## Source-Rich, Evidence-based Critical Thinking

Good teaching has always been evidence-based. However, availability of and speed of access to sources of evidence relating to almost any topic have increased dramatically with the advent of the Web. In the past, limitations in the availability of accessible sources militated for teachers asking questions and posing problems for which they knew such sources were readily available, for example, in the form of handouts, textbooks, or local library resources. It is now more realistic to expect learners to be able to find, with varying levels of assistance, evidence with which to address a much less restricted range of questions and problems.

As well as the sheer volume of potential evidence available via the Web, whether open corpus or in specialist repositories of texts, journal papers or learning objects, as we have seen in Chapter V search tools are increasingly powerful. In addition, it is possible for learners rapidly to receive personally selected updates of information via RSS or Atom feeds and to gain rapid access to information on topics and issues relevant to their interests subjects of study brought together from different sources via mashups.

Such richness of information sources brings with it exposure to a range of different types and sources of information, to multiple, often conflicting, views and perspectives, and to information of very varying quality. This requires the application of flexibility and versatility (the ability to learn from information sources not necessarily well suited to one's particular style and level of learning) and criticality (the ability to make sense of conflicting views and different types and qualities of *evidence*. Yet it is potentially, at the same time, an excellent environment in which (1) the need for such skills can be perceived, and (2) such skills can be developed.

Critical thinking is of particular relevance in a context where learning is taking place within a *knowledge creation* ethos. Relative to knowledge acquisition ethos, this entails a shift in the notion and role of traditional academic *authority* in learning, with a move from educational activity emphasising the taking in of authoritative content from experts to immersion in experience and engagement in reflection. The role of expert others moves to a focus on guiding the process of reflection, analysis, and interpretation.

## Collaborative, Community-Based, and Real World Learning

The collaborative and social networking tools described in the previous section afford increased opportunities for collaborative learning. Opportunities for working with people from different locations and with differing experience are enhanced—indeed, different groups can come together for different purposes. There is no longer a necessary emphasis on fixed cohorts of students brought together by the need to be co-present in a common place at particular times.

Learners with common needs and problems can also more easily interact, for example, to discuss learning problems, regardless of time and place. Traditional educational courses can be subject to critical comparison and debate between students studying similar subjects in different institutions nationally and internationally. Learning in the sense of the generation of knowledge by a community to solve problems authentic to that community; knowledge, which is essentially distributed within the community, existing in the interactions between its members is facilitated by the ability to relatively easily interact and collaborate via the development of shared resources and artefacts.

Social computing techniques also enable systems to gather dynamic knowledge about a (learning) community and the interactions taking place between its members. The systems can analyse this knowledge and make it available to members of the community. This knowledge can inform further interactions. As we will see in Chapter VIII, this approach can generate knowledge that is particularly useful within learning communities, for example, to put learners in contact with learning resources found to be particularly useful by other members of a learning community.

The Web offers the ability to easily interact and work collaboratively with other remotely located individuals and groups, sharing tools, resources, and artefacts. This facility enables close links between home, workplace, classroom, and community and offers the potential for breaking down artificial barriers between the classroom and the real world, and between theory and practice. The ability to engage in tasks that are likely to result in outcomes of more direct relevance to working and real world contexts, compared with, for example, performance, has the potential to engage learners' intrinsic motivation. Such new modes of learning require appropriate forms of assessment, which may themselves be blended, and include collaborative, multimedia, nonlinear text representations of solutions or records of interactions and procedures, as opposed to (or at least complementing) traditional essay, examination, or report-based assessments. There is also scope for blends of learner, peer, and community involvement in the assessment of the knowledge, artefacts, or procedures that are produced, that is, assessment involving the real owners and users of the products of learning.

## Mobile and Immersive Learning

The use of mobile communications technology can enhance opportunities for blended learning in that an experience (for example, presence at an exhibition, immersion in some simulated problem situation, or engagement in an augmented reality field trip) can be blended *at the time* with relevant commentary, data, analysis, and interpretation. Person-to-person communication can also take place with peers, tutors, and/or others. This technology enables *just-in-time* learning insofar as information and mediation can be delivered to learners wherever they happen to be at a particular time—in the workplace or elsewhere.

Developments in relation to virtual and augmented realities also mean that learners may participate in virtual events and investigate and act in simulated problem situations. They may have their experience of real environments and situations greatly enriched via the overlay of digital data, analysis, and commentary. These additional resources can be accessed while the learner is within the experience.

Such developments mean that learners can experience simulated real environments and situations that they could otherwise not experience, or could do so only with great difficulty, for reasons of danger, travel, or access restrictions. They can also experience environments that only exist virtually, for example, virtual realities set up specifically to meet the particular requirements of some training or educational purposes.

## Web Services in Education

Web services can, of course, provide educational services. Zhang, Song, and Zhang (2006), for example, propose a Web service-based architecture to support cross system and cross service personalisation of learning, entailing an ontology-based learner model designed to enable the seamless integration of existing services and user models. Web services are also central to an initiative entailing cooperation between the United Kingdom's JISC and Australia's Department of Education, Science and Training (DEST) to develop an e-learning framework (ELF). The intention is that this should become an international standard to support e-learning. The aim of the framework is to map out the key services required to support e-learning and to identify, for each, one or more open standards that can be used to guide implementation and development. The framework envisages the functions being provided by distributed Web services. The services would be used by user agents, which may include, for example, VLEs and LMSs; libraries and portals; e-learning authoring tools; timetabling systems; automated assignment marking systems; and so forth.

The framework has identified distinct sets of services, including those specific to e-learning as well as more generic services common to multiple application areas.

The following information is adapted from *The E-learning Framework* (http://www.elframework.org/).

**Learning Domain Services**

Automated assessments

Automated marking services

Course proposal, approval, and validation

Creation, access, and management of Resource List

Curriculum development and access to curriculum elements (structures and properties)

ePortfolio management Learning-activity management

Managing competency frameworks and mapping learning activities and achievements to competencies

Managing complex learning flows

Managing quality assurance documents (e.g., examiners' reports, second marking, etc.)

Submitting grades and marks

Reporting of institutional performance data to other agencies

Use of sequences of learning objects

Tracking learning performance information

**Common Services [selected illustrative categories only]**

AV conferencing;

Archiving;

Authentication;

Authorisation;

Calendaring;

Chat;

Context (e.g., discovering the activity a user is engaged in);

Digital rights management;

E-mail management;

Federated Search (searching across multiple types of repository);

Filing;

Format Conversion;

Forum;

Group (access to information concerning groups, courses, modules, activities, teams, departments, etc.);

Harvesting (resource discovery using metadata);

Messaging;

Metadata Management;

Metadata Schema Registry ;

Packaging;

Person details;

Presence (online status);

Rating/Annotation (creating and using secondary metadata including user ratings and annotations);

Resolver (e.g., redirection to other providers such as online bookshops, libraries, etc. based on OpenURL or similar metadata);

Scheduling (of physical resources, people, and space);

Search (single as opposed to federated searches);

Service Registry

Terminology (automated mappings between terminology within and across thesauri and classifications);

User Preferences;

Whiteboard;

Workflow management

Each service listed in the framework is linked to a description of the scope and precise definition of the service and, as they become available, links to appropriate specifications, associated files, implementations, other related initiatives, relevant reports, and open source implementation toolkits. Although intending to provide such open source toolkits, the intention is to facilitate the integration and interoperability of commercial as well as open source components, via standardisation relating to definitions, data models, behaviours, and protocols.

As we will see in Chapter VII and VIII, a number of educational informatics systems make use of a Web services architecture.

Figure 90 further extends the model introduced in Figure 48 at the end of Chapter IV. The details originally shown in the boxes labelled EDUCATIONAL PHILOSOPHIES..., MENTAL PROCESSES, and MENTAL STATES in Figure 48 have been collapsed in the version shown here. This is simply in the interests of clarity, and these details, although not shown here, still apply.

*Figure 90. Knowledge and information behaviour within an educational and ICT-based context*

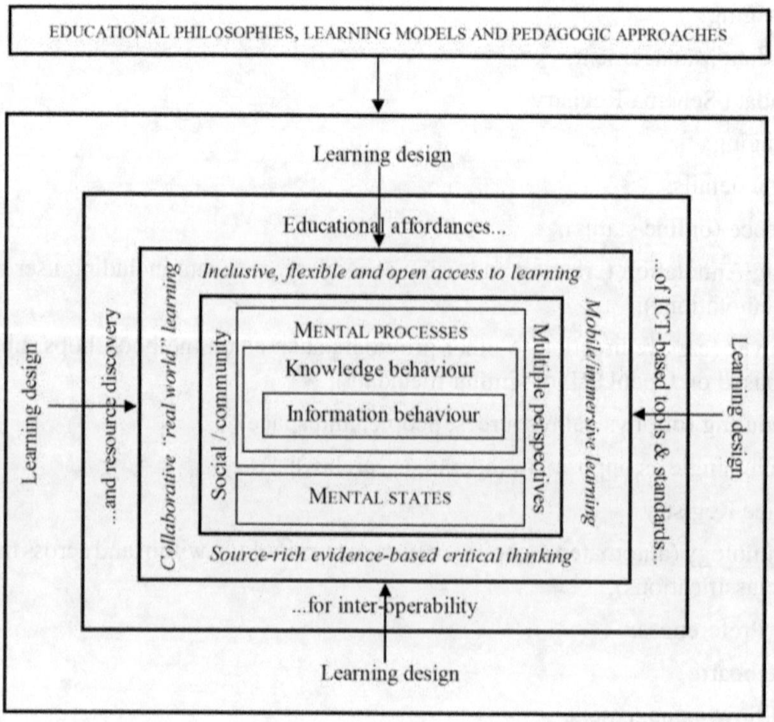


The model is now extended to include key ICT-related concepts introduced in this and the previous chapter. These include standards and tools impacting on and supporting (1) learning design, and (2) interoperability and resource discovery, which together support the sharing and reuse of learning materials and learning designs. This model will be further developed in Chapter IX to include educational informatics systems, which are ICT-based tools of which resource discovery based on pedagogical knowledge is an integral part. However, before this, the next two chapters introduce a number of educational informatics systems in detail. Chapter VII focuses on educational informatics systems designed with particular reference to individual learning. Chapter VIII explores educational informatics system which adopt a relatively social, community, and collaborative approach to learning.

# References


Abdullah, N. A., & Davis, H. C. (2005, July). *A real-time personalization service for SCORM.* Paper presented at the 5th IEEE International Conference on Advanced Learning Technologies, Kaohsiung, Taiwan.

*ADL reaches a milestone in SCORM development.* (2006). Retrieved August 1, 2007, from the ADL Web site: http://www.adlnet.gov/News/articles/index.aspx?ID=380

*ADL releases SCORM 2004 3rd edition public draft.* (2006). Retrieved August 1, 2007, from http://www.adlnet.gov/news/articles/375.cfm

*ADL SCORM content aggregation model—Overview.* (n.d.). Retrieved August 1, 2007, from the Learning Technology Standards Observatory Web site http://www.cen-ltso.net/Users/main.aspx?put=218

*ADL SCORM XML controlling document. SCORM CAM version 1.3 content packaging extensions XML XSD version 1.0.* (2004). Retrieved August 1, 2007, from http://www.adlnet.gov/downloads/58.cfm

Albert, D., & Hockemeyer, C. (1997). Adaptive and dynamic hypertext tutoring systems based on knowledge space theory. In B. du Boulay & R. Mizoguchi (Eds.), *Artificial intelligence in education: Knowledge and media in learning systems, Vol. 39 of frontiers in artificial intelligence and applications* (pp. 553-555). Amsterdam: IOA Press.

Albert, D., & Lukas, J. (1999). *Knowledge spaces. Theories, empirical research and applications.* Berlin: Springer.

*Assessment and learning in knowledge spaces* (ALEKS). (n.d.). PowerPoint presentation. Retrieved August 1, 2007, from http://141.225.14.27/home/zcai/IntroducingALEKS.ppt

Anderson, C. (2005). *The long tail. A public diary on themes around a book. What is the long tail?* Retrieved August 1, 2007, from http://longtail.typepad.com/the_long_tail/2005/01/what_is_the_lon.html

Anderson, P. (2007). *What is Web 2.0? Ideas, technologies and implications for education (TSW0701).* Retrieved August 1, 2007, from http://www.jisc.ac.uk/media/documents/techwatch/tsw0701b.pdf

Bailey, C., Zalfan, M. T, Davis, H. C., Fill, K., & Conole, G. (2006). Panning for gold: Designing pedagogically inspired learning nuggets. *Educational Technology & Society, 9*(1), 113-122.

Bohl, O., Schellhase, J., Sengler, R., & Winand, U. (2002, December 3-6). The sharable content object reference model (SCORM)—A critical review. In *Proceedings ICCE 2002—International Conference on Computers in Education, Auckland, New Zealand* (pp. 950-951). Los Alamitos, CA: IEEE Computer Society.

Brusilovsky, P. (2001). Adaptive hypermedia. *User Modeling and User-Adapted Interaction, 11*(1-2), 87-110.

Byers, P. (2006). *Is Web 2.0 anything more than just postmodernism*? Retrieved August 1, 2007, from http://opengardensblog.futuretext.com/archives/2006/09/is_web_20_anyth.html

Chabay, R. W., & Larkin, J. H. (Eds). (1992). *Computer-assisted instruction and intelligent tutoring systems: Shared goals and complementary approaches.* Hillsdale, NJ: Erlbaum.

Coar, K. (2007). *The open source definition*. Retrieved August 1, 2007, from http://www.opensource.org/docs/osd

Cohen, N. (2007, February 21). A history department bans citing Wikipedia as a research source. *The New York Times. Education.* Retrieved August 1, 2007, from http://www.nytimes.com/2007/02/21/education/21wikipedia.html?_r=3&oref=slogin&oref=slogin&oref=slogin

Conlan, O., Hockemeyer, C., Wade, V., & Albert, D. (2003). Metadata driven approaches to facilitate adaptivity in personalized elearning systems. *Journal of the Japanese Society for Information and Systems in Education*. Retrieved August 1, 2007, from https://www.cs.tcd.ie/Owen.Conlan/publications/JSISEv1.23_Conlan.pdf

Creative Commons. (n.d.). *Creative Commons licenses*. Retrieved August 1, 2007, from http://creativecommons.org/about/licenses/meet-the-licenses

Dalziel, J. (2003, December 7-10). Implementing learning design: The learning activity management system (LAMS). In G. Crisp, D. Thiele, I. Scholten, S. Barker, & J. Baron (Eds.), *Interact, integrate, impact. Proceedings of ASCILITE 2003, Adelaide, Australia* (pp. 593-596). Wollongong, NSW: The Australasian Society for Computers in Learning in Tertiary Education (ASCILITE). Retrieved August 1, 2007, from http://www.ascilite.org.au/conferences/adelaide03/docs/pdf/593.pdf

De Bra, P., Aroyo, L., & Chepegin, V. (2004). The next big thing: Adaptive Web-based systems. *Journal of Digital Information, 5*(1), Article No. 247.

Eaglestone, B., Ford, N., Brown, G. J., & Moore, A. (2007). Information systems and creativity: An empirical study. *Journal of Documentation, 63*(4), 443-464.

Elam, J. J., & Mead, M. (1987). Designing for creativity: Considerations for DSS design. *Information and Management, 13*(5), 215-222.

Ford, N. (2005). "Conversational" information systems: Extending educational informatics support for the Web-based learner. *Journal of Documentation, 61*(3), 362-384.

French, R. M. (2002). The computational modeling of analogy-making. *Trends in Cognitive Sciences, 6,* 200-205.

Gaizauskas, R., & Wilks, Y. (1998) Information extraction: Beyond information retrieval. *Journal of Documentation, 54*(1), 70-105.

Gardner, T. (2001). An introduction to Web services. *Ariadne, 29*. Retrieved August 1, 2007, from http://www.ariadne.ac.uk/issue29/gardner/intro.html

Greene, S. (2002). Characteristics of applications that support creativity. *Communications of the ACM, 45*(10), 100-104.

Greenfield, A. (2006). *Everyware: The dawning age of ubiquitous computing*. Berkeley, CA: Peachpit Press.

Heylighen, F. (2001). Bootstrapping knowledge representations: Via entailment meshes via semantic nets to learning webs. *Kybernetes, 30*(5/6), 691-722.

Hofstadter, D. (1995). *Concepts and creative analogies: Computer models of the fundamental mechanisms of thought*. New York: Basic Books.

IEEE. (2002, July 15). *Draft standard for learning object metadata. IEEE 1484.12.1-2002*. Retrieved August 1, 2007, from http://ltsc.ieee.org/wg12/files/LOM_1484_12_1_v1_Final_Draft.pdf

*IMS content packaging specification.* (2007). Retrieved August 1, 2007, from http://www.imsglobal.org/content/packaging/

*IMS question & test interoperability: An overview.* (2002). Final specification version 1.2. Retrieved August 1, 2007, from the IMS Global Learning Consortium Web site: http://www.imsglobal.org/question/qtiv1p2/imsqti_oviewv1p2.html

*IMS simple sequencing specification.* (n.d.). Retrieved August 1, 2007 from the IMS Global Learning Consortium Web site: http://www.imsglobal.org/simplesequencing/index.html

*IMS simple sequencing best practice and implementation guide.* (2003). Version 1.0 final specification. Retrieved August 1, 2007, from the IMS Global Learning Consortium Web site: http://www.imsglobal.org/simplesequencing/ssv1p0/imsss_bestv1p0.html

Joint Information Systems Committee (JISC). (2007). *MLEs and VLEs explained.* JISC Briefing Paper 1. Retrieved 1 August, 2007, from http://www.jisc.ac.uk/whatwedo/programmes/programme_buildmle_hefe/mle_lifelonglearning_info/mle_briefingpack/mle_briefings_1.aspx

Kolodner, J. (1993). *Case-based reasoning.* San Francisco: Morgan Kaufmann.

Koper, R., & Manderveld, J. (2004). Educational modelling language: Modelling reusable, interoperable, rich and personalised units of learning. *British Journal of Educational Technology, 35*(5), 537-552.

Laanpere, M., Põldoja, H., & Kikkas, K. (2004, August 30-September 1). The second thoughts about pedagogical neutrality of LMSs. In: *The 4th IEEE International Conference on Advanced Learning Technologies. Joensuu, Finland,* (pp. 807-809). Los Alamitos: IEEE.

Marakas, G. M., & Elam, J. J. (1997). Creativity enhancement in problem-solving: Through software or process? *Management Science, 43*(8), 1136-1146.

Masterman, L., & Lee, S. (2005). *Evaluation of the practitioner trial of LAMS: Final report.* JISC. Retrieved August 1, 2007, from http://www.jisc.ac.uk/uploaded_documents/LAMS%20Final%20Report.pdf

Mitchell, M. (1993). *Analogy-making as perception: A computer model.* Cambridge, MA: MIT Press.

Pangaro, P. (1997). *THOUGHTSTICKER: An idiosyncratic history of conversation theory in software, and its progenitor*. Belmont MA: Gordon Pask, Pangaro Inc. Retrieved August 1, 2007, from http://www.pangaro.com/published/thstr-fest.html

Pangaro, P. (2001). THOUGHTSTICKER 1986: A personal history of conversation theory in software and its progenitor, Gordon Pask. *Kybernetes, 30*(5/6), 790-806.

Pask, G. (1975). *Conversation, cognition and learning.* Amsterdam: Elsevier.

Pask, G. (1976). *Conversation theory: Applications in education and epistemology.* Amsterdam: Elsevier.

Pask, G. (1990). Some formal aspects of conversation theory and Lp. In F. Heylighen, E. Rosseel, & F. Demeyere (Eds.), *Self-steering and cognition in complex systems: Toward a new cybernetics.* (pp. 240-247). New York: Gordon and Breach.

Pask, G., & Gregory, D. (1986). Conversational systems. In R. J. Zeidner (Ed.), *Human productivity enhancement, Volume II* (pp. 204-235). New York: Praeger.

Ploetz, P. (2004). Faculty development and learning object technology: Bridging the gap. *Teaching with Technology Today, 10*(4). Retrieved August 1,2007 from http://www.uwsa.edu/ttt/articles/ploetz3.htm

Saeedi, M. H., & Sillince, J. (1999). Incorporating rhetorical and plausible reasoning in a system for simulating argumentation. *Knowledge-Based Systems, 12*(3), 113-127.

Shneiderman, B. (2002). Creativity support tools. *Communications of the ACM, 45*(10), 116-120.

Sillince, J. A. A. (1995). *Specification of naturalistic argumentation rules.* (Management School Discussion Paper No. 95.28). Sheffield, UK: University of Sheffield.

Smith, S. (1998). *Intelligent tutoring systems*. Retrieved August 1, 2007, from http://www.cs.mdx.ac.uk/staffpages/serengul/tutorial/Differential.student.models.htm

Stutt, A., & Motta, E. (2004). Semantic learning webs. *Journal of Interactive Media in Education,* (10). Special Issue on the Educational Semantic Web. Retrieved August 1, 2007, from www-jime.open.ac.uk/2004/10

Taagepera, M., Potter, F., Miller, G., & Lakshminarayan, K. (1997). Mapping students' thinking patterns by the use of knowledge space theory. *International Journal of Science Education, 19,* 283-302.

Urban-Lurain. (1996). *Intelligent tutoring systems: An historic review in the context of the development of artificial intelligence and educational psychology.* Retrieved August 1, 2007, from http://www.cse.msu.edu/rgroups/cse101/ITS/its.htm

Vreeswijk, G. A. W. (1993). Defeasible dialectics: A controversy-oriented approach towards defeasible argumentation. *Journal of Logic and Computation, 3,* 3-27.

Vreeswijk, G. A. W. (1995). IACAS: An implementation of Chisholm's principles of knowledge. In *Proceedings of the 2nd Dutch/German Workshop on Nonmonotonic Reasoning,* Utrecht, The Netherlands (pp. 225-234). Delft, Holland: Universiteit Utrecht.

Vreeswijk, G. A. W. (1997). Abstract argumentation systems. *Artificial Intelligence, 90,* 225-279.

Zhang, F., Song, Z., & Zhang, H. (2006, December 18-22). *Web service based architecture and ontology based user model for cross-system personalization.* Paper presented at the IEEE/WIC/ACM International Conference on Web Intelligence, Hong Kong.

Zimmer, R. S. (2001). Variations on a string bag: Using Pask's principles for practical course design. *Kybernetes, 30*(7), 1006-1023.

# Chapter VII

# Educational Informatics Systems: Individual Approaches

## Introduction

Educational informatics is defined within this book as:

*The development, use, and evaluation of digital systems that use pedagogical knowledge to engage in or facilitate resource discovery in order to support learning.*

Figure 91 shows how the previous chapters of this book have focused on each of the pillars on which educational informatics is founded. The nature of *learning* was explored in Chapters I and II, before we moved on to focus on *pedagogical* matters in Chapter III and *resource discovery* in Chapter IV. Chapters V and VI focused on *digital systems*, concentrating on information and communication technology (ICT) aspects of pedagogy and resource discovery respectively. The reader is referred to the Preface for a more detailed explanation of this definition.

*Figure 91. Definition of educational informatics and previous chapters*

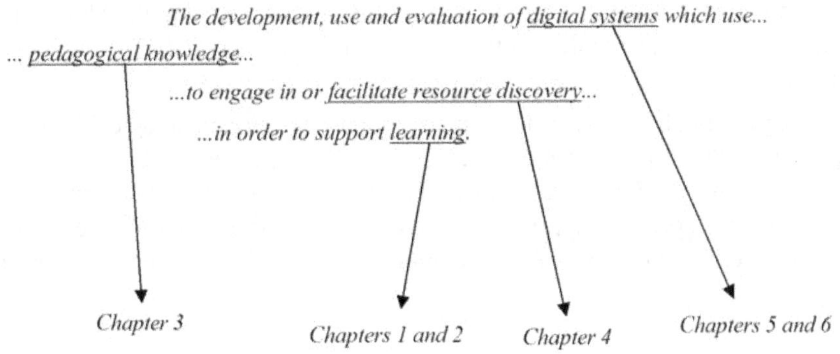


This and the following chapter present a selective review of recent developments in the development of educational informatics systems, which accord with the definition given previously. While Chapter VIII introduces a number of educational informatics systems that focus on social and collaborative aspects of learning, the present chapter focuses on the ways in which a number of educational informatics systems are being developed to offer a degree of personalisation of the learning experience to the individual learner, and on provision for learner control and the development of metacognition.

The simplest form of educational informatics system is a retrieval system that enables resource discovery via some pedagogic knowledge representation, for example, in the form of standard pedagogical metadata specifying, for example, educational level, pedagogical approach, and so forth. A number of educational repositories exist (Sampson & Karampiperis, 2006), which enable users to search for learning resources via the use of metadata that specifies various pedagogical features of those resources. Examples include ARIADNE (http://www.ariadne-eu.org/), CAN-CORE (http://www.cancore.ca/ en/), EducaNext (http://www.educanext.org/ubp), the Educational Network Australia (EDNA) (http://www.edna.edu.au/edna/go), the Exploratorium Digital Library Learning Resources Collection (http://www.exploratorium.edu/partner/nsdl/index.html), the Gateway to Educational Materials (GEM) (http://64.119.44.148/), the Globewide Network Academy (GNA) (http://www.gnacademy.org/), the Health Education Assets Library (HEAL) (www.healcentral.org), the LearnAlberta Portal (http://www.learnalberta.ca/Main.aspx), the Multimedia Educational Resource for Learning and Online Teaching (MERLOT) (http://www.merlot.org/merlot/index.htm), the National Learning Network (www.nln.ac.uk), the Science, Mathematics, Engineering and Technology Education Digital Library

(SMETE) (http://www.smete.org/smete/), the Scottish electronic Staff Development Library (www.sesdl.scotcit.ac.uk), and the World Lecture Hall (http://web.austin.utexas.edu/wlh/). A list of learning object repositories hosted at the University of Wisconsin is also available at http://www.uwm.edu/Dept/ CIE/AOP/LO_collections.html.

However, although such repositories—insofar as they use pedagogical knowledge expressed in the form of learning-related metadata to enable and facilitate resource discovery—meet the criteria necessary to qualify as educational informatics systems as defined here, they represent relatively simple forms. This and the following chapter introduce a number of more complex forms of the educational informatics system.

## Metadata-Enabled Learning Resource Discovery

Conole and Fill (2005) and Bailey, Zalfan, Davis, Fill, and Conole (2006) report developments designed to assist teachers in the creation of *learning nuggets,* which are described by metadata enabling their discovery and reuse. This sharing is restricted at present to four universities (unlike the other projects reported in this section, which focus on making learning resources available more widely via repositories). DialogPlus was a project partly funded by the Joint Information Systems Committee (JISC)/National Science Foundation (NSF) Digital Libraries in the Classroom Project. This project entails cooperation between geography departments in two English and two United States universities to produce and share what they refer to as learning nuggets. The process is supported by learning design taxonomies, a distinctive pedagogical metadata model, and software that not only supports the process of nugget creation, but also translates the results into Instructional Management System Learning Design (IMS LD) manifests. The project offers interesting comparisons with a number of apparently similar concepts. Learning nuggets echo the concept of learning objects, and the approach to designing learning activities is similar to that inherent in the Educational Modelling Language and related IMS LD standard.

The term *learning nugget* was coined in part to avoid some of the difficulties surrounding the notion of *learning object* particularly at the time the project began. Bailey et al. (2006) describe learning nuggets as follows:

*Nuggets are primarily comprised of tasks that learners will undertake in a particular context in order to attain specific learning outcomes. Contextual elements include subject area, level of difficulty, prerequisite skills or knowledge, and the environment within which the activity takes place. Declared aims and learning outcomes are ad-*

*dressed by a sequence of tasks, each of which may involve particular techniques, various roles and interactions, plus access to specified resources and associated tools. A task will take a prescribed length of time and may, or may not be assessed. Nuggets are, or should be, designed with a particular approach to learning and teaching in mind... (p. 114)*

Figure 92 shows the conceptual model of a learning activity. The main components are shown in bold. A learning activity consists of a descriptive aim, and associated learning outcomes. These outcomes are supported by different tasks. Bailey et al. (2006) note that although the particular sequence intended by the teacher is specified in the metadata, in practice this sequence is not enforced. This decision was made in the light of feedback to the effect that some students did not like to be sequentially restricted. It is interesting to note that in the case of the Learning Activity Management System (LAMS), teacher-defined sequences are enforced.

Tasks take place in a particular context, contextual elements including subject, degree of difficulty, prerequisite knowledge, and learning environment. Tasks are characterised by type (information handling, communicating, assimilating, etc.), length, technique (role play, reflection, field work, etc.), and type of interaction (for example, individual, one-to-one, one-to-many, student to student, etc.). Tasks are associated with particular roles (individual learner, group participant, presenter, etc.), resources (such as books, databases or Web pages, tools (for example, Web browser, search engine, media player, etc.), and types of assessment (diagnostic, formative, summative). They are designed to bring about particular types of learning outcome (for example, understanding, designing, evaluating, etc.)

The focus and approach are primarily teacher-based rather than driven by considerations relating to the needs of automation. This is reflected in the metadata model developed. Rather than use one of the mainstream metadata standards such as learning object metadata (LOM), the developers use their own relatively simple vocabulary. While acknowledging that such highly structured schemes are well suited to the requirements of machine indexing and retrieval, they contrast this with their own aim, which is (Bailey et al., 2006):

*...to provide a set of metadata fields that would be most appropriate to teachers to understand and use when describing and searching for other nugget objects. [...] This means the fields and data in our model have been chosen to represent a middle ground between being machine processable and being easily understood by the authors themselves. (p. 117)*

A selection of values available in the metadata taxonomy are shown in grey in Figure 107. Thus, for example, description of the particular technique used within

*Figure 92. Conceptual model of a learning activity (adapted from Bailey et al., 2006 and Conole & Fill, 2005)*

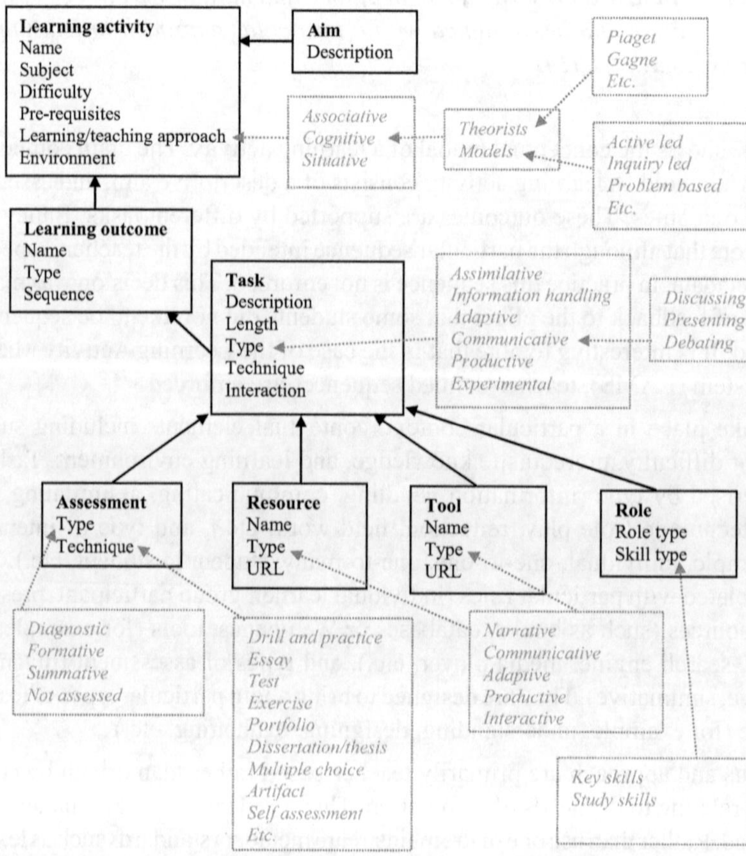


an assessment may be selected from metadata terms including *drill and practice*, *essay*, *test*, *exercise*, and so forth.

The nugget model shares a number of similarities with IMS LD, its main components being mappable to those of LD. For example, *learning activity* may be mapped to LD's *component*, *learning outcome* to *activity structure*, *task* to *learning activity*, and so forth. However, they differ in that they are primarily driven by the requirement to be readily intelligible to the practicing teacher—as opposed to the specialist learning designer or educational technologist. In practical terms, this has resulted in the inclusion of all its components in a single hierarchy, in which components must appear repeatedly if they are used repeatedly within a learning activity. IMS LD defines components separately, then references these definitions from instances within a learning unit. The nugget model also makes more use of relatively long, free-text descriptions of components. IMS LD also enables a higher level of abstraction to be expressed in the form of its *play* and *act* elements.

It has nevertheless been possible to develop an automatic mapping system, which is able to generate, from a nugget model specification, a basic IMS LD. This has been added to the RELOAD software. However, Bailey et al. (2006) consider use of their nugget-based system to be most appropriate at the stage when teachers are initially planning out learning activities. The ease, flexibility, and teacher friendliness of the nugget system militates for adoption by practising teachers. The same qualities, however, mean that complex mappings to IMS LD are not possible, and the authors recommend use of the automatic mapping facility to translate initial thinking to a basic IMS LD. Further complexity and standards-compliant metadata can then be added working within the IMS LD specification working within RELOAD or other LD-compatible authoring tools, to develop more complex and standards-compliant learning activities. However, the very features that stymie fuller mapping from the nugget model to LD are those that avoid a number of problems that arguably afflict learning sequences created using IMS LD and associated authoring tools—in particular, their default enforced linearity.

This work has also highlighted a number of issues relating to IMS LD, and Bailey et al. (2006) suggest, for example, the need to consider how IMS LD can allow the use of metadata at all levels of component (for example, to enable activity structures to have associated metadata specifying prerequisite information, learning objectives, etc.). They also draw attention to the need for IMS LD authoring tools to achieve a more seamless integration between LD and other external standards it references. Assessments, for example, are handled by the separate IMS Question and Test Interoperability (QTI) specification, and the authors make the point that in teachers' minds and practice, assessment is intimately entwined with other aspects of learning design as they create learning activities. They also note:

*In LD, that context is made explicit such that, in order to reuse a component, designers would be required to re-author much of the surrounding contextual metadata. In our project, we have found that the most desirable aspect of our nugget model is not principally to identify what resources are used, but rather how a specific subject is being taught by others. We believe that while the debate on long-term reusability of LD is still undecided, a tool such as ours can greatly increase the perceived reusability of learning design templates by providing a mechanism for abstracting the 'design' of learning activities separately from the business of making executable units of learning. (p. 120)*

Shabajee, McBride, Steer, and Reynolds (2006) report the development of a prototype "digital resource discovery portal," the objective of which was:

*to provide a usable and effective means for school teachers and students to access digital resources in support of their teaching and learning (linked to the local curriculum) from multimedia/interactive-media spread across multiple collections in Singapore. (p. 464)*

The system uses a Content Exchange Metadata Exchange Standard (CEMS) metadata application profile specially constructed to reflect the specific topics, types of resource, and educational levels of the Singaporean school curriculum (NCS, 2004). The *subject* element of this profile was extended with a thesaurus specifying a curriculum-specific controlled vocabulary.

The metadata application profile was converted using the Web Ontology Language (OWL) to form a richer ontological model of the curriculum structure including year groups, types of students, and courses. The linked curriculum thesaurus was also converted to the SKOS resource description framework (RDF)-based thesaurus format (Miles & Brickley, 2005). However, the system is also able to link to more detailed subject-specific curriculum ontologies created externally to reflect the degree of detail required to support specific curricula. One such demonstrator ontology was produced for the project in the area of history enabling learning resources to be tagged with metadata relating to specific people, places, and events. The system is also able to link to external information such as topical news and local events tagged as relevant to particular curriculum topics.

Learners can use a faceted search/browse approach whereby they can apply filters progressively to refine search results by facet including curriculum subject, type of resource (for example, lesson plan), type of media, educational level, availability and licensing terms, and by text search. Metadata terms link to items in the subject ontologies, enabling resource discovery to take advantage of Semantic Web-based inferencing. Thus a text search that includes a particular term describing an ontology element could retrieve resources tagged by terms that are related to that ontology element—for example, instances of a more general concept. By the same token, the addition of a new property to an ontology element would render all resources tagged by metadata linked to that element retrievable by the new property—without each resource requiring to be tagged with the new property. Figure 93 shows some of the components of the history domain ontology developed for the project.

Shown are selections from the classes *Person*, *Event*, *OfficialPosition,* and *Location*. Each class has a number of properties, which may link to other classes. For example, a property of the *Person* class is *involvedInEvent*, which links to the *Event* class. Reciprocally, the *Event* class has a property *thingInvolvedInEvent*, which links reciprocally to *Person*. The *thingInvolvedInEvent* property of the *Event* class also

*Figure 93. Part of a history ontology (adapted from Shabajee et al., 2006)*

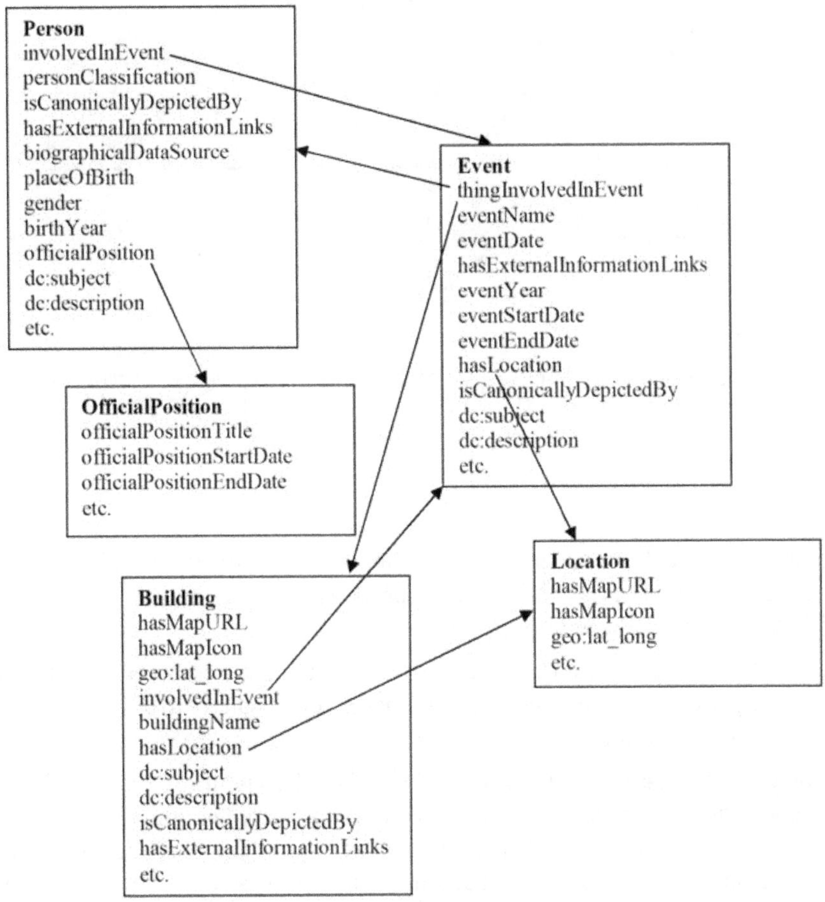


links to the class *Building*, which in turn has a property *hasLocation*, which links to the *Location* class.

Such an ontology enables both browsing and reasoning. Users can browse using relational links to navigate—for example, from a particular person to an event in which he or she was involved, through the location of the event to other events that occurred in the same place—and the people involved. Information can also be retrieved using inheritance. For example, a search for all events involving people born in a particular place does not require each relevant resource to be tagged with place-of-birth information for each person involved in the event. Only the names of the people would be required. The place of birth of each would be inherited via the ontology links as a property of the person. Another advantage is that new in-

*Figure 94. Architecture of the digital resource discovery portal*

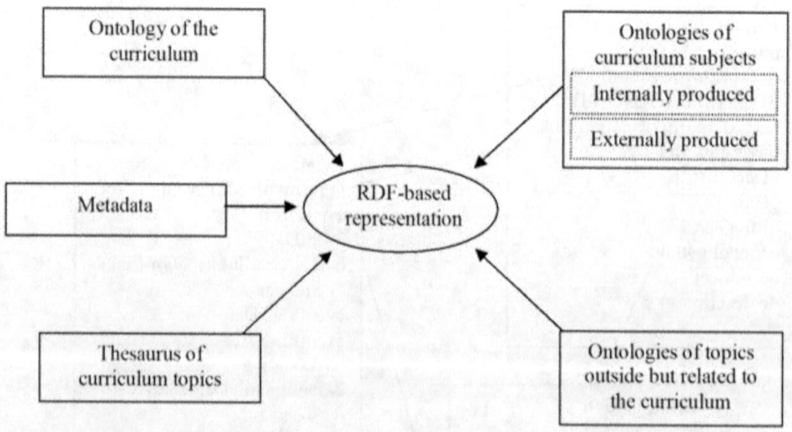


formation can easily be added. For example, if a new property is added to a class, all instances of that class can inherit the property, rather than having to be tagged individually with the new information.

Figure 94 shows the overall architecture of the system. The common RDF format is particularly useful, its open-ended data model enables changes to be made relatively easily and with minimum disruption.

Ontology awareness is also a key feature of TM4L. This is an environment designed to support the building and accessing of ontology-aware learning resource repositories using topic maps (Park & Hunting, 2002; Tramullas & Garrido, 2005). Topic maps are standards-based conceptual graphs similar to semantic networks. Internal and external learning resources are tagged by metadata, including LOM elements, and linked to ontologies that can be created by topic map authors. Authors can also create filters, or *themes*, to provide views of the concept maps to reflect different perspectives. As noted by Dicheva and Dichev (2006), the result is that:

> *a user's access to the learning collection is mediated by a multilayered browsable conceptual map of the subject domain. Strictly speaking, access to the learning collection is mediated by a set of browsable maps corresponding to the set of contexts or perspectives defined on the learning collection. Exploiting the map metaphor, the set of contexts or perspectives on a learning collection are analogous to the different types of maps used in practice, eg, physical, political, economic, climate and population maps. (p. 394)*

By applying themes, personalised views can be made available for different classes of learner (for example, those new to and those more experienced in a particular subject domain). The aim is to facilitate learners' resource discovery by enabling them to browse and search within the constraints of particular contexts specified by topic map authors, thus removing the need for them to sift through large volumes of materials that may be irrelevant due to the imprecision of more traditional keyword searching and browsing systems. The TM4L environment also provides support for the merging of ontologies.

Topic maps have emerged from a different "stable" than OWL-RDF ontologies. The latter are based on a World Wide Web Consortium (W3C) recommendation, whereas topic map standards have been developed by the International Organization for Standardization (ISO). They share similarities and differences, and work is ongoing to enable their integration. Topic maps arguably impose greater structure than semantic networks, and less structure than formal ontologies, although Vatant (2004) argues that the vast majority of developed topic maps express an inherent if not explicit ontology.

Topic maps impose a structure onto otherwise free semantic networks in that they require knowledge to be represented in terms of *topics*, *associations*, and *occurrences*. Topics can be any concept, and associations are relationships between topics. Occurrences link topics with information sources associated with them. This structure belies the basic intention behind the development of focus of topic maps, namely to facilitate the finding of information. The associations between a topic and its names and occurrences are collectively known as the *characteristics* of the topic. A simple topic map is shown in Figure 95.

A topic can be given different names, and different topics can be given the same name. Disambiguation is achieved by allowing the *scoping* of topic names. Different scopes specify the particular contexts within which the associations between particular topic names and occurrences are intended to be interpreted. Thus, for example, two different names for the same topic (say, a formal name and an informal name) can be interpreted in appropriately different ways depending on the scope (work or social) imposed on them. Or different occurrences of the same topic may be appropriate for different people (say, expert and novice).

A scope thus sets up, for a topic's characteristics, a type of namespace—or context in which the characteristics hold. Scopes can be specified that represent the union, or intersection, or different topics. The topics that together form a particular scope are termed a *themes*. Within an educational context, it may be appropriate to define themes such as *beginner* or *expert*, or themes for use as filters to adapt the resources located via the topic map according to particular needs or characteristics of learners.

*Figure 95.*

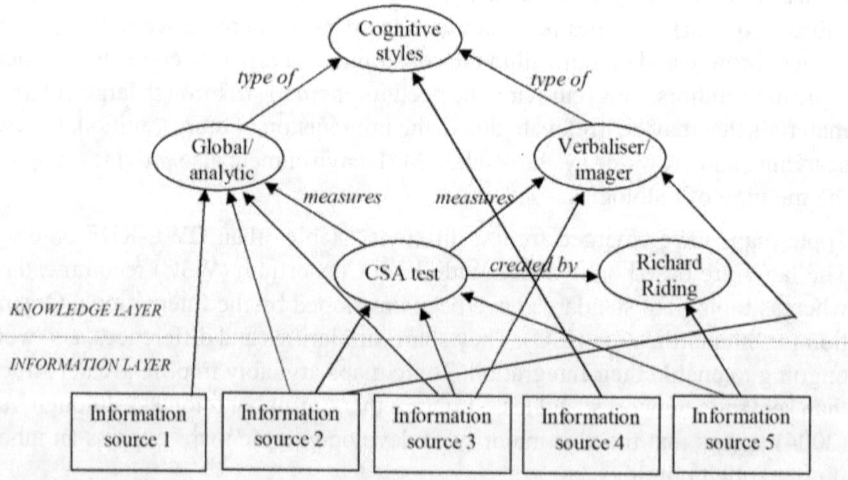


Ovals = topics
Arrows = associations
Boxes = occurrences

Topic maps are supported by XML Topic Maps (XTM)—a standard for representing topic maps in XML (http://www.topicmaps.org/xtm/index.html), and the Topic Map Query Language (TMQL) (http://www.isotopicmaps.org/tmql/).

## Adaptive Systems for Personalised Resource Discovery

One set of examples of educational informatics systems is provided by the relatively recent development of learning-specific adaptive systems, which enable high levels of pedagogical mediation to be applied to an increasingly large, remotely distributed, and shareable range of information sources available over the Internet. Such systems may integrate adaptive personalisation with standards such as SCORM to enable interoperability (Kazanidis & Satratzemi, 2007). The goal of such systems is the delivery of personalized courses, such systems offering the prospect of a blend of *individualised* and *autonomous* learning. However, before we take a look at some examples of such systems, let us first explore the difference between an intelligent adaptive tutoring system, which does *not* meet the criteria of being an educational informatics system, and one that *does*. Figure 96 shows the architecture of a generic intelligent adaptive tutoring system, which falls short of the definition of educational informatics since it does not "engage in or facilitate resource discovery."

The system shown in Figure 96 may be contrasted with that shown in Figure 97. This system uses metadata to locate and select information from collections of multiple independent sources. If such resource discovery is driven by some representation of pedagogical knowledge, then such a system would fall within the definition of educational informatics used here.

The sequence shown in Figure 98 shows how such a system works.

The learning resources can now be presented to the learner. As we will see in the examples presented later on, the learning resources accessed may reside in a particular repository, or in distributed and heterogeneously structured repositories. Increasingly, educational informatics systems are being designed to be able to access less structured open corpus materials on the Web. Also, various components of the system as shown in the figure above can themselves be distributed, residing on different servers across the Internet, and being offered as Web services to other systems.

*Figure 96. A generic intelligent adaptive tutoring system*

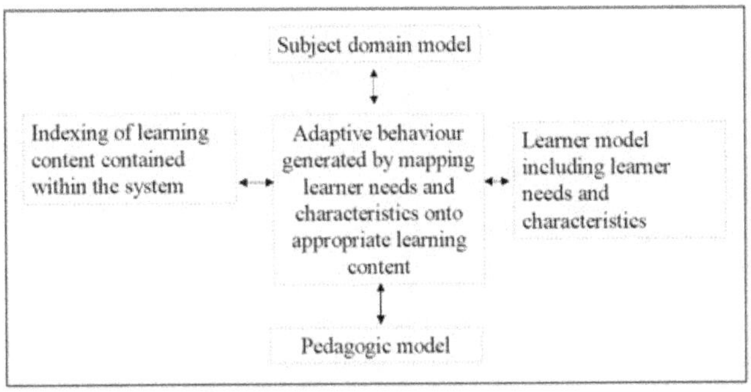


*Figure 97 An educational informatics system*

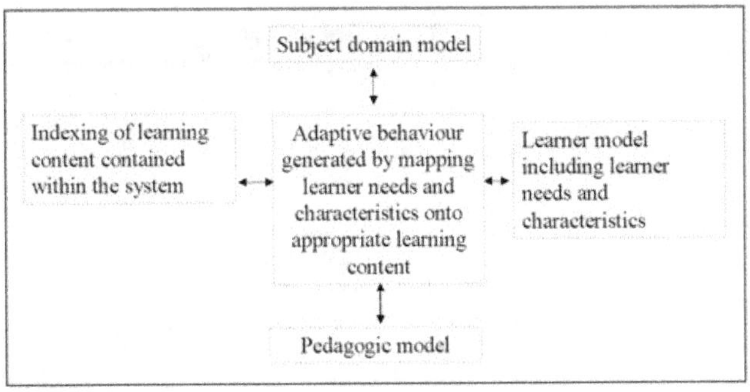

*Figure 98. A stereotypical adaptive educational informatics system in action*

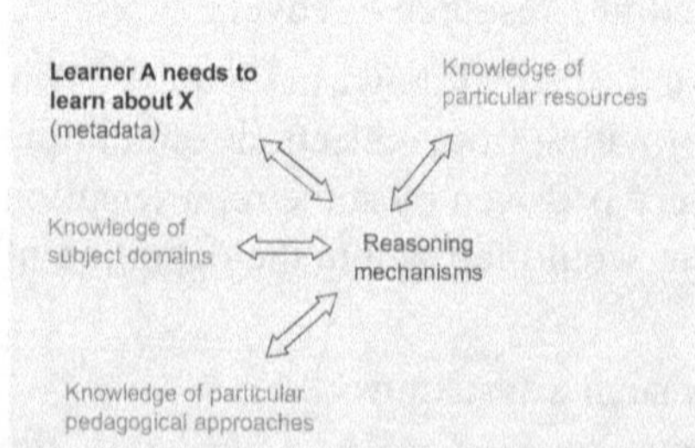


If we assume that a particular learner (learner A) needs to learn about a particular topic (X), then this information will be available to the system in metadata stored relating to what that particular learner has already learned, and what his or her next learning goal is.

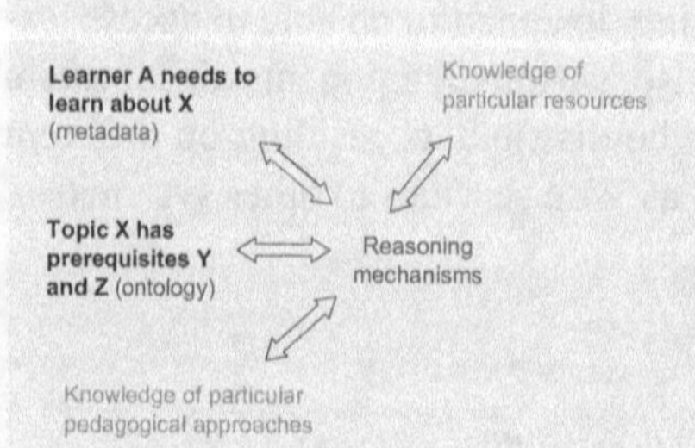


The system looks up the topic to be learned in a subject domain ontology, and discovers that this particular topic has two prerequisites (topics Y and Z).

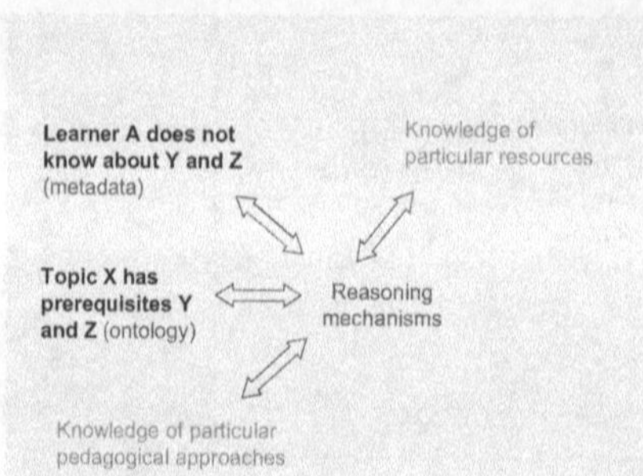


The system reconsults the learner metadata and retrieves the information that this particular learner has not already learned the prerequisite topics.

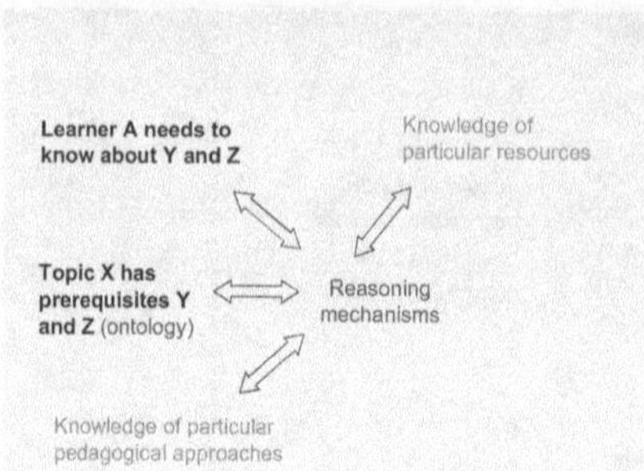


The prerequisite topics Y and Z are set as the next learning goals, which must be achieved before the original learning goal (X) can be tackled.

*continued on following page*

*Figure 98. continued*

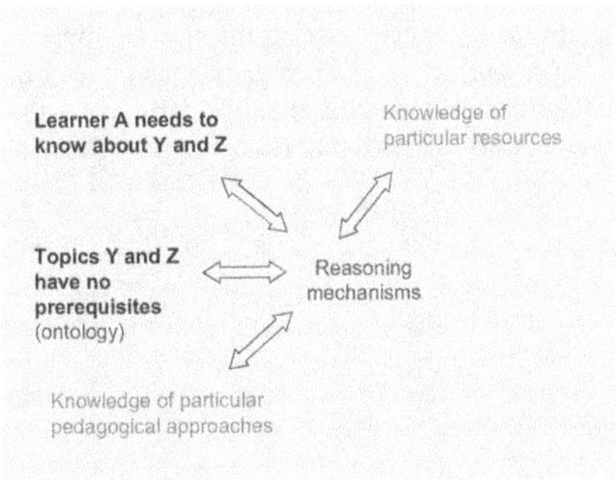


A reconsultation of the subject domain ontology reveals that topics X and Y do not themselves have any prerequisite topics, and therefore can be tackled immediately.

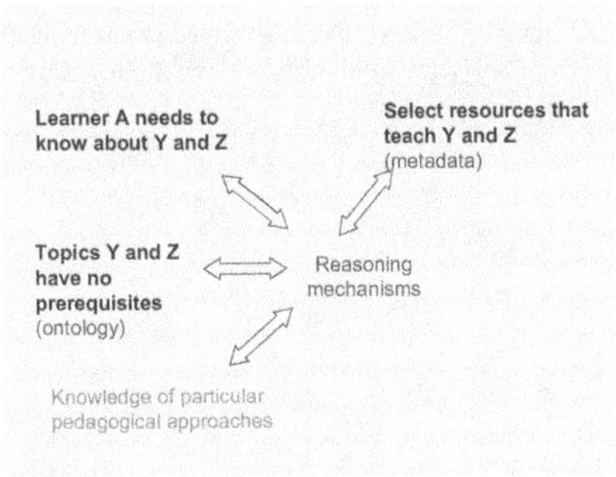


The system then engages in resource discovery, searching for learning materials that teach topics Y and Z. It may do so by searching the metadata records of one or more appropriate learning resource repositories.

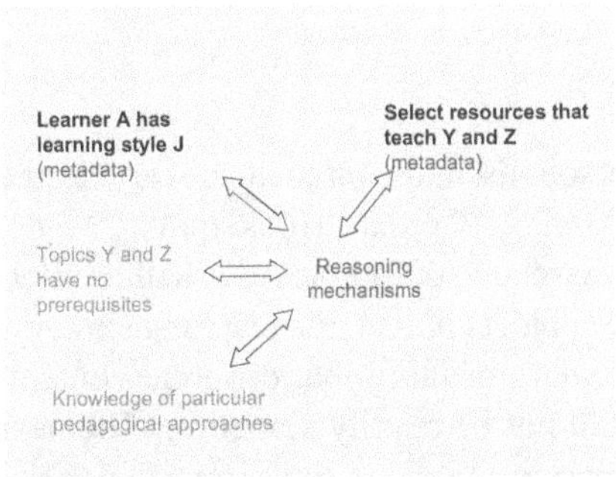


Before selecting the most appropriate learning resource, the system first reconsults the learner metadata which reveals that this particular learner has a preferred learning style (J).

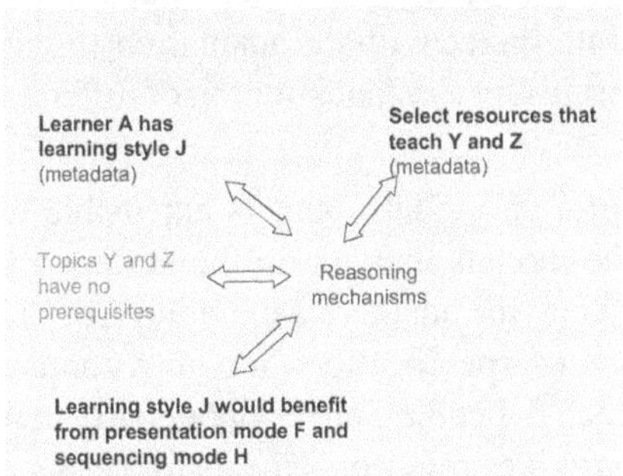


The system's pedagogical model links learning style J with particular presentation and sequencing modes F and H.

*continued on following page*

*Figure 98. continued*

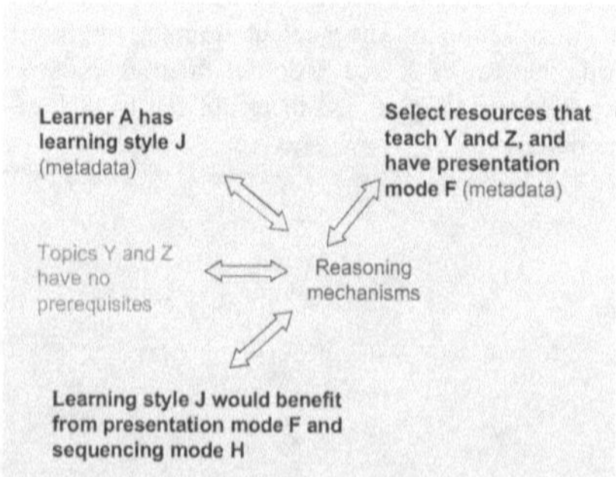


This information is used to select the most appropriate learning resources – i.e. which teach topics Y and Z, and which have a presentation mode which matches the individual learner's preferred learning style.

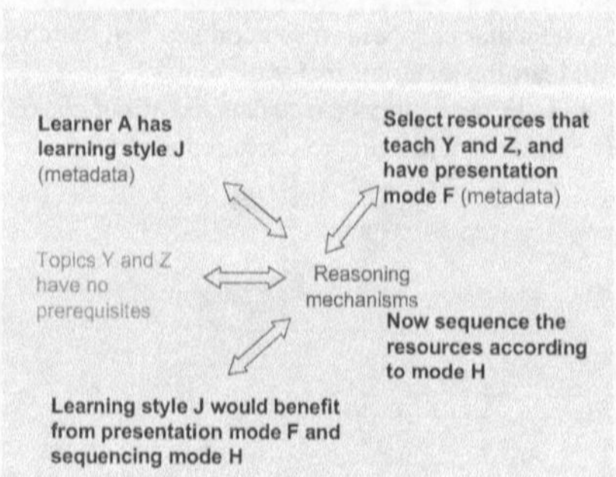


The learning resources are then arranged in a sequence which is appropriate for the learner's particular learning style.

An example of an adaptive system for personalised resource discovery is the Adaptive Personalized eLearning Service (APeLS) (Conlan, Hockemeyer, Wade, & Albert, 2003). Conlan, Wade, Bruen, and Gargan (2002) note how within intelligent tutoring systems, representations of the subject content, the teaching strategy, and the learner were essentially merged together, meaning that different content, never mind different teaching strategies, could not be readily slotted in. The next generation of intelligent computer-assisted learning tools, in the form of adaptive hypermedia systems did separate out content from the learner model—but still the teaching strategy was relatively inextricably interlinked with the adaptation engine and/or the content representation, thus preventing any easy substitution of different teaching approaches.

APeLS works with learner, content, and narrative models—but is extensible to include further models as required. All of the models making up the system are described by metadata, which are used to generate the adaptive behaviour. APeLS' adaptive engine generates particular *narratives*—specifications for how content should be sequenced—in relation to each learner, depending on his or her particular characteristics and knowledge state. These narratives refer to concepts, rather than specific information sources, thus enabling such sources to be updated, changed, or expanded independently of the conceptual narratives they instantiate at run time.

APeLS can take metadata describing an individual's learning needs, prior competences, and personal characteristics and construct a personalised course by discovering and sequencing appropriate learning objects discovered within one or more distributed specialist repositories. Input to a rule-based *adaptive engine* includes metadata relating to the learner, content in the form of learning resources, and narratives. A narrative is a description of the required conceptual pathway for a particular learner and is built prior to searching for particular learning resources, taking account, for example, of prerequisite concepts and their sequencing. Thus, the system's narrative model refers to concepts rather than specific resources.

APeLS provides independent, clearly separated, learner model, subject content model, and pedagogical model. These models can all be accessed by the generic adaptive engine. APeLS accesses a repository of learning objects in order to build a personalised course for the individual learner. Both learning objects and learner are described by metadata. Metadata for each learner provides details of his or her existing knowledge, learning objectives, and learning style. Such information is gleaned from the learner via a questionnaire that he or she completes before using the system. However, the learner can at any time revisit and resubmit this data collection instrument, thus being able to control to some extent his or her own learner model.

One parameter in the learner model relates to individuals' learning styles, which were introduced in Chapter II. The particular learning styles that have been used in work relating to APeLS include Kolb's and Honey and Mumford's styles. The following is an example of how an individual's score on the Honey and Mumford test might be coded in the XML-based learner model (adapted from Clarke, Wade, Conlan, & Dagger, 2003):

```
<andragogical>
    <learningstyle type="honey and mumford">
        <activist>25</activist>
        <reflector>25</reflector>
        <theorist>25</theorist>
        <pragmatist>100</pragmatist>
    </learningstyle>
</andragogical>
```

Learning objects are described using the IMS Learning Resource Metadata (IMS, 2002)—a metadata standard based on LOM (described in Chapter V). Since the IMS metadata scheme does not include data relating to adaptivity, an additional set of metadata is added that allows course designers to add adaptivity types. These include adaptation to learning style, to competencies taught by the object, and/or to competencies required of the learner.

The following XML representation is taken from Canavan (2004, p. 5) and shows how data relating to the learning style for which this particular learning object is suitable can be included in its metadata:

```
<pagelet>
    <general>
        <identifier>dbla04a</identifier>
        <title>DBMS Advantages</title>
        <keyword>DBMS Advantages</keyword>
        <keyword>Database management software advantages</keyword>
        <keyword>commercial products</keyword>
        <description>List of DBMS advantrages</description>
        <language>en</language>
    </general>
    <pedagogical>
        <objectivestaught>
            <objective>db.concepts.background.dbms_advantages</objective>
        </objectivestaught>
        <prerequisite>dbla04</prerequisite>
        <supportedlearningstyle>
            <type style="honey and mumford">
                <activist>25</activist>
                <reflector>25</reflector>
                <theorist>25</theorist>
                <pragmatist>100</pragmatist>
            </type>
        </supportedlearningstyle>
        <semanticdensity />
        <displayarea />
    </pedagogical>
    <technical>
        <location>dbla04a.html</location>
        <format />
        <requirements>
        <size />
```

```
    </technical>
</pagelet>
```

The system builds a list of candidate alternative resources that have the capacity to teach a particular narrative. This *candidacy* approach addresses the criticism that metadata can be too fine-grained in that it relates to specific learning resources as opposed to more abstract concepts (Dagger, Conlan, & Wade, 2003):

*This abstraction allows the course author and instructional designer to design the course in a more structured way without necessarily being concerned with the individual pieces of content that will be used to populate the final course.*

Candidate content groups can be formed containing alternative resources that share, for example, a common learning objective or prerequisite set of concepts. Such resources may reside in distributed repositories. A specific resource may subsequently be selected using a *candidate selector* set of rules (described by its own metadata) on the basis of further decision making according to other rules which take as input, for example, learning style or preferred teaching approach.

*For example, a narrative that adds concepts based on the learner's prior knowledge would, through the rule engine, look at the learner model repository to access the current learner's model. It would then query the learned competencies of that learner before adding the concept. If that concept was represented by a candidate content group with several learning resources the rule engine would execute a candidate selector to choose the appropriate learning resource. The candidate selector would use the rule engine to access the content model of each candidate pagelet before making its selection.*

The *pagelet* in the last line of this quotation refers to a unit of content that is more flexible than a page. The authors note that it is useful for the course designer to decide, prior to creating a narrative, on the level of granularity of the desired personalisation, which may be at different levels—for example, paragraph, section, page, and so forth.

Teaching strategies are thus represented by *narratives*—themselves described by metadata. A narrative embodies a subject expert's representation of the subject content to be learned, and the pedagogical approach to teaching it—for example, case-based learning, experiential learning, simulation, and so forth. Thus, the same learning objectives may potentially be achieved via several different narratives. The adaptive engine selects the most appropriate narrative in terms of which best suits the learner's requirements by reconciling metadata describing the narratives and metadata describing the learner. Relevant data might be, for example, the learner's expressed preference for a particular pedagogical approach.

Only when an appropriate narrative has been selected are specific learning materials identified. This is because the narrative is expressed not in terms of which specific learning materials should be used, but in terms of which *concepts* should be taught and how. Thus, the same narrative may be instantiated, or actually taught, by different specific learning objects. In response to a particular learning narrative, a *candidate content group* is generated, consisting of all the learning objects that could be used to satisfy that particular narrative. At this point, a candidate selector mechanism chooses the most appropriate learning objects to satisfy the selected narrative, taking into account the metadata describing the learning objects in the candidate content groups and, again, the learner metadata. At this stage, learner requirements are taken into account, for example, to select learning objects compatible with the learner's preferred learning style.

The following code is taken from Clarke et al. (2003), and shows how adaptivity type (in this case, relating to competencies taught) can be added to metadata describing a candidate group:

```
<candidategroup>
    <general>
        <identifier>cgmod052-001</identifier>
    </general>
    <members>
        <member>mod052-001</member>
        <member>mod052-001a</member>
        <member>mod052-001b</member>
    </members>
    <educational>
        <adaptivity>
            <adaptivitytype name="competencies.taught">
    <set type="ALL">
        <candidate>
            <langstring
                lang="en">db.datatypes.explanation
            </langstring>
        </candidate>
    </set>
            </adaptivitytype>
        </adaptivity>
```

```
    </educational>
</candidategroup>
```

APeLS is termed an adaptive personalised learning *service* because it is able to deliver its added value through a variety of different learning environments, such as WebCT and Blackboard. APeLS' services are SCORM compliant, and can be delivered to such a learning environment from a different server. APeLS and the learning environment would exchange data relating to each learner's identity and assessment scores. If the learning support facilities provided by a learning environment are not required, APeLS can also be used independently outside such a context. Conlan, O'Keeffe, Brady, and Wade (2007) have recently proposed adding educational *activities* as well as *content* to personalised adaptive systems.

The emphasis of APeLS on control and prespecification of learning objectives and pedagogical strategy does not immediately suggest compatibility with constructivist approaches to learning. Interestingly, however, Conlan et al. (2002) note that:

*Also observed was a behavior that was not originally anticipated—some students used the instrument to regenerate a personalized course for each study period. They interacted with the instrument is such a way that the personalized course produced contained only the content they wished to study for that period. This gave the students greater control over their learning, echoing some of the fundamental concepts of constructivism.*

O'Keeffe, Brady, Conlan, and Wade (2006) report the incorporation and further development of the APeLS system in the iClass project, funded by the European Commission's Framework 6 programme. The iClass service is in fact a framework of services designed to support teachers and learners in providing personalized learning experiences.

The iClass service is able to use learning content from distributed, and diversely organised, learning object repositories, even though these might make use of different metadata formats and ontologies. The service generates a personalized learning path of concepts by reconciling requirements specified by its models relating to learners, teachers, subject conceptual domain, and pedagogical strategy. In doing so it takes account of the learner's characteristics and the teacher's preferred pedagogical strategy (although teachers can if they wish request the system to select pedagogical strategies). Pedagogical strategies specify the type of learning object and relations between them that they require. For example, a *case study* strategy entails an introduction to the concept to be learned, presentation of a problem, provision of appropriate learning resources, and an example solution. In terms of standards, OWL is used for domain ontologies; IMS LD for structuring learning activities; IMS LIP for learner profiles; and SCORM for learning object manifests.

Like APeLS, iClass separates the generation of personalised conceptual learning paths from specific resources that can instantiate such paths. However, an important way in which iClass differs from APeLS is that pedagogy is explicitly represented in a separate model distinct from domain knowledge. Domain knowledge is represented in an OWL-based ontology that specifies concepts and relationships between concepts, which make up the subject domain. Separating out concept knowledge from pedagogical knowledge in this way enables domain experts to concentrate on developing ontologies without having to worry about any particular pedagogy by which the concepts might be taught. Thus, as far as is possible, the domain ontologies are pedagogically neutral. This also means that the same subject domain ontology can be used to generate learning paths using a variety of different pedagogies as required. Thus both pedagogies and domain knowledge can be reused.

As well as a learner model as does APeLS, iClass has a teacher model that stores information relating to, for example, the teacher's pedagogical preferences, and his or her specifications as to any particular type of learning material that should be included or omitted. The teacher will also specify the subdomain of the broad subject area that is to be taught, as well as the learning objectives to be addressed. However, the teacher may, if he or she wishes, hand control over the selection of learning objectives to the learner. Contextual information is also stored in iClass, relating for example to the particular device characteristics being used by particular learners.

The iClass *selector service* produces personalised learning paths. These are similar to APeLS narratives and are similarly conceptual—being divorced from the actual learning objects that will ultimately be delivered to the learner. The selector service comes into play after a subset of the subject domain has been specified by the teacher, and learning objectives have been set. The selector then chooses a pedagogical strategy based on data from the learner and teacher models and applies this strategy to the subject domain. A pedagogical strategy will determine how concepts should be presented to a learner in order to maximise learning.

For example, a case study pedagogical approach may entail the following presentation sequence: (1) an introduction to the concept to be taught; (2) information to set it in context; (3) a statement of a problem to be solved; (4) provision of support materials to help the learner in his or her problem solving; (5) and finally, an evaluation of solutions. Mapping the pedagogical strategy onto concepts depicted in the subset of the domain ontology may entail some restructuring—modification of the relationships between concepts, and possibly breaking down some concepts into more detailed constituent parts—in order to reflect pedagogical requirements. Taking all of this into consideration, the selector generates a personalised learning path.

The selector then interacts with the *learning object generator service*. The learning object generator service finds and/or creates appropriate learning objects to teach the concepts specified in the conceptual personalized learning path. It has access to metadata describing SCORM-based SCOs. Its job is thus to instantiate the conceptual learning pathway with actual learning resources. It does this by *validating* concepts specified in the pathway. Validation entails checking to see whether there are any appropriate learning objects. In doing so, the learning object generator takes into account information from the learner model relating, for example, to preferred learning style—and information from the contextual model relating, for example, to any limitations or requirements of the device via which the learner will be accessing the course.

If no suitable learning object can be found, the generator can attempt to generate a new learning object from smaller-granuled learning assets. If this is not possible, it can also explore different routes through the conceptual space to see if there is any other route by which the concepts can be taught without involving the failed component. Another strategy that the generator can apply is the application of some other (equally suitable in terms of the reconciliation of learner and teacher requirements) pedagogical strategy to see if it is more readily satisfiable from the repository of learning objects and/or the modification of existing learning assets to form new learning objects.

The learning object generator is able to call the *presenter service*, which actually presents learning materials using the sequencing and navigation prescribed by the personalised learning path. The presenter service is able to generate a package containing (1) the required learning objects, and (2) the instantiation of the pedagogical strategy in the form of an IMS LD specification detailing exactly how the content is to be delivered. As discussed in Chapter VI, the IMS LD is designed to be pedagogically independent in that it is able to accommodate a variety of different pedagogical approaches.

Castillo, Gama, and Breda (2006) report GIAS, a system designed to select learning resources from a repository which are appropriate to individual learners' current states of knowledge and their preferred learning styles. The system differs from others in that from a baseline initial psychometric assessment of learning style, it fine-tunes its model of each learner's style in response to feedback from interactions between the learner and learning resources. This on-going adaptation is necessary because of inherent uncertainty in any psychometric assessment of learning style, and also possible drift in learners' preferences over time and as a result of interactions with resources.

Metadata includes descriptions of resources in terms of the type of learning activity they represent (conceptual map, summary, historical review, lesson objectives, etc.), their medium of expression (text, picture, animated picture, audio, video etc.), and their level of difficulty. Learner descriptions include domain knowledge and learning style.

Learning resources in the repository are first filtered to exclude those unsuitable for the learner's current level of domain knowledge. Further filtering then takes place via the matching of features of the resource with learning style preferences. Prior to obtaining any feedback from learner interactions with resources, the system assesses each person's learning style using Felder and SoLOMan's *Index of Learning styles Questionnaire*. The system has a model that predicts the features of learning resources, which will be preferred by learners characterised by each particular style.

However, from an initial state of prediction based on descriptions of stereotypical learning style preferences derived from the literature, this model is able to fine-tune its predictions in relation to each particular individual learner, using feedback from on-going interactions between learner and resources. Data indicating which resource links are visited, and explicit ratings of resources by learners, are able to provide suitable input to an adaptive version of the Naïve Bayes probabilistic classifier—the Adaptive Bayes (Gama & Castillo, 2002) which takes account of new incoming data to update its current model.

Simon, Dolog, Miklós, Olmedilla, and Sintek (2004) also report the development of a personalised adaptive system, which provides unified intelligent access to the diversity of heterogeneous resources potentially accessible to support learning by employees in large organisations. These may include, for example, training materials developed in-house, locally available learning management systems, commercially available courses, in-house knowledge management systems, online bookstores, and so forth. The authors refer to such a range of resources as a "learning space," and report work to develop what they term "smart spaces for learning" entailing systems and approaches capable of providing not only a unified "view" of a learning space, but also the ability to generate personalised learning experiences via a "Personal Learning Assistant," which searches for appropriate resources using metadata describing potential learning resources, subject domains and learners.

As part of the ELENA project (http://www.ELENA-project.org), a prototype system has been set up integrating a range of sources of learning resources including:

- Educanext (a portal supporting the exchange of learning resources).
- The Universitärer Lehrverbund Informatik (ULI) project (a university teaching network entailing the exchange of course materials, courses and certificates).
- IMC CLIX (a commercially produced Learning Management System).
- IteachYou (a multimedia learning environment designed for the Internet or intranets).
- Arel (a service for relatively large organisations offering live and on-demand broadcasts by experts to virtual classes).

The Personal Learning Assistant provides personalised access to the learning space, enabling learners to search for and select appropriate learning resources. The system is predicated on the existence of RDF-based metadata describing services, resources, and learners. This metadata can be used as input to reasoning mechanisms using, for example, the TRIPLE Semantic Web RDF querying language (Henze, Dolog, & Nejdl, 2004; Sintek & Decker, 2002) to engage in intelligent reasoning. Such reasoning can map diverse metadata schemes (used by different communities providing metadata) to that preferred by the Personal Learning Assistant. The Personal Learning Assistant can take as input an individual's *learner profile* consisting of metadata relating to his or her learning needs, and existing accredited competencies (for example, levels of knowledge of particular topics measured on a particular test) in relation to those needs, and can then search the metadata describing the distributed learning resources on the network in order to achieve a match, generating personalised learning experiences for learners.

The learner profile is coded using the IEEE PAPI standard. The IMS LIP standard enables learner preferences to be expressed (e.g., language, location, disability, communication device preference). Work is also reported designed to incorporate metadata relating to learners' organisational roles and aspirations to which their employing organisation may have input (Gunnarsdóttir, Heimerl, Kieslinger, Simon, & Tsiortou S., 2004). Learning resources are described using the IEEE LOM standard, which enables their description in terms of, for example, their educational level, objectives, and prerequisites in terms of other learning resources, or competencies.

Melis et al. (2006) also report the development of a system designed to provide intelligent access to learning objects stored in diverse repositories using different metadata schemes. The system is based on an open services-oriented architecture, its components, and Web services being reusable in that they can be used by different applications. The system is specific to the teaching of mathematics, and it enables the use of learning objects that have been semantically marked up using the OMDoc standard (Caprotti, Carlisle, & Cohen, 2002). This allows the interpretation and validation of mathematical expressions (enabling, for example, feedback on exercises), and the use of various standard mathematical services.

Learning objects are tagged with metadata derived from Dublin Core and LOM. However, unsatisfied with the expressive power of LOM, the researchers developed an ontology of learning objects. This ontology is independent of any particular pedagogy, and specifies, for example, types of interactivity (exercise, exploration, real world problem, etc.), evidence (proof, demonstration), illustration (example, counter-example), and evidence (proof, demonstration).

However, the *mediator service* can also search for content located in distributed repositories and tagged using different metadata schemes. According to Melis et al. (2006):

*A typical query to the ActiveMath mediator inquires about the existence of elements that fulfill given constraints. An answer consists of a list of identifiers of matching elements. For instance, the query (getItems [class exercise] [property for deriva-*

*tion] [property difficulty low] [property field computer science]) returns all easy exercises for the mathematical concept derivation with a computer science context. (p. 409)*

The mediator service translates a query from a client component, formulated in its own metadata schema, into the mediator's own schema. It then searches remote repositories, translating the query into the different metadata schemas used by these repositories, before merging the results and passing them back to the client. This work complements other approaches to the mapping of different ontologies within an e-learning context such as that reported by Gasevic and Hatala (2006).

The *course generator* assembles learning objects using a hierarchical task network planner. In selecting appropriate learning objects it takes account of each learner's existing knowledge stored in its learner model, in order to identify prerequisite concepts to be taught. The planner can generate different learning sequences to reflect different tutorial strategies. The authors give an example sequenced according to Merrill's (2002) "first principles of instruction" (presented in Chapter III), which entails presentation of learning objects designed to provide motivation and basic familiarisation with the concept to be taught, followed by presentation of the concept, elaborations, examples, exercises, and finally concluding comments.

Abdullah and Davis (2005) note that SCORM has been criticised for its lack of ability to support individualisation in learning, and to adapt to learners' individual differences—for example, their learning styles. It restricts learners to "a static pool of learning resources organized in a predefined narrative structure" (p. 61). They acknowledge that a number of approaches have been taken to subvert SCORM sequencing, for example via the dynamic reassembly of SCORM learning objects to match learners' individual needs in terms of their prior knowledge (Shute & Towle, 2003), and by extending SCORM's sequencing rules to include an element of adaptation (Blackmon, Brooks, Roberts, & Rehak, 2004).

They have prototyped an alternative approach in which they preserve the sequencing of original SCORM-based learning materials, while providing access to additional personalised learning resources relevant to each learner's particular needs. Basically, an adaptive interface is interposed between the SCORM runtime environment and external Web-based resources. The adaptive interface takes input from a subject domain model, and a user model that stores information about each learner's characteristics including learning style, as well as dynamic information about the learner's activities within the SCORM player. Learners are able to change the information concerning their learning style in the user model if they wish.

The system analyses the SCORM manifest, which provides details of the learning materials and their organisation. Terms derived from the manifest are mapped to terms existing in the subject domain model, automatically creating a concept map. At any point in learning, the adaptive interface can associate the particular learning resource being viewed by the learner in the SCORM player with a term in the concept map. The concept name, and information detailing the learner's learning style, are then sent (as a Simple Object Access Protocol [SOAP] request) to a personalised link Web service (PLS). The PLS then queries the AuldLinky hyperlink server, which is able to search using both parameters relating to the learner's needs.

The result of the query is a list of URLs linked to additional information sources relevant to both the subject and learning style of the individual learner. This list is returned to the client via the PLS, and a hyperlinked description of each new source (derived from its metadata) is displayed in a frame at the bottom of the learner's SCORM player screen. Should the learner click a link, the new document appears in a pop-up window.

## Open Corpus Resource Discovery

A number of educational informatics systems are designed to enable resource discovery not only of materials stored in specialised repositories, but also open corpus material available on the Web. Dolog, Henze, Nejdl, and Sintek (2004), for example, report development of the "Personal Reader," which is also based on metadata-based reasoning mechanisms.

From the starting point of a learning resource being studied by a learner, the Personal Reader discovers resources that are related to the currently viewed resource. It can recommend resources that provide a different perspective on the topic—for example, a summary, more general or more specific material, or examples illustrating the concepts involved. It can do this at a local level utilizing closed corpus resources stored in a particular educational repository. However, at a global level it can also engage in the discovery of open corpus material available on the Web. The authors' aim is to work towards the vision of an adaptive web capable of leveraging open corpus material (Brusilovsky, 2001; Brusilovsky & Maybury, 2002; Henze & Nejdl, 2001).

Using standards-based metadata derived from standards-based ontologies can enable the exploitation of some of the potential of the Semantic Web. Figure 99 shows an example of the sort of ontologies being developed.

Metadata relating to resources, learners, learning activities, interactions, subject domains, and documents are represented as RDF triples. As in the case of the previously described Personal Learning Assistant, reasoning takes place using the TRIPLE RDF querying language. Metadata describing particular documents employs terms from a subject domain ontology, and thus prerequisite and other relationships between topics can be established. Users are also described using metadata relating to learning performance, competencies, and certification. Metadata describing a particular learner could indicate, for example, that he or she has obtained a certain score in a test after studying a certain concept.

The system uses adaptation reasoning rules (described more fully in Dolog et al., 2003) to discover and recommend additional resources conceptually and pedagogically linked to the current resource being viewed by the learner—such as an *example* of the concept under consideration. Examples of rules are given as follows:

*FORALL D, E example (D,E) <-*
*studyMaterial(D) AND example(E) AND*
*EXISTS C1 (D[dc:subject->C1]) AND*
*FORALL C2 (D[dc:subject->C2] -> E[dc:subject->C2]).*

This rule basically finds an example (E) which exemplifies all the concepts covered in some study material (D). The rule states:

*Figure 99. Ontology supporting the Personal Reader (adapted from Dolog, Henze, & Nejdl, 2003)*

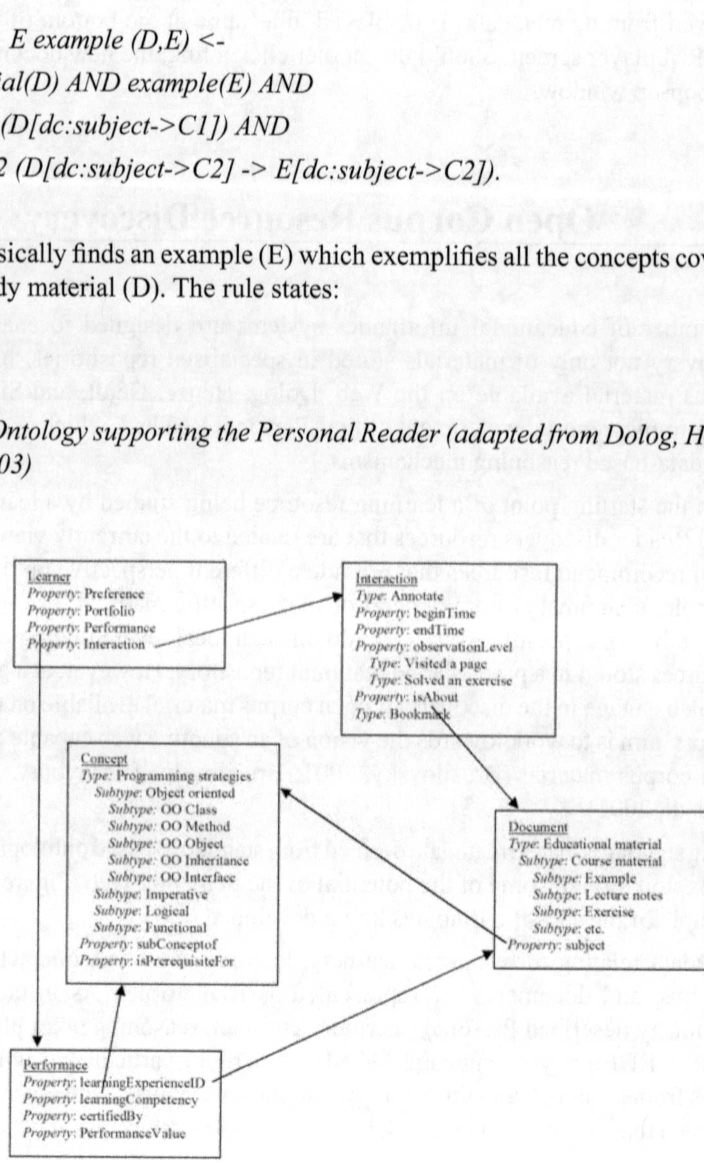

*Example (E) is an example of the content of the study material (D) if*

*D is indeed some "study material" [according to the "document" ontology] and E is indeed an "example" [again, according to the "document" ontology] and*

*Study material D contains a measurable concept C1 [there exists a Dublin Core (dc) metadata annotation of the type "dc:subject" for the concept] and*

*Each concept (C2) contained in study materials (D) is also covered in the example (E).*

*FORALL D, E weaker_example(D,E) <-*
*studyMaterial(D) AND example(E) AND*
*EXISTS C (D[dc:subject->C] AND E[dc:subject->C]).*

The previous rule finds a "weaker" example—that is, at least one of the concepts covered in study materials (D) is included in example (E). The rule states:

*Example (E) is a "weaker" example of the content of the study material (D) if*

*D is indeed some "study material" and E is indeed an "example" and*

*Study material D contains a measurable concept C and*

*Example (E) covers the same concept (C).*

*FORALL D, E, U best_example(D,E,U) <-*
*studyMaterial(D) AND example(E) AND user(U) AND example(D,E) AND*
*FORALL C ( (E[dc:subject->C] AND NOT D[dc:subject->C]) ->*
*p_obs(C, U, Learned) ).*

The previous rule finds the "best" example in terms of an example which takes into account what the learner already knows. The rule states:

*Example (E) is the "best" example of the content of the study material (D) for user (U) if*

*D is indeed some "study material" and E is indeed an "example" and example (E) is an example of the concepts covered in (D) [using the first "example" rule described above] and*

*Each concept (C) contained in the example (E) but not contained in the study materials (D)*

*Has been already learned by user (U) [according to that person's user profile—see later on].*

The last line in the previous rule will call another rule, shown hereafter, which determines if indeed there is a record in the particular learner's user (U) profile that he or she has already learned concept (C).

*FORALL C, U p_obs(C, U, Learned) <- user(U) AND concept(C) AND*
*EXISTS P (U[learner:hasPerformance->P] AND user_performance(P) AND*
*P[learner:learningCompetency -> C]).*

The previous rule states:

*User (U) has been observed to have learned concept (C) if user (U) is indeed a user [according to the "learner" ontology] and concept (C) is indeed a concept and*
*User (U) has a performance record (P) in his/her user profile and*
*That performance record (P) indicates that the user has achieved learning competency in concept (C).*

Examples can be recommended on the basis of what the learner has and has not already learned. Reasoning rules can use ontology relationships, which specify that, for example, a particular concept is a subconcept of another. This can be used, for example, to discover and recommend more general, or more specific resources.

As noted previously, as well as operating within the context of a closed corpus repository of learning materials, the Personal Reader system is also able to access open corpus materials such as those available on the Web. A minimal requirement for Personal Reader to be able to utilize any such open corpus resource is that it is described by metadata in RDF format. However, even granted that, problems may arise since the quality, completeness, and extent of metadata describing those resources may be very variable, and metadata schemes used may also differ from source to source. Thus the system has a number of strategies in place to discover and utilize open corpus materials. As when operating with a closed corpus repository, the first task is to obtain metadata describing the resource currently being studied by the user. On the basis of this, a query is constructed, which is then run using Edutella (Nejdl et al., 2002), TAP Semantic Web search (Guha, McCool, & Miller, 2003), or Lixto (Baumgartner, Flesca, & Gottlob, 2001).

An ontology mapping function makes use of the TRIPLE language to map metadata expressed in different schemes to that used by the system (Miklos, Neumann, Zdun,

& Sintek, 2003). However, even allowing for such a mapping, the variable nature of metadata describing open corpus resources means that any given resource may be only minimally or partially described compared to what the Personal Reader would optimally require.

Thus a query relaxation function has been developed that, if an insufficient number of resources is located, relaxes the query, for example, by using the underlying ontology to find broader, sibling, or narrower concepts, or by dropping a restriction such as resource type. The authors report that such heuristics can enable successful query reformulation even when metadata quality is low. Where metadata describing a particular resource does not indicate prerequisite concepts, to some extent these can be inferred from ontologies relevant to the subject of the resource (Dolog et al., 2004). An example of a relaxing rule is given as follows:

*FORALL C, CS similar_concept (C, CS, 1)*
*direct_super (C, CS) OR direct_super (CS, C).*

*FORALL C, CS, D, D1 similar_concept (C, CS, D)*
*D > 1 AND D1 is D - 1 AND similar_concept (C, CS1, D1) AND*
*(direct_super (CS, CS1) OR direct_super (CS1, CS)) AND not unify (C, CS).*

This rule states that

*For concept (C), another concept (CS) is a similar concept, located one level (1) away [in an appropriate subject ontology]*
*If the other concept (CS) is directly super-ordinate [in the ontology] to concept (C), or concept (C) is directly super-ordinate to the other concept (CS).*
*For concept (C), another concept (CS) is a similar concept, located (D) number of levels away [in an appropriate subject ontology]*
*If (assuming that it is not less than 2) we reduce the "number of levels away" by 1 (this new number is D1)*
*And for concept (C),* ***another other*** *concept (CS1) is a similar concept to the original similar concept (CS), located D1 levels away from the original concept (C) in the ontology*
*And concept (CS) is directly super-ordinate to concept CS1) or concept (CS) is directly subordinate to concept (CS1), and concepts (C) and (CS) are not the same.*

Additional rules are applied if rules such as the previous one have an excessively relaxing effect and produce too many queries. If this happens, one approach is to calculate the degree of similarity between, for example, titles in the following fields: dc:title, dc.subject, dc.description, and so forth.

Abel et al. (2006) report the extension of the Personal Reader system to the notion of the Personal Reader *Agent*. This is more flexible than the Personal Reader in that it allows users to choose, configure, and use configurable Web services. It also allows users to store and manage their saved configurations. Web services were introduced in Chapter VI. Configurable Web services provide RDF-based descriptions of how they may be configured in various ways according to the preferences of their users.

Personal Reader Agent first requests descriptions of all the Web services available in its Universal Description, Discovery, and Integration (UDDI) registry. These descriptions are shown to the user so that he or she may select those of interest. For each service selected by the user, the system reads the details of the available configuration parameters and presents these as HTML forms to the user. The system then calls the service with the relevant configuration details. The system not only allows the user to save his or her configuration for subsequent repeat use, but is also able to make recommendations of other people's configurations on the basis of an assumed similarity between them and the user. This similarity is based on an ontology of people and working groups known to the system. The assumption is that configurations made by one member of the same working group may be of interest to others.

Lawless, Wade, and Conlan (2005) also address the issue of enabling personalized adaptive systems to discover open corpus material. They report explorations designed to enable the previously described APeLS adaptive system to make use of unstructured or inconsistently structured open corpus content including that available on the Web and other open source repositories. They propose an extension of the APeLS system to incorporate a function that searches for open corpus content in such a way as to generate learning objects, which can then provide input to the existing APeLS adaptive facilities. Where the newly sourced content does not have structured metadata from a standard scheme recognized by the system, it must be analysed in order to generate a new learning object. The learning object generator is provided with metadata relating to both the learner and the specification of the learning object that is required (for example, learning objectives and prerequisite knowledge). The generator will use this data to make decisions about which parts of the newly sourced content to include, and how to structure them to form the learning object. Once created, the learning object can be tagged with metadata and made available to the APeLS adaptive engine as it attempts to generate a personalized course.

Chen, Magoulas, and Dimakopoulos (2005) report a study relevant to open corpus retrieval in which they investigated the way in which information retrieved by general search engines might more effectively be displayed to suit different users' cognitive styles. A sample of university students were tested for cognitive style using Ridings's *Cognitive Styles Analysis*, and given three information retrieval tasks, using Google, Lycos, and AltaVista. After completion of the tasks, and inspection of retrieved items, they were given a questionnaire asking about their reactions and preferences.

The authors report specific differences consistent with general hypotheses derived from a review of cognitive style literature. These general hypothesised differences were that, relative to field-dependent individuals, field-independent searchers would:

- Be less influenced by external structuring and formatting (hypothesis 1).
- Display a more active approach to locating relevant information (hypothesis 2).
- Be more analytic as opposed to global in their orientation to the displayed results (hypothesis 3).

The specific differences in preferences reported by the subjects are shown in Table 29, along with the related hypotheses.

The authors go on to propose (1) a set of guidelines for the design of display interfaces based on these results, and (2) a specific interface design which presents options relevant to different cognitive style preferences.

An inherent problem in any educational informatics system designed to adapt to individual user's cognitive styles is the need to obtain data allowing them to establish each person's style. A number of systems take the approach of asking users to complete some test prior to using the system, but the development of less obtrusive ways of establishing styles would be advantageous. If styles could be assessed using data derived from real-time learning activities on the part of the learner, this might offer the prospect not only of more convenient testing, but also of adjustments (fine-tuning and possibly corrections) being made by the system in response to ongoing learner activity over time.

In a related further study, Frias-Martinez, Chen, and Liu (2007) tested a number of approaches to such automatic cognitive style assessment. In a series of experiments, they tested the relative effectiveness of inductive classification approaches using decision trees and neural networks, a regression approach, and neuro-fuzzy system approaches. Quinlan's C4.5 machine learning algorithm, a multilayer perceptron neural network, two regression techniques, and two types of neuro-fuzzy systems were selected for testing.

The cognitive styles of a sample of university students were assessed, again using Riding's *Cognitive Styles Analysis*, and the students were then asked to perform a series of seven search tasks using the Brunel University library catalogue. The tasks

*Table 29. Field-dependent/-independent differences in retrieval display preferences (adapted from Chen et al., 2005)*

| | Field-dependent users prefer… | Field-independent users prefer… |
|---|---|---|
| Hypothesis 1 | Main subject categories and subcategories to be presented separately—subcategories on another page | Main subject categories and subcategories to be presented together, subcategories appearing under the main categories |
| Hypothesis 2 | Subject categories and related results to be displayed according to relevance | Subject categories and related results to be displayed in alphabetical order |
| Hypothesis 3 | More main subject categories with fewer levels of subcategory | Fewer main subject categories, but containing more levels of subcategory |

were designed to require both specific searching and browsing behaviour. A proxy server recorded details of searcher interactions with the catalogue, thus generating input variables that could be used to test different approaches to the automatic classification of cognitive style. The results of the automatic classification of styles were compared with those of the *Cognitive Styles Analysis*.

It is interesting that this test assesses global (field dependent) and analytic (field independent) cognitive styles based on performance on a series of visual tests of the individual's ability to (1) dis-embed a shape from a more complex pattern in which it is embedded, and (2) judge whether two complex patterns are or are not identical. The measures used to classify styles automatically were derived from each individual's logged interactions with the library catalogue. These variables consisted of frequencies of use of:

- The *Basic Search* facility
- The *Advanced Search* option
- The "word or phrase" option in *Basic Search*
- The "author," "title," and "periodical" options in *Basic Search*
- The "New Search" option
- The "Go Back" option

The authors found that a regression approach outperformed the classification approach, and that a *soft computing* neuro-fuzzy approach could further improve accuracy. Frias-Martinez et al. (2007) conclude that:

*The results obtained by using a neuro-fuzzy approach in this context have shown that the system can be applied to automatically generate user models for cognitive personalization, thus avoiding the main inconvenience of constructing cognitive personalizedinterfaces. We consider that these improvements open the door to actually implement high-scale personalized digital librariesbased on cognitive styles. (p. 250)*

García, Amandi, Schiaffino, and Campo (2007) also report attempts at the automatic detection of students' learning styles using Bayesian networks, which are used to model different aspects of learner behaviour as they interact with an e-learning system, and inductively to derive categorisations of style.

## From Supplantation to Metacognition

The educational informatics systems discussed in Chapters VII and VIII make intelligent use of pedagogical knowledge in order to engage in resource discovery. In doing so, they take certain decisions on behalf of the learner—in other words, to an extent *supplant* certain of the learner's intellectual processes. However, a number of educational informatics systems adopt a different approach in that they seek to increase the degree of learners' control over their own learning processes.

For example, Papanikolaou and Grigoriadou (2006) propose an instructional framework designed to give learners control over the level of autonomy with which they learn. After choosing a learning goal to work on, the learner is provided with choice in relation to learning approach and the level of guidance he or she would like to receive. If the learner chooses a prescriptive approach, the system generates a learning sequence. It selects learning objects according to each person's learning style and provides navigation advice tailored to each learner's level of competence in the topics being taught. It also gives learners the opportunity to take more control by changing their own profile relating to competence and preferred style, and/or switching off the system's adaptive and advisory features.

If the learner chooses a constructivist approach, then the system provides project-based tasks. This mode includes a *problem manipulation space* in which the learner can generate a hypothesis and search for appropriate information to support it. The system provides support in the form of suggesting appropriate Web resources and peers who may be able to help. These suggestions are based on the system's knowledge of each learner's existing level of knowledge and his or her learning style. The learner can switch to prescriptive mode if he or she wishes at any time. The system thus enables learners to take varying levels of control over certain aspects of their learning. The constructivist learning mode entails a looser degree of control by the system in that open corpus materials are recommended within the context of more learner-driven information seeking.

Czarkowski and Kay (2006) report the development of Tutor3, which is also designed to make its adaptivity transparent to and controllable by users. The authors note that this is desirable to the extent that it may engender more trust in the system on the part of users, compensate for any errors or limitations in the adaptations, and be useful in facilitating reflective learning. The authors note that transparency also to some extent addresses issues raised by Kobsa (2002) relating to legal requirements for people to be able to access personal details stored about them, to understand the way in which they are being used, and if necessary to modify them.

Learning content is marked up using the Adaptive Text Markup Language (ATML) designed by the authors. This enables descriptions of adaptive components of learning resources to be attached to the resources themselves as metadata. This data is then used to enable a matching between learner characteristics and required adaptations. A document may thus contain different content for display in response to different learner requirements, which are stored in the user profile. Learners are initially asked about their learning goals and preferences, and this information is stored in each learner's profile. Such knowledge relates, for example, to the person's learning objectives, interests and preferences—for example: to learn new material or to revise; to engage in minimal levels of learning "just enough to pass"; or to master the material thoroughly; preference for abstract definitions, concrete examples; and so forth.

The ATML markup language enables different sections of a document to be tagged with information specifying for which learner profile features they are appropriate. Thus, for example, only appropriately tagged content will be presented to a learner who has expressed a preference for a minimalist approach to learning, or if the learner's current learning objective is to revise, then he or she will be passed to a set of multiple choice revision questions. The approach is similar to but simpler than that used in the AHA system (De Bra & Ruiter, 2001). There exists a wide range of adaptive methods and techniques available to the designers of educational systems, and notion of transparency in adaptation is likely to receive increasing attention. Brusilovsky (2003), for example, based on empirical evidence that individuals with differing levels of domain knowledge may react differently to different adaptive approaches, makes the case for meta-adaptive systems that are able to adapt the nature of adaptation to individual users.

Rather than enabling learners to control the type and level of supplantation they receive from the system in relation to the processes of resource discovery, the approach described hereafter seeks to bring about strategic behaviour on the part of learners so that they can themselves more effectively engage in resource discovery. It does this by seeking to make accessible learners' own implicit metacognitive knowledge in order to bring about information-seeking activity appropriate to the particular learning task on which he or she is engaged.

This approach to educational informatics is employed in work reported by Cole designed to build what may be described as *metacognitive devices* into an information retrieval system. The reader is referred to the definition and discussion in Chapter III of *metacognition* and its relationship with concepts including *cognitive, autonomy*, *versatility*, and *learning to learn*. The system reported later on may be considered to represent an attempt to build *metacognitive*, as opposed simply to *cognitive* devices to the extent that the intention of the researchers was to use the devices to help learners develop knowledge and skills that are generalisable beyond the specific content being learned in the experiments. It may be contrasted with approaches such as that reported, for example, by Kassab and Lamirel (2007) in which the system attempts to estimate, from its knowledge of individual information seekers, the nature of their information needs in terms of the relative balance they may require between recall and precision.

Cole's work is predicated on recognition of the inherently imprecise nature of "information needs" and builds on a range of library and information science-based theoretical perspectives including those of Kuhlthau, Taylor, Belkin, and Oddy. Taylor (1968) suggested that awareness of one's information needs may vary from unconscious to explicitly known and clearly expressible. Importantly, in the early stages of working on an assignment, while the overall problem or topic may be clear, the associated information needs may be far from so, and not explicitly known or expressible by the learner. Cole follows Belkin, Oddy, and Brooks (1982a, 1982b) in acknowledging the paradox (discussed in Chapter IV) whereby information seekers are required to express what they do not know. This is the case particularly where a learner is in the early exploratory stages of an assignment—for example, Kuhlthau's "focusing" stage—a stage at which, Cole argues, many university students approach an information retrieval system to help them in essay assignments.

Cole, Cantero, and Ungar (2000) note that:

*We can envisage Kuhlthau's six stage ISP as a series of visits to the academic library where on each visit the undergraduate reads something that shifts his or her information need, abstract space or cognitive state as he or she progresses from stage 1 to stage 6 of the essay writing process. (p. 484)*

Kuhlthau (2004, 2006) has identified six stages students go through when they are doing their college assignments; these are shown in Table 30. The particular knowledge and information needs of students as they pass through these stages are very different, and Cole and his colleagues are working to create "devices" that stimulate students to engage in appropriate information behaviour relative to the various stages. Their initial work has focused on stage 3, in which the student is extending his or her personal knowledge about the topic.

*Table 30. Kuhlthau's information search process (adapted from Cole et al., 2000)*

| Stage | Description | Task | Information need |
|---|---|---|---|
| 1 Initiation | The student becomes aware of a lack of knowledge. | To "recognize a need for information" | "Background" information |
| 2 Selection | The student chooses the general topic to be tackled. Prospective topics are considered. | To "identify and select the general topic" | "Relevant" information |
| 3 Exploration | The student extends his or her personal understanding of the general topic. He or she needs to orient him/herself and to try to form a focus. | To "investigate information on the general topic in order to extend personal understanding" | "Relevant" information |
| 4 Formulation | In the light of information found, the student forms a focus. | To "form a focus from the information" | "Relevant/focused" information |
| 5 Collection | The student gathers information relevant to the focus of the assignment. | To "gather information related to the focused topic" | "Relevant/focused" information |
| 6 Presentation | The student completes and presents the finished assignment. | To "complete search and prepare to present findings" | "Relevant/focused" information |

Cole argues that the expressed information need (forming a query to an information retrieval system) may not correspond at all well with what may subsequently turn out to be much more appropriate at a more advanced stage of learning. He argues that the refinement and increased awareness of the learner's information need may emerge during, and as a result of, interaction with an "enabling" information retrieval system.

The ultimate aim (Cole et al., 2000) is of a tool which can be added to the front-end of an information retrieval system which:

> *...if administered to the undergraduate at the beginning of his or her interaction with the IR system, will allow the system to make this diagnosis, then select the 'enabling' device that is most appropriate to that particular student at that particular time. The 'enabling' device ... is also a query formulation device: it draws-out from the student the concepts most pertinent to the task of writing an undergraduate essay for the student's topic; it then sorts/weights the concepts into a truly 'effective' query to the IR system. (p. 499)*

Cole has developed models and associated prototype relating to the notion of an enabling information retrieval system. This work is included here as an educational informatics system since it entails the use of pedagogical knowledge—in this case, knowledge of how learners' implicit metacognitive knowledge can be leveraged by the use of enabling devices in order to facilitate more effective resource discovery. The conceptual and prototype experiments have also been developed with reference to a specifically educational task. The system provides searchers with a degree of metacognitive stimulation in the form of a template task structure model relating specifically to a particular type of essay typically set for undergraduate social sciences/humanities courses.

This work is based inter alia on Brookes' (1977, 1980) conjecture that communication entails a two-level process. The first involves an analysis of what the sender of a communication is intending to say. The second represents the receiver's integration of the author's message within the broader context of the task in which he or she is engaged (Cole & Mandelblatt, 2000, p. 1035).

The system prompts the learner to engage in Brookes' second level of analysis, providing a degree of support in the form of a *task intervention device.* This consists of specific instructions aimed at helping searchers better align their queries to the information system and the structural requirements of their essay tasks (Cole, 2000):

> *The IRS offers the device to the student when the student indicates the nature of his or her information task to the system. In summary, the device schematizes a type of essay structure commonly used in history called the compare-and-contrast essay. Second, the device forces the student to think of the essay as an integrated whole, centered on an argument or thesis statement ... While filling in the device, ... the student must cognitively integrate the structure of a compare-and-contrast essay into what he or she already knows about his or her essay topic. The result for the student of being stimulated by the IR device to assemble then taskfocus his or her response to the IRS's informative message is the transformation of the student's cognitive state or way of thinking about the essay. The student's cognitive state is then ready to receive the information contained in the next IRS message in a more productive, application-focused manner. (p. 423)*

The device has also been embedded in a more complex strategy elaborated in Cole et al. (2000) and Cole, Beheshti, Leide, and Large (2005).

Cole et al. (2000) contend that for each of Kuhlthau's six stages, an enabling information retrieval system should present to the user a distinct enabling device. A central feature of these devices is that they should stimulate the learner to expand and reduce their levels of uncertainty depending on the stage in which they find themselves at any time. Uncertainty expansion is appropriate at stage 3, when it is proposed that when interacting with an IR system, the learner is not dealing with unknown information:

*To make an IR system function, the user must label his or her information need, which is information the user does not yet know, with search terms derived from information the student already knows something about. With these types of search terms, what the student gets from the IR system is citations to information with which the student is already more or less familiar. (Indeed, citations to completely unknown information will be deemed irrelevant and ignored by the student.) In this sort of information retrieval situation, it is probable that when the student selects search terms to access new information in the system the student is not primarily dealing with unknown information but rather information he or she already knows but is not fully conscious of knowing at that particular moment. It is tacit knowledge.*

Figure 100 illustrates the basic idea of Cole et al.'s (2000) uncertainty *expansion* device, while the essence of his uncertainty *reduction* device is shown in Figure 101.

The need to reduce, rather than expand uncertainly comes, according to Cole and his colleagues, in stage 4, when the student is required to establish a firm focus for his or her assignment. Cole (2001) reports statistically significant improvements in

*Figure 100. Essence of Cole's uncertainty expansion device (adapted from Cole et al., 2000)*

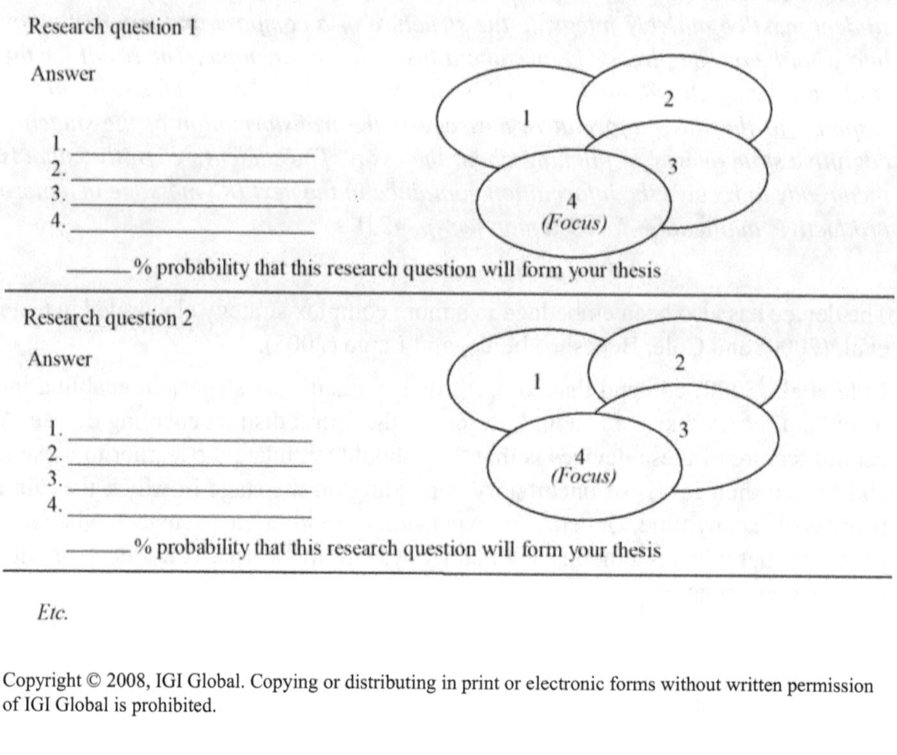

*Figure 101 Cole's uncertainty reduction device (adapted from Cole et al., 2000)*

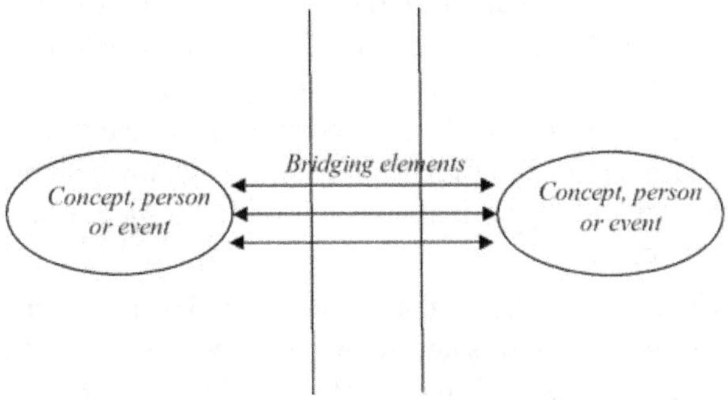


students' grades when using these devices compared to a control group, is a study of 60 Concordia University students.

According to Cole et al. (2000):

*Because of the cognitive approach's definition of information, such systems go further than traditional 'intelligent' IR systems; they 'enable' the user to perform his or her task by actually stimulating cognitive activity in the user. Part of this cognitive activity is the user inferencing knowledge about the task at hand while he or she is online interacting with the IR system—a highly desirable mental activity that is a sign of expert-like thinking (Cole, 1998 [...]; Noordman & Vonk, 1992; Noordman, Vonk & Kempff, 1992) (p. 486)*

More recent work is reported by Cole and Leide (2006) exploring the metacognitive potential of "metaphor instantiation" as the basis for developing information retrieval systems capable of helping people new to a topic learn more effectively from interacting with an information retrieval system through developing more appropriate information retrieval queries. This work also focuses on stimulating learners' own metacognition. They seek to address the problem that topic novices must query an information retrieval system on the basis of their own existing knowledge of concepts of which they wish to learn more, whether entering their own keywords or using concepts located in a system thesaurus. As Cole and Leide (2006) note:

*For domain novice users, these concepts are taken from what little they know about the domain—concepts users think they know a little about but primarily want to find out more about. The concept terms in the query, representing the user's information need, are the user's own, fluctuating conceptualizations of categories of objects, events or subject topics, found in his/her own memory (Barsalou, 1992). (p. 173)*

These concepts do not necessarily map accurately onto those used to describe relevant documents in an information retrieval system. Metaphor instantiation is "a memory device for facilitating unfamiliar information processing" (Cole & Leide, 2006, p. 172), and Cole and Leide report investigations seeking to explore its potential use as a component of an information retrieval system designed to provide a temporary scaffolding structure from a known to an unknown domain, sufficient to enhance information seeking until a more appropriate structure can be established as the result of learning.

The research is in its early stages and has concentrated on researchers in the area of history. They have made progress developing a methodology for eliciting (1) metaphoric descriptions of users' research problems and (2) search terms derived from these metaphors. The resulting lists of search terms display interesting variations, and work is progressing to evaluate the effectiveness of search terms derived from different sources of metaphor, namely those derived from the user's perceptions of his/her research topic, of his/her research problem situation, and of the problem situation of the people on whom the researcher's study is focusing.

This work falls within educational informatics in that it is geared to developing new information retrieval systems, which utilise pedagogic principles derived from a review of research in cognitive science. This hypothesis is that stimulation of users, by an information retrieval system, to generate deeper understanding of the knowledge needs underlying their information needs can result in the generation of queries to the information retrieval system, which are more appropriate and effective than would be generated without such a device.

The devices used by Cole constitute what Allert, Richter, and Nejdl (2004) term "second-order learning objects." They differentiate between first-order learning objects that essentially support reproductive learning, and second-order learning objects that support productive or generative learning. Reproductive learning entails adaptation on the part of learners to their environment: Generative learning may entail changes in the environment as a result of learning processes. First-order learning objects are designed around the learner achieving some specific learning objective. Second-order learning objects are designed to empower the learner to engage in enquiry and innovation—the situated identification of problems and the generation of solutions. They support strategies such as reflection, planning, decision making, and problem solving and may result in the development and change of the learning objects themselves. This type of learning is particularly appropriate to the *knowledge creation* perspective described in Chapter III and requires the accommodation of open-ended and ill-structured goals and activities that defy complete planning, control, and predetermination. Examples of second-order learning objects include: metacognitive strategies, creativity techniques, strategic planning methods, and problem-solving strategies.

Ford (1986) reported an early system that used rule-based expert system techniques to support procedure building in this way. Learners were required to express procedural aspects of their learning in the form of rules. The stipulation that the rules should execute correctly in the inference engine was designed to ensure logically sound procedural understanding. At present, within rather restricted domains, such a facility could also argue with the user in an attempt to strengthen procedure building. As discussed in Chapter VI, a number of argumentation systems have been developed (e.g., Saeedi & Sillince, 1999; Sillince, 1995; Vreeswijk, 1993, 1995, 1997), which might be employable for such purposes. One might also envisage support within a virtual environment for the development of more global description-building aspects of understanding via tools facilitating the acquisition of a view of the subject domain in terms of broad interrelationships between concepts. Shortcomings in the level of integration of developing concepts, symmetries, analogies, and points of difference between concepts (characteristically missed by the extreme operation learner) could become more visible—indeed, could be pointed out—to this type of learner.

Indeed, based on Pask's work, Ford (2000) proposed a computer-based system designed to provide a range of types of support, with options entailing a progressive decrease in the level of supplantation in order to facilitate learners' acquisition of metacognitive learning to learn knowledge and skills in the sense of learning to compensate for possible stylistic weaknesses. Ford proposes a support system in which global description building and analytic procedure building views and support tools could be deployed for individuals (1) who lack strength in relation to either description building or procedure building, or (2) who would benefit from adopting a holist or serialist approach despite being strong in both description building and procedure building. Recall that these differences were introduced in Chapter II.

There is some evidence that even versatile learners who are strong in both description building and procedure building nevertheless may have biases towards holist or serialist learning strategies, which imply different sequences which can lead to the same full (versatile) understanding. As noted in Chapter III, when information is presented in a way which matches an individual's holist or serialist bias, learning has been found to be significantly enhanced. Conversely, mismatching has been observed to have a disruptive effect on learning (Ford, 1995; Pask & Scott, 1972). Such effects have been found even for high achieving postgraduate students who are competent in the skills of both description and procedure building (Ford, 1985). This implies that even versatile learners who successfully engage in both description and procedure building may need to do so using predominantly either a holist or a serialist sequence and approach.

Ford proposed a computer-based system that would offer support particularly to learners who have a weakness in either description building or procedure building—but which would also be useful to versatile learners requiring a predominantly holist or serialist learning approach. The system would enable different patterns and sequences of access to (1) global views of a topic, with *enrichment* material suited to holist learners; and (2) relatively analytic views with an emphasis on close logical connections between aspects of the topic, and close attention to the exposition of supporting evidence as required by the serialist.

The level of user control over the level of mediation exercised in relation to the accessing of information sources could vary from autonomous through recommended to prescribed. If a learner selected an autonomous mode, he or she would be able to choose patterns of access to resources for him or herself. Learners may alternatively choose to be guided. However, the extent to which individuals are likely to choose strategies that are optimal for their particular information styles is an open question. For example, in a study by Ford and Ford (1992, 1993), when given extensive freedom during interactions with a computer-based training system, a proportion of postgraduate students chose ineffective strategies, others choosing more effectively. Another option would be for access patterns to be prescribed for users by the system. However, such a system would require (1) a mechanism for accurately assessing each user's stylistic competence, and (2) a robust model capable of generating, on the basis of such an assessment, an effective access pattern for each user.

A variation on this approach would be to replace prescribed options with recommended options, which could take the form of default navigational *next moves* suggested by the system—but capable of being overridden by the user if desired. It may also be possible to support individuals who are weak in description or procedure building. A user stronger in description building than in procedure building could be helped to achieve a more secure evidence-based understanding of an area via tools enabling the exploration, testing, and validation of procedural aspects of topics and subtopics. Support for such a learner weak in procedure-building competence could be provided in the form of components of a virtual environment that engage in, for example, the computation of argumentation. Such support could subject users' developing understanding to a level of logical verification sufficient to ensure that they avoid the characteristic pathology of the extreme comprehension learner—namely, an inability to build closely argued detailed evidence to support the broad conceptual overview of concept interrelationships. Such support is shown in Figure 102.

Systems that engage in a particular intellectual activity can to some extent support learners who are weak in its competence by supplanting or facilitating that activity. As discussed in Chapter III, supplantation entails engaging in the activity on behalf of the user so that his or her need for the particular competence is reduced. Facilitation entails providing tools that enhance the user's own engagement in the intellectual activity—for example, by providing encouragement, structure, review, validation, and feedback.

Ford (2000) suggested the use of neural network-based identification of learning styles (Figure 103), since this approach may enable real-time inductive classification of learners by style based on real learning data. A neural network-based system could also inductively analyse the relationship between style classifications, learner behaviour, and performance levels and feed the results of such an analysis back to

*Figure 102. A supplantation/support system (adapted from Ford, 2000)*

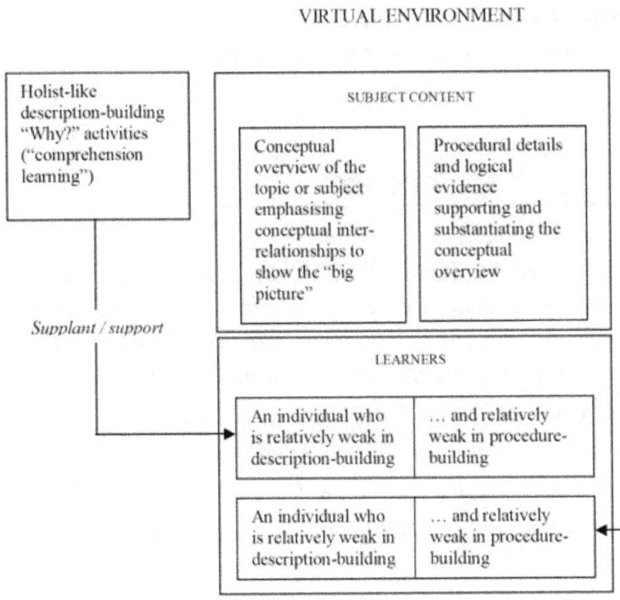


*Figure 103. A neural network-driven adaptive system (adapted from Ford, 2000)*

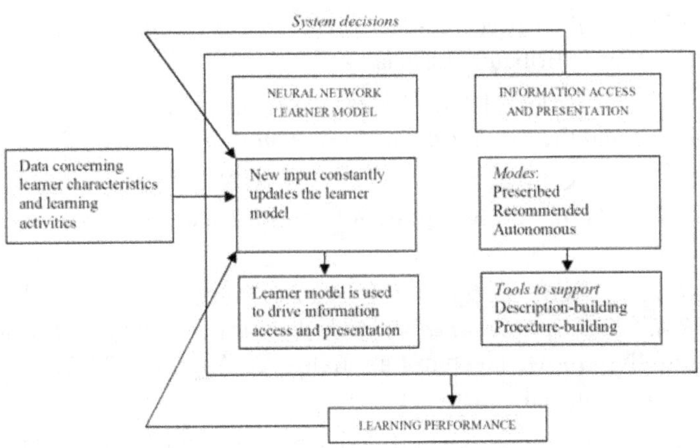


learners and/or into the model used by the system to drive its adaptive behaviour. Indeed, related work by Frias-Martinez et al. (2007) on the automatic classification of cognitive styles using a neural network, along with a range of other automatic techniques, was reported earlier in this chapter.

The educational informatics systems introduced here have focused predominantly on the individual learner. However, educational informatics systems have also been developed that emphasise social, collaborative, and community-based aspects of learning; these systems form the focus of the next chapter.

## References

Abel, F., Brunkhorst, I., Henze, N., Krause, D., Mushtaq, K., Nasirifard, P., et al. (2006, October). *Personal reader agent: Personalized access to configurable Web services*. Paper presented at ABIS 2006—14th Workshop on Adaptivity and User Modeling in Interactive Systems, Hildesheim, Germany.

Allert, H., Richter, C., & Nejdl, W. (2004). Lifelong learning and second-order learning objects. *British Journal of Educational Technology, 35*(6), 701-715.

Bailey, C., Zalfan, M. T., Davis, H. C., Fill, K., & Conole, G. (2006). Panning for gold: Designing pedagogically inspired learning nuggets. *Educational Technology & Society, 9*(1), 113-122.

Baumgartner, R., Flesca, S., & Gottlob, G. (2001, September 17-19). *Declarative information extraction, Web crawling, and recursive wrapping with Lixto.* Paper presented at 6th International Conference on Logic Programming and Nonmonotonic Reasoning, Vienna, Austria.

Barsalou, L. W. (1992). *Cognitive psychology: An overview for cognitive scientists.* Hillsdale, NJ: Lawrence Erlbaum Associates.

Belkin, N. J., Oddy, R. N., & Brooks, H. M. (1982a). ASK for information retrieval: Part I. Background and theory. *Journal of Documentation, 38*(2), 61-71.

Belkin, N. J., Oddy, R. N., & Brooks, H. M. (1982b). ASK for information retrieval: Part II. Results of a design study. *Journal of Documentation, 38*(3), 145-164.

Blackmon, W., Brooks, J., Roberts, E., & Rehak, D. (2004). *The overlap and barriers between SCORM, IMS Simple Sequencing, and adaptive sequencing*. Carnegie Mellon Learning System Architecture Lab. Retrieved August 1, 2007, from http://www.lsal.cmu.edu/lsal/expertise/papers

Brookes, B. C. (1977). The developing cognitive viewpoint in library and information science. *Journal of Informatics, 1,* 55-62.

Brookes, B. C. (1980). Measurement in library and information science: Objective and subjective metrical space. *Journal of the American Society for Library and information science, 31,* 248-255.

Brusilovsky, P. (2001). Adaptive hypermedia. *User Modeling and User-Adapted Interaction, 11*(1-2), 87-100.

Brusilovsky, P. (2003). Adaptive navigation support in educational hypermedia: The role of student knowledge level and the case for meta-adaptation. *British Journal of Educational Technology, 34*(4), 487-497.

Brusilovsky, P., & Maybury, M. (2002). From adaptive hypermedia to the adaptive Web. *Communications of the ACM, 45*(5), 30-33.

Canavan, J. (2004*). Personalised e-learning through learning style aware adaptive systems*. Dissertation submitted in partial fulfilment of the requirements for the degree of MSc in Computer Science, University of Dublin.

Caprotti, O., Carlisle, D., & Cohen, A. (2002). *The OpenMath standard.* Retrieved August 1, 2007, from http://www.openmath.org/cocoon/openmath/standard/om11/index.html

Castillo, G., Gama, J., & Breda, A. M. (2006). An adaptive predictive model for student modelling. In G. D. Magoulas & S. Y. Chen (Eds.), *Advances in Web-based education: Personalized learning environments* (pp. 70-92). London: Library and information science Publishing.

Chen, S., Magoulas, G., & Dimakopoulos, D. (2005). A flexible interface design for Web directories to accommodate different cognitive styles. *Journal of the American Society for Information Science and Technology, 56*(1), 70-83.

Clarke, L., Wade, V., Conlan, O., & Dagger, D. (2003, November 7-11). *Personalisation for adult eLearning—An AHS approach.* Paper presented at E-Learn 2003, World Conference on E-Learning in Corporate, Government, Healthcare and Higher Education, Phoenix, AZ. Retrieved August 1, 2007, from https://www.cs.tcd.ie/Owen.Conlan/publications/elearn2003_v1_Clarke.pdf

Cole, C. (1998). Information acquisition in history Ph.D. students: Inferencing and the formation of knowledge structures. *Library Quarterly, 68,* 33-54.

Cole, C. (2000) Interaction with an enabling information retrieval system: Modeling the user's decoding and encoding operations. *Journal of the American Society for Library and Information Science, 51*(5), 417-426.

Cole, C. (2001) Intelligent information retrieval: Part IV—Testing the timing of two information retrieval devices in a naturalistic setting. *Information Processing and Management, 37*(1), 163-182.

Cole, C., Beheshti, J., Leide, J. E., & Large, A. (2005). Interactive information retrieval: Bringing the user to a selection state. In A. Spink & C. Cole (Eds.), *New directions in cognitive information retrieval* (pp. 13-41). Dordrecht, The Netherlands: Springer.

Cole, C., Cantero, P., & Ungar, A. (2000). The development of a diagnostic-prescriptive tool for undergraduates seeking information for a social science/humanities assignment: Part III. Enabling devices. *Information Processing and Management, 36,* 481-500.

Cole, C., & Leide, J. E. (2006). A cognitive framework for human information behaviour: The place of metaphor in human information organizing behaviour. In A. Spink & C. Cole (Eds.), *New directions in human behaviour* (pp. 171-202). Dordrecht, The Netherlands: Springer.

Cole, C., & Mandelblatt, B. (2000). Using Kintsch's discourse comprehension theory to model the user's coding of an informative message from an enabling information retrieval system. *Journal of the American Society for Library and information science, 51*(11), 1033-1046.

Conlan, O., Hockemeyer, C., Wade, V., & Albert, D. (2003). Metadata driven approaches to facilitate adaptivity in personalized elearning systems. *Journal of the Japanese Society for Information and Systems in Education*. Retrieved August 1, 2007, from https://www.cs.tcd.ie/Owen.Conlan/publications/JSISEv1.23_Conlan.pdf

Conlan, O'Keeffe, Brady, & Wade. (2007, July 18-20). Principles for designing activity-based personalized eLearning. In *Proceedings of the Seventh IEEE International Conference on Advanced Learning Technologies (ICALT 2007),* Niigata, Japan (pp. 642-644). Retrieved August 1, 2007, from http://doi.ieeecomputersociety.org/10.1109/ICALT.2007.209

Conlan, O., Wade, V., Bruen, C., & Gargan, M. (2002, May). *Multi-model, metadata driven approach to adaptive hypermedia services for personalized e-learning*. Paper presented at the Second International Conference on Adaptive hypermedia and Adaptive Web-Based Systems, Malaga, Spain. Retrieved August 1, 2007, from https://www.cs.tcd.ie/ Owen.Conlan/publications/AH2002v0.99e11_Conlan.pdf

Conole, G. C., & Fill, K. (2005, June). *A toolkit for creating effective learning activities*. Paper presented at EdMedia Conference, Montreal, Canada.

Czarkowski, M., & Kay, J. (2006). Giving learners a real sense of control over adaptivity, even if they are not quite ready for it yet. In G. D. Magoulas & S. Y. Chen (Eds.), *Advances in Web-based education: Personalized learning environments* (pp. 93-125). London: Library and Information Science Publishing.

Dagger, D., Conlan, O., & Wade, V. (2003, September). *An architecture for candidacy in adaptive elearning systems to facilitate the reuse of learning resources*. Paper presented at E-Learn 2003, World Conference on E-Learning in Corporate, Government, Healthcare and Higher Education, Phoenix, AZ.

De Bra, P., & Ruiter, J. P. (2001, October 23-27). AHA! Adaptive hypermedia for all. In W. A. Lawrence-Fowler, J. Hasebrook (Eds.), *Proceedings of WebNet 2001—World Conference on the WWW and Internet,* Orlando, FL (pp. 262-268). Chesapeake, VA: Association for the Advancement of Computing in Education (AACE).

Dicheva, D., & Dichev, C. (2006). TM4L: Creating and browsing educational topic maps. *British Journal of Educational Technology, 37*(3), 391-404.

Dolog, P., Henze, N., & Nejdl, W. (2003, August). *Logic-based open hypermedia for the Semantic Web*. Paper presented at the Workshop on the Semantic Web and Hypertext, Hypertex 2003 Conference, Nottingam, UK. Retrieved August 1, 2007, from http://www.cs.aau.dk/~dolog/pub/htsw2003.pdf

Dolog, P., Henze, N., Nejdl, W., & Sintek, M. (2004, August): The personal reader: Personalizing and enriching learning resources using Semantic Web technologies. In *Proceedings of AH2004—International Conference on Adaptive hypermedia and Adaptive Web-Based Systems,* Eindhoven, The Netherlands. Berlin: Springer Verlag.

Ford, N. (1985). Learning styles and strategies of postgraduate students. *British Journal of Educational Technology, 16,* 65-79.

Ford, N. (1986, November). *Novel uses of simple expert system technology in improving training and education.* Second International Expert Systems Conference, Learned Information, London.

Ford, N. (1995). Levels and types of mediation in instructional systems: An individual differences approach. *International Journal of Human-Computer Studies, 43,* 241-259.

Ford, N. (2000) Cognitive styles and virtual environments. *Journal of the American Society for Information Science, 51(6),* 543-557.

Ford, N., & Ford, R. (1992). Learning strategies in an ideal computer assisted learning environment. *British Journal of Educational Technology, 23*(3), 195-211.

Ford, N., & Ford, R. (1993). Towards a cognitive theory of information accessing: An empirical study. *Information Processing and Management, 29*(5), 569-585.

Frias-Martinez, E., Chen, S., & Liu, X. (2007). Automatic cognitive style identification of digital library users for personalization. *Journal of the American Society for Information Science and Technology, 58*(2), 237-251.

Gama, J., & Castillo, G. (2002). Adaptive bayes. In F. Garijo, J. Riquelme, & M. Toro (Eds.), *Advances in Artificial Intelligence—IBERAMIA 2002* (LNAI 2527, pp. 765-774). Berlin, Germany: Springer Verlag.

García, P., Amandi, A., Schiaffino, S., & Campo, M. (2007). Evaluating Bayesian networks' precision for detecting students' learning styles. *Computers and Education, 49*(3), 794-808.

Gasevic, D., & Hatala, M. (2006). Ontology mappings to improve learning resource search. *British Journal of Educational Technology, 37*(3), 375-389.

Guha, R., McCool, R., & Miller, E. (2003, May 20-24). Semantic search. In *WWW2003—Proceedings of the 12th international conference on the World Wide Web,* Budapest, Hungary (pp 700-709). New York: ACM Press.

Gunnarsdóttir, S., Heimerl, U., Kieslinger, B., Simon, B., & Tsiortou, S. (2004). *Current issues of training management in European enterprises*. Retrieved August 1, 2007, from http://www.zsi.at/attach/Training_Mgt.PDF

Henze, N., Dolog, P., & Nejdl, W. (2004). Reasoning and ontologies for personalized e-learning in the Semantic Web. *Educational Technology and Society, 7*(4), 82-97.

Henze, N., & Nejdl, W. (2001). Adaptation in open corpus hypermedia. *International Journal of Artificial intelligence in Education, 12,* 325-350.

IMS. (2002). *Learning resource meta-data specification. Version 1.3—Final specification—HTML*. Retrieved August 1, 2007, from http://www.imsglobal.org/metadata/index.html

Kassab, R., & Lamirel, J. C. (2007, March 11-15). Towards a synthetic analysis of user's information need for more effective personalized filtering services. In *Proceedings of the 2007 ACM Symposium on Applied Computing,* Seoul, Korea (pp. 852-859). New York: ACM Press.

Kazanidis, I., & Satratzemi, M. (2007, July 18-20). Combine adaptive education hypermedia and SCORM compliant learning management systems. In *Proceedings of the Seventh IEEE International Conference on Advanced Learning Technologies (ICALT 2007),* Niigata, Japan (pp. 330-331). Retrieved August 1, 2007, from http://doi.ieeecomputersociety.org/10.1109/ICALT.2007.97

Kobsa, A. (2002). Personalized hypermedia and international privacy. *Communications of the ACM Archive. Special Issue: The Adaptive Web, 45*(5), 64-67.

Kuhlthau, C. C. (2004). *Seeking meaning: A process approach to library and information services* (2nd ed.). Westport, CT: Libraries Unlimited.

Kuhlthau, C. C. (2006). *Information search process*. Retrieved August 1, 2007, from http://www.scils.rutgers.edu/~kuhlthau/information_search_process.htm

Lawless, S., Wade, V., & Conlan, O. (2005, October, 24-28). *Dynamic contextual elearning—Dynamic content discovery, capture and learning object generation from open corpus source*. Paper presented at E-Learn 2005, World Conference on E-Learning in Corporate, Government, Healthcare and Higher Education, Vancouver, B.C. Retrieved August 1, 2007, from https://www.cs.tcd.ie/Owen.Conlan/publications/eLearn_2005_lawless.pdf

Melis, E., Goguadze, G., Homik, M., Libbrecht, P., Ullrich, C., & Winterstein, S. (2006). Semantic-aware components and services of ActiveMath. *British Journal of Educational Technology, 37*(3), 405-423.

Merrill, M. D. (2002). First principles of instruction. *Educational Technology Research & Development, 50*(3), 43-59.

Miklos, Z., Neumann, G., Zdun, U., & Sintek, N. (2003, October). *Querying Semantic Web resources using triple views.* Paper presented at the 2nd International Semantic Web Conference (ISWC), Sundial Resort, Sanibel Island, FL.

Miles, A., & Brickley, D. (2005, November 2). *SKOS core guide, W3C editor's working draft*. Retrieved August 1, 2007, from http://www.w3.org/2004/02/skos/core/guide/

NCS. (2004). *Making IT happen. Presentation on development and outcomes - metadata standard and taxonomy for education content exchange*. Retrieved August 1, 2007, from http://www.itsc.org.sg/events/metadata04/Details.pdf

Nejdl, W., Wolf, B., Qu, C., Decker, S., Sintek, M., Naeve, A., et al. (2002, May). *EDUTELLA: A P2P networking infrastructure based on RDF*. Paper presented at the 11th World Wide Web Conference, Honolulu, HI.

Noordman, L. G. M., & Vonk, W. (1992). Reader's knowledge and the control of inference in reading. *Language and Cognitive Processes, 7,* 373-391.

Noordman, L. G. M., Vonk, W., & Kempff, H. J. (1992). Causal inferences during the reading of expository texts. *Journal of Memory and Language, 31,* 573-590.

O'Keeffe, I., Brady, A., Conlan, O., & Wade, V. (2006). Just-in-time generation of pedagogically sound, context sensitive personalized learning experiences. *International Journal on E-Learning, 5*(1), 113-127.

Papanikolaou, K. A., & Grigoriadou, M. (2006). Building an instructional framework to support learner control in adaptive educational systems. In G. D. Magoulas & S. Y. Chen (Eds.), *Advances in web-based education: Personalized learning environments* (pp. 127-146). London: Library and Information Science Publishing.

Park, J., & Hunting, S. (2002). *XML topic maps: Creating and using topic maps for the Web.* Boston, MA: Addison-Wesley.

Pask, G., & Scott, B. (1972). Learning strategies and individual competence. *International Journal of Man-Machine Studies, 4,* 217-253.

Saeedi, M. H., & Sillince, J. (1999). Incorporating rhetorical and plausible reasoning in a system for simulating argumentation. *Knowledge-Based Systems, 12*(3), 113-127.

Shabajee, P., McBride, B., Steer, D., & Reynolds, D. (2006). A prototype Semantic Web-based digital content exchange for schools in Singapore. *British Journal of Educational Technology, 37*(3), 461-477.

Shute, V., & Towle, B. (2003). Adaptive e-learning. *Educational Psychologist, 38*(2), 105-114.

Sillince, J. A. A. (1995). *Specification of naturalistic argumentation rules* (Management School Discussion Paper No. 95.28). Sheffield, UK: University of Sheffield.

Simon, B., Dolog, P., Miklós, Z., Olmedilla, D., & Sintek, M. (2004). Conceptualising smart spaces for learning. *Journal of Interactive Media in Education,* (9).

Special Issue on the Educational Semantic Web. Retrieved August 1, 2007, from www-jime.open.ac.uk/2004/9

Sintek, M., & Decker, S. (2002). Triple—An RDF query, inference, and transformation language. In I. Horrocks & J. Hendler (Eds.), *Proceedings of the International Semantic Web Conference (ISWC)*(pp. 364-378). Berlin, Germany: Springer Verlag,.

Taylor, R. S. (1968). Question-negotiation and information seeking in libraries. *College and Research Libraries, 29,* 178-194.

Tramullas, J., & Garrido, P. (2005). Constructing web subject gateways using Dublin Core, RDF and topic maps *Information Research, 11*(2) paper 248. Retrieved August 1, 2007, from http://informationr.net/ir/11-2/paper248.html

Vatant, B. (2004, May). *Ontology-driven topic maps*. Paper presented at XML Europe 2004, Amsterdam. Retrieved August 1, 2007, from http://www.idealliance.org/papers/dx_XMLe04/papers/03-03-03/03-03-03.pdf

Vreeswijk, G. (1995). IACAS: An implementation of Chisholm's principles of knowledge. *Proceedings of the 2nd Dutch/German Workshop on Non-monotonic Reasoning,* Utrecht, The Netherlands (pp. 225-234). University of Utrecht.

Vreeswijk, G. A. W. (1993). Defeasible dialectics: A controversy-oriented approach towards defeasible argumentation. *Journal of Logic and Computation, 3,* 3-27.

Vreeswijk, G. A. W. (1997). Abstract argumentation systems. *Artificial intelligence, 90,* 225-279.

## Chapter VIII

# Educational Informatics Systems: Social Approaches

## Introduction

This chapter concentrates on a number of educational informatics systems that focus explicitly on social, collaborative, and community-based aspects of learning. These aspects arguably align better with the social and knowledge creation perspectives on learning introduced in Chapter III. In some ways, the systems presented here bring into relief some of the limitations of the relatively individual-focused approaches introduced in the previous chapter.

Ultimately, however, educational informatics is essentially a social collaborative enterprise, since one of its key defining features is a concern with the discovery, sharing and reuse of learning resources within and between learning communities. The difference between systems included in this and the previous chapter is relative rather than absolute, relating to the degree of emphasis on collaborative features built into the systems.

## Alternative Pedagogies

There are a number of well-rehearsed criticisms of educational systems predicated on the use of learning objects and metadata as described thus far. Allert (2004), for example, considers current educational metadata schemes to be severely limited in terms of the type and range of pedagogical knowledge they can express. Schemes such as learning object metadata (LOM), although claiming to be neutral, in fact display epistemological and ontological assumptions that restrict them to particular pedagogic perspectives.

Schemes such as LOM seek to describe features of a learning object created for use in a particular context, in such a way that it can be discovered and reused by others in other contexts. The intention is to encapsulate the *aboutness* of the object, and characteristics of it that may determine its potential educational usefulness and learnability, in its metadata. This metadata can then be used as input variables to an equation whereby learners are matched with learning resources that are *about* the topic the learner wishes or needs to learn about, and which are suitably matched with learner characteristics such as learning style and prior knowledge. LOM describing the topic which the learning object is designed to teach can be mapped onto ontologies which may indicate, for example, prerequisite topics. The result of the equation is a personalised selection and sequence of learning objects designed effectively and efficiently to teach the learner the required knowledge.

As Allert (2004) notes, LOM:

*aims at an absolute description of an object and assumes de-contextualization. Meaning is completely deduced from the object itself, which means that the entire meaning lies within the object. LOM's concept of semantics is based on epistemological and ontological assumptions comparable to those of the acquisition metaphor of learning.*

This is at odds with a view of learning in which the broader context where learning takes place affects the nature and effectiveness of that learning. The same learning resource may be differentially effective when used in different contexts. From this perspective, the notion of decontextualisation in relation to learning objects and their metadata is less than helpful. Rather than representing "noise" to be factored out so that the essential content of a learning object can be more accurately described, context is central to meaning.

Mwanza and Engeström (2005) note that:

*we considered the task of understanding and describing activities in context as an integral part of the metadata abstraction. This is due to the fact that acquired contextual insight is considered to be crucial to the appropriate categorisation and description of education content.* (p. 454)

They argue that failing to take into account such context may result in a misunderstanding of learners' real needs. Within particular communities, sociocultural and pedagogic norms, which provide the context for searching for and using learning resources can be implicit, potentially causing ambiguities and misunderstandings where resources are used across contexts. Indeed, cultural differences are an important factor affecting e-learning more generally (Edmundson, 2007).

Indeed, the whole enterprise whereby personalised learning is delivered via matching decontextualised LOM with metadata describing learners and their needs is itself arguably based on epistemological and ontological assumptions that align it with a particular and limited perspective on teaching and learning. These assumptions map particularly well onto the "acquisition" as opposed to "participation" (Sfard, 1998) or "knowledge-creation" (Paavola, Lipponen, & Hakkarainen, 2002) metaphor for learning discussed in Chapter III.

Viewed from a *participant* perspective on learning, the prime goal of learning is not the acquisition by the individual of knowledge and skills that can be applied in new contexts. Rather, it is building communities in which knowledge is collaboratively constructed through participation in shared learning activities and social processes. The perspective is rooted in the notion of *situated* learning in which knowing is *located* in social interaction and participation. Allert (2004) quotes Hanks' (1991) explanation that:

*The individual learner is not gaining a discrete body of abstract knowledge which (s)he will then transport and reapply in later contexts. ... There is no necessary implication that a learner acquires mental representations that remain fixed thereafter, not that the 'lesson' taught consists itself in a set of abstract representations.* (p. 14)

Allert (2004) notes that Paavola et al. (2002) have extended Sfard's (1998) participation metaphor to what they term the knowledge creation metaphor, which focuses on *innovation* and is particularly applicable to modern communities characterised by constant change and transformation. From such a knowledge creation perspective (Paavola et al., 2002):

*learning is seen as analogous to processes of inquiry, especially to innovative processes of inquiry where something new is created and the initial knowledge is either substantially enriched or significantly transformed during the process* (p. 1)

Such learning entails tackling poorly structured problems and outcomes that can not be accurately planned and predicted in detail. Learning is seen as too complex to be viewed via any simple predictable cause and effect relationship as the direct result of teaching.

Mwanza and Engeström (2005) consider it necessary to be able to express such pedagogical contexts in metadata. Although LOM can express certain pedagogical information about a learning object, this facility is underdeveloped. Indeed, others such as Huang, Webster, Wood, and Ishaya (2006) have commented that:

*In terms of standardisation, LOM ... and Sharable Content Object Reference Model (SCORM) ..., the most popular e-learning standards, have not taken pedagogy support as one of their core issues in specification.* (p. 354)

However, Mwanza and Engeström (2005) note that LOM does enable its top level categories to be extended:

*a key advantage of using the LOM standard is evident in the provision for extending LOM top-level categories ... this implies that extensions can be created and added to LOM top-level categories so as to introduce theory-driven subcategories and elements drawn from specific theories of learning and social–cultural perspectives.* (p. 460)

They have used this facility to propose extensions to LOM, based on *expansive learning theory*, which requires pedagogical and social context to be taken into account. This theory was developed by Engeström (1987), based on the more general *activity theory*, itself receiving increasing attention in both education (Collis & Margaryan, 2004) and library and information science (Wilson, 2006). As activity theory views human activities as developmental processes, so expansive learning views learning as emerging from the creation of new artifacts by learners and teachers engaged in real life problem solving.

Mwanza and Engeström (2005) note that within activity theory:

*Participants in an activity are portrayed as subjects interacting with objects to achieve desired outcomes. Meanwhile, human interactions are mediated with each other and with objects of the environment through the use of tools, rules, and division of labour. Mediators represent the nature of relationships that exist within and between participants of an activity in a given community of practices.* (p. 457)

They thus add, as extensions to LOM's educational category, key concepts deriving from expansive learning including: *subjects*, *tools*, *objectives*, *rules*, *community*, *division of labour*, and *desired outcomes*.

The lack of ability of metadata standards to accommodate situated learning is addressed by Specht (2006), who reports work developing adaptive systems to support situated learning as part of the European Union-Funded Remotely Accessible Field Trips (RAFT) project. As with other systems, learners are described in terms of their knowledge, preferences, interests, and capabilities. However, metadata describing resources includes not only LOM categories but also a series of environmental parameters appropriate to supporting learners engaged in field trip activities. As information is collected, metadata is attached relating to environmental factors such as its location, position, and so forth. The information is made available to the field trip participants. The prototype Situated Mobile Learning Support (SMILES) system enables the recording and accessing of such resources. Specht (2006) provides the following example of the use of such environmental metadata:

> *... learners could browse a database of pictures in a biology field trip filtered by the location and the time of the year. Using this approach students could explore and learn about simple questions liker "Which flowers grow here at what time of the year?" Additionally, metadata such as the precise time when the picture was taken and the weather conditions on that day can give interesting materials for exploring and learning about important factors of flower growth.* (pp. 345-346)

This work represents the extension of metadata to include features specifically designed to support situated learning.

Limitations have also been noted in relation to standards such as the Educational Modelling Language (EML) to the extent that they display inherent assumptions. EML, on which the Instructional Management System Learning Design (IMS LD) is based, was developed to enable the specification of learning designs. It represented an attempt to avoid the danger of building in a particular pedagogical perspective. Indeed, at the top level, EML offers a pedagogical meta-model that enables the modelling of different pedagogical approaches (Hummel, Manderveld, Tattersall, & Koper, 2004). This pedagogical meta-model was derived from a mapping of commonalities between a wide range of learning and learning design theories and models covering behaviourist, cognitivist, and constructivist perspectives.

Sicilia (2006) and Sicilia and Lytras (2005), on the basis of their work investigating ontological structures for generic constructivist and sociocultural learning, also criticize the EML approach—in the form of IMS LD. They do so on the grounds that, while it is neutral to and can accommodate different pedagogical perspectives, it does not allow the expression of them explicitly. While there is no problem expressing a range of different learning designs, the underlying rationale, which led to a particular design—that is, the assumptions and theoretical perspective behind it—cannot be expressed. Such representations are crucial, they argue, for linking theories to practice and for evaluating the validity of theoretical assumptions. They report work developing ontologies that explicitly represent constructivist and sociocultural learning frameworks and allow the expression of learning design rationales.

Allert (2004) has also criticized EML in view of its activity-based nature. Assumptions of the EML meta-model are that learners learn by engaging in goal-directed activities in some environment consisting of a set of objects, services, and/or people. Learning may be facilitated insofar as the learner is motivated, provided with an appropriate environment, and possesses the necessary prerequisites and abilities. Irrespective of pedagogical approach, people acquire *roles* and engage in learning and/or support *activities* (which may be aggregated into *activity structures*) within an *environment* in pursuit of particular *outcomes*. Determination of which activities are associated with which roles is made by a *method* created to achieve particular learning objectives. A method consists of one or more *plays*, which themselves are made of one or more sequential *acts*, and may include IF… THEN… ELSE… rules.

Specifications such as the EML enable the description of strategic pedagogical procedures and processes designed to move learners from one state of knowledge to another. These descriptions can also be fed into the personalised learning equation, for example, to sequence the selected learning materials to suit a preferred pedagogic strategy. They describe learning in terms of pedagogical means and ends, and the planning of educational activities in order to achieve preplanned objectives via causal relationships. However, as Allert (2004) notes:

> *innovative learning processes are contextualized, generative, ill-structured, and long lasting processes, which do not directly lead to a predetermined objective. ... A sufficient model therefore must be able to describe open systems, ill-structured non-deterministic processes of change.* (p. 16)

Thus, although able to accommodate a range of pedagogical perspectives, and to set learning objects within their broader pedagogical context, certain of what in the EML are considered basic assumptions do arguably resonate more with certain pedagogical positions than with others. This view is at odds with pedagogical perspectives that emphasise relatively open-ended knowledge creation as previously described.

Allert (2004) proposes a multi-layered relativistic modelling approach that seeks to overcome the inherent limitation of activity-centred models. Within her proposed system (Figure 104), the same object (level 0) may be annotated with metadata describing (1) characteristics that can be decontextualised and that represent universal defining features of the object, and (2) different roles that the same object may play in different pedagogical contexts (both described at level 1). At a higher level (level 2), different pedagogical approaches are themselves explicitly represented. A given object (level 0) may be linked to different roles (level 1), each of which may be linked to a different pedagogical approach (level 2).

*Figure 104. Multi-layered modelling approach (adapted from Allert, 2004)*

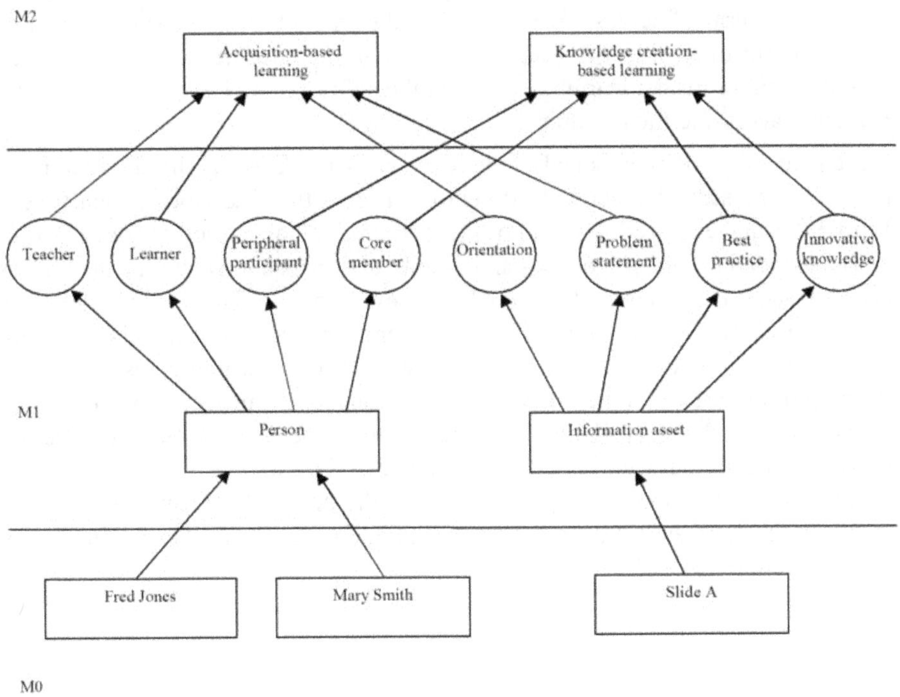


## Educational Informatics Systems that Learn

A more radical bottom-up approach to building shared knowledge entailing learning on the part of the system is taken by McCalla (Brooks & McCalla, 2006; McCalla, 2004) in his "ecological" paradigm for the development of educational systems. This is an approach to providing adaptive personalised learning which not only makes use of standard pedagogical metadata, but also dynamically collects and cumulates other metadata relating to resources, learners, and the interactions between the two, at the time of use. The approach also entails the mining of this data in order to generate new pedagogical knowledge as required for different purposes.

Metadata is gathered at the time of use of the resource as opposed to being preassigned by human experts. As a learner accesses a particular resource, metadata is attached to that resource, which relates to the learner, the resource and the interaction between the two. *Learner* information may include, for example, cognitive and affective characteristics, and learning goals. *Resource* information may include interpretations of what the resource is about as specified by the learner, and also as inferred by text processing algorithms as well as descriptions assigned from recognized metadata schema and ontologies. *Interaction* information may include recorded patterns of access, *dwell time* (i.e., the amount of time spent by the user viewing the learning object), the learner's evaluation of the usefulness of the resource in addressing his or her learning need, and the software and hardware used by the learner in accessing the resource.

More metadata will be attached to the resource as it is used by different learners, and/or by the same learner on different occasions. In other words, each time a learning resource is used, a *model* of the learner and the interaction is attached to it. The model represents a context- and time-bound snapshot. Next time the learner accesses the same resource, the model will have changed. The learner model has two main elements. The *characteristics* component records relatively enduring learner features including age, cognitive style, current learning goals, history of learning resources previously studied, past learning assessments, and so forth. The *episodic* component of the learner's model records aspects of the learner's interactions with the current learning resource, including for example, his/her evaluation of the resource in terms of its perceived difficulty and so forth, and data relating to any test the learner has completed in relation to the resource. Data collection is illustrated in Figure 105.

*Figure 105. An ecological approach to metadata generation*

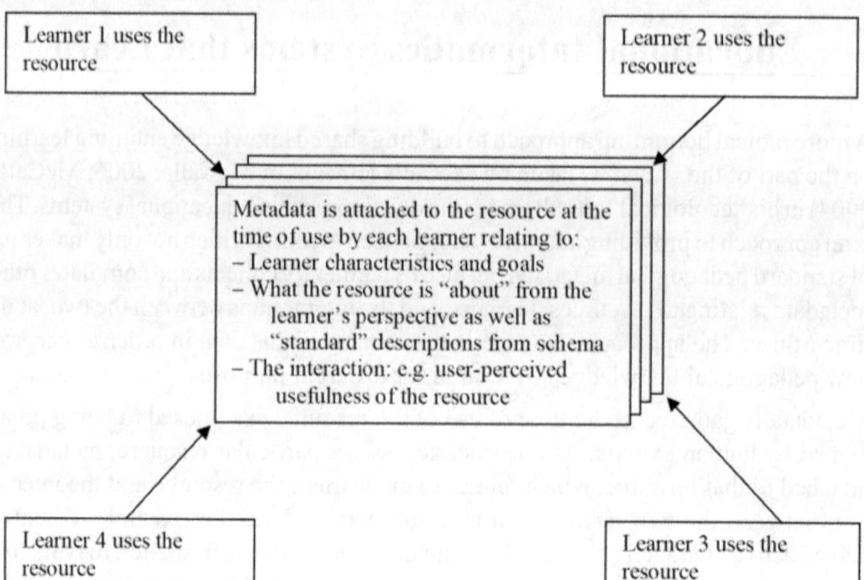

Over time, each learning resource will accumulate many models. This data can then be subjected to data mining in order to discover patterns that are useful in achieving particular tasks. Examples of such tasks are described hereafter, and may entail, for example, information retrieval and personal recommendation, discovering resources (including people) most suited, across a range of parameters including pedagogic, to providing personalized assistance to learners, and even aspects of resource collection management including the weeding of less useful resources as other more useful ones are added to the collection. McCalla (2004) notes that:

*The approach is ecological because over time the system is populated with more and more information, and something like natural selection based on purposes determines what information is useful and what is not. ... In a phrase, the approach involves attaching models of users to the information they interact with, and then mining these models for patterns that are useful for various purposes. The information and the data mining algorithms interact with one another in an ecosystem where the relevance and usefulness of information is always being adjusted to suit the changing needs of learners and teachers and to fit changes in the external environment and the system's perceptions.*

A model of the learner is kept, which records his or her characteristics along with records of his or her interactions with learning objects over time. After every interaction with another learning object, an *instance* of the learner model is associated with the learning object. This means that (1) the learning object is associated with instances of the learner model of each learner who has interacted with it, and (2) each learner model contains data relating to all his or her interactions with different learning objects.

Thus, metadata contained in an instance of a learner model can include: information relating to the goal(s) that brought the learner into contact with the particular learning object; affective and social as well as cognitive learner characteristics; the learner's views about the learning object and its usefulness; the learner's level of knowledge relating to the subject content of the learning object (this may be assessed, for example, by a test taken as part of the interaction with the learning object); statistical data relating to the interaction, such as dwell time, keystrokes, and so forth; technical aspects of use, including the hardware and software used by the learner to access the learning object; and contextual information including links to the learner model instances associated with learning objects with which the learner has previously interacted.

In this way, a large volume of data is obtained that can be mined for various purposes. Indeed, the purposes need not be determined in advance. This has the potential to enable real-time adaptation to the on-going needs of learners. Brooks and McCalla (2006) note that:

*In sum, then, the ecological approach promotes the notion that information gradually accumulates about learning objects, the information is about the use of the learning object by real learners and this information is interpreted only in the context of end use. The approach is ecological because over time the system is populated with more and more information and algorithms emulating natural selection (based on purposes) that can determine what information is useful and what is not.* (p. 55)

Thus the system both generates pedagogic knowledge via the mining of data from learner interactions with resources, and in turn uses this acquired knowledge in order to facilitate the discovery and selection of further resources.

Tang and McCalla (2003) also report a system based on this approach, designed to search CITESEER and recommend relevant papers to research students. Each time a paper is read by a learner, an instance of the learner's model is attached to the paper's metadata. The system also enables the learner to annotate the resource, this information feeding in to model (recording the learner's interactions with resources). The retrieval of relevant papers in response to a request by a particular learner proceeds via the matching of that learner's model (in terms of both its *characteristics* and *episodic* components) with those of other learners who share relevant characteristics and who have evaluated the papers positively in relation to their own use of them. By examining appropriate aspects of the learner models (particularly their evaluations relating to usefulness) attached over time to particular papers, any on-going changes in their perceived relevance can be mapped. As McCalla (2004) notes:

*More sophisticated and intelligent examination of the papers in the repository through the lens of the students' experiences with them could allow all manner of inferences to be drawn about papers, including what they are about, how they relate to each other, how the research discipline is changing, what papers appeal to what types of readers, etc.*

Such facilities could, for example, enable the weeding of a resource collection as the usefulness of certain papers is perceived to wane over time as new papers appear.

Work is reported (McCalla, Vassileva, Greer, & Bull, 2000; Niu, McCalla, & Vassileva, 2005; Vassileva, McCalla, & Greer, 2003) further developing approaches to the learner modeling that is a key feature of ecological systems. What they term the *active learner modelling* paradigm entails the development and application of partial and context-bound learner models in which knowledge of any particular learner is fragmented among the various distributed agents that collect it. The agents can then use their particular knowledge to negotiate with other agents in order to fulfill whatever learning task is being worked on at the time. This entails analysis of raw data computed as required and specific to particular purposes and contexts of use.

Negotiation by distributed active agents in pursuit of particular goals is also the essence of the *I-Help* system (Brooks & McCalla, 2006; McCalla et al., 2001). This system supports learners by finding suitable people to help them with the particular learning problem they are experiencing. Each learner is represented by an agent, which maintains a model of its owner. When a learner issues a request for help, his or her agent negotiates with the agents of others to find the best match. After the help interaction, the consumer of the help provides feedback on the effectiveness or otherwise of the help, and this information is fed into the user models of both the consumer and the provider of the help.

The metadata used in the matching process by each agents includes: (1) information provided by the learner, in the form of self-assessments of his or her level of knowledge in particular areas, and availability; (2) the feedback evaluations described previously; (3) knowledge at the system level of the frequency of both online availability; and (4) levels of past participation in the public discussion component of *I-Help*, of the agent owner. These multiple fragmented learner models are constantly updated and negotiate among themselves to find an optimal solution to a particular problem dynamically at the time this is required. This work has been further developed in the form of the Helper's Assistant framework (Kumar, Greer, & McCalla, 2005). The LORNET project (McCalla, 2004) also displays the application of the active learner modelling developed in the I-Help system to learning objects. This project seeks to enable such objects themselves to become active agents, able to negotiate with both other learning objects, and agents representing learners.

Researchers at the laboratory for the Advanced Research in Intelligent Educational Systems (ARIES) at the University of Saskatchewan have developed a content management system, iHelp courses, which delivers learning objects to learners using the IMS Content Packaging standard. They have implemented metadata collection based on an ecological approach as previously described. Before and after use, learners are given online multiple-choice quizzes to assess their level of knowledge about the subject content. This information is converted into resource description framework (RDF) format by the Massive User Modelling System (MUMS) (Brooks, Kettel, & Hansen, 2005; Brooks & McCalla, 2006), and mapped onto a subject domain ontology, represented as an RDF graph.

The data is also mapped onto an ontology of educational objectives, which is based on the work (described more fully in Chapter I), by Bloom, Krathwohl, and Anderson analysing different information processing types in which learners may be required to engage, such as recall, comprehension, analysis, and so forth (Anderson & Krathwohl, 2001; Bloom & Krathwohl, 1956). This means that metadata is collected relating to both the subject content and the information processing types entailed in the learner's interaction with a learning object. RDF representation of such learner metadata is much more flexible than, for example, LOM, since it is extensible in a more open-ended way (recall from Chapter V how RDF tuples can chain together, the value of one triple becoming the object of another). The metadata thus derived from interaction between learner and learning object can then be linked to that learning object. Brooks and McCalla (2006) note that the MUMS tool also:

> *allows ready customisation of data mining algorithms to analyse these data and naturally facilitates the integration of information discovered by these algorithms.* (p. 59)

Part of the research effort is also to investigate the appropriateness of, and develop where necessary, data mining algorithms for various different educational purposes. Brooks and McCalla (2006) list a number of such goals, and reference related work:

> *– a study aid, for example, to retrieve for a learner relevant papers from a cache of such papers for a graduate student trying to learn about an area of research (e.g. Tang and McCalla, 2003)*
>
> *– a recommender system, to recommend some content to a learner that is relevant to his her current task (e.g. Recker and Wiley, 2001)*
>
> *– an instructional planner, to plan out a sequence of content pages of relevance to a learner, sort of an individualised curriculum of study*
>
> *– a group formation tool, to suggest to the learner a group of other learners relevant to solving a particular task or learning about a particular subject (e.g. Winter and McCalla, 2003 [...])*
>
> *– a help seeker, to find another learner who can help the learner solve a problem he/she has encountered (e.g. the I-Help system (Greer et al., 1998))*
>
> *– a reminder system, to keep a learner updated with new information that is relevant to the learner's goals*
>
> *– an evaluation tool, to allow learners' interactions with educational content to be studied by instructional and cognitive scientists, in particular to look at the experiences of all learners or particular types of learners with some educational content*
>
> *– an end-use tagging system, to automatically derive educational content tags from pre-established ontologies based on the experiences of the actual users of the content and that can be parameterised by end-use variables such as the type of learner, success/failure of the educational content for each type of learner, etc. A variant of this possibility is the ability to refine, modify or change pre-assigned metadata based on inferences from end use an 'intelligent' garbage collection system to determine the ongoing relevance of educational content and, if necessary, to suggest modifications or even that it be deleted as no longer being useful to learners (e.g. as discussed by Bannan-Ritland et al. (2000)).* (pp. 55-56)

The ecological approach as propounded by McCalla (2004) in many ways runs counter to the movement towards standardisation and associated interoperability in that it represents a move away from centrally provided, consensus authority-based metadata schemes that emphasise a priori decisions by experts relating to both categories and likely uses of metadata. The ecological approach also entails a number of problems—not least the trade-off between a potentially vast and rapidly growing volume of data and the computational effort required to mine this data for useful patterns, particularly in real-time. Brooks and McCalla (2006) envisage a situation in which the emphasis shifts away the generation, interpretation, and use of metadata as an essentially human activity to one in which metadata is generated by machines for interpretation and use by intelligent software agents.

They acknowledge that coexistence and the advantages of symbiosis between traditional and ecological metadata approaches may in the future add significant value to the current situation. One possibility is that software agents may be able to summarise complex data produced as a result of applying ecological approaches and export it—albeit at the expense of considerable semantic degradation—in a form compatible with the elements of traditional metadata schemes like LOM.

## Community-Based Learning

A number of researchers are working to apply Web 2.0 concepts to learning. One example is the use of social tagging. As noted in Chapter VI, social tagging systems such as flickr, del.icio.us, YouTube, and the academic-focused CiteULike offer the facility for users freely to associate content with their own tags. This enables them a degree of personalised control and organisation in that they can then retrieve content via their own descriptive keywords. However, the individual may also be able to benefit from the harnessing by the system of aspects of the collective intelligence of the community of users. Thus, an individual user can view the tags associated with a given information source assigned by other users, and information relating to the relative popularity of tags. The frequency with which particular sources are viewed can also be made known to each user. Such information can be used by the individual in his or her navigational choices thus making use of what has been termed *social navigation.*

Other systems such as Gibeo and Marginalia allow the more extensive annotation of Web sources. AnnotatEd is an educational annotation system designed to support the annotation and social navigation of Web-based educational information sources. This system forms the basis of the Open Annotation and Tagging System (OATS), which is intended to add value to the iHelp courses system (introduced earlier in this chapter). The iHelp Courses system (Bateman, Brooks, & McCalla,

2006) already enables users, when viewing a particular learning object, to engage in chat and discussion displayed at the bottom of their screens, relating specifically to that learning content. In this way, learners can actively engage with the views of others.

OATS enables individual learners easily to tag and annotate textual learning objects by simply highlighting text (Bateman, Brooks, McCalla, & Brusilovsky, 2007; Bateman, Farzan, Brusilovsky, & McCalla, 2006). When the learner clicks on this highlighted text, a pop-up menu appears, offering the facility to add tags, view (and delete) any existing tags that the learner has previously assigned, and view tags that other learners may also have assigned to the selected text. The same pop-up menu also offers an option to add notes—free text annotations. The learner can mark notes as private to him or herself, or public. As with tags, any previously assigned annotations made by the individual learner, and any public annotations created by others, are visible. Details are given relating to who generated the annotation(s) and when.

It is also possible to view both personal tags and those used by others making up the learning community using the system—the most frequently used being presented first. For any selected tag, the learner is able to view all the pages—or if preferred, all highlighted text sections—that he or she has marked with that tag. The learner is also able to view, again in order of popularity, all the tags used by the community of learners, and by clicking any of these tags can add it to his or her personal tags associated with the highlighted text. A search facility is also provided, allowing the learner to search for pages, notes, and tags.

The system is intended to be integrated into the iHelp system at the University of Saskatchewan. However, it is intended to be able to be used as a Web service, accessible to—but independent of—other e-learning systems including learning management systems, as Bateman, Brooks, and McCalla (2006) put it: "to decouple value-added functionality from the LMS or learning portal." However, they also acknowledge that a security requirement of AJAX (which is used to implement the service) that the Web service must be located on the same server as the learning management system does compromise the claim that OATS is truly decoupled and has necessitated solutions entailing the use of proxies.

CommonFolks (Bateman, Brooks, & McCalla, 2006) is a system designed to facilitate the tagging of learning resources with metadata. It seeks to make the task sufficiently easy to avoid deterring nonspecialist metadata authors, such as students, from being willing to engage in metadata tagging of learning resources they use. At the same time, the system aims to inject sufficient semantic quality and structure to render the metadata useful for machine processing. This will militate for the generation of rich metadata by large numbers of learners, which can be used in adaptive e-learning systems. CommonFolks metadata is written in RDF.

The system takes advantage of both social tagging approaches and ontologies. Social tagging was described in Chapter VI and entails users freely associating unstructured descriptive words to phenomena such as images, videos, or documents. Social tagging enables the harnessing of knowledge derived from the analysis of collective indexing behaviour and requires no training or expertise, but may be idiosyncratic and unstructured. Indexing using ontologies brings the benefits of structure and standardisation but requires considerable learning effort on the part of those wishing to make use of them in indexing.

CommonFolks makes use of the fact that there is an existing semantic lexicon for the English language, WordNet. WordNet is a type of ontology—a structured list of English words detailing for each its meaning and relationships to other words. Nouns, verbs, adjectives, and adverbs are grouped into *synsets*, or sets of synonyms, and a lattice of semantic relationships between synsets is created. The following is an example of terms linked by the *is a* relationship (http://en.wikipedia.org/wiki/WordNet):

```
dog, domestic dog, Canis familiaris
    => canine, canid
        => carnivore
            => placental, placental mammal, eutherian, eutherian mammal
                => mammal
                    => vertebrate, craniate
                        => chordate
                            => animal, animate being, beast, brute, creature, fauna
                                => ...
```

Each different meaning of a term has its own hierarchy. A number of other relationships are specified—for example: hypernyms, hyponyms, holonyms, meronyms, troponyms, entailments, antonyms, synonyms, and so forth.

The CommonFolks system has a lattice of words and connections between them. The CommonFolks lattice also contains the WordNet lattice. When a user wishes to tag a particular learning resource, he or she may enter a word as a tag—just as with social tagging systems such as del.icio.us or flickr. If the word is not already known to the system, the user can search or browse the lattice in order to find the most appropriate *parent* for the new term—that is, a term to which the new term is related by the *is a* relationship. If other users of the system have already used the term, then the parents that they have chosen will be displayed, along with an indication of which has been the most popular choice.

For example, suppose that a user wishes to tag a new *learning nugget* designed to teach beginners about information retrieval. He or she may discover from the system that other users have used this tag, and associated it with *learning object*—that is, as far as they are concerned, learning nugget *is a* learning object. Other users may have associated learning nugget with *learning resource*, and so on. The system may indicate that the most popular choice is learning object.

The user may then either select one of these suggestions or choose his or her own new parent. The tag is now integrated into the wider structure of relationships in the lattice, specifying not only that learning nugget is a learning resource, but linking it by inheritance with all the relationships linked to learning resource and their ancestors in the relevant lattice hierarchies. At this stage, the particular learning resource (identified by a URI) can be linked with the tag, using an RDF triple:

<http://www.shef.ac.uk/ed-info/examples/IR> <is a> <learning nugget>

The user may now wish to associate the item with a tag describing its subject matter—*information retrieval*. Again, he or she may consult the system for suggestions for an appropriate tag, and be informed that other people have used *is about* while others have used *has subject*. The user makes his or her choice (which can be changed retrospectively at any time), and the resource becomes tagged as follows:

<http://www.shef.ac.uk/ed-info/examples/IR> <has subject> <information retrieval>

Had information retrieval not been known to the system—that is, not already contained within the lattice—the user could have added it, again searching or browsing the network to locate an existing associated term to give it context. This addition, and others made by other users, would extend the lattice. CommonFolks monitors each user's use of tags and will alert him or her to any inconsistencies or contradictions as new tags are added.

The approach is inductive in the sense that, rather than start with an ontology, then select terms to describe learning objects as in the more conventional approach, metadata generation within CommonFolks starts with tags, which will either already exist in—or be added to—the lattice. As Bateman, Brooks, and McCalla (2006) note:

*Rather than designing an ontology and then providing instances that fit the ontology for given resources, we are able to skip the design process and begin using instances to describe our resource, since instances will be added to or exist in the WordNet lattice. We can later infer a domain ontology for a set of tags (instances used to describe resources) at any point, based on our own or the communities' annotations.*

The authors acknowledge that the system is still at the prototyping stage, with annotations at present restricted to words existing in WordNet. In 2006, WordNet included 155,327 words, arraged in 117,597 synsets covering 207,016 word-sense pairs (http://wordnet.princeton.edu/man/wnstats.7WN#sect2).

Learner control as opposed to high levels of supplantation is characteristic of a number of systems designed to facilitate community-based learning. Such systems act as intermediary tools which communities can use to assist in resource discovery and learning. They may entail the rendering more explicit and accessible of pedagogical features of information sources.

Stutt and Motta (2004), for example, report a vision of—and early empirical work relating to—the development of semantic learning webs in which semantic browsers and semantic constructors enable community-based knowledge neighbourhoods to engage in the creation of knowledge charts enabling knowledge navigation. (These terms are explained hereafter.) Learning is a prime function of knowledge neighbourhoods:

> *A Knowledge Neighbourhood can be viewed as a location in cyberspace where learners can congregate into groups or larger communities with the goal of acquiring knowledge about some topic.* (p. 20)

Indeed, the starting point for their work (Stutt & Motta, 2004) is focused on "learner needs":

> *...it is possible to give an even more abstract account of learner needs which we can use to guide our thoughts about future learning environments. At a more cognitive level students need environments which are congruent with what goes on in learning. From what we have said already we can distinguish between three types of learner needs: for structure, relatedness and interpretation. These correlate more or less with the first two items in Laurillard's (2002) characterization of learning as: apprehending structure, integrating parts, acting on the world, using feedback, and reflecting on goals.* (p. 6)

This work entails a less explicit form of pedagogical knowledge (as defined in the Preface to this book), in that it relates to forms of reasoning via which we learn—for example, argumentation structures by which particular information sources contribute to and interact with evolving idea generation and scholarly debate. *Knowledge charts* are representations of argumentation structures contained within information sources. Part of a knowledge chart is shown in Figure 106. Level 1 shown in Figure 106 represents arguments relating increases in $CO_2$ emissions to rises in temperature and sea level. Level 2 represents a scientific debate concerning this relationship.

It is possible for users to drill down to a greater level of detail relating to particular claims and counter claims. For example, Stutt and Motta (2004) note that

*Figure 106. Part of a knowledge chart (adapted from Stutt & Motta, 2004)*

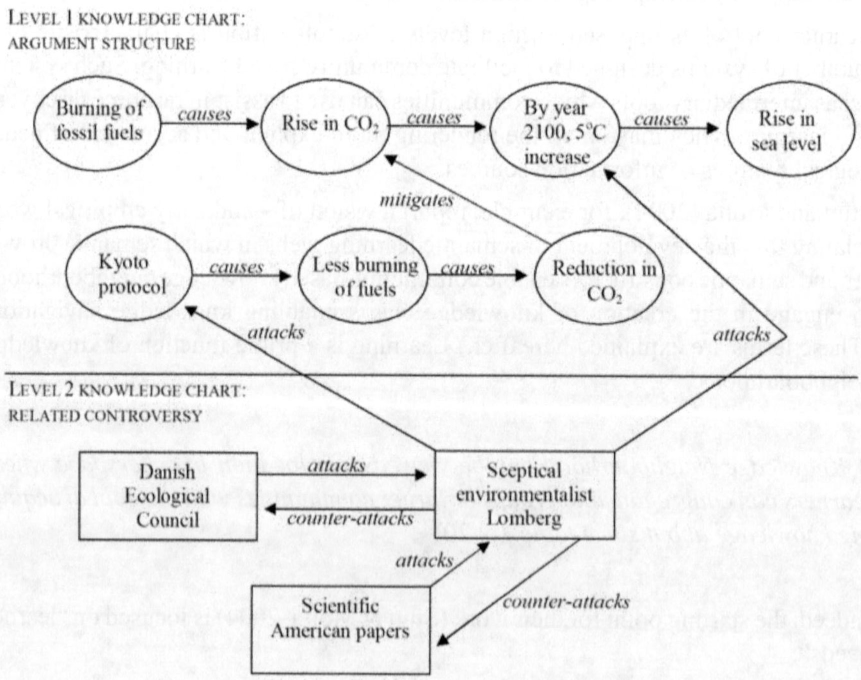


LOMberg argues that the reason $CO_2$ rise is unlikely to lead to increase of 5°C by 2100 is because Intergovernmental Panel on Climate Change (IPCC) models are inadequate—also, that the Kyoto protocol may reduce the burning of fuels but at an acceptable cost, and in any case reducing $CO_2$ at a negligible level. Representations of these more detailed aspects of the argument are accessible should the user wish to explore them.

Resource discovery is facilitated by knowledge representations geared to making explicit (and navigable) the ways in which we come to understand or make sense of information (i.e., learn). Knowledge charts, to which information resources are linked via metadata, render the information sources discoverable in terms of how the user might better understand and contextualise this understanding in terms of how the knowledge fits into its broader context—for example, its role is an on-going scientific debate. The learning-related features of *structure*, *relatedness,* and *interpretation* are precisely what knowledge charts are intended to help the learner develop. Stutt and Motta (2004) also envisage the addition of ontologies relating to specific pedagogic purposes attributed to particular knowledge charts, via extension of EML.

Knowledge charts are ontology-based representations of agreed knowledge within particular communities. Stutt and Motta (2004) describe them as "the ontologically permeated representations of a community's knowledge or point of view." However, the ontologies on which they are based are not restricted to domain concepts and relationships. The types of ontology envisioned relate to types of knowledge in terms of their underlying reasoning structures, and as such represent a type of pedagogical knowledge—knowledge of how we may come to understand, or learn about, complex topics. Such types include, for example, *argumentation* and *debate*, reasoning by *analogy*, constructing *narratives* by which phenomena can be understood, *simulations*, or *cause/effect* models. At one level, an ontology would describe basic knowledge types, and each knowledge type, in turn, would have its own ontology. For example, an argumentation/debate ontology could include concepts such as claim, refutation, support, and confirmation, as well as *debate moves* linked by rhetorical relations. A narrative ontology may include actors, events, and so forth.

Stutt and Motta (2004) propose that metadata describing information resources be extended to enable resources to be linked to appropriate knowledge charts. Marking up may be done by humans and/or via the development of software such as that being developed to enable the extraction of argument and story structures from texts (e.g., Vargas-Vera & Celjuska, 2003;Vargas-Vera & Moreale, 2003). Knowledge charts thus represent reasoning structures found within (single or multiple) documents.

Semantic browsers are designed to use domain ontologies to identify and highlight important concepts in a document, so that the user can follow links from such concepts to related knowledge maps. The maps enable both navigation and interpretation, allowing the user not only to access explanations of the concepts entailed, but also to set the concepts within a broader context, for example, by showing their role and relationships within an on-going scholarly debate. By selecting elements of the knowledge chart, users can navigate in order to explore related or more detailed component arguments, or access original documents. Domingue and Dzbor (2004) and Dzbor, Domingue, and Motta (2003) report the development of such a semantic browser in the form of Magpie developed at the UK Open University's Knowledge Media Institute.

Knowledge charts would be created and used by members of particular knowledge neighbourhoods. These are virtual knowledge-generating and learning communities relating to particular areas of interest. Knowledge charts could be a means to enable such neighbourhoods to communicate with each other insofar as they represent "boundary objects" (Arias & Fischer, 2000). Such boundary objects would facilitate the linking of ontologies envisaged by Berners-Lee's (2004, quoted in Yli-Luoma & Naeve, 2006):

*The Semantic Web will have to be as messy as the World Wide Web. Instead of common ontologies, local ontologies will be stitched together at the edges into a quilt of ontologies.*

Such "stitching" would require a degree of semantic integration or mapping of different ontologies (e.g., Akahani, Hiramatsu, & Satoh, 2003; Gasevic & Hatala, 2005, 2006; Silva & Rocha, 2003). But as well as the linking of discrete ontologies generated by different communities so that they can reference and communicate with each other, there will be an increasing need to come to terms with a diversity of competing ontological perspectives within communities requiring negotiation entailing establishing and recording parameters of agreement and disagreement.

Indeed, Sheth, Ramakrishnan, and Thomas (2005) (quoted in Lytras & Naeve, 2006) recognize the fundamental complexity inherent in the notion of *meaning* that underlies attempts to agree on common representations of what we *know* about domains, topics and objects:

> *Semantics has been a part of several scientific disciplines, both in the realm of computer science and outside of it. ... Most of these areas have very different views of what 'meaning' is, and these views all build on some metatheoretical and epistemological assumptions. These different views imply very different views of cognition, of concepts and of meaning. ... Ontologies for everything seem to be the new buzzword of our decade. However, this ontology mania requires a community consensus and agreement. In a recent interview with Tom Gruber for AIS SIGSEMIS Bulletin—(Gruber, 2004)—he emphasises that 'Every ontology is a treaty—a social agreement—among people with some common motive in sharing.'* (pp. 479-481)

Such negotiation is addressed by Naeve (2005), who proposes the building of ontological bridges between different perspectives by means of "conceptual calibration." Echoing Pask's work on *conversation theory* (introduced in Chapter I), this entails establishing agreement on what is agreed, what is not agreed, and how such agreements and disagreements should be recorded.

The notion of alternative perspectives and disputed understandings is central to the scholarly ontologies (or ScholOnto) project at the UK Open University's Knowledge Media Institute. As part of this project, a number of tools have been developed, including ClaiMapper, which enables users to create *argument maps* relating to information sources and their interconnections, and ClaimFinder, which facilitates searching across the claims mapped by ClaiMapper. ClaiMaker is a server supporting the representation, discovery, and navigation of scholarly discourse and argumentation (Uren, Buckingham Shum, Bachler, & Li1, 2006).

ClaimSpotter (Buckingham Shum, Uren, Li, Sereno, & Mancini, 2007; Sereno, Buckingham Shum, & Motta, 2005) is an environment designed to support the annotation of scholarly documents with metadata derived from an ontology of discourse. This discourse relates to naturalistic scholarly argumentation—that is, the way in which we make sense of, discuss, and negotiate the type of complex ideas that are open to debate and interpretation, as typically found in academic documents.

This work falls within the realm of educational informatics as defined here in the same way as does the work previously described by Stutt and Motta (2004), in that the ontology and metadata document annotations represent a type of pedagogical knowledge (as defined in the Preface), and as discussed hereafter, the system uses this knowledge to enable resource discovery to support learning.

The ontology of scholarly discourse includes relations such as the extent to which an idea supports or challenges other ideas (proves, refutes, is evidence for, is evidence against, agrees with, disagrees with, is consistent with, is inconsistent with); how it relates to a particular problem or issue (addresses, solves); how it affects other ideas (predicts, envisages, causes, is capable of causing, is prerequisite for, prevents, is unlikely to affect); is similar or dissimilar (is identical to, is similar to, is different to, is the opposite of, shares issues with, has nothing to do with, is analogous to, is not analogous to); is taxonomically related (part of, example of, subclass of, not part of, not example of); or linked by more general relationships (is about, uses/applies/is enabled by, improves on, impairs, etc.)

Rather than with relatively factual, static aspects of a document as described by standard metadata schemes, Sereno et al. (2005) are interested in:

> *...the annotation of documents with knowledge resulting from a sensemaking process. Consider a scholarly document. What its salient points are, how it relates to previous works in a community, and how innovative it is might not appear immediately. Carefully reading the paper, identifying the themes of interest, arguing with the position defended, building on the previous papers we, as scholars, have read beforehand, understanding why a particular paper is cited..., drawing our own connections to other papers which are (or not) cited. . . all these steps, among others, are involved in an interpretation process, a sensemaking process. Not to mention that this interpretation might change over time as our research interests evolve, and of course that two readers might see different aspects in the same document.* (p. 199)

Different users can annotate a document with potentially contradictory interpretations. The interpretations are accessible to other users of the system, which enables the discovery of documents that are related in terms of their perceived argumentation structures to a document being considered by a user. Documents unrelated formally may be discovered via relations solely existing in user interpretations. Not only can such relationships be discovered, but the nature of the relationship is made explicit. Users can also discover the various ways in which a particular issue has been addressed by a community, and/or identify other people supporting or contesting particular ideas.

The annotations are represented as triples linking a source concept and a destination concept via a relationship. The relationships must be selected from the discourse ontology. The concepts are unconstrained and can consist of a word or paragraph of free text. ClaimSpotter provides support for annotators by flagging examples of the ontology relationships where they exist in a document and identifying tentative potential concepts that the annotator may wish to consider. It does this by analysing the text to find, for example, author-provided keywords, noun groups, and other specified sequences of words. Importantly, the system provides only suggestions to annotators, who are free to ignore or use them, and to generate their own concepts as they wish.

Based on Pask's conversation theory, and work on the THOUGHTSTICKER system reported by Pangaro in Chapter VI, Ford (2005) proposes a speculative "conversational information system" designed to support both mediated and autonomous learning. This system is included in the present chapter, which focuses on social systems, since the system would enable different Paskian entailment meshes to be "plugged in," and would essentially act as what Ford termed a "conversation brokering" service. Learning would be facilitated by enabling and supporting conversational interactions between learners constituting particular communities of interest and whatever entailment meshes were present in the system at a given time.

Notions of *authority, expert,* and *novice* can be viewed as potentially fluid, shifting over time as a result of Paskian conversations. Such different levels of knowledge representation can essentially coexist, and mechanisms within the system proposed, based on the properties of entailment meshes, can be subjected to comparison, coherence checking, negotiation, and dynamic change. In this way, an individual may come to the system as a novice wanting to learn from the knowledge of authoritative others. He or she may equally approach the system as critical evaluator and negotiator of new shared meanings. As the individual's knowledge changes and develops, so can the role in which he or she uses the system.

Entailment meshes can not only represent the conceptual structures (the understandings) of different individuals, but also enable the checking that meshes are *well formed*—that is, possess certain required properties such as coherence and cyclicity, which militate for high levels of *learnability* within conversation theory. The properties of a well-formed entailment structure enable ambiguities, gaps, and contradictions to be identified automatically as new knowledge is added. They can also enable and facilitate comparisons between different understandings, and the identification of agreements and disagreements between conversational participants. Such structures can in this way allow the representation of the different, but equally valid, understandings that constitute different perspectives, and different constructed *realities* of different individuals.

Figure 107 shows the structure of such a system. The system would not contain or seek to establish some authoritative knowledge representation of a subject domain, as in many current adaptive educational informatics systems. Rather, it would provide rules which specify the requirements of a *well-formed* entailment mesh—in any subject domain—by which it is formally *coherent*, along with rules governing conversations between different p-individuals, who would include learners and resource authors. Clearly, the system would need to provide authoring facilities to enable the creation of appropriate entailment meshes by the conversational participants. As Ford (2005) notes:

*The system would thus interact with users on the basis of complex rules such as those pioneered by Pask governing the cyclicity, consistency and connectivity of well-formed entailment meshes. These enable conflict, gap and ambiguity detection and the provision of interactive dialog to support their resolution. They are also required in order to enable the revision of meshes in their entirety in response to ongoing changes resulting from conversational interactions, to ensure their holistic integrity.*

The system would be designed to offer a range of types and levels of support. At one level, it would assist authors. Authors would be supported in their production of entailment meshes for the thesis they are expounding—in a particular information source or series of information sources—which would conform to Pask's requirements for high levels of understandability. Recall from Chapter VI that Pask developed clear rules to ensure that entailment meshes are characterised by properties including consistency and cyclicity, which militate for such high levels of understandability. The system could also help authors to detect—and resolve—ambiguities, gaps, and contradictions in the entailment meshes they are producing.

As noted previously, entailment meshes could be produced at different levels. At one level, they may relate to particular theses expounded in particular information sources. At a higher level, entailment meshes with a more global focus could incorporate, or link to the lower level meshes. Such meshes could be produced via

*Figure 107. A Paskian conversation brokering system*

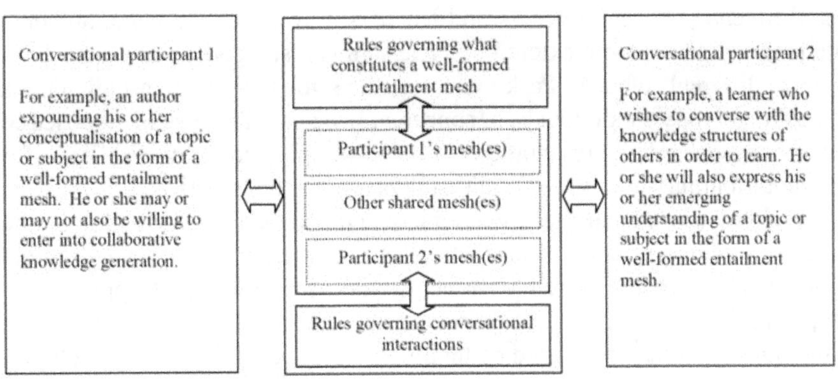

the use of the same, or a remote but similar THOUGHTSTICKER-type system. This support could be provided via a Web service, and remotely created entailment meshes could be retrieved and plugged in to the system.

Learners could therefore access and interact with author meshes. Recall from Chapter VI that entailment meshes support the generation of *unfolding* navigable concept maps, which from any access point offer full mesh qualities associated with high learnability. Assuming a critical mass of entailment mesh-based learning resources in the system, learners could search for them by using an information retrieval component of the system, which at the simplest level would match keywords with meshes containing them. Retrieval criteria could also include, for example, the degree to which meshes represent an agreed expert view on a particular topic or domain, possibly using the social navigation approaches discussed previously. Other criteria could be customised to serve different learning needs and contexts. Meshes could also be discovered via more sophisticated querying in which an existing mesh could be used as the query input to graph-matching techniques. Such mechanisms would essentially overlay the basic system of meshes, offering a variety of access routes and levels of mediation and support in discovering and using them.

The learner could then make use of the meshes in a number of different ways. In relatively passive mode, he or she could simply navigate around an author's mesh, exploring topics—their *why?* and *how?*—to learn about that author's conceptualisation of the topic or domain. The unfolding map facility would enable entry to a mesh at any point, for example, in response to a keyword query, as well as considerable flexibility of exploration. However, differing levels of guidance and mediation could be provided. The system would also allow learners to drill down (and up) to linked resources, including assessment facilities if these would appropriate and desired.

However, learners could interact more actively, using the system to generate their own entailment meshes. They could make use of the system's authoring support facilities to check gaps, ambiguities, and contradictions in their own evolving understanding. At a higher level of interactivity, learners could also engage in formal conversations with author meshes, establishing agreements and disagreements.

The difference between learners and teachers, novices and experts, authors and interpreters may to some extent blur. The same person could interact at different times in different roles. As Pask indicated, the same biological m-individual may possess numerous p-individuals, or conceptual systems. The system proposed could not only host shared representations of the developing conceptualisations of multiple contributing authors, but could support interactions between them. Authors could, if they wished, engage in greater interactivity and agree to modify their own conceptual representations in the light of conversational interactions. It might be possible to offer multi-layered dynamic networks of meshes, with appropriate version control and appropriate read/write permissions enabling different versions of author meshes, where permitted by their owners, to be modified as a result of such interactions.

One possible scenario might entail a learner initially accessing the system. He or she might start to build an entailment mesh representing his or her initial understanding of—and/or questions about—the topic or domain in focus. This process could be facilitated by the sort of interactive questioning provided to mesh authors by, for example, the THOUGHTSTICKER consistency-checking facilities described in Chapter VI. The learner may then use retrieval and discovery facilities in order to search for meshes produced by the authors of relevant information sources. Relevant meshes could then be retrieved and plugged in to the system. As a result of interactions with such meshes, the learner could progressively represent his or her evolving understanding in the form of an increasingly sophisticated mesh.

Ford (2000) has argued that, since we need to be able to store, access, and interpret a great multiplicity of information, which is generated from a variety of different perspectives (for example, from the points of view of system designers, researchers, teachers, and learners) and which entails a great range of different levels and types of knowledge, we need some sort of dynamic, interactive, multi-perspective, and flexible *evidence map*. Such an evidence map would ideally also enable us to record the cumulation, integration, disputation, and other forms of interaction between, these disparate sources of knowledge. Although in the following quotation Ford emphasises the utility of such a system to researchers in the field of information retrieval, such a system would arguably be of much wider use to a great variety of stakeholders. Ford (2000) argues that:

*Researchers from a range of different disciplines ... need to be able to find relevant IR research findings in response to searches formulated in terms of their own particular problems and perspectives. Such multi- and inter-disciplinary searches would benefit from a range of ontologies designed to map such requests onto more specialised IR terminology. However, as well as a range of heterogeneous reviews and ontological mappings of search terminologies, we also need multi-perspective and multi-purpose conceptual mappings more complex than those provided by ontologies.* (pp. 634-635)

He comments that although systematic reviews and meta-analyses do to an extent provide integrated views of particular areas of knowledge, they also impose a particular structure and perspective. Ideally, an appropriately flexible system which could respond to questions such as the following:

*Let me explore topic X in terms of aspect Y, from perspective Z. I want to keep X and Y exactly as I have defined them, but would like to explore variations in Y.*

Ford (2000) suggests investigating, as a possible system for implementing such an evidence map, ZigZag—a hypertextual paradigm devised by Nelson (1998, 1999, 2001, 2004). According to Moore and Brailsford (2004), this system:

*... excels at making the complex comprehensible by laying bare the underlying structure of information. It makes far greater provision for storing and visualising the fundamental interconnectedness of information than other, more conventional, methods of hypertextual representation. ... ZigZag hyperstructures allow the relationship between fundamental pieces of information/media along diverse lines of whatever implicit or explicit scaffolding the user or system may specify.*

Moore and Brailsford (2004) have conducted some exploratory work using the ZigZag system in bioinformatics—an area which they note is characterized by particularly high levels of intrinsic complexity. These authors found that the ZigZag system was able to render such very complex structures more readily browsable and comprehensible.

Nelson (2004) describes the basic approach as follows:

*From orthogonally connected data items (zzcells) and untyped connections (zzlinks), we build a cross-connected fabric of data (zzstructure) that is visualizable, interactive, and programmable. ... It is essentially spatial. It is based on criss-crossed lists of cells which are assigned to dimensions. Along these dimensions the cells are viewable, traversible, and subject to operations. ... Not only is it desirable to view zzstructures in 3D, but it should be possible easily to view more than three ... [dimensions] at once. ... All cells exist in all dimensions. Conversely, each new dimension embraces every cell. ... as soon as a dimension is created, connections can be made along that dimension to any cell in the system.*

Two of the main characteristics potentially offered by this the *zzstructure* referred to in the previous quotation are flexibility enabling users to take alternative views of complex, multi-faceted data. New perspectives can also be easily added as new dimensions, without the information already stored in the system needing to be reconfigured. Such facilities could be particularly useful in enabling the navigation of the type of complex, multi-faceted, multi-perspective evidence map proposed by Ford. In this way, users could explore complex knowledge from alternative perspectives, and with different questions in mind. Interactive Wiki-like contribution facilities, along with appropriate access rights and version control relative to particular user communities, could allow the interactive development of the evidence map.

If in some way linked or integrated with the type of Paskian conversational system proposed earlier in this chapter, it may be possible for such a system, as well as enabling flexible navigation, also to facilitate comparisons and the identification and mapping of conflicts and discrepancies between different items of knowledge. It may also be possible to map differences in the types of evidence on which different items of knowledge are based, and differences in approaches and perspectives. It could potentially enable dynamic interaction between contributors entailing the negotiation of shared agreements and disagreements. This could allow the evidence map to be extended and refined with different views reflecting, from different users' points of view, the modification, consolidation, confirmation, disputation, and rejection of knowledge items, and approaches and perspectives propounded in the evidence map by others—whether individuals, groups, or communities.

Prototypes of the ZigZag system have been developed and tested (for example, Moore & Brailsford, 2004), as have prototypes of Paskian conversational systems based on entailment structures (for example, Heylighen, 2001; Pangaro, 1997; Zimmer, 2001). Clearly the complexities and potential problems of implementation are great, and at this stage the proposal to base such an evidence map on zzstructure representations is highly speculative. Also, it is far from clear how, and if, conversational information systems might be linked to or integrated with zzstructure data representations. It may be that one type of representation could overlay the other.

This and the previous chapter have explored a range of educational informatics systems, building on the work reported in the previous chapters relating to systems designed to support learning design, teaching, and resource discovery. Chapter IX will focus on more general themes that emerge from these developments, relating to a number of fundamental questions, problems, and issues concerning research and development. It will examine what may be fundamental limitations in the nature of any direct contribution computers can make to what are essentially human creative processes. It will also explore a number of pragmatic problems associated with research, taking as a mini case study difficulties surrounding research into learning styles—which represent an increasingly popular variable used, in conjunction with others, to drive adaptive system behaviour.

## References

Akahani, J., Hiramatsu, K., & Satoh, T. (2003, October 21-23). *Approximate query reformulation for ontology integration*. Paper presented at the Semantic Integration Workshop Collocated with the 2nd International Semantic Web Conference (ISWC03), Sanibel Island, FL.

Allert, H. (2004). Coherent social systems for learning: An approach for contextualized and community-centred metadata. *Journal of Interactive Media in Education,* (2). Retrieved August 1, 2007, from www-jime.open.ac.uk/2004/2

Anderson, L. W., & Krathwohl (Eds.). (2001). *A taxonomy for learning, teaching, and assessing: A revision of Bloom's Taxonomy of Educational Objectives*. New York: Longman.

Arias, E., & Fischer, G. (2000, December). *Boundary objects: Their role in articulating the task at hand and making information relevant to it*. Paper presented at the International ICSC Symposium on Interactive and Collaborative Computing (ICC '2000). Retrieved August 1, 2007, from http://www.cs.colorado.edu/~gerhard/papers/icsc2000.pdf

Bannan-Ritland, B., Dabbagh, N., & Murphy, K. (2000). Learning object systems as constructivist learning environments: Related assumptions, theories, and applications. In D. A. Wiley (Ed.), *The instructional use of learning objects: online version*. Retrieved Retrieved August 1, 2007, from http://reusability.org/read/chapters/bannan-ritland.doc

Bateman, S., Brooks, C., McCalla, G., & Brusilovsky, P. (2007, May 7). *Applying collaborative tagging to e-learning*. Paper presented at the Workshop on Tagging and Metadata for Social Information Organization, held in conjuction with the 16th International World Wide Web Conference, Banff, Canada. Retrieved August 1, 2007, from http://fox.usask.ca/files/tagging_elearning_bateman.pdf

Bateman, S., Brooks, C., & McCalla, G. (2006, June 20). Collaborative tagging approaches for ontological metadata in adaptive e-learning systems. In *Proceedings of the Fourth International Workshop on Applications of Semantic Web Technologies for E-Learning (SW-EL 2006) in conjunction with 2006 International Conference on Adaptive hypermedia and Adaptive Web-Based Systems (AH2006)*, Dublin, Ireland (pp. 3-12). Retrieved August 1, 2007, from http://fox.usask.ca/files/bateman_brooks_mccalla_SWEL2006_final.pdf

Bateman, S., Farzan, R., Brusilovsky, P., & McCalla, G. (2006, November 8-10). *OATS: The open annotation and tagging System*. Paper presented at the Third Annual International Scientific Conference of the Learning Object Repository Research Network, Montreal, Canada. Retrieved August 1, 2007, from http://fox.usask.ca/files/OATS-lornet.pdf http://fox.usask.ca/files/OATS-lornet.pdf

Berners-Lee, T. (2004, May 17-20). *Will the Semantic Web scale?* Keynote address at the WWW2004 Panel Debate, New York.

Bloom, B. S., & Krathwohl, D. R. (1956). *Taxonomy of educational objectives: The classification of educational goals, by a committee of college and university examiners. Handbook I: Cognitive domain*. New York: Longman.

Brooks, C., Kettel, L., & Hansen, C. (2005, October). *Building a learning object content management system*. Paper presented at the World Conference on E-Learning in Corporate, Government, Healthcare and Higher Education (E-Learn 2005). New York: Association for the Advancement of Computing in Education (AACE).

Brooks, C., & McCalla, G. (2006). Towards flexible learning object metadata. *International Journal of Continuing Engineering Education and Life Long Learning, 16*(1-2), 50-63.

Buckingham Shum, S. J., Uren, V., Li, G., Sereno, B., & Mancini, C. (2007). Modelling naturalistic argumentation in research literatures: Representation and interaction design issues. *International Journal of Intelligent Systems, 22*(1), 17-47.

Collis, B., & Margaryan, A. (2004). Applying activity theory to computer-supported collaborative learning and work-based activities in corporate settings. *Educational Technology Research & Development, 52*(4), 38-52.

Domingue, J., & Dzbor, M. (2004). Magpie: Supporting browsing and navigation on the Semantic Web. *Proceedings of the 9th international conference on intelligent user interface.* Funchal, Madeira, Portugal (pp. 191-197). New York: ACM Press.

Dzbor, M., Domingue, J., & Motta, E. (2003, October). Magpie—Towards a Semantic Web browser. In K. S. Dieter Fensel & J. Mylopoulos (Eds.), *Proceedings of the Second International Semantic Web Conference (ISWC)*(LNCS 2870, pp. 738-753). Sanibel Island, FL: Springer Verlag.

Edmundson, A. (2007). *Globalized e-learning cultural challenges.* Hershey, PA: Information Science Publishing.

Engeström, Y. (1987). *Learning by expanding: An activity-theoretical approach to developmental research.* Helsinki, Finland: Orienta-Konsultit Oy.

Ford, N. (2000). Improving the "darkness to light" ratio in user-related IR research. *Journal of Documentation, 56*(6), 624-643.

Ford, N. (2005). "Conversational" information systems: Extending educational informatics support for the Web-based learner. *Journal of Documentation, 61*(3), 362-384.

Gasevic, D., & Hatala, M. (2005, October 2-5). *Searching context relevant learning resource using ontology mappings.* Paper presented at the SW-EL workshop at the 3rd International Conference on Knowledge Capture (K-CAP05), Banff, Canada.

Gasevic, D., & Hatala, M. (2006). Ontology mappings to improve learning resource search. *British Journal of Educational Technology, 37*(3), 375-389.

Greer, J., McCalla, G., Cooke, J., Collins, J., Kumar, V., Bishop, A., et al. (1998). The intelligent helpdesk: Supporting peer-help in a university course. *Proceedings of the Fourth International Conference on Intelligent tutoring systems (ITS 1998)* (pp. 494-503). Berlin: Springer-Verlag.

Gruber T. (2004). Every ontology is a treaty—A social agreement—Amongst people with some common motive in sharing: an interview with Tom Gruber. *AIS SIGSEMIS Bulletin, 1*(3), 4-8.

Hanks, W. F. (1991). Foreword. In J. Lave & E. Wenger (Eds.), *Situated learning, legitimate peripheral participation* (9th Reprint, 2001). Cambridge: Cambridge University Press.

Heylighen, F. (2001). Bootstrapping knowledge representations: Via entailment meshes via semantic nets to learning webs. *Kybernetes*, *30*(5/6), 691-722.

Huang, W., Webster, D., Wood, D., & Ishaya, T. (2006). An intelligent semantic e-learning framework using context-aware Semantic Web technologies. *British Journal of Educational Technology, 37*(3), 351-373.

Hummel, H., Manderveld, J., Tattersall, C., & Koper, R. (2004). Educational modelling language and learning design: New opportunities for instructional reusability and personalised learning. *International Journal of Learning Technology, 1*(1), 111-126.

Kumar, V., Greer, J., & McCalla, G. (2005). Assisting online helpers. *International Journal of Learning Technology, 1*(3), 293-321.

Laurillard, D. (2002), *Rethinking university teaching: A conversational framework for the effective use of learning technologies* (2nd ed.). London: Routledge Falmer.

Lytras, M., & Naeve, A. (2006). Semantic e-learning: Synthesising fantasies. *British Journal of Educational Technology, 37*(3), 479-491.

McCalla, G. (2004). The ecological approach to the design of e-learning environments: Purpose-based capture and use of information about learners. *Journal of Interactive Media in Education,* (7). Special Issue on the Educational Semantic Web. Retrieved August 1, 2007, from http://www-jime.open.ac.uk/2004/7/

McCalla, G., Greer, J., Vassileva, J., Deters, R., Bull, S., & Kettel, L. (2001, May). Lessons learned in deploying a multi-agent learning support system: The I-Help experience. In *Proceedings of AIED 2001: International Conference on AI in Education.* Published as J. Moore, C. Redfield, & W. L. Johnson (Eds.), *Artificial intelligence in Education: AI-ED in the wired and wireless future* (pp. 410-421). Amsterdam: IOS Press.

McCalla, G., Vassileva, J., Greer, J., & Bull, S. (2000, June). Active learner modeling. In *Proceedings of ITS 2000: Intelligent tutoring systems,* Montréal, QC, Canada (pp. 53-62). Berlin: Springer Verlag.

Moore, A., & Brailsford, T. (2004, May 27). Unified hyperstructures for bioinformatics: Escaping the application prison. *Journal of Digital Information, 5*(1), Article No. 254. Retreived August 1, 2007, from http://jodi.tamu.edu/Articles/v05/i01/Moore/

Mwanza, D., & Engeström, Y. (2005). Managing content in e-learning environments. *British Journal of Educational Technology, 36*(3), 453-463.

Naeve, A. (2005). The human Semantic Web: Shifting from knowledge push to knowledge pull. *International Journal of Semantic Web and Information*

*Systems, 1*(3), 1-30. Retrieved August 1, 2007, from http://kmr.nada.kth.se/papers/SemanticWeb/HSW.pdf

Nelson, T. H. (1998, May 12-13). *What's on my mind? (ZigZag overview article)*. Paper presented at the First Wearable Computer Conference, Fairfax, VA. Retreived August 1, 2007, from http://www.xanadu.com.au/ted/ZigZag/xybrap.html

Nelson, T. H. (1999). *Welcome to ZigZag (the ZigZag tutorial)*. Retreived August 1, 2007, from http://xanadu.com/ZigZag/tutorial/ZZwelcome.html

Nelson, T. H. (2001, August 14-18). *Deeper cosmology, deeper documents (technical briefing)*. Paper presented at the 12th ACM conference on Hypertext and Hypermedia, Århus, Denmark.

Nelson, T. H. (2004). Cosmology for a different computer universe: data model, mechanisms, virtual machine and visualization infrastructure. *Journal of Digital Information. Special Issue on Future Visions of Common-Use Hypertext, 5*(1), Article No. 298. Retreived August 1, 2007, from http://jodi.tamu.edu/Articles/v05/i01/Nelson/

Niu, X., McCalla, G., & Vassileva, J. (2005, July 25). *Purpose-based user modelling in a multi-agent portfolio management system.* Paper presented at the Workshop on Decentralized, Agent-Based and Social Approaches to User Modeling (DASUM-05), held in conjunction with the Tenth International Conference on User Modeling, Edinburgh, UK.

Paavola, S., Lipponen, L., & Hakkarainen, K. (2002). Epistemological foundations for CSCL: A comparison of three models of innovative knowledge communities. In G. Stahl (Ed.), *Computer support for collaborative learning: Foundations for a CSCL community. Proceedings of the Computer-supported Collaborative Learning 2002 Conference* (pp. 24-32). Hillsdale, NJ: Erlbaum.

Pangaro, P. (1997). *THOUGHTSTICKER: An idiosyncratic history of conversation theory in software, and its progenitor*. Retrieved August 1, 2007, from http://www.pangaro.com/published/thstr-fest.html

Recker, M., & Wiley, D. (2001). A non-authoritative educational metadata ontology for filtering and recommending learning objects. *Interactive Learning Environments Journal, Special Issue on Metadata,* 1-17.

Sereno, B., Buckingham Shum, S., & Motta, E. (2005). ClaimSpotter: An environment to support sensemaking with knowledge triples. In *Proceedings of the 10th International Conference on Intelligent User Interfaces,* San Diego, CA (pp. 199-206). ACM Press.

Sfard, A. (1998). On two metaphors for learning and on the danger of choosing just one. *Educational Researcher, 27*(2), 4-13.

Sheth, A., Ramakrishnan, C., & Thomas, C. (2005). Semantics for the Semantic Web: The implicit, the formal and the powerful. *International Journal on Semantic Web and Information Systems, 1*(1), 1-18.

Sicilia, M. (2006). Semantic learning designs: Recording assumptions and guidelines. *British Journal of Educational Technology, 37*(3), 331-350.

Sicilia, M., & Lytras, M. (2005). On the representation of change according to different ontologies of learning. *International Journal of Learning and Change, 1*(1), 66-79.

Silva, N., & Rocha, J. (2003, October 20-23). *Service-orientated ontology mapping system*. Paper presented at the Workshop on Semantic Integration of the International Semantic Web Conference, Sanibel Island, FL.

Specht, M. (2006). Contextualized learning: Supporting learning in context. In G. D. Magoulas & S. Y. Chen (Eds.), *Advances in Web-based education: personalized learning environment* (pp. 331-352). London: Library and information science Publishing.

Stutt, A., & Motta, E. (2004). Semantic learning webs. *Journal of Interactive Media in Education,* (10). Retrieved August 1, 2007, from www-jime.open.ac.uk/2004/10

Tang, T., & McCalla, G. (2003, July 20-24). *Smart recommendation for an evolving e-learning system. proc. workshop on technologies for electronic documents for supporting learning*. Paper presented at the International Conference on Artificial intelligence in Education (AIED 2003), Sydney, Australia.

Uren, V., Buckingham Shum, S., Bachler, M., & Li1, G. (2006). Sensemaking tools for understanding research literatures: Design, implementation and user evaluation. *International Journal of Human-Computer Studies, 64*(5), 420-445.

Vargas-Vera, M., & Celjuska, D. (2003) *Ontology-driven event recognition on stories* (KMI Technical Report KMI-TR-135). Retrieved August 1, 2007, from http://kmi.open.ac.uk/publications/pdf/kmi-03-11.pdf

Vargas-Vera, M., & Moreale, E. (2003). *A question-answering system using argumentation* (KMI Technical Report KMI-TR-132).

Vassileva, J., McCalla, G., & Greer, J. (2003). Multi-agent multi-user modeling in I-Help. *Journal of User Modeling and User-Adapted Interaction, 13,* 179-210.

Wilson, T. D. (2006). A re-examination of information seeking behaviour in the context of activity theory. *Information Research, 11*(4). Retrieved August 1, 2007, from http://InformationR.net/ir/11-4/paper260.html

Winter, M., & McCalla, G. (2003, July 20-24). *An analysis of group performance in terms of the functional knowledge and teamwork skills of group members*. Paper presented at the International Conference on Artificial intelligence in Education (AIED 2003), Sydney, Australia.

Yli-Luoma, P. V. J., & Naeve, A. (2006). Towards a semantic e-learning theory by using a modelling approach. *British Journal of Educational Technology, 37*(3), 445-459.

Zimmer, R. S. (2001). Variations on a string bag: Using Pask's principles for practical course design. *Kybernetes, 30*(7), 1006-1023.

# Chapter IX

# Real World Learning

## Introduction

This chapter focuses on limitations in our knowledge of learning, learning design, and the design of information and computer technology (ICT)-based learning support systems. We need to overcome these limitations in order to enable us to improve our own learning, the design of other people's learning, and the design of learning support systems that will work effectively in the real world. The chapter starts by focusing on some of the problems besetting research into humans, and the need to recognise the serious limitations of knowledge derived from such research when it comes to practical application in real world teaching and learning.

It explores, as a mini case study, a notion that is central to much educational informatics research and development, namely personalisation, and within this, a construct that a number of researchers and developers have used and are using as a driver of adaptive behaviour—learning style. The chapter goes on to present another mini case study in which the applicability of a well established and influential theoretical framework for learning design in higher education—Laurillard's *conversational framework*—is evaluated in a real world blended learning context.

There follows an examination of some key problems facing the development of educational informatics systems and the generation of knowledge of how best we might deploy such systems in a symbiotic relationship with learners. The chapter explores this relationship, assessing the extent to which computers are inherently limited in providing support for the relatively serendipitous, unpredictable, and unplannable mental activity that appears to underlie higher order critical and creative thinking. Helping learners to develop their own powers of metacognitive *learning to learn* knowledge and skills will be increasingly essential as we are faced with an increasing range of systems, tools, and facilities enabling us to access and confront ever vaster amounts of information.

As students, teachers, researchers, and system developers, we are all learners. As learners we must become practitioner-researchers engaging in self-organised learning, whether we are working in mediated or autonomous learning contexts. The chapter concludes by discussing how, within this role, we might generate new knowledge in order to help us make more informed choices and decisions concerning our own learning, designing the learning of others, and developing improved ICT-based support systems.

# Theory and Practice

## Learning Styles and Effects in Real World Teaching and Learning

As we have seen in the previous chapters of this book, considerable research effort within the field of educational informatics has been devoted to attempts to personalise the learning experience. Personalisation is also a key element of calls for funded research into technology-enhanced learning and of proclaimed educational policy of governments. The notion of learning styles seems a particularly attractive focus for the development of educational systems designed to adapt to individual learners' needs. From the range of learning styles studied, those identified by Pask are arguably particularly directly mappable onto the design and presentation of learning content and have the most extensive empirical support relating to complex learning—including direct empirical evidence of the learning effectiveness of taking style into account in teaching.

If some learners learn, say, by taking a holist route, and others a serialist route through the same subject matter, then we can use technology to provide these different routes for different learners and thus individualised learning. Indeed, Pask's experiments provided evidence that learning is greatly enhanced when learners learn in matched conditions—that is, from a system which matches the presentation of learning materials to learners' individual learning styles. Further experiments have replicated aspects of Pask's work on learning styles, including the effects of matching and mismatching (for example, Ellis, Ford, & Wood, 1993; Ford, 1985, 1995; Ford, & Chen, 2001; Wood, Ford, Miller, Sobczyk, & Duffin, 1996).

However, although a number of Pask's findings were supported in other studies, a number of questions were also raised. For example, *statistically* significant findings observed in constrained experimental conditions may not necessarily be *ecologically* significant in real teaching and learning contexts. We do not know whether, and if so to what extent, learning in matched conditions may be superior to learning in more normal conditions—which may not be particularly matched or mismatched to a particular learner's style. We do not know what might be the effects of allowing learners to choose their own navigation routes, for example, via the use of hypermedia learning materials in which they have autonomous use of navigational tools to select their own routes through subject content. We do not know if learners—some, most, many, or few—would choose an effective route or not, and what factors might influence such decisions. As noted later on, learning style *preferences* may not necessarily equate to learning style *competencies*.

Nor do we know the extent to which *natural* (i.e., nonexperimental) learning environments currently make use of learning materials and approaches that are in practice matched or mismatched with the learning styles of Pask. The dramatic effects of matching and mismatching information presentation with learning styles found by Pask and Scott (1972) were obtained in highly constrained learning conditions. For example, learners were forced to return to the beginning of their learning materials every time an error was made, until a clear run was achieved. Further research is needed to discover whether matching instruction with learning styles can enhance learning effectiveness in comparison with more normal forms of instruction, that is, that which is not deliberately mismatched with students' learning styles for experimental purposes.

Also, measures of learning performance in research into learning styles have often consisted of simple recall of factual information. Although such recall may often form a component in the repertoire of assessment in real study conditions, even relatively large performance differences relating to recall at this level may be of negligible importance compared to those found using less reproductive, more sensitive forms of assessment. Although in Pask's experiments, realistically complex academic content was used, it may be that different effects, or no effects, may be found when students are working over longer time scales in relation to, for example, a substantial piece of coursework, an entire module or programme. It is interesting to note that in a learning style study by Ellis et al. (1993), although significant effects relating to learning styles were found using measures of factual recall, no significant effects were found using measures requiring the practical application of knowledge, or the generation of answers requiring the integration of multiple sources of information used.

Statistical significance of correlations between learning styles and learning behaviour and performance may derive not from large behaviour or performance differences, but rather from the consistency with which small differences are found. As Landauer (1987, 1991) has noted, effects found in laboratory conditions may be insignificant in scale in real world situations—and thus of little value to applied system design. In the case of the experiments reported here, just what such differences may signify—if anything—for performance by students on real courses learning in real study conditions is hard to determine. Effects may be negligible or nonexistent in terms of essay grades, let alone assessment of more global aspects of course performance. In Pask and Scott's (1972) original experiment, the effects of matching and mismatching learning style with information presentation style were dramatic, although the sample size was small, and learning performance was measured using a relatively simple test of recall.

Measurement of learning styles is also far from problematic. Problems include, for example, accuracy and consistency of measurement. There are inconsistencies between instruments which arguably attempt to measure the same or very similar constructs. For example, in a study by Ford (1985), significant effects of holist and serialist matching and mismatching were related to scores on a relatively untested inventory—the Study Processes Questionnaire (SPQ), designed to assess holist/serialist biases)—but not to Entwistle's relatively well tested Short Inventory of Approaches to Studying (SIAS)—designed to measure comprehension, operation and versatile learning styles). Nor did the two measures correlate—that is, holist/serialist biases as measured by the SPQ did not correlate significantly with comprehension/operation learning styles as measured by the SIAS. Again, in the previously mentioned study by Ellis et al. (1993), global/analytic differences in hypertext navigation correlated with the SPQ, but not with the SIAS. There seems no clear explanation for the lack of correlation between the two instruments. Indeed, one might expect some correlation on the basis of Pask's empirical and theoretical observations linking the two sets of constructs, the comprehension learner tending to behave like the holist, the operation learner like the serialist. Indeed, one of the main criticisms made by the Coffield Report (Coffield, Moseley, Hall, & Ecclestone, 2004) into 13 popular learning styles is that instruments designed to measure them are seriously deficient in terms of validity and reliability, though the full version of Entwistle's inventory Approaches and Study Skills Inventory for Students (ASSIST) is a well tested and relatively reliable instrument. Popescu, Trigano, and Badica (2007) also comment on the questionable reliability and validity of learning style measures, as well as the lack of any unified learning style model. They go on to propose the use of a model that integrates the essential characteristics of a number of existing models, and that is not used to stereotype learners, but rather to inform data also obtained from learner interactions with the learning system.

Another important issue relates to the difference between competence, behaviour, and preference. Some measures such as Entwistle's inventory are based on students' introspections about their predominant patterns of normal study behaviour and their study preferences. Others, such as Pask's Spy Ring Test, Witkin's Embedded Figures Test, and Ridings Cognitive Styles Analysis, however, are measures of competence based on performance. These constructs would seem to be conceptually independent in that students' perceptions of their study behaviour do not necessarily accurately reflect their independently observed behaviour, and their study preferences do not necessarily correspond with their competencies. Nor do students' observed behaviours necessarily reflect either competence or conscious preferences. A number of other factors—factors that are not necessarily either logical or conscious—may come into play to influence actual behaviour.

Recall that a number of the educational informatics systems described in Chapters VII and VIII utilise the outputs of learning style measures in order to personalise the selection and presentation of learning materials in an attempt to provide a level of personalisation in students' learning experiences. However, it would seem that we are in reality a long way from being able to use learning style measures to real life learning in such a direct way.

## Cognitive Ergonomics: Matching vs. Mismatching

Regardless of the difficulties and limitations associated with the measures used to attempt to characterise learners in various ways—for example, in terms of their learning styles—the very enterprise whereby we attempt to devise educational informatics systems, which make use of such characterisations in order to match learning content and presentation to them, is also far from problematic. The notion of learning to learn, for example, implies learners developing an ability to learn in conditions that are not necessarily optimised to match their learning styles, preferences, biases, and existing skills. Making the learning environment cognitively ergonomic—requiring minimum cognitive overhead per *unit* of learning output—is arguably to make that learning environment hostile to such development. Just as the athlete in training must seek a mismatch between relaxation and the resistance-based working of key muscles, so arguably a degree of manageable mismatch may be a necessary stimulus to and enabler of the development of learning to learn skills and attitudes.

Recall that mismatch is at the very heart of learning itself—that is, some mismatch (an incongruity or anomaly) between concepts that requires resolution via some integrating theme. Some *critical confusion* may act as a stimulation to learning and development. However, it is interesting to note in this context that Perry (1970), in his seminal work on the development among college students of relativistic reasoning (discussed in Chapter II) noted that as students develop from dualistic perspectives increasingly to appreciate multiple perspectives and to engage in relativistic reasoning, too much of a mismatch between what is acceptable to them in terms of their existing knowledge, attitudes, and beliefs may cause retrenchment in which they revert to a previous stage of their intellectual development.

Indeed, it seems reasonable to assume that what constitutes the nature and degree of a constructive mismatch—whether this mismatch is between a learner's learning style and the way learning content is selected and presented, or between his or her stage of critical reasoning development and the nature and level of conflicting ideas presented to him or her—may be as difficult to specify as it is important in terms of helping the learner to extend and develop whilst avoiding retrenchment. Figure 108 shows this process in diagrammatic form. It seems likely that the point at which retrenchment may occur—the point at which mismatching becomes excessive—may be determined by factors intimate and possibly idiosyncratic to each learner. These factors are likely to include the degree of perceived conflict between new information and (a) the learner's existing knowledge, attitudes, and beliefs; (b) the level of critical relativistic reasoning which he or she has reached; and (c) mental states such as tolerance of ambiguity, self-efficacy, and anxiety.

These issues are tied in to the notion of supplantation. Recall from Chapter III that a system designed to supplant certain cognitive activities seeks to perform those cognitive activities *for*, or *on behalf of*, the learner. Educational informatics systems that attempt to maximise cognitive ergonomics—optimising the degree to which teaching is matched to learner characteristics—are attempting to supplant the cognitive activity required to reorganise learning is a way which more readily integrates with each learner's cognitive structure.

Such an approach would seem particularly appropriate in learning contexts in which the goal is to maximise the efficiency with which factual knowledge is acquired. It may also be appropriate in the early stages of learning, which is designed ultimately to facilitate learning to learn skills, as part of a strategy whereby supplantation is

*Figure 108. Development and retrenchment*

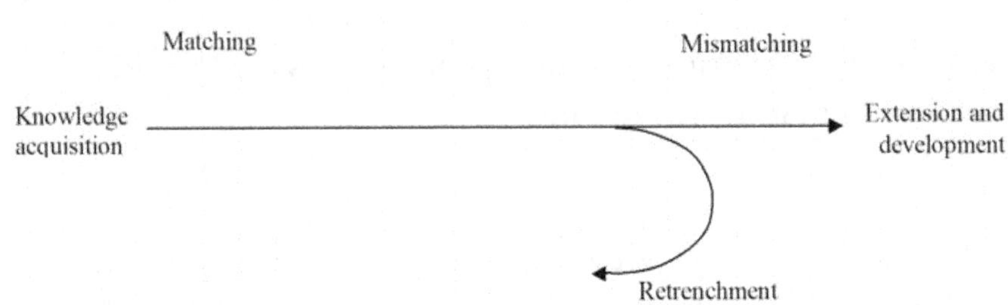

progressively reduced and controlled levels and types of mismatch are introduced. The range of cognitive processes performed by intelligent computer-based systems on behalf of their users is increasing. Examples include the many recommender systems, agents, and systems that engage in anticipatory background retrieval. Advances are also being made in relation to ambient computing, in which decisions may often be made on behalf of users.

This would seem to be an eminently desirable direction of development within educational informatics in those contexts where the needs of learners are clear and simple, and where inferences are relatively factual rather than value-laden or potentially contentious. Not only does such development offer the prospect of machines taking over some of the drudgery of time-consuming and intensive routine cognitive processing, but also, insofar as expert behaviour can be built into relevant systems, users can to an extent perform like experts, thus maximising their effectiveness. However, as suggested earlier in this book, when it comes to complex and real world learning and related information seeking, building supplantation into computer systems and measuring its effectiveness become somewhat more complex and problematic.

Beyond a certain level of complexity, learning, and information seeking are to a significant extent multifaceted, dynamic, fuzzy, and context-bound phenomena. These qualities pose problems for those who seek to identify and isolate precise variables and the specification of relationships between them. They contrast dramatically with the relatively simple, but objectively measurable and reliable, conceptions of learning and information seeking typical of many studies that seek to establish user models on which to base the development of computer systems within education, library/information science, and educational informatics.

If learning and information seeking were indeed so simple, then the development of systems that facilitate more effective performance via the supplantation of certain of the learner's or information seeker's cognitive activities might be a less difficult task. But in reality, these activities may often be more complex, fuzzy, and problematic than is taken into account in many user-based experiments. A common problem is that in order to characterize learning and information behaviour in objective and generalisable ways, researchers must often oversimplify them.

## Evaluating Learning Design Theory in a Real World Blended Learning Environment

This and the previous section explore, via the use of mini case studies, some of the problems that can beset our quest to generate meaningful and robust knowledge concerning the validity, applicability, and effectiveness of learning and learning design theories for real world teaching and learning contexts. The previous case study illuminated problems affecting the study and application of learning style theories. The following case study focuses on the evaluation of learning design in real world contexts.

Two studies of Laurillard's conversational framework (1993, 2002) are described in order to illustrate the type of difficulties that can arise in finding information that can inform decisions relating to the application of theories to real world teaching and learning. The conversational framework has been chosen in view of its widespread impact and influence. Indeed, it is described by Allison et al. (2007) as "one of the most influential theories in European Higher Education of the past 20 years" (p. 480). It is also particularly relevant to this book since it is based on one of its key themes—Pask's conversational model. The conversational framework was introduced in Chapter III.

As with the previous mini case study, the intention is not to provide a wide-ranging or representative review of evaluative studies. Rather, two studies are selected in order to illustrate more general problems and issues that can arise when we try to find information from research studies that will enable us to generate knowledge useful in practical contexts. Buckley and Donert (2004) report a study that includes, as one of its goals, an evaluation of the usefulness of the conversational framework as an evaluative tool for a distance learning course relating to geographical information. The study was small scale, based on an analysis of 23 online questionnaire responses; interviews with 14 students and 5 tutors; and e-mail messages exchanged by the students over a 12-month period. Buckley and Donert conclude that:

*... the Conversational Framework was been found to be useful for assessing the academic learning environment and interactions between the tutors and users. It provides insights into the extent and meaningfulness of interactions between tutors and students and between students themselves. Laurillard's (1993) model allows for the investigator to assess the extent to which users have control over aspects of the learning process and the responsiveness and potential for adaptation of those involved in administering and designing the course. It also provides a useful framework for evaluating the process of learning, in particular the potential of course materials for encouraging a reflective and considered approach to learning. It has great potential as an evaluative tool, particularly in the area of assessing students' thoughts on the quality of feedback and the procedures in place for developing learning. The model allows for assessment of the opportunities provided for student reflection based on feedback from self-assessment exercises and tutor feedback during the course and for assignments.*

Although the evaluation is generally very positive, they also note a limitation in relation to the emphasis of the framework on conversations between individuals as opposed to collaborative group activity.

The second study is one by Heinze, Procter, and Scott (2007), who wished to evaluate the usefulness of the conversational framework in the context of a part-time higher education blended learning course on information technology. It was selected since the authors considered it, as noted in Chapter III, as a particularly attractive framework to apply within the context of blended learning. They also employed a small sample, using action research and grounded theory, over a two-year period. Data were collected from: (a) interviews with lecturers before and after their experience of the course; (b) three focus groups with lecturers; (c) six focus groups with students, one after each semester over the two years; (d) six semi-structured interviews with students; and messages exchanged between the students on the discussion board on the VLE used to support the course.

Heinze et al. (2007) are somewhat more reserved than were those of the previous study concerning the usefulness of the conversational framework. They conclude that:

> *Data suggest that the Conversational Framework is a useful starting point when considering a theoretical foundation for Blended learning, but it is not ideal. It became apparent that the theory relies heavily on student and staff willingness and ability to take part in the dialogue.* (p. 117)

A number of problems were identified:

- Although interviewees recognised the need for a theoretical framework to support the implementation of blended learning in practice, a number felt that they were not prepared or able to spend the time and effort reading about a framework.
- Those lecturers who had read Laurillard's book in which she propounds the framework found it difficult to appreciate how it could be related to practice.
- Staff who attempted to implement the framework considered that it was limited in that its successful implementation required *ideal* students.
- Students were not able to see the difference that use of the conversational framework made to a module.

The authors conclude that a viable theoretical framework should:

- Be grounded in well-established pedagogical theories.
- Be easily understandable and capable of being implemented by busy lecturers.
- Be applicable to both large and small classes.
- Be able to be adapted to suit students of different academic abilities.
- Emphasise the links between formative and summative assessment.

They go on to propose an alternative form of conversational framework which represents a reversion to a model that is closer to the conversational model original proposed by Pask (Figure 18 of Chapter I) as extended by Thomas and Harri-Augstein (2001) and Thomas (Figure 30 of Chapter III). Particularly notable is the addition of assessment, and the learner's interaction with it.

It is not at all uncommon to find such different results from studies ostensibly focusing on the same phenomenon. However, no two phenomena are entirely the same. It is a matter of judgement to determine how applicable findings and interpretations of research conducted in one context and with one purpose are to another context and purpose. There are always differences as well as any similarities between the two. In critically evaluating the potential applicability of research—particularly where sources of information provide inconclusive and/or conflicting evidence—the learner

*Figure 109. Blended learning skeletal conversational model (adapted from Heinze et al., 2007)*

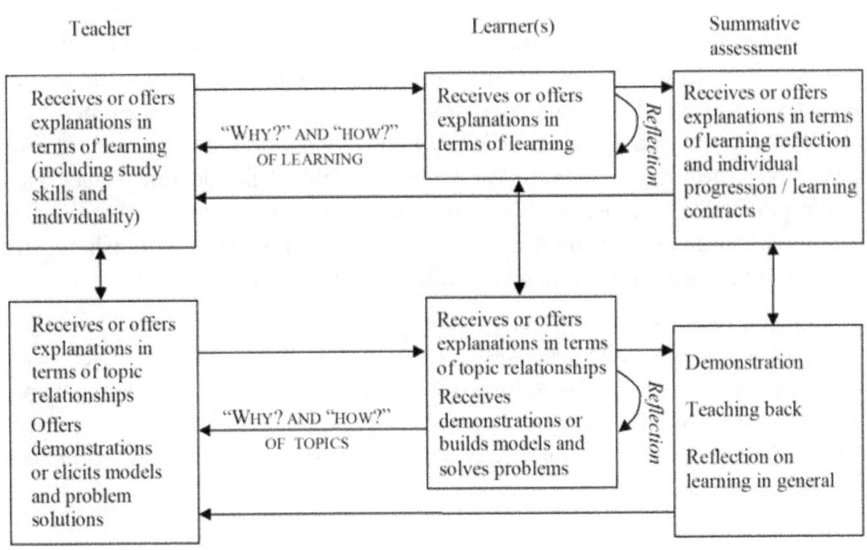

(whether student, teacher, learning designer, or system developer) is essentially trying to establish an integrating theme, or optimal resolving balance between competing tensions which relate to:

- The context in which he or she wishes to apply knowledge derived from research (in the aforementioned mini case studies, a learning theory or learning design).
- The evidence provided in one or more sources of research information, which as noted previously may be conflicting and/or inconclusive in terms of convincing the learner.
- His or her own knowledge and experience.

Recall that this complex and iterative process was represented in Figure 29 in Chapter III. Issues relating to different types of research-based evidence, and how learners may go about acquiring them, are discussed in more detail in the final section of this chapter.

## Educational Informatics Support for Critical Thinking and Creativity

So far in this chapter we have explored limitations in our knowledge relating to how people learn (learning theories), and how learning might best be brought about (learning design theories). The nature of the limitations in our knowledge relates particularly to questions of how applicable and effective such theories might be in relation to learning contexts which apply to us—whether in our teaching of others or our own learning. We need to know, for example: which learning theories and learning designs to choose, and how applicable they are to our own teaching and learning situations—what modifications might be appropriate in translating their use from that reported in evaluative studies to our own context, and so forth.

This section focuses on limitations relating to ICT-based support for learning—in particular for higher order individual critical and creative thinking. There would seem to be an inverse relationship between the capability of computer systems to supplant intellectual activities and the degree to which those activities are characterised by individuality and creativity. Figure 110 shows a number of dimensions that we can use to think about learning.

*Figure 110. Levels of critical thinking (adapted from Ford et al., 1999)*

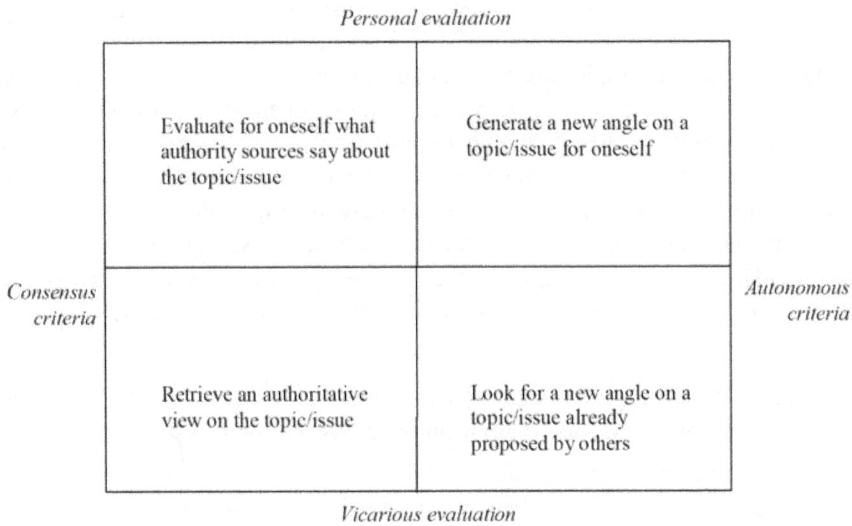


Figure 110 represents different types of knowledge need, each with differing implications for the sort of information required to support it. The bottom two quadrants relate to learning situations in which the evaluation of the quality and validity in relation to some topic, issue, or problem has already been established (or claimed) by someone else. In the bottom left quadrant, the learner's need is to discover, in relation to the topic or issue under investigation, the general consensus of views on key issues. In information retrieval and resource discovery terms, this might imply, for example, an authoritative encyclopaedia article or textbook.

The learner may diverge from such an *authority consensus* position by moving upwards and/or to the right in Figure 110. Moving from the lower-left to the upper-left quadrant entails the application of critical thinking in that the learner will evaluate authority sources for him or herself, and indeed may encounter differences in perspectives and opinions between authorities. Moving from the lower-left to the lower-right quadrant entails an express intention to seek out different perspectives and opinions as already espoused by others in and possibly beyond the field of study. The top-right quadrant combines the application of autonomous evaluation criteria and the search for a new perspective or opinion of one's own. If successful, this relatively divergent thinking may lead to genuinely creative output.

The more one moves away from the bottom left quadrant either right or upwards, the more demand is made on information retrieval, resource discovery, and other information and learning support tools. Focussing on information retrieval, specifying searches in terms of the characteristics of the different quadrants in Figure 110 may require of an information system more than it is capable of satisfying. Document collections searched by a retrieval system may in fact contain the type of information required by a learner—but it may simply not be specifiable in search formulations. For example, *quality*, defined in terms of the appropriateness and rigour of its research design, is not a feature of documents that is directly indexed, or readily inferable. However, medical search filters, structured abstracts, thesauri which acknowledge the importance of research methodological indexing, information extraction systems, and other approaches are making inroads into this problem in certain fields where quality can be fairly readily consensually referenced to some gold standard. Underspecifying searches can lead to a high *signal to noise* ratio. However, most information retrieval systems are far from capable of:

- Indicating for a given document the extent to which it has been critically evaluated by others, and if so, using what criteria.
- Allowing users to specify, as search parameters, quality criteria generated to be personally relevant to their own particular needs and perspectives.

*Figure 111. ICT-based support for relatively convergent and divergent thinking*

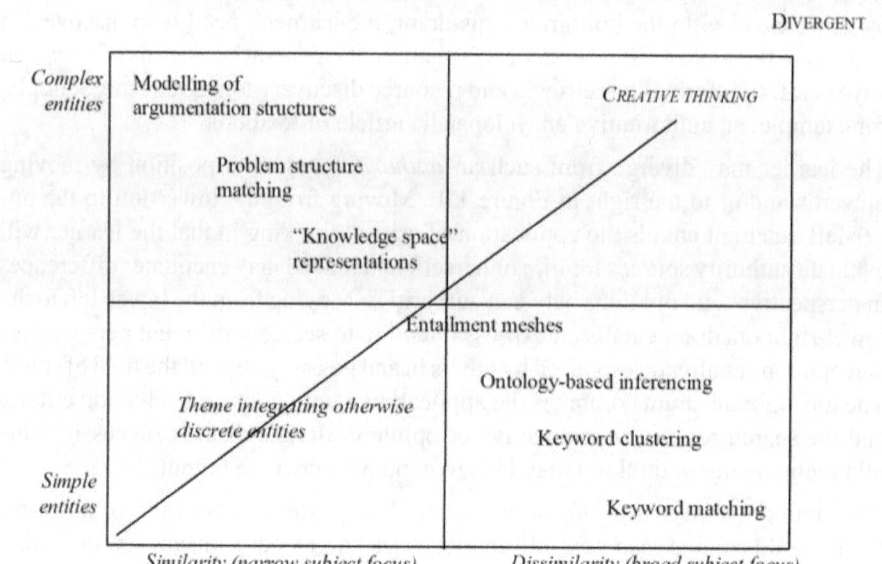

The feasibility of providing computer-based support for intellectual activity becomes more problematic as one moves in Figure 110 away from the bottom-left quadrant from relatively convergent to more divergent thinking. Figure 111 maps a number of already well developed computer-based approaches to supporting relatively convergent and divergent forms of intellectual activity. This figure does not relate to the *personal* versus *vicarious evaluation* dimension shown in Figure 110. However, it does indicate different levels of creativity, mapping onto the model of creativity originally presented in Figure 13 in Chapter I. Recall from that chapter that creativity was defined in terms of the levels of dissimilarity and complexity characterising the entities that are brought together by an integrating theme.

If we can further develop computer-based systems that are able to search for, discover, and manipulate semantically deep knowledge representations relating, for example, to the underlying structures of problems and problem solutions, and to patterns of argumentation, and so forth, over a wide range of topics and subject areas, this could be extremely useful in supporting the identification and testing of tentative theories (integrating themes). In view of the definition of creativity used here, which relates not only to the level of complexity but also the diversity of entities which become integrated via some new theme, an ability to provide such support across a wide and diverse (as opposed to narrowly constrained) range of topics and subjects might be of great value in supporting relatively creative thinking.

The development of systems more able to support creative thinking in this way would require further work on the representation of semantically deep knowledge structures, and the ability to manipulate them using powerful reasoning mechanisms. Relevant work is progressing steadily in areas such as information extraction, case-based reasoning, analogical reasoning, and argumentation. However, generally the more detailed the structures we try to formalise, the narrower is the subject scope they relate to.

One way of addressing the problem of narrowness of scope is to increase interoperability between domains, as opposed to (or as well as) attempting to develop less detailed but more integrative meta-knowledge representations. Current work on the development of ontologies, and means of linking and interconnecting them (as described in Chapter VII) falls into this category. Earlier work has also been reported (Chen, Zhang, & Houston, 1998) that attempts to build semantic interoperability in order to:

> *enable users to search information on unfamiliar subjects by inputting terms from their (known) domain and have the system determine semantically similar terms in the target (unknown) domain.* (p. 16)

Interoperability would seem to be a potentially important support to divergent thinking to the extent that it enables and facilitates ready navigation and exploration of knowledge representations across diverse subject areas.

However, it is important that technological development is accompanied by efforts to help users develop their own learning and information seeking knowledge and skills, and their metacognitive ability to self-improve such skills. This will enable learners to maximise the potential benefits of, while compensating for the limitations of, the systems, tools, and facilities increasingly becoming available to them as new developments come on stream.

Ultimately, only the individual learner can decide what is, for him or her, the most effective balance between convergent and divergent thinking in relation to a given problem, learning need, or learning situation. Also, creativity is essentially not a thing that can be predicted and planned. It is by its very nature to a large degree a spontaneous and unplanned occurrence. The idea that we can, or even should attempt to, provide increasingly direct machine support for it, by progressively analysing and *homing in* on its mechanisms and developing appropriate knowledge representations and reasoning algorithms in order to supplant various of its components, seems to be inherently limited. Development of novel knowledge representations and reasoning algorithms may indeed be helpful, but less directly as components of a range of information-accessing and support tools that give learners the opportunity to seek, identify, and test out tentative themes; to search for new directions; and to develop new approaches. Perhaps the most productive way forward may be to make available to learners a range of support tools that can enable them to access the richest possible diversity of information from which creative ideas may emerge, and to provide them with the knowledge and skills to be able to use them effectively.

There would appear to be a considerable mismatch between the notions of serendipity and divergence, which characterise creative thinking, and the way in which information systems work and what they are essentially designed to deliver. However, there may still be value in attempting to developing systems that are better able to provide support for such unpredictable mental activity. As noted in Chapter I, various stages in the processes of creative thinking have been identified. Certain of these stages may entail more mundane, routine, controlled, conscious, and focused activity involving the gathering of information—some of which may represent the raw material that ultimately may lead to and fuel the sudden flash of insight or inspiration. Concentration on the less conscious, less predictable, and controlled moment of insight may cause us, when we think of creativity, to ignore what might be the essential groundwork that provides the fertile mental environment for recognising and seizing some new integrating theme.

Despite such an apparently fundamental separation between the generation of creative thoughts, and the focused systematic searching for information, it may be that such spontaneous flashes are ultimately to a large extent dependent on information accumulated via these more mundane and routine processes. If we can develop systems that can improve the quality and creative potential of such *feeder* information, then we may be able better to support the processes that ultimately lead to creative output. An analogy may be made with preparation for athletic or sports performance. An inspirational performance on the field of play may be inextricably linked with sound preparation, systematic work, and a planned approach to training and nutrition. This may underlie the adage: "The harder I work, the luckier I seem to get!"

Current information systems do clearly provide support for creative thinking, since people who make use of them do acquire information that is subsequently used to develop new ideas and directions. However, relatively few studies have focused explicitly on the way in which relatively divergent and creative thinking may be affected, or helped, by such systems. An exception is the study of the use by researchers of an information retrieval system reported by Spink and Greisdorf, who (as described in Chapter IV) found an inverse relationship between reported high levels of relevance, and the reported generation of new ideas and directions on the part of researchers. Retrieved items judged as highly relevant contributed to the work of the researchers in relation to relatively convergent aspects of their thinking—helping them confirm what they already knew, and to maintain and reinforce existing directions. It was the *less* highly relevant information sources which contributed more to relatively divergent and creative thinking—helping them to generate new ideas and explore new directions.

In relation to Spink and Greisdorf's study, Ford (1999) commented that:

> *There may indeed be some chemistry in failed high relevance which results in creatively useful information clustering in the middle ranks of best match searches. It is possible that a mid-ranked document has just enough (but not too much) relevance to aid creativity without being so totally unrelated as to be useless. Currently, a lack of relevance is as close as we can get to specifying the requirements of IR systems to support relatively creative thinking. However, it would be more useful if we could specify positively the elements desired rather than negatively simply accepting documents that fail to score highly in response to a search. If we are searching for information that would give us a new angle on 'dogs biting men', then retrieving items simply on the basis that they are not about 'dogs biting men' would be unlikely to turn up the proverbial 'man bites dog' story. We should be attempting to enable the relatively divergent, as well as the more convergent thinker to specify more positively retrieval parameters more directly related to his or her needs.*

In broad terms, one approach to creating new systems is to build on past techniques and extend what is possible, in the hope that new developments may be found useful by certain people for certain tasks. This approach may be contrasted with the alternative in which explicit models of information needs and information behaviour are the main drivers of development. What seems clear, however, is that the potential for productive interaction between system developers and user modellers is far from being fully realised. System designers may often feel that user modellers have little of practical use to say to them concerning the design of retrieval tools. User models are often constructed with little reference being made to system features.

Another broad distinction may be drawn between different approaches to improving information seeking. These approaches in fact complement each other rather than being mutually exclusive. One seeks to enhance information seeking effectiveness by focusing on the development of ever smarter computer systems, which aim to *supplant* certain intellectual activities on the part of the individual (i.e., systems that perform certain intellectual processes *for* the individual). The other approach seeks to improve effectiveness by enhancing the individual's own powers of information seeking skills and metacognition—self-awareness of his or her own processes, strengths, and weaknesses, enabling him or her to exploit the strengths, while compensating for the weaknesses of computer-based resource discovery and searching tools.

Arguably, the level of sophistication of intelligent systems, which aim to supplant certain intellectual activities, is not sufficiently advanced in terms of supporting complex information seeking within the context of sophisticated levels of learning, to reduce the vital complementary role of metacognitive approaches. Research into knowledge and information behaviour may help in both these processes—developing improved systems that better map onto people's information-seeking requirements and enhancing the information seeking skills and powers of the individual.

Above a certain level of complexity, an individual's intimate knowledge needs, and associated information needs may be very subtle, and possibly unknowable in any very meaningful sense to a relatively crude user model driving an educational informatics system. At this level, attempting to enhance the learner's own awareness of his or her knowledge needs, and his or her associated skills in the use of appropriate systems (whether computer-assisted learning, information retrieval, or educational informatics systems) may be much more appropriate than trying to build systems that attempt to second-guess the subtlety of learners' needs and the intellectual activity needed to bring about effective learning outcomes.

The previous section emphasised the limitations of systems designed to supplant certain of the learner's intellectual activities. However, *smart* computer systems may be extremely useful in reducing the amount of drudgery relating to relatively routine tasks. While in other fields of endeavour smart systems (for example, expert systems) can also help novices "punch above their weight" and perform like experts in terms of intellectual activity, and can even occasionally enhance the performance of experts, learning is more problematic as a focus for the development of such systems. It is problematic since, as noted in Chapter III, autonomy—by definition the converse of supplantation—is an essential goal of teaching and learning. Effective *learning* is not synonymous with effective *performance*. This is not, of course, to say that smart systems do not have a useful role in supplanting intellectual activities that are not the focus of the learning. Thus, for example, if a smart information retrieval system is able to retrieve documents, which are more relevant to a learner's needs than would be retrievable using a less smart system, then the supplantation entailed in the processes of retrieval is obviously useful.

We need to develop a symbiotic relationship between learners and educational informatics systems in which such systems offer supplantation in certain activities and for certain tasks but without compromising the learner's ability and opportunity to develop his or her metacognitive knowledge and skills to support learning to learn. Helping learners to be able to effectively take control might help to reduce the semantic gap between their knowledge needs and associated information needs, and the *understanding* of those needs by computer-based systems. However, this raises the question of the extent to which the learner does in fact possess the knowledge required to orchestrate the use of available systems, tools, and components, in order to achieve effective learning.

## Making Sense of Research: Generating Useful Real World Knowledge

So far in this chapter we have explored limitations in our knowledge relating to:

- Theories of how we learn (learning theory).
- Theories of how learning might best be brought about (learning design theory).
- ICT-based support tools and techniques for learning—particularly critical and creative thinking.

A common theme is our need to overcome these limitations by generating new knowledge that will enable us to make informed choices in relation to our teaching, our learning, our learning design, and our design of ICT-based support tools. This section focuses on ways in which we might generate such knowledge, and in this task we must all be constant learners. As learners, we can acquire such knowledge in a variety of ways. Let us take as an example the situation referred to at the end of the previous section. This concerned the need for learners to be able to generate knowledge that could enable them to make informed choices relating to their use of different ICT-based systems, tools, and components.

Adopting what, as we will see in Chapter X, Thomas and Harri-Augstein (2001) term a "stage 1" scientific method approach, we could seek out objective, generalisable information relating to the characteristics, behaviour, and performance of system tools and components. Such information would derive from experimental studies high in validity, reliability, and generalisability, of which there are many examples in the fields of educational computing and information science. The knowledge derived from such information might enable us to make informed choices concerning which tools to use and how to use them in order to obtain optimal results. If such information concerning the characteristics and performance of particular tools and system components is indeed objective and generalisable, then we may feel reassured that it is likely that these characteristics and performance are likely to apply in the context of their particular use of them.

It seems reasonable to suppose that to an extent system tools and components will indeed behave in predictable ways, and will be possible to specify their behaviour and performance accurately. But other important aspects of such behaviour and performance may not be so readily susceptible to objective measurement and the establishment of reliable, generalisable specifications of how they will behave and perform in different contexts. It is possible that tools and components will also to an extent deliver different performance when used in different contexts. Indeed, it is the very objectivity and generalisability sought by researchers when they set up experiments using a stage 1 scientific method that render the results of those experiments less ecologically valid when applied in more complex real life contexts. This may be engendered by the simplification of problem conception, and the isolation of variables required to enable the necessary statistical analyses. Truly context-independent findings may thus be of limited usefulness.

A second approach whereby we might acquire relevant knowledge would be to apply what Thomas and Harri-Augstein (2001) refer to as "stage 2" scientific method (as noted previously, these stages will be introduced in detail in Chapter X). This would entail seeking information from studies that have adopted a position embraced by much qualitative interpretive research, entailing the acknowledgment and exploitation of the richness and diversity of context. Context-rich information may offer greater ecological validity. Context-rich case studies, for example, might take into account the subtleties of complex learning and associated information needs for particular learners in particular contexts. Such information offers the prospect of being *transferable* rather than *generalisable*, transferability entailing some resonance between contexts.

Resonant transferable information obtained by the study of one context may be relevant and to some extent applicable (possibly with some modification) by another learner with similar needs but working in another context. The potential for such transferability depends on a sufficiently rich and detailed description of the original context to enable an assessment of how similar it is to, and what features it shares with, the new context within which it may be applied. Such information, however, suffers from a converse limitation in that the richer and more complex the context it incorporates in its explanations, the less universally applicable it may be. Highly context-specific information is transferable to other contexts only if there exists a rich mapping of elements.

Unless the descriptions of a great many complex scenarios were stored and available, finding relevant information capable of being transferred to a given new situation could be problematic. The difficulty of finding appropriate relevant information would also increase with the novelty or uniqueness of the learning need and context of the person seeking it. Also, even granted such potentially transferable information could be discovered, the process of determining the extent to which it could be transferred to the new context would require a considerable amount of in-depth reading of rich contextual descriptions.

Järvelin and Ingwersen (2004) note a similar problem in relation to information retrieval system design. They are of the opinion that:

*... even limited knowledge on real information seeking and retrieval may reveal typical uses, strengths and weaknesses of various systems, and how their users perceive them. This provides a better basis for design than the de-contextualized standard assumptions and measures.*

However, Järvelin and Ingwersen (2004) also point out, in relation to the claim that more context-rich information should be generated, the counter argument that:

*... there are too many seeking contexts with too many possible combinations of systems, so that the design and evaluation of information retrieval systems becomes unmanageable. Therefore, it is better to stick to the tradition of information retrieval design and evaluation. If one knows no more than one's own unsystematic recollection of personal information retrieval system use, the suggested design and evaluation approach may be of tall order, indeed.*

Another way in which we could acquire knowledge to enhance their ability to take control of systems, tools, and components would be to adopt Thomas and Harri-Augstein's (2001) "stage 3" scientific method. This would entail acting as self-organised learners in the critical acquisition of relevant knowledge. An appropriate approach might entail engagement in our own reflexive action research, designed to generate personally relevant (and appropriately tested and validated) knowledge of how systems, tools, and components might work best for us, how we might use and deploy them to best advantage in relation to our own personal needs, characteristics, and abilities, and how we might improve these abilities over time.

Levy (2003) succinct explains the potential of action research for enabling the generation of personally relevant, and practically useful, knowledge:

*Recognising the uniqueness and complexity of specific educational situations, action researchers assume that professional competence is more than just a matter of routinely applying universal rules of practice or purely technical know-how prescribed by some external source of guidance. Instead, competence is taken to be a matter of being able to perceive, and take forward, the right course of action when in a particular situation ... it is based on knowledge that is embedded in personal experience and that is essentially concrete, context-specific, and open to re-interpretation. [...] In terms of methodology, educational action research is grounded in interpretive and reflective practice. Practitioner-researchers investigate and evaluate educational situations inductively, looking afresh at their own educational assumptions, values, aims and actions.* (p. 90)

Such critical reflection, entailing the challenging of one's own assumptions, values, aims, and actions may be facilitated by learning conversations within a learning community. However, such conversations may also take place as Paskian "inner dialogues." Recall from Chapter I that conversations between different p-individuals can take place within the brain of a single person—representing inner dialogues as people come to understand (Scott, 2001).

Viewed from a stage 3 scientific method perspective, the development of effective learning and information seeking knowledge and skills, as well as of metacognitive knowledge and skills enabling learning to learn, is a process of generating and testing personally relevant—and personally validated—knowledge by means of experimentation and critical reflection, whether this is conducted individually or with others.

Levy (2003) describes the type of knowledge that may be generated from such activity:

*[A]ction research therefore does not aspire to the construction of propositional knowledge (episteme), or to the production of purely technical know-how. Instead, the aim is to construct validated, 'practical' knowledge (the Aristotelian concept of phronesis) through critical analysis of specific ... situations within the context of action – that is, through praxis ... This is seen as a dialectical process that is constitutive of effective action and new knowledge...* (p 90)

Levy (2003) explains that this type of personally validated knowledge can be applicable beyond the individual, and that theory created through *praxis*—sometimes termed *living theory*—is shareable within communities, which are able in this way to build up a shared knowledge base.

The level of knowledge and skill required to make effective choices and to exercise effective control of complex educational informatics systems, tools, and components, within the context of complex and dynamically evolving information needs, militates for learners to apply self-organised learning principles entailing become their own practitioner-researchers. As Ford (2004) concludes:

*Ultimately, we must all build the personal knowledge structures that drive and guide our behavior, and in doing so must determine the nature and extent of the evidence we deem sufficient to inform our actions. In the context of complex information needs, this is likely to entail not only processing information generated by significant others such as IR researchers and system designers, but also the generation of personally relevant and validated knowledge generated through one's own experimentation and experience—whether or not moderated by some significant other(s).*

However, if we are to enable and facilitate effective learning by practitioner-researchers, then we need to pay attention to the environments—including the hidden messages they may convey—within which people learn. This applies to learners at all levels, whether students at school or university, teachers, researchers, or developers.

To the extent that we wish to promote engagement in relatively creative thinking, we need environments that maximize the complementary interplay between the forces of constraint and freedom, convergent and divergent though, each requiring the liberating and constraining energies of the other. There is some evidence that more creative forms of thinking may rely on a degree of freedom from anxiety, time, and other pressures—and from being too intensely focused. As Ford (1999) notes:

*Often descriptions of instances of creative thought suggest a sudden perception or realisation—a flash of insight when things come together—occurring when the person is not intensely focused on the particular problem.* (p. 532)

Recall from Chapter I the assertions that:

*... our brains are at their most efficient when allowed to switch from phases of intense concentration to ones in which we exert no conscious control at all.* (Gregory, 1987, p. 171)

*Only under certain conditions will [...] insights arise [...] [Questions and answers] are raised and sought even if on a subliminal level of consciousness, and sometimes for quite a time, before the vital question or answer breaks through to consciousness.* (Strauss & Corbin, 1997, p. 29)

*Figure 112. Working environments on the generation of new ideas (adapted from Ford, 2004)*

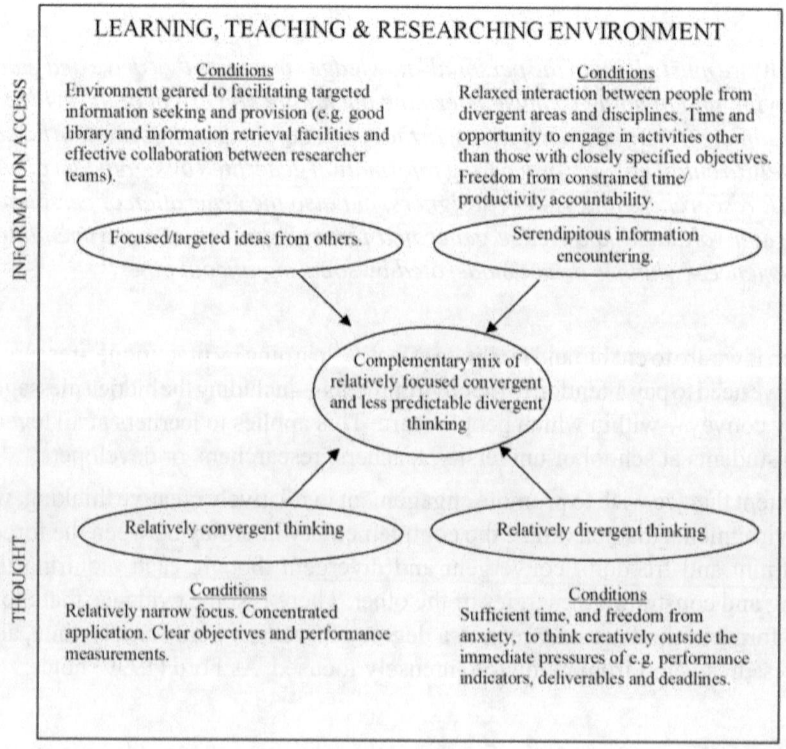


Environments may have profound effects on the availability or absence of conditions conducive to relatively creative thinking. The availability of such conditions may facilitate learners' ability to escape from their own often hidden and untested assumptions, and those of the learning/teaching/research community in which they function. Figure 112 maps conditions conducive to relatively convergent and divergent thinking.

Within knowledge-based organisations, such as educational and research institutions, the conditions to the left of Figure 112 are inherently more manageable—that is, susceptible to planning, scheduling, and predicting—than those to the right. Access to good library resources and information-seeking facilities, and the gathering together of teams of people with cognate interests, may facilitate the extent to which learners (whether students, teachers, or researchers) can seek specific information and target—and be targeted by—colleagues with closely related interests.

However, the types of information access and thought shown to the right of Figure 112 are arguably of equal importance in that they are particularly influential in enabling new perspectives and thinking "outside the box." These conditions are much less susceptible to management (planning, scheduling, predicting, and control). However, creative potential may arguably be fostered indirectly by providing environments that at least do not stifle it.

Individuals working within organizations operate within complex force fields that may exert subtle (and not so subtle) influences on their activities. Research cultures, management styles, and institutional appraisal and career progression incentives may all affect the perceptions, thoughts, and activities of those working within them. The institutions within which they operate themselves operate within a broader context of force fields emanating from, for example, funding organizations, professional organisations, and governments.

It is important to note that within such contexts people may react to—possibly behaving according to the perceived expectations of—those responsible for managing and appraising them. There may be subtle and hidden interactions between (a) people's thoughts about what they are doing—for example, their teaching and research aims and goals, and (b) *meta-level* thoughts in which they think about the context in which these activities are taking place. Such meta-level thoughts may relate, for example, to issues such as the way in which their performance is assessed, their career progression, and the way in which they are managed.

As we will see in the next chapter, such interactions between different levels of thinking (what in Chapter X will be termed *object* and *meta* levels, or *level 1* and *level 2*) can cause considerable problems for *observations* concerning humans. Being the focus of observation is interpreted broadly here to include, for example, being studied, assessed, or managed. Such problems may arise from the fact that people who are the focus of observation may react to their observers and the observation in hidden and subtle ways, of which they and their observers may be unaware. These reactions may entail the mixing of the two levels of thinking, and the nature of the behaviour that is observed. Such interactions may also entail implicit and untested assumptions on the part of both observer and observed, of which one or both are unaware, and may lead unwittingly to self-fulfilling expectations, practices, and research designs.

Essential components of effective learning, teaching, and researching are: (a) to attempt to expose to explicit scrutiny one's own implicit assumptions, and any effects that meta-level thoughts relating to an observation (on the part of observer and/or observed) may have on the nature of what is observed; and (b) to justify, via the same scrutiny, the sufficiency of evidence and appropriateness of judgments supporting one's thoughts and actions.

However, learners, teachers, and researchers may reasonably expect those who manage them, and who are responsible for establishing and maintaining the intellectual, organisational, and physical environment in which they work, to do likewise. Meta-level effects may result from implicit messages communicated, for example, via management decisions relating to systems of incentives, rewards, and control—including the ways in which research efficiency and effectiveness are assessed. Different such messages may militate more, or less, for the types of activity depicted in the left and right halves of Figure 112.

They may reasonably expect the evidence-bases that support the adoption and maintenance of the particular styles and cultures of management, appraisal, and assessment to which they are subjected—by which they are managed and judged, stimulated, and stifled—are themselves subjected to similar levels of explicit scrutiny to those required of them in their judgments and activities. Such scrutiny is required in order to monitor the extent to which the evidence bases, and the methodologies by which evidence is conceived, collected, analyzed, and used to draw conclusions by those responsible for managing, organising, and assessing their activities, may themselves be deemed to be free from implicit untested assumptions and tautological—possibly self-fulfilling—thinking.

The next chapter concludes our exploration of educational informatics by distilling a number of themes and issues—including those touched upon just now—which emerge from this review of techniques, tools, approaches, and standards developed within education, library/information science, and educational informatics. The chapter goes on to focus on differences in research perspectives and approaches, and conceptions of acceptable *evidence*, and to consider how these might be addressed in order to enable educational informatics to progress.

## References

Allison, C., Nicoll, R., Purdie, S. D. J., Eisenstadt, M., Komzak, J., & Denham, C. (2007, July 18-20). Grid enabled collaborative learning. In *Proceedings of the Seventh IEEE International Conference on Advanced Learning Technologies (ICALT 2007),* Niigata, Japan (pp. 480-484). Retrieved August 1, 2007, from http://doi.ieeecomputersociety.org/10.1109/ICALT.2007.153

Buckley, C., & Donert, K. (2004). Evaluating e-learning courses for continuing professional development using the conversational model: A review of UNIGIS. *European Journal of Open, Distance and E-Learning*. Retrieved August 1, 2007, from http://www.eurodl.org/materials/contrib/2004/Buckley_Donert.html

Chen, H., Zhang, Y., & Houston, A. L. (1998). Semantic indexing and searching using a Hopfield net. *Journal of Library and Information Science, 24*(1), 3-18.

Coffield, F., Moseley, D., Hall, E., & Ecclestone, K. (2004). *Learning styles and pedagogy in post-16 learning. A systematic and critical review*. London: Learning and Skills Research Centre.

Ellis, D., Ford, N., & Wood, F. (1993). Hypertext and learning styles. *The Electronic Library, 11,* 13-18.

Ford, N. (1985). Learning styles and strategies of postgraduate students. *British Journal of Educational Technology, 16,* 65-79.

Ford, N. (1995). Levels and types of mediation in instructional systems: An individual differences approach. *International Journal of Human-Computer Studies,* 43, 241-259.

Ford, N. (1999). Information retrieval and creativity: Towards support for the original thinker. *Journal of Documentation, 55*(5), 528-542.

Ford, N. (2004). Creativity and convergence in library and information science research: The roles of objectivity and subjectivity, constraint, and control. *Journal of the American Society for Information Science and Technology, 55*(13), 1169-1182.

Ford, N., & Chen, Y. (2001). Matching/mismatching revisited: An empirical study of learning and teaching styles. *British Journal of Educational Technology, 32*(1), 5-22.

Ford, N., Miller, D., Booth, A., O'Rourke, A., Ralph, J., & Turnock, E. (1999). Information retrieval for evidence-based decision-making. *Journal of Documentation, 55*(5), 528-542.

Heinze, A., Procter, C., & Scott, B. (2007). Use of conversation theory to underpin blended learning. *International Journal of Teaching and Case Studies, 1*(1/2), 108-120.

Järvelin, K., & Ingwersen, P. (2004). Information seeking research needs extension towards tasks and technology. *Information Research, 10*(1), paper 212. Retrieved August 1, 2007, from http://InformationR.net/ir/10-1/paper212.html

Landauer, T. K. (1987). Relations between cognitive psychology and computer system design. In J. M.Carroll (Ed.), *Interfacing thought* (pp. 1-25). Cambridge, MA: MIT Press.

Landauer, T. K. (1991). Let's get real: A position paper on the role of cognitive psychology in the design of humanly useful and usable systems. In J. M. Carroll (Ed.), *Designing interaction: Psychology at the human-computer interface* (pp. 60-73). Cambridge, UK: Cambridge University Press.

Laurillard, D. (1993). *Rethinking university teaching: A framework for the effective use of educational technology*. London: Routledge.

Laurillard, D. (2002). *Rethinking university teaching: A conversational framework for the effective use of learning technologies*. London: Routledge.

Levy, P. (2003). A methodological framework for practice-based research in networked learning. *Instructional Science, 31*(1-2), 87-109.

Pask, G., & Scott, B. C. E. (1972). Learning strategies and individual competence. *International Journal of Man-Machine Studies, 4,* 217-253.

Perry, W. (1970). *Forms of intellectual and ethical development in the college years: A scheme*. New York: Holt Rinehart & Winston.

Popescu, E., Trigano, P., & Badica, C. (2007, July 18-20). Towards a unified learning style model in adaptive educational systems. In *Proceedings of the Seventh IEEE International Conference on Advanced Learning Technologies (ICALT 2007),* Niigata, Japan (pp. 804-808). Retrieved August 1, 2007, from http://doi.ieeecomputersociety.org/10.1109/ICALT.2007.263

Scott, B. (2001). Conversation theory: A constructivist, dialogical approach to educational technology. *Cybernetics & Human Knowing, 8*(4), 25-46.

Thomas, L., & Harri-Augstein, S. (2001). Conversational science and advanced learning technologies (ALT): Tools for conversational pedagogy. *Kybernetes, 30*(7/8), 921-954.

Wood, F., Ford, N., Miller, D., Sobczyk, G., & Duffin, R. (1996). Information skills, searching behaviour and cognitive styles for student centred learning: A computer-assisted learning approach. *Journal of Library and information science, 22*(2), 79-92.

# Chapter X

# Going Forward:
## Research Issues and the Future

## Introduction

This chapter analyses some of the key themes and issues that emerge from the review of research and development presented in the previous chapters. It goes on to examine issues relating to research methodologies, exploring the question of how educational informatics might effectively be progressed. A parallel is drawn between broad dimensions of difference relating to perspectives and approaches observed in this review, and dimensions of difference observed in relation to cognitive styles.

These differences have implications for the nature and level of what is considered acceptable *evidence* on which to progress. They may also underlie conflicts sometimes experienced between proponents of different approaches to research constituting, in their extreme form, the phenomenon of *paradigm wars*. The model of learning developed throughout the previous chapters is further extended to include key aspects of these differences, and to take into account the need for dialectic exploration of the nature and causes of disagreements and differences.

The chapter ends with speculation about the future development of the Web, and possible implications for teaching and learning. The future Web may enable us to learn how we might optimise the potential synergies between the competing forces of individuality and consensus, freedom and authority, and autonomy and mediation.

## Different Perspectives on Educational Informatics Developments

Computer-based systems can now realistically cater to individual differences such as learning styles and strategies by enabling learners to take different routes through a given body of subject matter, and by permitting different levels of freedom in adopting such routes, from teacher-prescribed sequencing of information to learner-controlled navigation.

However, we still arguably lack robust models of learners that can guide such developments. It often appears as though our ability to build clever systems outstrips our knowledge of the more complex and subtle world of real learners' real learning needs and characteristics of social learning interactions complementing individual learning processes. We cannot easily generalise from experimental studies to the real learning and teaching world when viewed broadly and in context. The reality is more complex and full of uncertainties than is acknowledged in many research studies and development projects.

Possibly because of the complexities of user-based research, and the consequent lack of clear robust user models that can inform system design in meaningful ways, many computer systems are built on the basis of what is possible, with relatively scant attention being paid to the need to base developments on sound and appropriately complex models of human behaviour. Indeed, aspects of Rosenberg's (1987, quoted in Urban-Lurain, 1996) critique of the state of research in relation to intelligent tutoring systems (ITS) in the late 1980s still resonate strongly today in relation to the need—by no means generally satisfied—to ground technologically impressive developments in robust and realistically complex models of learners and learning. The following quotation arguably still applies to much research and development if we substitute educational *informatics systems* for *ITS*:

*Some shortcomings of ITS became apparent as researchers realized that the problems associated with creating ITS were more intractable than they had originally anticipated. Rosenberg notes that most papers about ITS make few references to the education literature; the majority are grounded in the computing literature. He asserts that much ITS work suffers from two major flaws:*

*The systems are not grounded in a substantiated model of learning. Model formulation should be preceded by protocol analysis, but very little analysis is done, almost none of it qualitative. ITS models should be validated by the teachers and students who will use the systems, but ITS researchers do not appear to consult these experts.*

*Testing is incomplete, inconclusive, or in some cases totally lacking. Data on computerized tutorials is, at best, mixed. The almost universally positive claims for ITS and other computerized instructional systems—most notable in the education literature—are based on results from severely flawed tests. (Rosenberg, 1987)* (p. 11)

*It was obvious that the basic premises of ITS research needed revision.*

Certainly within library/information science, the criticism has often been voiced that the designers of information systems take little account of research in user studies. It may simply be that the tentative nature of many findings particularly from qualitative studies of complex human learning and information-seeking behaviour do not readily map onto the requirements of system development. Within the field of information retrieval (IR), for example, Ford (2000) has commented on our lack of realistically complex yet robust user models in terms of a "darkness to light ratio." These comments are reminiscent of more postmodern perspectives to be contrasted with a view assuming a steady cumulation of knowledge:

*The limitations of our knowledge relating to human-system interaction are revealed when we consider the extent to which we are able to answer what to the system developer and user are fundamental basic questions such as: how can we help people search more effectively? What empirical research there is into users tells us very little about how to design and improve systems. Complex IR systems have been and are being built—but they are often based on relatively untested theoretical assumptions about users, not on any valid and robust empirically-based understanding of them. Developments in IR system design increase strategic options open to the user—but tell us nothing of how such options may be deployed to achieve optimally effective searching... Our desire to develop practically useful knowledge may encourage us to be over-optimistic in relation to the generalizability of what are essentially very sporadic research efforts. This over-optimism may mask the scale of the darkness to light ratio and the fact that we are falling very short in terms of the critical mass required to support the generalizable knowledge we seek. (p. 626)*

However, arguably such comments may apply to the lack of achievement in user modelling more generally—and certainly in educational informatics. Human-computer interaction (HCI) studies have focused on issues such as user preferences and cognitive ergonomics, but arguably have not impacted more substantive aspects of system design in terms of deep understanding of individual/social and cognitive/affective processes entailed in complex decision making, information seeking, and learning. Again in relation to information retrieval, Järvelin and Ingwersen (2004) have drawn attention to the relative exclusion, from traditional system evaluation studies, of information seekers and the work and other task contexts giving rise to information needs, and criteria for the judgement of the effectiveness of their information seeking. Equally, user studies have not included any meaningful consideration of system design requirements.

Insofar as they do have anything to say to system designers, several recent models of key aspects of human information behaviour stress the complexity of information seeking and assessments of effectiveness and usefulness. Beyond a certain level of complexity in information seeking and learning, there is no easy mapping of user needs and characteristics onto features of system design by which the effectiveness of that information seeking and learning may be optimised.

As noted in the Preface, educational informatics represents the intersection of library/information science, information and computer technology (ICT), and education. These areas of activity possess rich traditions not only of research findings, but also of different approaches to research. Unfortunately there has been a lack of constructive dialogue between researchers and developers working on different aspects of these fields and from different perspectives. It will arguably be important as educational informatics develops to draw on the strengths of such differences, while minimising the entrenchment and disharmony that difference can sometimes engender.

These areas also boast a rich variety of conceptions of the nature of acceptable evidence, and of what constitute valid and useful research goals. Of the three constituent research traditions feeding into educational informatics, arguably education boasts the most eclectic history of conceptions of and approaches to research. The move in education to include qualitative interpretative research approaches predated that in library/information science, as has progression to encompass constructivist action research—now common in education but less widespread rare in library/information science.

Educational informatics shares with education the *breadth* of focus in terms of its concern with people—at individual, social, institutional, and professional levels. This breadth has implications in particular for conceptions within educational informatics of valid *aims and purposes* of research. Educational informatics is centrally concerned with *people*—in the sense that any concern with computer systems must be explicitly referenced to users. It is also centrally concerned with people *interacting with meaning*—that is, engaging with informational content relating to particular subjects and problem domains. Both of these foci have implications particularly for the *nature* of research in terms of approaches and issues of validity and generalisability.

Indeed, the research reviewed in this book does display a great variety of approaches, and associated differences of epistemological perspective, resulting in a range of emergent themes. A number of dimensions of difference in perspectives and approaches are apparent in the research and developments reviewed previously. Although observable within educational informatics, these dimensions are not restricted to this specific field of activity and reflect relatively fundamental differences in the way different researchers and other stakeholders in education, library/information science, and ICT—and their convergence within educational informatics—approach: (a) the description of intellectual content in order to enable its discovery; (b) the representations of knowledge underlying such descriptions; and (c) the way in which discovered information can and should be used in the educational process. These differences are summarized as follows:

- From one perspective, complex intellectual content (information sources) can be productively analysed into discrete components for use in contexts other than that in which, and for which, the content may have been originally created. The role of metadata is to provide an objective description of context-free aspects of content, such that others working in different contexts can assess their relevance and potential usefulness to them.
- From another perspective, however, complex content cannot effectively be decomposed and the components decontextualised, since it is the gestalt (the whole which is more than the sum of the parts) and the context of production and use which give them meaning and effectiveness. For this reason, an essential aspect of metadata is their capacity to provide rich contextual descriptions. Rather than being considered as "noise," context is an essential component of meaning.
- The function of metadata may be considered to be the centralised provision of a an authoritative description of an information source, generated prior to and anticipating its discovery and use, and remaining static (i.e., not subject to constant change).
- This may be contrasted with a view of metadata as more user-centric, and divergent in the sense that a given source may be described by different co-existing (possibly conflicting) metadata, generated by users at the time of the interaction. Such metadata may also be fluid—subject to constant change with every new interaction.
- An ontology (and other knowledge representation formalisms) may be viewed as an attempt to establish a universally agreed, authoritative view of a domain.

- However, this may be contrasted with a view of ontologies as representing diverse, divergent, and provisional ontological knowledge possessed by individuals and communities, including multiple and potentially conflicting views, and supporting the social negotiation of agreements and disagreements in relation to them.
- System-held knowledge (in the case of educational informatics systems, pedagogic knowledge) may be used to control and sequence certain intellectual processes in order to bring about specified and predictable outcomes. Such outcomes may be viewed primarily as being relatively convergent, in the sense of conforming with agreed, clearly prespecified objectives.
- Alternatively, the complexity of intellectual processing may be acknowledged and preserved in a lack of attempt by the system to control and sequence them for users. This is replaced by acceptance of, and an attempt by the system to support, more open-ended, uncertain, and unpredictable outcomes, in the sense of individualistic and open-ended—and therefore relatively uncertain and unpredictable—goals.
- From one perspective, the system may aim to do certain things and make certain decisions *for* the user—representing a degree of supplantation. The goal of the system is to do things relatively directly *for* the user, rather than empower the user to do things for him or herself. The problem may be seen essentially as an objective technical/logical in that it relates to the need better to analyse—and specify in a form that the computer can process and manipulate—the individual's thought processes and characteristics. It may be viewed as a need to devise better reasoning and decision-making rules, and more accurate measures of individual differences such as learning styles and levels of prior knowledge. This focused and analytic perspective is relatively narrow and may tend to map onto a focus on the individual rather than communities.
- This may be contrasted with systems designed to empower users in the sense of attempting to stimulate their metacognitive awareness, knowledge, and skills. Although by no means necessarily so, this broader view may tend to map particularly well onto a more social focus on communities and interactions within them. The problem may be seen less as a question of applying more logic and improving the technology, and more as one of needing better to understand the complexities and subtleties—including the apparent resistance to computation and supplantation—of such social interactions, and to be able to handle problems associated with subjectivity.

These distinctions are summarized in Table 31.

The two columns in Table 31 are to some extent in tension with one another. Indeed, these differences seem to echo some of the differences noted in relation to

*Table 31. Emergent themes in the research and development reviewed in this book*

| | |
|---|---|
| Learning elements can be decontextualised | Context should be preserved since to remove it is to denude of meaning |
| Closed authority-based centrally produced metadata | Open fluid user-centric and idiosyncratic metadata |
| Ontologies as representations of established authority consensus | Ontologies as representations of potentially conflicting and provisional multiple perspectives |
| Control, planning, predictability, and certainty in learning. | Unpredictability, open-endedness, and uncertainty in learning |
| Development proceed by analysis and isolation of variables, and accurate specification of procedures (focusing on the parts). | Development proceed by focusing on and preserving and reconfiguring the whole (gestalt). |
| Convergent thinking (learn agreed material to agreed standards) | Divergent thinking (creativity) |
| Focus on the individual's cognitive processes. | Focus on social interactions. |
| Technical/logical/objective focus. | Social/intuitive focus. Entails handling subjectivity. |
| Dependence: Goal is for the system to supplant selected cognitive processes | Autonomy: Goal is to empower people/communities to learn how to learn |

*Table 32. Dimensions of difference observed in cognitive styles and approaches to research more generally*

| | |
|---|---|
| Description building (*why?* questions) | Procedure building (*how?* questions) |
| Divergent thinking | Convergent thinking |
| Idiosyncrasy | Conformity (adherence to authority standards) |
| Preserve complex context limiting generalisability | Seek universally valid generalisable knowledge |
| Focus on the whole (the gestalt) | Focus on the component parts |
| Emphasis on the social/intuitive | Emphasis on the technical/logical |
| High tolerance of uncertainty (the possible) | Search for certainty (the probable) |
| Acceptance of the value of subjectivity | Emphasis on the search for objectivity |

research approaches more widely, in education, information science, computing, and beyond. They also appear to map remarkably closely onto the cognitive style differences—and the differences in regional brain differences which, it was suggested, might to some extent influence such differences—presented in Chapter II. These differences are summarised in a more abstract way in Table 32.

Research activity that is characterised by the features listed in the right column of Table 32 seems to offer a secure type of evidence in which knowledge can be built up cumulatively, step-by-step on relatively secure foundations, with its emphasis on objectivity and measurable generalisability. Understandably, much research in the development of computer-based systems in education, library/information science, and educational informatics to date has adopted such an approach. At one level it seems sensible to concentrate on those parts of phenomena that are most readily understandable and that offer us the surest prospect of establishing cumulatively useful building blocks of understanding.

However, while this may be productive up to a point, it is also important to remember that this paints only a part of the picture. Research characterised by features to the left in Table 32 can shed softer multi-angle lighting on a phenomenon under scrutiny. Although this may entail more shadows and uncertainties, it can be a useful complement to the apparently bright and clear—yet somewhat harsh and linear—searchlight afforded by research characterised by features to the right. Indeed, different research perspectives and approaches can generate fundamentally different kinds of knowledge, each with its distinctive strengths and weaknesses. Ford (1999) has commented on the dilemma posed by these differences:

> *Overly-analytic states of knowledge are characterised by fragmentation—at worst, isolated facts lacking integration into any coherent wider conceptual picture. ... As a result, much research in information science has arguably provided highly reliable answers to highly meaningless quest ions. The take-up of qualitative research approaches is now widespread in user oriented research. But without critical interaction with complementary perspectives the increasing use of subjective analysis of introspections using small samples of information users threatens to supply highly meaningful quest ions with highly unreliable answers. Some balance and integration must be achieved between the two extremes.* (p. 1151)

The differences outlined previously echo those discussed in Chapter II in relation to learning styles identified by Pask. It was noted there that procedure building relates to the detailed step-by-step logical evidence and arguments supporting the "big picture," while description building entails construction of the latter, via a more exploratory, holistic process. Indeed, if different research perspectives and approaches are the products of human cognition, then it is perhaps not surprising if these differences echo those identifies in research into cognition itself.

However, in relation to learning theory, Pask goes on to note that both components are necessary to achieve full understanding. As Entwistle (1981) notes:

*Any weakness either in the plan, or in ... the operations and procedures which will satisfy the implicit demands of that plan, will prevent the building being satisfactorily completed (understanding being reached).* (p. 93-94)

In regards to the extreme operation learner, if he or she fails to complement his or her procedure building with adequate amounts of description building, he or she will display a characteristic learning pathology—in essence, failing to see the wood for the trees. Whereas the extreme comprehension learner, failing to complement description building with adequate levels of procedure building, will display the characteristic pathology of over-generalisation. This entails the generation of a speculative but richly interconnected conceptual overview of the area being studied. However, this may be invalid when subjected to scrutiny in terms of more detailed supporting evidence.

## Types of Evidence

If we accept the admittedly speculative link between these stylistic differences relating to human cognition, and stylistic differences characterising research perspectives, then Pask's observations of the need to combine these complementary components would lend support to the notion that greater understanding may be achieved by combining different types of research evidence.

Beyond a certain level of complexity, our understanding of learning and related information seeking leaves much to be desired in terms of providing system designers with complex, valid, and robust models capable of driving the generation of computer-based systems capable of significantly enhancing the quality of information seeking and learning.

As noted previously, there is even much dispute about how me might, and should, go about generating the evidence on which such models might be built. It may indeed be that the necessary improvements in our understanding can to a large extent be generated via the development and testing of hugely complex computer-based models entailing large numbers of variables and complex interactions. It may be that quantitative, relatively reductionist studies, in sufficiently large numbers, with sufficiently wide coverage, and conducted with sufficient methodological rigour, may ultimately cumulate to provide the sort of substantial and sophisticated knowledge we need in order to build truly effective educational informatics systems.

It may be that, when viewed in retrospect in years to come, the most significant developments in our understanding of what are currently cognitive and affective unknowns of learning and information seeking may be seen to have derived from such approaches, their evidential strength deriving from powerful features such as statistical significance and generalisability. However, we may look back and conclude that the most significant progress was due to less quantifiable, less objective evidence offering more holistic, context-bound, and sensitive understanding, its value deriving from the resonance-based *transferability* characterising much qualitative interpretive research rather than statistically based generalisation.

Equally, however, it may be the interplay and interaction *between* such different perspectives and research approaches that we acknowledge to have been a key determinant of further significant inroads in our quest better to understand learners and learning. Within the component sciences contributing to educational informatics there exists a great multiplicity of evidence relating to learners, learning, and information seeking generated from a variety of different perspectives, and researchers with different roles and agendas (including system designers, researchers, educationists, learners, information professionals, and users).

There is also evidence of both synthesis and antithesis between such different perspectives and approaches. Synthesis may take different forms, the ways in which different research approaches may be deployed in relation to one another being varied. Strategies for methodological pluralism include, for example: (a) critical dialogue relating to a common phenomenon from different paradigmatic perspectives; (b) the use of different paradigms within a single study; (c) the mapping of different paradigms onto different kinds of problem; or (d) methodological relativism, in which any paradigm is considered to be as good as any other.

Antithesis may range from bias towards and preference for a particular approach, to partisan and entrenched hostility between proponents of different research *camps* in the form of paradigm wars (Ford, 2000; Kuhlthau, 2005). While many commentators emphasise the need for methodological pluralism, others have questioned the viability and desirability of such integration. Less common have been calls for more systematic exploration of the very nature of tensions between different perspectives.

An exception is Thornley (2005) who, writing about conceptual problems and conflicts within information retrieval, proposes the dialectical model as "a way of understanding meaning as a dialectical conflict between the subjective and the objective" (p. 197), which "exist in a mutually antagonistic and dependent relationship" (p. vi). She suggests that:

*The continuing dissatisfaction with theoretical development in IR, and also perhaps in IS, can now be interpreted as a frustration with attempts to create a stable synthesis in a subject matter which cannot contain such a synthesis. [...] A dialectical understanding of the relationship between 'what is' and 'what is not' can help explain why stable synthesis is so difficult to achieve in IR. The nature of its subject matter, meaning and information is characterised by this relationship, which means that any position in IR which aims for synthesis will always be unstable. The aspects of meaning and information, which it either ignores or explicitly rejects, will also be essential to its position.* (pp. 247-248)

The dialectical model, however, offers a potential solution in that it:

*... relies on the hypotheses that the subjective/objective divide is important, that it can be characterised as a mutually antagonistic and dependent relationship, and that this plays a central role in both meaning and information.* (p. 256)

and that it represents:

*an improvement on previous work in this area because it provides a way of working with the many contradictory concepts within IR without trying to create an untenable synthesis.* (p. vii)

To take a visual analogy, Figure 113 shows a familiar optical illusion. Conceal the bottom half of the image with a sheet of paper, leaving the top half visible. Look at the image for a few moments, then reverse the procedure, leaving only the bottom half visible.

*Figure 113. An impossible object*

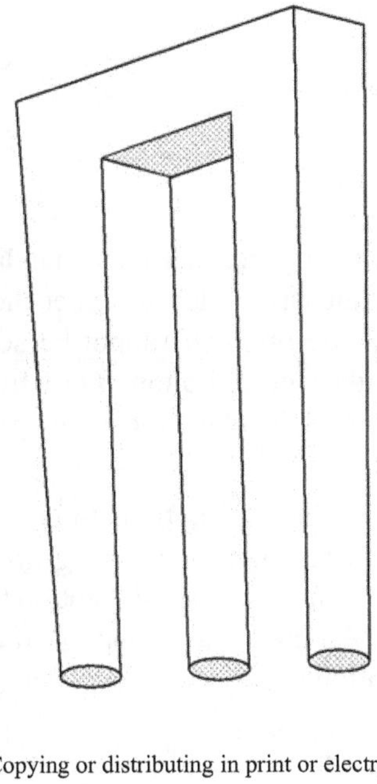

*Figure 114. Integrating themes at different levels of abstraction*

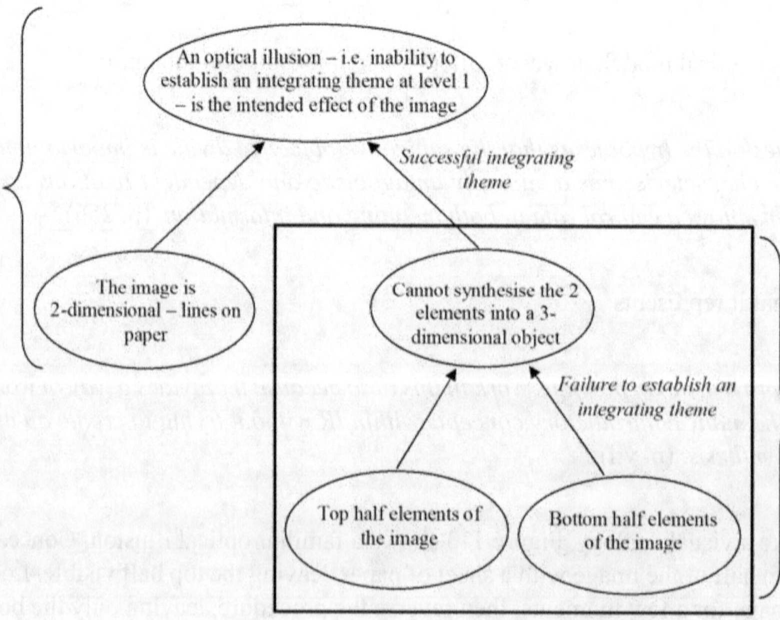


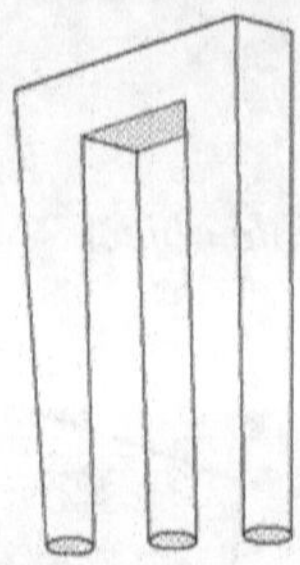

The point of this exercise is to suggest that understanding the nature of what is depicted is not advanced by intensive study of either the top half in isolation, or the bottom half in isolation. The *problem* cannot be solved by intensifying the level of scrutiny applied to either top or bottom. Only by examining the image as a whole can the dialectic nature of the phenomenon be perceived and the nature of the incongruity tackled.

Such a broader perspective enables assumptions to be made explicit, questioned, and resolved via the application of a higher-level *integrating theme*. In this case, it is apparent that the incongruity stems from the assumption that Figure 113 represents some sort of physical reality. Making the assumption explicit and applying a meta-analysis in which this assumption is only one component, allows the emergence of the meta-interpretation that Figure 113 is *about* the effect of assumptions on human perception rather than being about the depiction of a physical object. Applying an integrating theme at a meta-level in order to make sense of this illusion is shown in Figure 114. The optical illusion is used here as a visual analogy of more general issues relating to differences of perspective and approach as we try to *make sense* of things by converting information into knowledge.

Such an approach is inherent in the basic processes whereby we build more sophisticated understanding. We may do this via the realisation of limiting assumptions inherent in a particular frame of reference with which we approach some phenomena, and the development of a more abstract frame of reference which takes account of and attempts to overcome such limitations. Indeed, the previous review of educational informatics developments contains examples where increasingly *meta* abstractions (designed to represent and model ontological aspects of pedagogical knowledge) have been developed, each attempting to overcome limitations perceived in some previous abstraction.

The need to shift from a physical (object representation) to a psychological (perceptual illusion) frame of reference in the example shown in Figures 113 and 114 is quickly obvious in this simple case. However, the tensions between different research camps alluded to previously suggest that it may not always be easy to effect such shifts in the context of complex research phenomena. In this context, developing an appropriate meta-level frame of reference may require an explicit mapping of relationships between different *evidential purposes*—for example, to chart the possible or predict the probable; to build watertight theory or pragmatically impact practice; to describe the unique or explain the universal. Only by focusing more explicitly and directly on the precise nature of apparent incongruities, may there be enabled a degree of cumulative (and/or interactive) contribution to knowledge from heterogeneous types of evidence generated from different perspectives.

The model shown in Figure 115 extends the model presented in Figure 90 in Chapter VI. Figure 115 maps onto this model the key dimensions of difference in perspective observable in educational informatics research discussed previously. The two poles of each dimension, depicted by the spokes, exist in some tension with one another. Thus, learning aiming at the development of, and/or the use of autonomy and metacognition on the part of the learner (at the bottom right of Figure 115), is in tension with learning approaches that emphasise the learner's dependence on teachers, and *supplantation* in which information processing is to a relatively high degree done, whether by human teacher or machine, *for* rather than *by* the learner (top left).

There is also tension between, for example within the area of resource discovery, approaches to describing the content of information and resources using social tagging techniques—which are essentially distributed and relatively idiosyncratic (top right), and standards for metadata, classifications and ontologies systems which are produced and controlled more centrally, and which offer agreed authoritative *rulings*

*Figure 115. Differences in perspectives of, and approaches to, learning and system development*

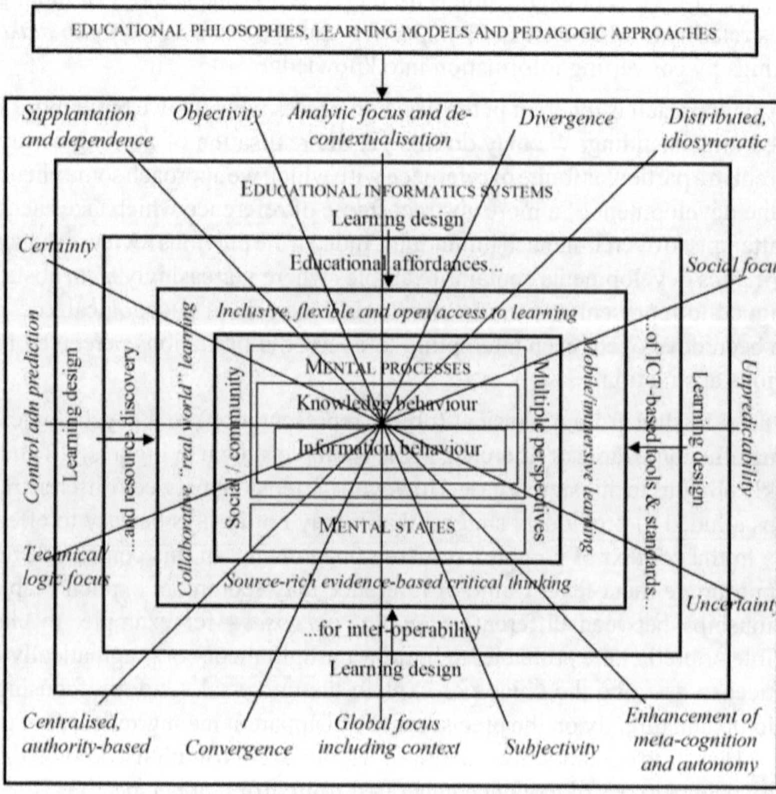


on the way content should be described (bottom left). Within education more generally there is similar tension, for example, between providing single "authoritative" interpretations of ideas centralised within a teacher or educational system, and the distributed negotiation of multiple relativistic perspectives—which may tend towards the idiosyncratic in the case of divergent and creative thinking.

Figure 115 depicts distinctions in the way different stakeholders and individuals may think about educational informatics systems—that is, the purposes and nature of the systems that are being and should be developed. However, there is a difference of focus between (level 1) *thinking about* educational informatics systems, and (level 2) *thinking about how we think about* educational informatics systems. Figure 115 relates to level 1.

*Figure 116. Two-level conversational model applied to research (adapted from Harri-Augstein & Thomas, 1991)*

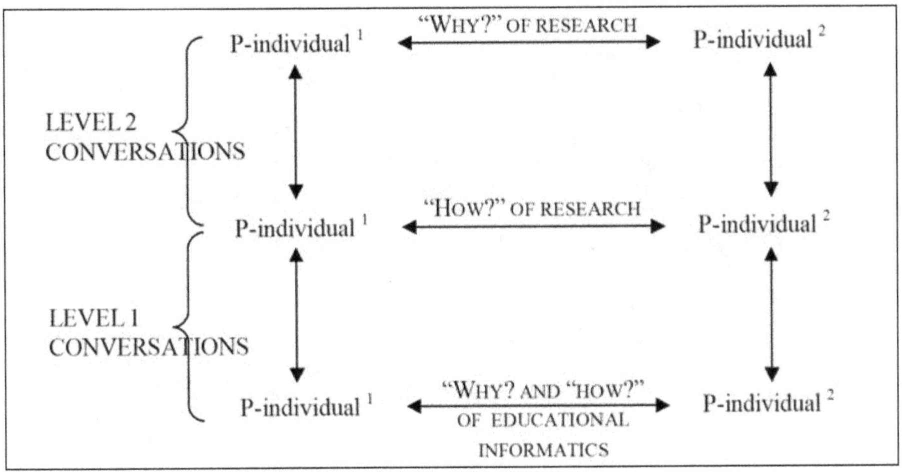


At level 1, the dimensions shown in Figure 115 can map and inform conversations about the object of our research—educational informatics—for example, concerning why and how we might develop educational informatics systems to support creativity. However, at a more abstract meta-level (level 2), we might engage in conversations about level 1 conversations—for example, to discuss the adequacy of our research approaches, the possible advantages, disadvantages, and implications of—and the nature of disagreements between—alternative theoretical perspectives.

Recall that in Figure 30 in Chapter III, Pask's model of conversations about learning (level 1) was extended by Harri-Augstein and Thomas (1991) to include a meta-level representing *conversations about* conversations about leaning (level 2). Figure 116 applies this two-level conversational model to *research*.

The dimensions represented by the spokes in Figure 115 are related to level 1 conversations. However, they are also applicable to level 2 conversations. Recall that Table 32 outlined a number of dimensions of difference applying essentially to level 2—that is, to perspectives of and approaches to research and development, and the nature of acceptable evidence that different stakeholders and individuals may deem necessary and sufficient as a basis for progression. Recall also that these differences were very similar to those identified in this review of research and development of educational, resource discovery, and educational informatics systems shown in Table 31—and relating essentially to level 1 conversations. Figure 117 incorporates these different levels of conversation into the model of perspectives of and approaches to learning and system development.

*Figure 117. Differences in level 1 and level 2 conversations about learning and system development*

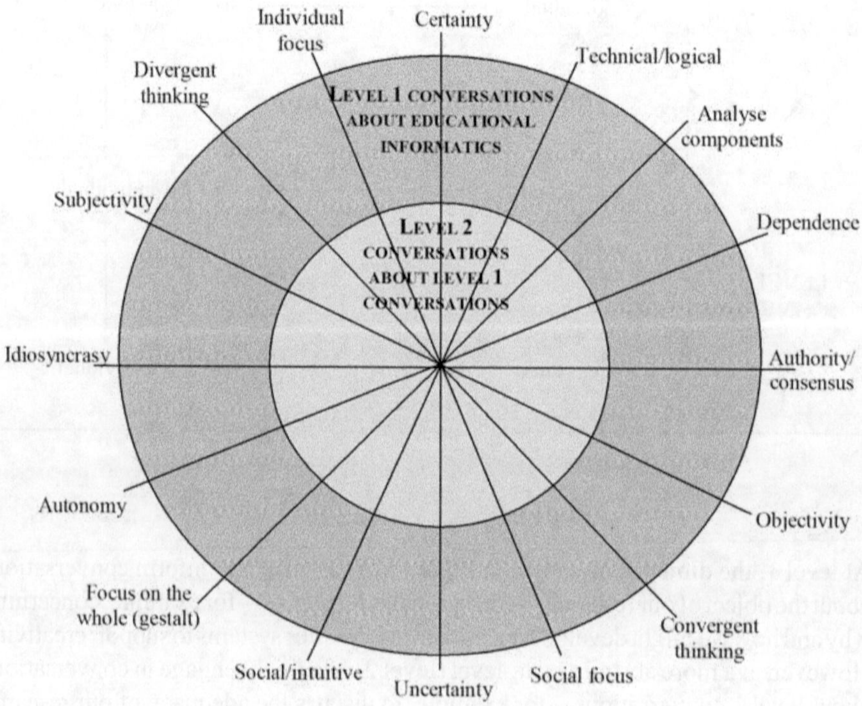


Level 1 conversations thus focus on educational informatics—how we can build more effective systems. Level 2 conversations are dialectic and focus on the nature of the conflicts and agreements between the different biases reflected in the different poles of the dimensions (the *spokes* of the wheel). These different levels of conversation echo the differences between *object*-level and *meta*-level languages stressed by Pask and discussed hereafter. This differentiation between object- and meta-level conversations is further represented in Figure 118.

Particularly where there are tensions and conflicts of opinion, for example, in the interpretation of data, it is important to engage in meta-level (level 2) conversations questioning the nature of disagreements and subjecting research approaches and methods to constant critical scrutiny and reappraisal. But why should this be so when we have well-established research paradigms, methodologies, and methods that lay out good research practice, and procedures designed to maximise validity, reliability, and neutrality?

*Figure 118. Why? and how? conversations at levels 1 and 2*

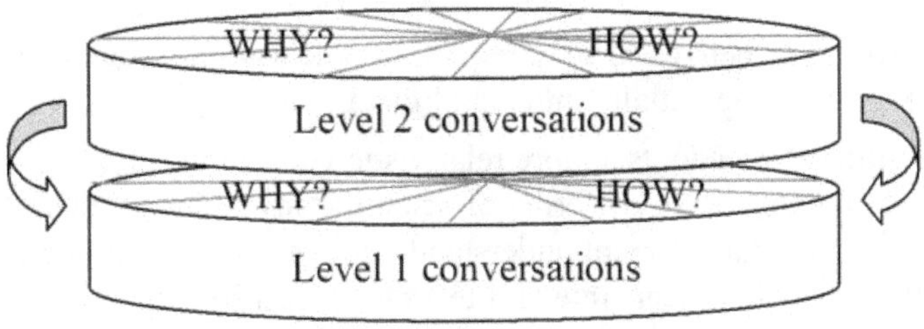


According to Thomas and Harri-Augstein (2001), such constant scrutiny and re-appraisal are essential components of what they term "stage 3" scientific method. They use the term "scientific method" in a less restrictive sense than that in which it is often used which they describe as "stage 1."

Stage 1 scientific method typically entails the isolation of variables from their natural context, coupled with carefully controlled experimental design in order to exclude any *extraneous* influences. Key goals are objectivity (avoiding the influence of subjective judgements) and reliability (ensuring that effects observed on one occasion may also be observed on different occasions). Unexpected effects are attributed to the influence of variables which, for whatever reason, failed to be identified and either excluded from or taken into account by the experimental design.

Stage 2 scientific method entails recognition that phenomena exist, operate within, and are affected by their broader contexts. It explicitly acknowledges this by including context within research design. Much so-called *qualitative* research includes an emphasis on avoiding de-contextualisation of elements of a phenomenon under investigation, and preserving it as an interacting gestalt, changes in parts affecting the whole configuration of behaviour. As Thomas and Harri-Augstein (2001) note:

*The power of the stage 1 form of scientific method was that, by enabling a community of scientists to construct shared systems of meaning, it encouraged the systematic growth of knowledge in which one generation could stand on the shoulders of the previous one building from their pooled experience. The weaknesses of this approach stem from the belief that any one system of knowledge could be complete within itself. The power of the stage 2 form of the scientific method is that it insists on the continuity and wholeness of nature and the need for knowledge to reflect this. It accepts the coherent totality of each person's experience. Thus, in pure science, physics throws light on chemistry and chemistry informs biology. More importantly in the practical living world each application of science must recognise the actual context of that application. (p. 924)*

Unexpected effects or behaviour may require the inclusion of more context in an attempt not to exclude potentially influential factors.

Stage 3 scientific theory adopts a more relativistic view, in which the provisionality and context-bound nature of forms of scientific investigation themselves are recognised. Not only our different understandings about aspects of the world, but also the ways in which we generate and test them must be subject to continuous conscious evolution. This evolution entails testing *meanings*. Scott (2006) argues that "meaning" can be modelled (and thus tested) in terms of "the pragmatic consequences of holding certain beliefs to be true" (p. 310). Where the observed consequences (of our own and/or those of others with whom we converse) do not match what our beliefs lead us to expect, we must revisit not only the conditions surrounding the observations and our interpretations of the findings, but also the ways in which we generate meanings—our experimental methods, methodologies, and theorising processes.

Thus, the ways in which we seek understanding and explanation are constantly subject to critical scrutiny, modification, and development. This activity is moderated by the testing and feedback loops (discussed in the section *Reality Checking for Quality Control*). The reaction to unexpected effects is in effect an extended stage 2 reaction in that it entails extending the focus of critical investigation to the even wider context of the nature and methods of the investigation itself. This process is designed to avoid the danger of the build-up of hegemonic claims relating to well-established methodologies and systems of knowledge while avoiding the anarchy of unfettered postmodernism.

Stage 3 scientific theory is an overarching framework for thinking about knowledge generation across diverse areas of science. It essentially entails metacognitive processing—thinking about the successes and limitations of the cognitive processes whereby we generate new understandings, and how they might be amended, extended or conceived otherwise in order to improve the match our meanings and our observations.

Thomas and Harri-Augstein (2001) report the results of such stage 3 activity in relation to their longstanding study of human learning. They note that any study of humans is affected by characteristics not shared by research into inanimate phenomena. This characteristic makes it highly likely that stage 1 or stage 2 approaches can only ever lead to the achievement of a relatively low plateau of understanding of human thought and behaviour. It centres on the fact that when humans know that they are being observed (studied), they themselves observe this observation.

# Contingent Dependencies and Object and Meta-Languages

When humans know that they are being observed, they may also think about and react to their observers and the observation. Thus what is observed by the researcher (the subjects' behaviour and action) may be due not only to the effects of whatever phenomenon the researcher thinks he or she is observing, but also at least in part to the subjects' thoughts and reactions to being observed. Such effects are termed here *contingent dependencies*. Subtle, and by no means necessarily perceptible, interactions between observed and observer may cause contingent dependencies to arise. For example, conscious or unconscious assumptions and expectations on the part of the observed may affect the nature of the very behaviour that is being observed. As Thomas and Harri-Augstein (2001) note:

*This is essentially a conversational situation. Our behaviour does not produce the consequences we perceive. We assume that another agent is at work. The agent is attributing meaning to our behaviour and themselves behaving accordingly. It is this construing of us while we are construing them that has made social science so apparently difficult when pursued through the scientific methods of the physical sciences. In accepting the physical science paradigm, the efforts of social scientists have been dissipated in trying to eliminate the independent agency from our subject matter. While we 'know' that as people we cannot do this, as scientists we have persisted because the scientific method (as defined by the physical sciences) seemed to depend on our doing so. (pp. 930-931)*

In relation to addressing the problems associated with contingent dependencies, it is extremely important to be able to distinguish between "object language" and "meta-language" (Pask, 1975a, 1975b, 1976c; Schuurman & Veermans, 2001). Object language refers to the language used to talk about the object of direct study—the phenomenon under investigation, as viewed from a particular perspective. For example, a research investigation may focus on the effects on learning behaviour of a particular teaching approach from a particular pedagogic perspective. Conversations about this focus—what is observed, and possible interpretations of the findings—take place in the *object language*.

However, it is also important to be able to talk about, for example, the adequacy and limitations of the research approach and theoretical perspective being adopted. It may be useful to consider the potential usefulness of alternative perspectives and theoretical perspectives in relation to the study. In other words, it may be necessary to discuss the characteristics, advantages, and disadvantages of the object language itself—and to consider the use of some alternative object language. This conversation would take place in the *meta-language*.

If object language and meta-language are not clearly separated, unintended contingent dependencies may result, and any intended dependencies (for example, the effects of some experimental intervention) cannot be clearly seen. This may happen, for example, if the subjects of an experiment react to the observer and the observation in terms of anticipations, expectations, emotions, or attitudes. Where subjects being observed react—consciously or unconsciously—to what they think is expected of them, or in terms of what they believe will be perceived by others as *reasonable* in the observed situation in which they realise they are—they are mixing object language and meta-language.

Object language is concerned with the activity or behaviour that the researcher wishes to observe, and about which he or she wishes to generate knowledge. Meta-language is concerned with the observation. Ford, Miller, and Moss (2003) draw attention to the possibility of such an interaction when reporting the results of a study on Web searching. Links were found between individuals who were typed by a "reproductive" study orientation and who tended to search using Boolean operators:

*The reproductive-oriented person is by definition likely to have a preoccupation with the relatively extrinsic requirements and judgments of significant others—particularly those involved in assessing their academic work. Indeed a reproductive approach is inherently geared to regurgitating information in such a way as to satisfy the extrinsic requirements of assessment as opposed to engendering understanding. High levels of fear of failing may increase this preoccupation. It is thus possible that individuals characterized by a reproductive study orientation may have perceived the adoption of a Boolean approach as:*

*What they thought was desired (even though no such desire was expressed) by a research team exploring Web-based information seeking within a specialist department of library and information studies, and which they knew to contain academic staff teaching on their programs; and/or*

*Offering relatively explicit visible evidence (especially in cases of a lack of success in terms of results) of effort and professional competence to significant others—in this case, again the research team.*

*The latter notions are, however, entirely speculative at this stage, and would require further investigation of the intentions, perceptions, and motivations behind searchers' behavior.*

Pask makes the point (Schuurman & Veermans, 2001) that we cannot necessarily assume that the human subjects of research will necessarily clearly differentiate between object language and meta-language. If this is the case, then we cannot necessarily avoid undesired and unanticipated contingent dependencies. Pask's solution was to embrace such contingent dependencies—and the interactions between object and meta-language—more explicitly. As noted by Schuurman and Veermans (2001):

*Pask wanted to exploit possible contingent dependencies and proposed a mechanism to make well-defined contingencies structural features of an intended manipulation interactions between object language and meta language [are] generally considered inadmissible in research because contingent dependencies between observer and observations are supposed to be external to experimental manipulations. In general it is mandatory to avoid contingent dependencies, because they create artifacts. According to Pask those artifacts are admissible and in fact sought for, but one must keep a proper record. (pp. 881-883)*

In other words, Pask proposed that interactions between object language and meta-language should be explicitly addressed and recorded. There should be explicit discussion about this issue between observer and observed. Thus, for example, experimental subjects should talk about their reactions to being put in an experimental situation, and about their expectations and feelings about this. There should be explicit agreement between observer and observed relating to these interactions. If we know that a particular outcome (A) depends not only on a direct experimental intervention (B) but also some interaction (C) between object language and meta-language (some contingent dependency), we can only learn about the true effects of intervention (B) on outcome (A) if we also know all about the interaction between object and meta-languages (C). Importantly, this interaction (B) can include explicit negotiations and agreements relating to what might be a desirable outcome (A) and to how it might be achieved through the research. These ideas are embedded in Pask's conversation theory. They are also fundamental considerations underlying the development and justification of *action research*.

However, contingent dependencies can also emerge from interactions between object language and meta-language on the part of the observer. For example, the researcher may hold implicit and unconscious assumptions about the nature of the observed and the observation. This problem is addressed by Dervin (1983, 1991, 1992, 1993, 1998, 1999a, 1999b), whose ideas, like those of Pask, are embedded in a complex body of work constituting her sense-making methodology (see also her "sense-making methodology" site at http://communication.sbs.ohio-state.edu/sense-making/).

Dervin notes, for example, that researchers often look for relatively stable enduring phenomena, which are thus observable across time (for example, cognitive styles, attitudes, culture). She considers such an a priori emphasis on what she terms "across time-space phenomena" to be excessively restrictive since humans are both potentially stable (as shown by our habits, and rigidities) and potentially fluid (as indicated by our flexibility and innovation). Emphasising across time-space constants may result in research methodology that is ultimately tautological in that it may constitute an a priori assumption that is not subjected to testing within the research—that is, it is not explicitly challenged. In fact, it may not be formulated within the research design in terms of a challengeable proposition.

Dervin (1999) proposes measures designed to militate against contingent dependencies caused by untested implicit assumptions on the part of the observer. She lists examples of such commonly untested assumptions and suggests methods to avoid being constrained by them. The researcher should:

*[S]erve a mandate of self-conscious self-reflexivity. This requires even more than a concern for the potential tyrannies of interpreting the worlds for others. It requires the positioning of self as a focus of investigation, as an exemplar of the human condition this does not imply that researchers suppress their own interpretations, or the access to understandings that the privilege of their chosen life paths gives them. Rather, it implies that these are humbled and tested in dialogue and that the researcher becomes a vehicle of dialogic practice. (pp. 734-735)*

The responsibility of the researcher—and the fact that such quality control is essentially an issue of human judgment, as opposed to something which can be "passed off" to some claim of "objectivity"—is echoed by Thomas and Harri-Augstein (2001):

*Our first conversationally scientific discovery is that science is a human activity. This means that attempts to depersonalise either the process or the products of science will always be counter-productive if not downright dangerous. Hence our attempt to report our research in first person terms. This does not prevent us from being rigorous, systematic researchers, cogniscent of the work of others. But it does prevent us from abdicating personal responsibility by hiding behind an unwarranted objective authority of established thinking or traditional practises. It also forces us to reconstrue the meaning of such terms as "validity", "reliability" and "objectivity". Validity, no longer as statistical, pre- and post-studies but as viability, i.e. as effectiveness of performance. Reliability, not as repeatability within a fixed scenario but as the appropriateness of ongoing performance in terms of the agents, values and purposes. Objectivity, not as absolute truth but as shared subjectivity. (p. 929)*

# Reality Checking for Quality Control

This section examines ways that have been proposed for trying to introduce a level of quality control into conversations, whether these are about learning, teaching, or researching.

An essential element of conversations—at both object level and meta-level—is some sort of quality control or reality check, entailing the testing of understandings that emerge from those conversations. Pask stressed that an essential component of effective teaching and learning was the use of some modelling facility in which conversational participants could *demonstrate* their understandings to each other. As mentioned in the previous section, Scott (2006) considers that meaning can be modelled in terms of "the pragmatic consequences of holding certain beliefs to be true" (p. 310). More generally, Scott considers that the testing of understandings in terms of their pragmatic consequences in the real world is essential if we are to avoid an "anything goes" state of affairs—a danger seen by some writers as inherent in certain aspect of the current Web 2.0 vogue.

Scott goes on to describe Rescher's (1973, 1977) model in which he elaborates not only the fundamental distinction between *why?* and *how?* questions inherent in conversations, but also the function of pragmatic testing at both levels. Rescher proposes two cycles of interconnected activity as shown in Figure 119 .

*Figure 119. Aspects of Rescher's model and Scott's interpretation of it (adapted from Scott, 2001b)*

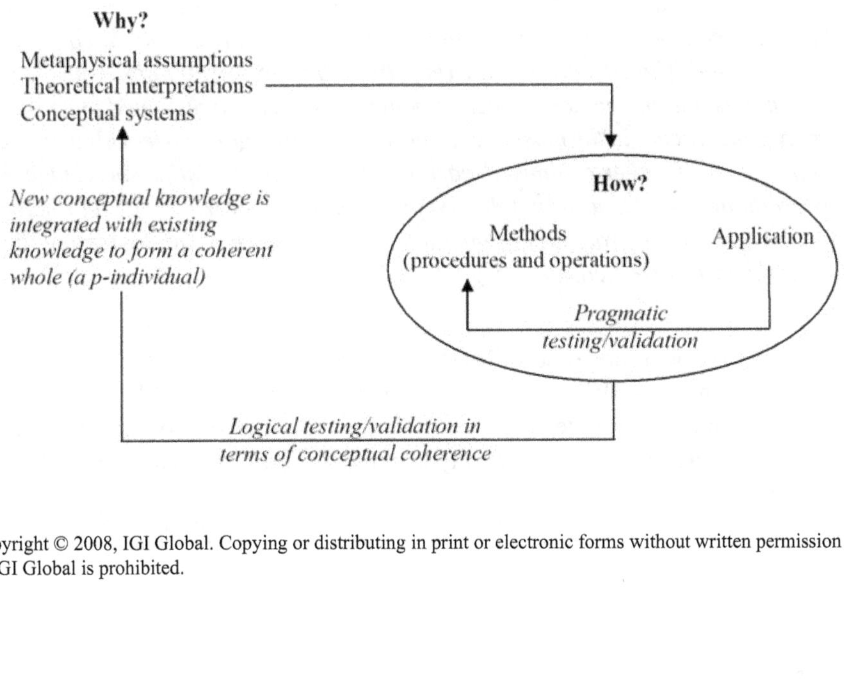

As in *conversation theory*, the whole cycle is recursive—recall that a conversation between two a p-individuals can itself be a p-individual. Scott (2001b) notes that:

> *By revealing the process of epistemic validation in science, Rescher has given due acknowledgement to the primacy of affect, praxis. At the same time, he has shown how cognitive methodology may evolve such that a logic and rationale can guide praxis. Although the outcome of praxis is the final arbiter of the effectiveness of those methodologies, the methodologies (cognition, metacognition) are such that they provide not only an apparatus for substantiating theses about the world but also provide an apparatus for their own rational evolution and refinement. The logic of scientific discovery thus pulls itself up by its own bootstraps. There remains a real sense in which logic (cognition) has primacy.* (p. 349)

Thomas and Harri-Augstein (2001) consider that there is a danger within formal education—a danger which much institutional education unfortunately fails to avoid—of underemphasising the engagement of learners in these feedback loops, which is an essential component in the process of meaning making.

> *Unhappily most of our educational processes have come to ignore and de-value this systematic, reflexive, conversational meaning constructing process. Instead the specific findings and methodologies of the sciences are taught by experts to novices and the less expert. In the short term this may appear to be an efficient and economic way of achieving academic standards. But it is gradually becoming recognised that something essential is being lost. [...] Theory, experiment and socially effective applications have parted company, to the extent that they cease to feedback effectively one into the other. The conversational process has broken down, to be replaced by the popularisation and exploitation of scientific knowledge [...] The "lessons" which science teaches, even the sacred scientific method itself, has become deeply misunderstood. The adventure of the reflective learning conversation which invents its meanings and its methods better to achieve its deeply questioned purposes has largely gone, except in the most trivial sense. The self-organised learning of science is replaced by the other-organised learning of derivative scientific knowledge. Even postgraduate students usually follow a prescriptive pathway, directed by scientific gurus. The primary processes of imagination and invention are lost in the pursuit of secondary transmitted knowledge. (p. 925)*

The conversational model described by Thomas and Harri-Augstein (2001) highlights the dangers and limitations inherent in putting artificial barriers between classroom and real life, between theory and practice, and between teaching and research, emphasising their essentially integrated nature within the context of stage 3 scientific method.

A number of implications are associated with this need to integrate theory and real world feedback from the testing of emerging understandings, to embrace and make explicit interactions between object and meta-level language, and to open up to critical dialogue even relatively well established research assumptions and approaches. These implications are that:

- Artificial barriers between classroom and real life, theory and practice, teaching and research—if they lead to an underemphasis of pragmatic real world testing of emerging understandings—may have undesirable effects.
- Objectivity is essentially *shared subjectivity*, and the provisionality of our knowledge and methods relating to human science should not be underestimated or ignored by attributing to such science ultimately spurious claims to some universally valid measures of objectivity and reliability.
- Research concerning humans is inescapably a human activity, and the effects of human judgement on the part of observed, observer and the interaction between them, should be made explicit and acknowledged. Such considerations render particularly valuable in the study of human behaviour and activity the notion of action research.

Taking on board the previous bulleted points is characteristic of what Thomas and Harri-Augstein (2001) have termed the "self-organised learner"—a term that applies equally to teacher, learner, and researcher since they are all engaged, at various levels, in the same basic process of processing information in order to generate new knowledge. Thomas and Harri-Augstein (2001) describe self-organised learners thus:

*Self-organised learners are people who can converse with their environment in ways that enable them to construct and share meanings which will work effectively for them. Other-organised learners become stuck with the meanings which their education has sold them. They are blind to the full consequences of applying their knowledge in ways that produce results which that knowledge does not predict. [...] For us the metaphor of the scientist as self-organised learner (SOLer) is a powerful concept. Such scientists construct their theories about the world as they act within it to progressively validate and expand their understanding, thus becoming increasingly viable and effective. SOL has relevance for scientific research and permeates beyond our current understanding of physical science, to psychology and social systems. It has consequences for the way we should support new generations to learn about existing knowledge while learning to conduct their own unique, personally relevant experiments. (p. 925)*

# Towards the Learning Web

The powerful combination of machine reasoning techniques and ontology-based knowledge representations enables developers to build intelligence into Web applications. As increasing volumes of information are published on the Web in a form making it readily manipulatable by machine reasoning techniques, the Web will increasingly be able to offer direct question-answering to complement the present default search engine response of retrieving information sources in which we may find answers—or from which we may, often in combination with other sources, piece them together.

The combination of deductive and inductive reasoning techniques also offers powerful potential. Deductive reasoning using, for example, the type of IF... THEN... rules introduced in Chapter V, enables aspects of human expertise—judgement and decision making—to be built into digital systems. This expertise can then be applied remotely 24/7, for example in the form of Web services for use by and integration within other applications and services.

Systems that deliver information and learning resources across the Web can also collect data on the interactions between those who use them. With significant caveats relating to ethical issues, learning delivery systems can thus at the same time be pedagogical research tools, gathering unprecedented volumes of data from *real* learners engaged in *real* learning. Deductive analysis can potentially enable the testing of hypotheses, models, and theories of learning and learning design—again, on an unprecedented scale. However, inductive analysis can result in the discovery of patterns of interaction enabling the generation of novel hypotheses, models, and theories.

The volume and range of information representing diverse opinions and perspectives published on the Web are increasing rapidly. As more and more of these information sources are represented in a form rendering them directly susceptible to machine reasoning, for example as resource description framework (RDF) triples or graphs, the author perspectives that they represent can be used by others to filter their own navigation of the Web.

Figure 120 shows a variety of layers of information sources available on the Web. People's *knowledge states* are shown at the top of the figure. These include not only, for example, knowledge that authors wish to express but also the knowledge and information needs of learners and information seekers. People *express* these knowledge states in a variety of ways. Authors may express their ideas and perspectives by publishing information sources. Information seekers may express their needs in the form of queries to search engines.

These expressions may themselves be represented at a more abstract level. Individual information sources and aggregations of them may be represented in the form of metadata. More complex representations such as knowledge charts and topic maps

*Figure 120. The Web as layers of potentially interrelated perspectives*

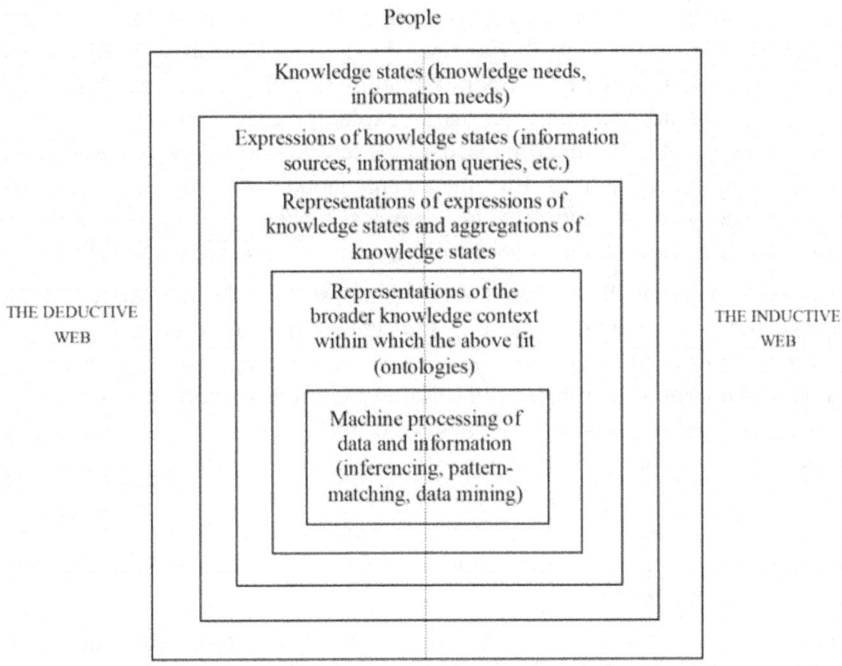


can express the intellectual structure of the knowledge state expressions at a more sophisticated level in terms of, for example, their argumentation or pedagogical structure. Such knowledge state expressions may represent facts, opinions, perspectives, models, and theories that seek to predict and explain the phenomena they treat.

Ontologies are representations of the broader knowledge context into which representations of particular knowledge state expressions fit. They are one step removed from the latter in that, while their terms can be used to describe particular expressions (particular arguments or views), they are not tied to these expressions.

Insofar as they are expressed in a form enabling manipulation by inference engines, these different layers of expression can be used by others to filter their *views* of the Web. Such expressions represent the mini *world view* or mental model of the domain held by their authors. Since in principle anyone can publish a knowledge state expression at any of the levels shown in Figure 120, specifying their mental model of any domain, argument, perspective, or theory, such views of the Web can proliferate into a vast and complex array of potential filters and navigation pathways for others to use. This myriad of perspectives on unlimited topics and domains would be potentially subject to manipulation by machine reasoning techniques, which could generate further representations entailing combinations, integrations, and modifications of them.

Mediating tools could manage the process whereby Web users could select filters and navigate documents on the Web via views imposed by their different perspectives. We are all familiar with the facility provided by Google Earth, whereby users can fly over geographical areas, dive down to explore an area in more detail, and ask for different views to be superimposed on the terrain—to show, for example, road networks, and other facilities. Imagine an analogous system in which users could navigate conceptual as opposed to geographical space, superimposing at different levels particular views filtered by one or more interconnected perspectives.

We could navigate the Web filtered according to, say, a particular pedagogical perspective—or a combination of several subject domain and *problem-solving structures* perspectives. At a certain *zoom out* level it may be possible to perceive, for example, similarities in problem and solution structures pertaining across different domains. The possible viable combinations of filters relating to particular learning designs, learning theories, learner needs, goals and characteristics, pedagogical adaptation approaches, and argumentation structures are vast. At present our efforts at educational personalisation, where we attempt to allow or prescribe different routes, modes, and media via which learners explore conceptual spaces, are gross and clumsy compared to what might be possible.

We can, however, imagine a *learning Web* in which there are available a bewildering array of potential pathways through the learning of a vast range of content. Such a Web could potentially contain content and possible pathways to suit almost every combination of learner need and characteristic, pedagogical approach, and learning design. Such a proliferation of information sources, pathways, and perspectives increases the volume, complexity, and diversity of conceptual space. The problem, of course, is one with which we are all too familiar in relation to finding information on the Web—the obfuscation of the particular needle we need by the vastness and chaotic nature of the haystack—described by Heylighen (2007) as "the chaotic organization of the present Internet, and the concomitant 'data smog'".

Heylighen (2007) argues that as technology advances, the ease with which people (and machine agents) can interact becomes greater. Greater levels of interaction bring with them greater potential for conflict (tensions and incongruities). However, evolutionary forces have a mediating effect in terms of reducing of such conflict. This process is helped by "stigmergy," defined by Heylighen as "the unintended collaboration between agents resulting from their actions on a shared environment" (p. 286). Stigmergy may be quantitative or qualitative. Quantitative stigmergy promotes greater efficiency in doing what we already do. Qualitative stigmergy facilitates the development of new ideas and directions.

Quantitative stigmergy entails the Web learning collectively from the activities of its users, and using this learning to improve the efficiency with which users can perform the same actions. An example from biology is the strengthening of certain links between neurons in the brain as a result of frequent successful activity. The strengthening of these links means that potential choice of which links should be activated in future similar tasks is reduced since activity using the strengthened links is prioritised. Thus similar mental activity may be achieved with greater processing efficiency.

Heylighen quotes as a Web-based example Google's *PageRank* algorithm, which prioritises (gives higher weightings to, thus listing first in the hit list resulting from a search) Web pages which have many links coming in to them from other Web pages themselves deemed to be of high quality as measured by the same process. Links are thus strengthened between query keywords and Web pages containing them which are deemed to be of higher quality than others. Such strengthening of successful links represents an essentially convergent process in that it is reinforcing existing well-used pathways.

Qualitative stigmergy relates to more conscious collaborative activity using a shared medium, entailing the creation of new knowledge. Heylighen (2007) quotes Wikipedia as an example of such activity, in which independent agents interact collaboratively—without the need for hierarchical control and coordination except to establish basic principles and working methods—and collectively to create something that is more than merely the sum of its parts.

Stigmergic forces militate for the emergence of mediating structures—whether in the form of reinforcement of productive pathways, or the development of new shared knowledge. Such mediating structures essentially work to reduce tensions and resolve incongruities—tending to develop greater order from chaos. The examples of quantitative and qualitative stigmergy outlined previously represent small-scale localised activities compared to stigmergy functioning at a global Web level. However, Heylighen (2007) envisages the Web developing to a stage in which such forces operate at this global level, with mediating effects applying to the Web as a whole. They would work intelligently to manage, and to maximise the synergy of, Web-based interactions. At this developmental stage, the Web's global mediating processes and structures would represent metacognitive activity, and in Heylighen's view would constitute a "Global Brain."

The parallels drawn by Heylighen (2007) between such an emerging Global Brain and the type of neural network introduced in Chapter I bring us full circle. A pervasive theme of the book has been the resolution of tensions between conflicting forces via the generation and testing of integrating themes. Such activity constitutes a fundamental process in the way that individual humans strive to make sense of the world around them. It may be that similar processes, operating at a global level within the medium of the Web, can offer a degree of optimism that we may be able to harness the potential benefits of the vast, complex, diverse, and flexible conceptual space that is the Web—counterbalancing the forces of chaos and confusion that will abound without such mediation.

It may be that we can envisage a learning Web in which individuals and communities can learn in optimally effective—and optimally challenging and stretching—ways, in accordance with their needs and capabilities such that their needs are satisfied and their capabilities enhanced. Current developments suggest that such a vision may not be entirely unrealistic.

# References


Chen, H., Zhang, Y., & Houston, A. L. (1998). Semantic indexing and searching using a Hopfield net. *Journal of Library and information science, 24*(1), 3-18.

Dervin, B. (1983, May). *An overview of sense-making research: Concepts, methods, and results to date.* Paper presented at International Communication Association Annual Meeting, Dallas, TX. Retrieved August 1, 2007, from http://communications.sbs.ohio-state.edu/sense-making/art/artdervin83.html

Dervin, B. (1991). Comparative theory reconceptualized: From entities and states to processes and dynamics. *Communication Theory, 1,* 59-69.

Dervin, B. (1992). From the mind's eye of the user: The sense-making qualitative-quantitative methodology. In J. D. Glazier & R. R. Powell (Eds.), *Qualitative research in information management* (pp. 61-84). Englewood, CO: Libraries Unlimited.

Dervin, B. (1993). Verbing communication: A mandate for disciplinary invention. *Journal of Communication, 43*(3), 45-54.

Dervin, B. (1998). Sense-making theory and practice: An overview of user interests in knowledge seeking and use. *Journal of Knowledge Management, 2*(2), 36-46.

Dervin, B. (1999a). Chaos, order, and sense-making: A proposed theory for information design. In R. Jacobson (Ed.), *Information design* (pp. 35-57). Cambridge, MA: MIT Press.

Dervin, B. (1999b). On studying information seeking methodologically: The implications of connecting metatheory to method. *Information Processing and Management, 35,* 727-750.

Ellis, D., Ford, N., & Wood, F. (1993). Hypertext and learning styles. *The Electronic Library, 11,* 13-18.

Ford, N. (1999). The growth of understanding in information science: Towards a developmental model. *Journal of the American Society for Information Science, 50*(12), 1141-1152.

Ford, N. (2004). Creativity and convergence in library and information science research: The roles of objectivity and subjectivity, constraint, and control.

*Journal of the American Society for Information Science and Technology, 55*(13), 1169-1182.

Ford, N., & Chen, Y. (2001). Matching/mismatching revisited: An empirical study of learning and teaching styles. *British Journal of Educational Technology, 32*(1), 5-22.

Ford, N., & Ford, R. (1992). Towards a cognitive theory of information accessing: An empirical study. *Information Processing and Management, 29*(5), 569-585.

Ford, N., Miller, D., & Moss, N. (2003). Web search strategies and approaches to studying. *Journal of the American Society for Library and information science and Technology, 54*(6), 473-489.

Harri-Augstein, S., & Thomas, L. F. (1991). *Learning conversations.* London: Routledge.

Harrington, A. (Ed.). (1999). *The placebo effect: An interdisciplinary exploration.* Cambridge, MA: Harvard University Press.

Heylighen, F. (2007). Accelerating socio-technological evolution: From ephemeralization and stigmergy to the global brain. In G. Modelski, T. Devezas, & W. Thompson (Eds.), *Globalization as an evolutionary process: Modeling global change* (pp. 286-335). London: Routledge.

Landauer, T. K. (1987). Relations between cognitive psychology and computer system design. In J. M. Carroll (Ed.), *Interfacing thought* (pp. 1-25). Cambridge, MA: MIT Press.

Landauer, T. K. (1991). Let's get real: A position paper on the role of cognitive psychology in the design of humanly useful and usable systems. In J. M. Carroll (Ed.), *Designing interaction: Psychology at the human-computer interface* (pp. 60-73). Cambridge, UK: Cambridge University Press.

Parsons, H. M. (1974). What happened at Hawthorne? *Science, 183,* 922-932.

Smith, R. (1996). What clinical information do doctors need? *British Medical Journal, 313,* 1062-1068.

Thornley, C. V. (2005). *A dialectical model of information retrieval: Exploring a contradiction in terms.* Unpublished doctoral dissertation, University of Strathclyde.

Wood, F., Ford, N., Miller, D., Sobczyk, G., & Duffin, R. (1996). Information skills, searching behaviour and cognitive styles for student centred learning: A computer-assisted learning approach. *Journal of Library and information science, 22*(2), 79-92.

# About the Editor

**Nigel Ford** is a professor in information science at the University of Sheffield, UK. His research interests include: effective teaching and learning in higher education; educational informatics; cognitive and learning styles; user modelling for adaptive systems; information seeking; and creativity. He has led a number of funded research projects in the areas of student-centred learning; cognitive and learning styles; and information seeking. He has published extensively in international peer-reviewed journals and has authored four books on aspects of artificial intelligence. He is Director of Research for the Department of Information Studies at Sheffield, and is head of its Educational Informatics Research Group.

# Index

## M



## N



## O

**P**



**R**



**S**



**T**

www.ingramcontent.com/pod-product-compliance
Lightning Source LLC
LaVergne TN
LVHW062110200926
848484LV00007B/1636
* 9 7 8 1 5 9 9 0 4 7 4 1 6 *